McCormack's Gui
life in Contra Costa a
understandable. The ce..
sented in a readable style.

Scholastic Aptitude Test (SAT) scores, rankings for public schools, what to look for in private and public schools, a profile of Catholic schools, a directory of private schools — they are all inside. The perfect guide for Contra Costa and Solano parents or people shopping for homes or apartments.

The 1993 edition of "Contra Costa & Solano" tells which months have the most rain, which the least, when to expect the fog.

Community profiles. Home values, rents. Housing trends.

Hospital services and day care. Directory of major local hospitals and day-care providers.

Places to visit, things to do. Parks, museums, sports for children and adults.

The commuting scene. BART guide. Tactics to save time and sanity.

Looking for work? "Contra Costa & Solano" tells what jobs are in demand. Salary sampler.

Vital statistics. Population, income. Republicans and Democrats. Crime, ethnic makeup, history.

Solano County schools, towns, commute, home values, more.

Don McCormack is a former newspaper reporter, editor and columnist. Cops, courts, planning, schools, politics — he has covered them all.

Publisher and editor Don McCormack formed McCormack's Guides in 1984 to publish annual guides to California counties. A graduate of the University of California-Berkeley, McCormack joined the Contra Costa Times in 1969 and covered police, schools, politics, planning, courts and government. Later with the Richmond Independent and Berkeley Gazette, he worked as a reporter, then editor and columnist.

Co-editor and co-publisher Allen Kanda lives in San Mateo County. A University of Washington graduate with a degree in chemical engineering, Kanda joined the Richmond Independent in 1973 and worked as a reporter, then editor for the Richmond Independent and Berkeley Gazette.

This book is dedicated to Nancy, Dan and Meghan. Ship in sight.

DISCLAIMER

Although facts and statements in this book have been checked and rechecked, mistakes — typographical and otherwise — may have occurred. Census data, test scores, and other information have been updated to the time of publication using cost-of-living figures, mathematical averaging and other tools, which by their nature must be considered estimates. This book was written to entertain and inform. The authors, the editors and the publisher shall have no liability or responsibility for damages or alleged damages arising out of information contained in the 1993 "Contra Costa & Solano" edition of McCormack's Guides.

All rights reserved. No portion of this book may be copied, reproduced or used, except for brief quotations in a review, without the permission of the publisher.

Copyright © 1992 & 1993 by McCormack's Guides, Inc.

Indexed   ISBN 0-931299-34-9

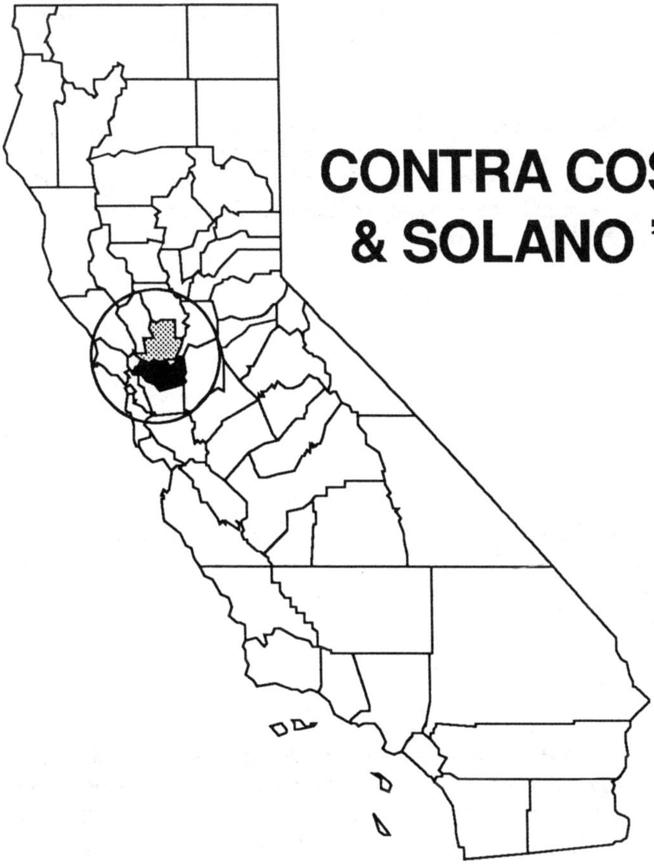

CONTRA COSTA & SOLANO '93

Edited by Don McCormack
and Allen Kanda

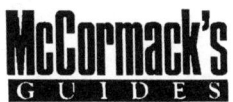

McCormack's GUIDES
3211 Elmquist Court, Martinez, CA 94553
Phone: (510) 229-3581 & Fax: (510) 228-7223

Contents

Part 1 — Contra Costa County Schools & Cities

1 Contra Costa County at a Glance — 8
Population, income, vital statistics. History. Politics.

2 Contra Costa School Rankings — 26
Public school rankings. Elementary, middle, high schools.

3 Contra Costa City Profiles — 50
Home prices and rents in Contra Costa towns and cities. Thumbnail sketches of each town and city.

Part 2 — Solano County Schools & Cities

4 Solano County at a Glance — 92
Population, income, vital statistics. History. Politics.

5 Solano County School Rankings — 102
Public school rankings. Elementary, middle, high schools.

6 Solano City Profiles — 112
Home prices and rents in Solano towns and cities. Thumbnail sketches of each town and city.

Part 3 — Education, Day Care & Health Care

7 How Public Schools Work — 129
SAT scores, district enrollments, ethnic enrollments, key vacation dates, how to help your child in school.

8 Private Schools & Colleges — 146
What to expect. Directory of private schools. College listings.

Better Homes Realty Offers Quick And Easy Relocation Services

We'll help get you into your new home, or out of your old one.

Better Homes Realty dominates the East Bay with each office independently owned and operated. When we help you look for a home, we know where to look . . . after all, we live here too.

Our Preferred Financing Program is another Better Homes benefit. Service is fast, rates and terms competitive, and with a choice of mortgage options.

Our prequalifying program will tell you how much you can afford. Professionalism and experience, a network of support systems, and an exceptional line of consumer services, all help make your next move quick and easy.

Call for a free brochure and listing information on all priced homes.

ALAMO
1451 Danville Blvd.
Alamo, CA 94507
(510) 820-4800

CONCORD
2339 Almond Ave.
Concord, CA 94520
(510) 680-0211

CONCORD
1333 Willow Pass Rd., Ste. 110
Concord, CA 94520
(510) 676-7400

DANVILLE
360 Diablo Road
Danville, CA 94526
(510) 837-2200

LAFAYETTE
3701 Mt. Diablo Blvd.
Lafayette, CA 94549
(510) 284-9500

LIVERMORE
187 So. J Street
Livermore, CA 94550
(510) 373-6616

PLEASANT HILL
140 Gregory Lane, Ste. 110
Pleasant, CA 94523
(510) 938-4554

SAN RAMON
2551 San Ramon Valley Blvd. #203
San Ramon, CA 94583
(510) 820-8800

WALNUT CREEK
1838 Tice Valley Blvd.
Walnut Creek, CA 94596
(510) 939-1131

WALNUT CREEK
1511 Treat Blvd., Ste 100
Walnut Creek, CA 94598
(510) 939-7920

WALNUT CREEK
300 Ygnacio Valley Rd.
Walnut Creek, CA 94596
(510) 937-4880

You can *Count* on us!

**Out of state? Call
1-800-642-4428**

Each office is independently owned and operated

9	**Day Care** Directory of day-care providers.	163
10	**Hospitals & Health Care** Overview of local medical care and insurance — HMOs, PPOs, traditional, government. Directory of hospitals.	174

Part 4 — Fun & Leisure in Contra Costa & Solano

11	**Restaurants** Directory of Contra Costa and Solano restaurants.	193
12	**Fun & Games** Museums, parks. Get the most out of local recreation.	225
13	**Regional Recreation** What to see and do in Northern California. A's, Giants.	233

Part 4 — Living & Working Contra Costa & Solano

14	**Newcomers Guide** How to vote, register your child for school, get a driver's license and other useful tips.	239
15	**New Housing** Developments in Contra Costa, Solano, nearby counties.	244
16	**Jobs, Salaries & Food Prices** Sampler of local food prices and salaries. Job outlook.	259
17	**Commuting Help** Driving miles. Commuting tactics and strategies.	267
18	**Weather** How the weather works. Rainfall. Temperatures.	276
19	**Crime** FBI crime ratings for cities in Contra Costa and Solano counties. A perspective on crime.	282

Cover Photo: Artist's rendering of the new south wing of the Mt. Diablo Medical Center in Concord. See Hospitals & Health Care chapter.

before.

Founders Title Company.
We're changing our name!
Same great service, same great people.
New name, that's all!

after.

OLD REPUBLIC TITLE COMPANY

OLD VALUES, NEW VISIONS.

8 CONTRA COSTA COUNTY AT A GLANCE

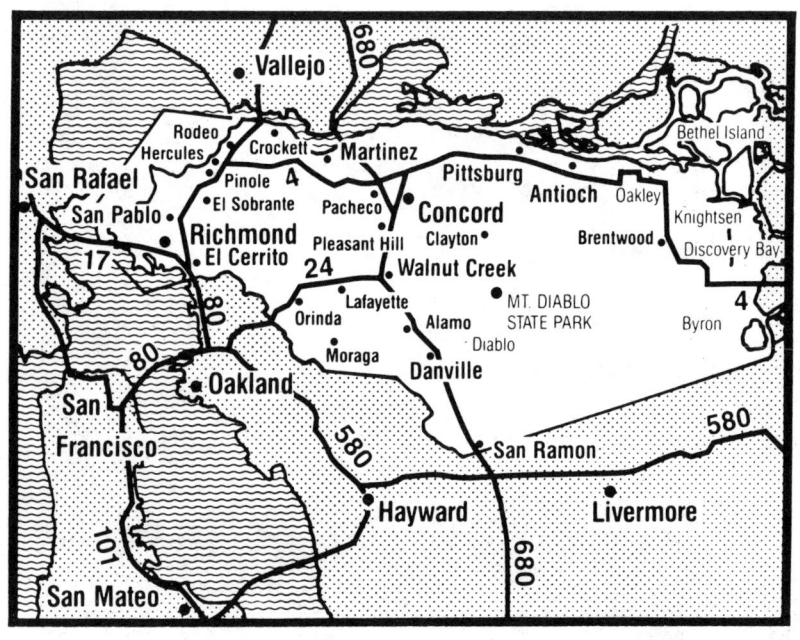

Contra Costa County

1/Contra Costa at a Glance

Ninth Most Populous in California — History, Size, Income, Politics, Homegrown Celebrities

LOCATED IN THE EAST BAY of the San Francisco region, Contra Costa is a suburban-commercial county of 836,781 residents, the great majority of whom live in 22 cities or towns.

The county's climate is temperately dry. Rain confines itself to the winter and in amounts rarely exceeding 20 inches annually. Three or four times a winter snow will grace the top of Mt. Diablo, the county's highest mountain (3,849 feet), and a landmark of the region. But perhaps only once a decade do the flakes reach the flatlands and valleys where the people live. Except for a few summer days, humidity irritates few.

Contra Costa is bordered on three sides by water. Fishing, boating and waterskiing are popular sports. Many towns have marinas.

School rankings are generally middling to high, crime middling to low. But there are exceptions. Contra Costa is a pleasant county, not a problem-free county.

Rectangular in shape, Contra Costa covers 733 square miles, about half the size of Rhode Island. It's the ninth most populous county in the state and the ninth from the bottom in size.

People and Traffic

North to south, Contra Costa runs about 25 miles, east to west about 43 miles. When freeways are clear, you can drive end to end, on either axis, in less than an hour. Unfortunately, the freeways are rarely clear. Traffic congestion bedevils the county, a perennial problem. BART (rail commute) and buses help move people from place to place.

Up until about 1950, most Contra Costans mowed fields, tended vineyards

Contra Costa County Population

City or Area	Male	Female	Total	*Total
Alamo	6,110	6,167	12,277	NA
Antioch	30,664	31,531	62,195	66,600
Bayview-Montalvin	1,977	2,011	3,988	NA
Bethel Island	1,072	1,043	2,115	NA
Blackhawk	3,115	3,084	6,199	NA
Brentwood	3,743	3,820	7,563	8,800
Clayton	3,614	3,703	7,317	8,025
Concord	54,786	56,562	111,348	113,000
Crockett	1,569	1,659	3,228	NA
Danville	15,398	15,908	31,306	32,950
Discovery Bay	2,737	2,614	5,351	NA
E. Richmond Heights	1,594	1,672	3,266	NA
El Cerrito	10,833	12,036	22,869	23,050
El Sobrante	4,804	5,048	9,852	NA
Hercules	8,233	8,606	16,829	18,100
Kensington	2,350	2,624	4,974	NA
Lafayette	11,565	11,936	23,501	23,550
Martinez	15,759	16,049	31,808	32,400
Moraga	7,671	8,181	15,852	16,300
Oakley	9,353	9,021	18,374	NA
Orinda	8,174	8,468	16,642	16,850
Pacheco	1,572	1,753	3,325	NA
Pinole	8,517	8,943	17,460	18,100
Pittsburg	23,659	23,905	47,564	49,450
Pleasant Hill	15,377	16,208	31,585	31,700
Richmond	41,709	45,716	87,425	92,600
Rodeo	3,677	3,912	7,589	NA
San Pablo	12,071	13,087	25,158	26,400
San Ramon	17,556	17,474	35,030	36,200
Tara Hills	2,490	2,508	4,998	NA
Vine Hill	1,601	1,613	3,214	NA
Walnut Creek	28,038	32,531	60,569	62,000
West Pittsburg	8,785	8,668	17,453	NA
Remainder	23,285	21,950	45,235	NA
Countywide	393,448	410,284	803,732	836,900

Source: 1990 Census and Demographic Research Unit of the California Department of Finance. **Key**: NA (not available). *Jan. 1, 1992 population estimates by California Department of Finance.

and picked walnuts, or worked in the large plants — Shell, Chevron, U.S. Steel, C&H Sugar — located in the river cities.

The plants are still there. The farms have just about disappeared, although a good deal of open space remains. Large office complexes — Bank of America, Chevron, Pac Bell — have relocated to the county, bringing with them thousands of white-collar jobs.

During World War II, the population soared when thousands migrated to the county to work in the local industries.

In the 1950s, the freeways came and Contra Costa went suburban.

The county started 1940 with about 100,000 residents. It started 1950 with 298,000. Since then the population has almost tripled.

Schools — Higher Education

Contra Costa has three community colleges, a satellite community college, two full-fledged private universities and a satellite campus of a California State University. Many other private colleges and institutions offer courses in the county.

The University of California-Berkeley is located just over the county line, UC Davis, about 45 miles up the river.

Almost every city has one or several private schools but the great majority of students are educated in public schools. In recent years, state funding for

12 CONTRA COSTA COUNTY AT A GLANCE

Average Household Income

City	1990	*1995	*2000
Alamo	$137,398	$144,700	$153,200
Antioch	47,090	50,300	54,200
Blackhawk	137,398	144,700	153,200
Brentwood	47,173	50,900	56,500
Clayton	76,365	79,000	81,200
Concord	50,417	52,500	57,500
Crockett	45,891	47,500	50,200
Danville	101,654	105,000	111,500
El Cerrito	56,196	58,600	61,100
Hercules	62,600	64,900	68,300
Lafayette	92,974	97,800	105,500
Martinez	54,053	56,600	59,200
Moraga	93,309	96,300	101,300
Orinda	112,951	117,400	122,300
Pinole	52,084	54,000	55,900
Pittsburg	42,331	44,600	46,500
Pleasant Hill	56,647	58,800	61,000
Richmond	41,922	43,900	45,800
Rodeo	45,891	47,500	50,200
San Pablo	33,284	34,100	36,000
San Ramon	79,245	83,200	87,400
Walnut Creek	62,184	64,500	67,100
Rural East County	58,762	61,800	65,300
Remainder	89,245	90,900	93,500
Countywide	59,432	62,200	65,800

Source: Association of Bay Area Governments, *"Projections 92."* Average income per household includes wages and salaries, dividends, interest, rent and transfer payments such as Social Security or public assistance. Based on 1990 Census data, income is stated in 1990 dollars. *Projections.

public schools has fallen short of what's needed, and Contra Costa's schools have suffered.

But many school districts have passed construction bonds to make up the state's shortfall, and education remains a high priority in the county. One study, done about six years ago, showed Contra Costa leading all other California counties in sending its young people to college.

Parks and Recreation

Cities and various agencies have poured millions into parks, recreation, education and culture. Walnut Creek several years ago opened a Regional Center for the Arts.

Shakespeare, in the form of a theater and annual festival, recently set up camp near Orinda.

Cosby, Brubeck, Willie Nelson, the Boston Pops, Neil Diamond, and many other stars, have played the Concord Pavilion. UC Berkeley is a cornucopia of the arts: concerts, recitals, dance, plays, and more.

Sturgeon, striped bass and catfish fill the waters. Many towns have public swimming pools and private pools are common.

Hiking and horse trails wind throughout the county. Baseball, basketball, soccer, bocce ball (a favorite in Martinez), golf, bridge, racquetball, softball, tennis, Jazzercise, water skiing, water polo, sailing, camping, duck hunting, wind surfing, dining, dancing, theater, music—name almost any activity and Contra Costa will provide it. Or it will be within a short drive.

The Sierra and first-class skiing are 3-4 hours to the east. San Francisco, with its opera and symphony, is just across the Bay. The Oakland A's

---

ONE FOR MADONNA

When Madonna's book, "Sex," hit Orinda Books (store) in 1992, owner Janet Boreta decided to put curiosity to the service of a good cause.

The book was wrapped in plastic. No buy, no peek. Janet bought one for the store, threw away the wrapper, and charged $1 for peeking, the money to go to the local fire department. "A hot book," she deadpanned.

Relocating?

National Relocation Assistance Corporation  **NRAC.**

NRAC has the answers!

Unique Visual Presentation
Where to Live Orientation
•
Services Provided at No Charge to Homebuyers
•
Rental Assistance
•
Complete Demographic Analysis of Entire Bay Area
•
Mortgage & Financial Counseling
•
Commute Times
•
Weather Patterns
•
School Information
•
Temporary Corporate Housing
•
Spousal Employment Assistance

NRAC
of Northern California, Inc.

Your Relocation Professionals

2682 Bishop Drive, Ste. 209
San Ramon, CA 94583

(510) 275-9500

Coming & Going
(Driver's License Address Changes)

County	Moved To Contra Costa from	Moved Out of Contra Costa to	Net
Alameda	12,927	8,852	4,075
Alpine	1	6	-5
Amador	47	80	-33
Butte	345	536	-191
Calaveras	53	180	-127
Colusa	19	25	-6
Del Norte	36	62	-26
El Dorado	202	309	-107
Fresno	335	360	-25
Glenn	24	36	-12
Humboldt	115	201	-86
Imperial	33	51	-18
Inyo	9	3	6
Kern	168	201	-33
Kings	36	47	-11
Lake	117	200	-83
Lassen	17	29	-12
Los Angeles	2,726	2,172	554
Madera	42	71	-29
Marin	788	613	175
Mariposa	9	23	-14
Mendocino	87	131	-44
Merced	84	98	-14
Modoc	8	14	-6
Mono	7	8	-1
Monterey	243	230	13
Napa	227	332	-105
Nevada	105	255	-150
Orange	971	799	172
Placer	166	380	-214
Plumas	32	53	-21
Riverside	308	334	-26
Sacramento	1,080	1,645	-565
San Benito	16	13	3
San Bernardino	322	279	43
San Diego	944	1,039	-95
San Francisco	4,445	2,674	1,771

Note: Data covers fiscal year July 1, 1991-June 30, 1992.

CONTRA COSTA COUNTY AT A GLANCE 15

Coming & Going
(Driver's License Address Changes)

County	Moved To Contra Costa from	Moved Out of Contra Costa to	Net
San Joaquin	598	845	-247
San Luis Obispo	240	248	-8
San Mateo	2,445	1,175	1,270
Santa Barbara	249	307	-58
Santa Clara	1,907	1,412	495
Santa Cruz	222	264	-42
Shasta	147	293	-146
Sierra	2	6	-4
Siskiyou	41	67	-26
Solano	1,999	3,042	-1,043
Sonoma	486	713	-227
Stanislaus	238	392	-154
Sutter	29	55	-26
Tehama	39	80	-41
Trinity	17	21	-4
Tulare	78	119	-41
Tuolumne	70	142	-72
Ventura	232	188	44
Yolo	260	417	-157
Yuba	28	72	-44
All Counties	36,421	32,199	4,222
Out of State	9,463	9,251	212
Total	45,884	41,450	4,434

Source: California Department of Finance. Data covers fiscal year July 1, 1991-June 30, 1992. Out-of-state counts have been adjusted for non-compliers.

swing their bats and the Warriors shoot baskets in a sports complex about a half-hour from Walnut Creek.

For college football and basketball, there's St. Mary's and UC-Berkeley.

The Problems:

So pleasant does Contra Costa sound, so enticing are its offerings that it is easy to forget its shortcomings.

Growth has given birth to problems of growth: traffic congestion, preserving open space, garbage disposal, water supply. Several cities now severely restrict development.

In crime, Contra Costa has some of the safest cities in the state and a few

Education Level of Population Age 18 & Older

City or Town	HS	SC	AA	BA	Grad
Alamo	14	25	6	31	20
Antioch	33	27	8	10	3
Bayview-Montalvin	33	28	5	7	1
Bethel Island	40	18	7	5	4
Blackhawk	14	22	8	36	16
Brentwood	29	22	8	8	4
Clayton	17	25	10	31	13
Concord	28	27	9	17	7
Crockett	26	25	9	17	5
Danville	16	26	8	31	14
Discovery Bay	27	30	11	18	8
East Richmond Heights	17	26	8	26	13
El Cerrito	19	19	7	25	19
El Sobrante	31	24	8	12	6
Hercules	19	27	10	25	7
Kensington	7	16	4	33	37
Lafayette	13	20	7	34	22
Martinez	23	28	10	19	7
Moraga	12	27	8	32	19
Oakley	31	28	8	9	3
Orinda	9	19	5	37	27
Pacheco	34	26	8	11	3
Pinole	29	28	10	14	5
Pittsburg	29	27	8	10	3
Pleasant Hill	21	28	10	23	10
Richmond	25	24	7	13	7
Rodeo	31	24	8	11	4
San Pablo	27	20	7	7	3
San Ramon	19	27	9	28	11
Tara Hills	35	25	10	10	2
Walnut Creek	18	24	7	29	15
West Pittsburg	30	23	7	9	2
Contra Costa County	24	25	8	19	10

Source: 1990 Census. Figures are percent of population age 18 and older, rounded to the nearest whole number. Not shown are adults with less than a 9th grade education or with some high school education but no diploma or GED. **Key**: HS (adults with high school diploma or GED only, no college); SC (adults with some college education); AA (adults with an associate degree); BA (adults with a bachelor's degree only); Grad (adults with a master's or higher degree).

neighborhoods that are genuinely crime infested. Most cities and neighborhoods have crime rates about average for middle-class suburbs. Be cautious and take precautions.

Nature has blessed Contra Costa — and dealt it a joker. Active faults fracture every coastal and near-coastal county from San Diego through Marin. Contra Costa straddles several major faults. It's not a matter of if, it's a matter of when.

The prudent Californian prepares for quakes. For a quick overview of do's and don'ts, see the beginning pages of your phone book.

Despite earthquakes, and the problems of growth and crime and congestion, it is hard to visualize the average Contra Costan fretting his or her life away. The diversions are too many and too sweet.

A Short History

The Indians, called Ohlones, lived here for thousands of years. Spanish expeditions arrived in 1772 and 1776, the first American, John Marsh, in 1837.

By 1850, most of the Indians were dead, victims of bullets, disease and misguided benevolence. Also by 1850, the Mexican rancheros were on their way out. What they didn't sell, they lost to swindlers and squatters. For the next 90 years, Contra Costa cut grain and picked grapes and walnuts, save for the shore cities which built oil refineries and other industries.

After World War II, freeways were built. Bye, bye farms, hello suburbia.

The Highlights

10,000 to 3000 B.C. The Indians

REAL ESTATE LOANS

Moving into the area? Relocating across town?

Western Financial Savings Bank F.S.B. makes financing easy!

♦ **Home Loans**
    ♦ **Equity Lines of Credit**
♦ **Construction Loans**
    ♦ **Auto Loans**
♦ **Home Improvement Loans**
    ♦ *Special Community Homebuyer Program*

We want to be your financing partner... Call us today!

WESTERN FINANCIAL SAVINGS BANK F.S.B.

Walnut Creek: **(800) 448-7111**
San Jose: **(408) 241-8734**
Sacramento: **(800) 289-8016**
San Rafael: **(415) 499-0104**

Religion in Contra Costa County

Denomination	No.	Members	Total
American Baptist	18	3,995	5,004
Assemblies of God	19	2,778	4,905
Baptist General Conference	3	1,007	1,261
Catholic	34	NA	180,000
Christian & Missionary Alliance	5	463	1,070
Church of Christ	3	415	520
Disciples of Christ	4	685	911
Christian Reformed	1	209	320
Church of Christ, Scientist	9	NR	NR
Church of God (Anderson, Ind.)	2	57	64
Church of God (Cleveland, Tenn.)	3	341	427
Church of God (Prophecy)	2	62	78
Latter-day Saints	46	NA	19,636
Church of the Nazarene	6	1,053	2,215
Church of Christ	21	2,267	2,861
Congregational Christian	1	42	53
Conservative Baptist	4	NR	NR
Episcopal	17	4,159	6,236
Evangelical Free	6	1,162	1,476
Evangelical Lutheran	16	5,107	6,826
Free Methodist	3	262	262
Free Will Baptist	5	480	601
Friends	1	62	72
Greek Orthodox	2	NR	NR
Apostolic Catholic Assyrian	0	11	47
Foursquare Gospel	7	1,698	2,127
Lutheran-Missouri Synod	14	3,328	4,535
Open Bible Standard	7	NR	NR
Orthodox Church in America	1	NR	NR
Pentecostal Church of God	7	315	958
Pentecostal Holiness	4	243	304
Christian Brethren	4	340	655
Presbyterian (USA)	15	10,362	12,979
Presbyterian Church in America	2	51	72
Primitive Baptists	1	7	9
Salvation Army	3	139	149
Seventh-Day Adventist	7	2,319	2,905
Seventh-Day Baptist	1	51	64
Southern Baptist	35	9,579	11,998
Unitarian-Universalist	1	334	444

CONTRA COSTA COUNTY AT A GLANCE 19

Religion in Contra Costa County

Denomination	No.	Members	Total
United Church of Christ	9	2,309	2,892
United Methodist	21	6,530	8,179
Wesleyan	1	47	127
Wisconsin Evangelical Lutheran	1	42	56
Jewish*	4	NA	21,000
Independent, Non-Charismatic*	2	NA	600
Countywide	378	78,259	324,874

Source: Glenmary Research Center, Atlanta, Ga. **Key**: No. (number of churches in the county); Members (communicant, confirmed, full members); Total (all adherents); NA (not applicable); NR (not reported). *Estimates.

arrive. Tribes include the Karquin, the Cholbones, the Julpunes and the Saklan. Using bows and arrows, they hunt deer, antelope, grizzlies and condors. The bays and rivers teem with salmon. Nets are used to catch geese and ducks. Acorns are ground to make bread.

1772. The first Spaniards, seeking easy trails, visit Contra Costa.

1776. While Americans are fighting their Revolutionary War, Captain Juan Bautista de Anza explores county and is greeted by friendly Indians. Spanish policy is to domesticate Indians at the San Francisco mission and convert them to Christianity. Measles and other diseases kill many taken to the mission. Before long, the Indians rebel and small battles are fought.

1821. Mexico wins her freedom from Spain and, to encourage settling in Contra Costa, awards large estates, several about 17,000 acres, to soldiers and government supporters, but many will not put down roots until the 1830s. The settlers, their ranges overrun with cattle introduced by the Spaniards, turn to ranching.

1837. Dr. John Marsh arrives and buys an estate 10 miles by 12 miles near Brentwood from a Mexican ranchero discouraged by hostile

Residential Loans

Call for a free Home Loan Pre-Approval

Current rates listed on the Chronicle's Mortgage Hotline
(415) 512-5000
Category 9613

Real Estate Broker
Ca. Dept. of Real Estate

Purchases to 95%
Refinances
No Point Loans
Competitive Rates
Free Lock-ins

3470 Mt. Diablo Blvd, Suite A150
Lafayette, CA 94549
(510) 284-5705

Voter Registration

City or Town	Democrat	Republican	NP
Alamo Area	1,798	3,779	581
Alhambra Area	563	464	76
Antioch	19,787	10,345	3,635
Bethel Island Area	741	453	123
Brentwood Area	956	717	171
Byron Area	1,575	2,478	499
Clayton	2,120	2,629	598
Concord	29,847	22,300	7,037
Crockett	1,346	484	208
Danville	6,897	12,841	2,466
Danville Area*	1,705	5,140	856
El Cerrito	9,530	3,395	1,407
El Sobrante	4,024	1,614	602
Hercules	4,366	2,070	1,133
Kensington	2,489	1,005	339
Lafayette	6,267	8,278	1,604
Martinez	10,714	7,009	2,225
Moraga	3,739	5,963	1,104
Oakley	4,970	3,004	876
Orinda	4,681	6,720	1,194
Pinole	5,687	2,686	1,006
Pittsburg	13,903	4,774	2,060
Pleasant Hill	9,193	7,682	2,248
Richmond	34,419	5,668	3,441
Rodeo	2,627	874	493
San Pablo	6,020	1,184	698
San Ramon	7,056	10,807	2,659
Walnut Creek	16,445	21,813	4,535
Pittsburg Area**	3,424	1,214	541
Unincorporated Areas	44,506	32,943	8,901
Countywide	237,306	170,448	470,310

Source: Secretary of State of California & Contra Costa County Registrar of Voters, November, 1992. **Key:** NP (Voters who declined to state any political party affiliation.)
*Danville Area includes Blackhawk and other unincorporated neighborhoods.
**Pittsburg Area includes West Pittsburg and other unincorporated neighborhoods.

Indians. The price: $500. Yankee invasion begins.

1849. Following the Mexican-American War, California becomes a state. Farmers and gold miners settle in the county, switching the economy to

Presidential Voting in Contra Costa County

Year	Democrat	D-Votes	Republican	R-Votes
1948	Truman*	50,277	Dewey	36,958
1952	Stevenson	69,060	Eisenhower*	67,453
1956	Stevenson	71,733	Eisenhower*	74,971
1960	Kennedy*	93,622	Nixon	82,922
1964	Johnson*	113,071	Goldwater	65,011
1968	Humphrey	101,688	Nixon*	97,486
1972	McGovern	111,718	Nixon*	139,044
1976	Carter*	123,742	Ford	126,598
1980	Carter	107,398	Reagan*	144,112
1984	Mondale	140,994	Reagan*	172,331
1988	Dukakis	169,411	Bush*	158,652
1992**	Clinton*	187,993	Bush	106,998

Sources: Contra Costa County Registrar of Voters and California Secretary of State.
*Election winner nationally. **Ross Perot (69,399).

farming. Coal is discovered three years later near Pittsburg.
   1870-1900. Railroads come to Contra Costa County. Warehouses are built at Port Costa and used in a wild scheme to corner the wheat market. The county

GRUPE MANAGEMENT COMPANY

EXECUTIVE LIVING

CORPORATE RELOCATION NETWORK

Specializing in quality temporary housing

Fully furnished corporate suites • Rental car, personal computer, facsimile machine • Related relocation services available • Corporate discount programs

Call our professional staff at EXECUTIVE LIVING today and let them cater to your relocation needs!

San Francisco (800) 878-7579
Sacramento (800) 466-1993
Stockton (209) 473-6241

Population Profile by Occupation

City or Town	EX	PF	TC	SA	CL	SV	AG	MF
Alamo	31	22	3	20	11	6	1	7
Antioch	13	10	4	13	17	13	1	29
Bayview-Montalvin	10	8	4	9	20	15	2	34
Bethel Island	17	5	5	13	15	15	3	30
Blackhawk	43	16	3	21	7	4	1	6
Brentwood	12	11	3	9	13	14	6	31
Clayton	29	18	3	15	16	8	*0	11
Concord	17	13	5	13	18	12	2	22
Crockett	15	16	5	11	19	10	2	24
Danville	26	19	4	19	14	8	1	10
Discovery Bay	24	15	4	18	16	6	1	15
East Richmond Hts.	18	25	5	9	15	8	1	21
El Cerrito	19	29	5	11	15	8	1	12
El Sobrante	14	12	3	11	18	12	2	29
Hercules	18	15	6	12	21	10	*0	18
Kensington	19	48	6	8	9	5	*0	5
Lafayette	26	26	4	15	12	8	1	9
Martinez	18	18	5	13	17	10	1	18
Moraga	26	25	3	16	14	8	1	7
Oakley	13	9	4	12	17	11	1	33
Orinda	29	30	3	16	9	6	1	6
Pacheco	12	6	6	13	21	9	1	22
Pinole	15	12	5	11	22	10	*0	25
Pittsburg	11	9	4	10	22	13	3	27
Pleasant Hill	21	18	5	14	18	9	1	15
Richmond	13	15	5	10	21	14	1	21
Rodeo	14	12	3	10	22	11	1	27
San Pablo	8	6	4	9	22	17	2	22
San Ramon	24	16	5	13	16	8	1	12
Tara Hills	12	9	4	12	22	12	*0	30
Walnut Creek	23	22	4	16	16	8	1	10
West Pittsburg	12	7	4	10	20	14	4	29
Contra Costa County	18	16	4	13	17	11	1	19

Source: 1990 Census. Figures are percent of population, rounded to the nearest whole number. **Key**: EX (executive and managerial); PF (professional specialty); TC (technicians); SA (sales); CL (clerical and administrative support); SV (service occupations, including household, protective and other services); AG (agricultural including farming, fishing, forestry); MF (manufacturing including precision production, craft, repair; also machine operators, assemblers, inspectors, equipment cleaners and handlers, helpers and laborers). *Less than 0.5 percent.

greets the new century with 18,046 residents.

1900s. The early decades. Santa Fe picks Richmond for its western terminal. Standard Oil, later to be Chevron, opens in Richmond one of the biggest refineries in the world. Shell Oil builds a refinery at Martinez, U.S. Steel a plant at Pittsburg. World War I spurs industry.

1937. Caldecott Tunnel opens, encouraging residential construction in the Central County.

1940s. World War II. Richmond becomes a major shipbuilding center, Pittsburg, a troop staging area, Port Chicago, a munitions depot. Workers recruited from other states will stay, veterans will come back. Within a decade, the county's population triples to 300,000.

1950s. Freeways march across the county, completing what the Caldecott began. New towns, Pleasant Hill, San Ramon, spring up.

1960s and 1970s. Baby boom sags. BART opens. Suburbia spreads to East Contra Costa County. Los Medanos College is built. Customers flock to the new shopping malls, Sun Valley and later Hilltop. The Concord Pavilion opens.

1980s. Suburbia says no to some growth. Developers fret. Center for Higher Education opens in San Ramon. Freeways snarl. Much debate over how to solve modern problems, foremost traffic.

1990s. BART begins work on extension to East Contra Costa County. Public university campus opens in Concord. Recession slows residential construction but population contin-

MOVING?

Find Your New Home Through The Preferred Relocation Experts

Because your concerns are our priority, the people at **John M. Grubb Company** are committed to making your relocation smooth and easy.

We provide a *free* video tour and package of current information on housing, schools, financing, plus a host of other helpful services.

Discover how hassle-free relocation can be...

 Housing Information Package

 Area Video Tour
Relocation Counseling by Phone or in Our Center
 Financing and Mortgage Information
 Full Service CORPORATE Relocation Program

CONTACT THE PREFERRED
RELOCATION EXPERTS

1-800/445-2200

REALTORS
THE RIGHT DECISION

 6 John M. Grubb Offices to Serve You Locally.
3,400 Relo Offices To Serve you Nationwide!

Contra Costa County Ethnic Makeup

City, Town or Area	White	Af.Am.	Hisp.	Asn./Pl	N. Am.
Alamo	11,065	68	474	632	32
Antioch	47,454	1,563	9,719	2,788	566
Bethel Island	1,969	20	100	4	22
Blackhawk	5,150	93	243	680	17
Brentwood	4,866	50	2,405	118	42
Clayton	6,483	73	388	357	15
Concord	86,033	2,528	12,765	9,219	634
Crockett	2,747	34	355	64	22
Danville	27,663	252	1,288	2,008	84
Discovery Bay	4,894	61	275	86	31
El Cerrito	14,094	2,055	1,518	5,079	76
El Sobrante	7,528	530	928	759	91
Hercules	5,887	2,107	1,758	7,011	43
Kensington	4,216	143	152	436	11
Lafayette	21,175	132	761	1,355	65
Martinez	26,103	1,033	2,676	1,746	221
Moraga	13,718	106	553	1,432	30
Oakley	13,368	260	3,950	587	154
Orinda	14,937	137	403	1,117	34
Pinole	11,426	1,204	1,715	2,963	126
Pittsburg	22,433	8,117	11,288	5,363	276
Pleasant Hill	26,733	429	2,099	2,143	165
Richmond	26,757	37,461	12,690	9,870	437
Rodeo	4,773	816	94	970	39
San Pablo	8,743	5,246	6,737	4,049	264
San Ramon	11,029	261	613	894	40
Walnut Creek	52,938	618	2,869	3,980	131
West Pittsburg	9,670	1,986	3,768	1,816	184
Countywide	560,146	72,799	91,282	73,810	4,441

Source: 1990 Census. **Key**: Af.Am. (African-American); Hisp. (Hispanic); Asn./Pl (Asian/Pacific Islander); N. Am. (Native American including American Indian, Eskimo and Aleut). Not included, a small number identified by census as "other race."

ues to rise. Tentative approval given to San Ramon area project: over 10,000 homes.

As Contra Costa Votes ...

So generally does the nation. Only twice in the last 34 years has the county differed in choice of presidents. In 1968, by a few thousand votes, it chose

Hubert Humphrey over Richard Nixon and in 1988, Michael Dukakis over George Bush by 10,000-plus votes.

Local Talent

Celebrities? Sports stars? Contra Costa County has produced its share.

Born or raised in Contra Costa County were Richard Crenna, Concord ("Sand Pebbles," "The Real McCoys," "Our Miss Brooks"); Aldo Ray, Crockett ("The Naked and the Dead"); comedian Ronnie Schell, Richmond; Dave Brubeck, Concord; actress Katherine Ross, Walnut Creek ("Butch Cassidy and the Sundance Kid"); actress Markie Post, Walnut Creek ("Night Court"); John and Tom Fogarty, El Cerrito, Creedence Clearwater Revival band; Squire Fridell, Orinda, "King of TV Commercials;" and Blossom Seeley, San Pablo, a singer of the Twenties and Thirties.

Gridiron Heroes

Local gridiron Hall of Fame includes Norm Van Brocklin, Walnut Creek; Gino Marchetti, Antioch; Jim Turner, Crockett, who kicked three field goals in Super Bowl III (Jets 16, Colts 7); and John Henry Johnson, Pittsburg, inducted in 1987 into the Pro Football Hall of Fame, joining Van Brocklin and Marchetti.

In 1992, Gino Torretta of Pinole won the Heisman Trophy.

The Boys of Summer

Baseball stars: Lefty Gomez, Rodeo (Yankees); Willie McGee, Richmond (Giants); Tug McGraw, Martinez (Mets, Phillies); Dale Sveum, Pinole, (Milwaukee Brewers); Michael Felder, Richmond (Giants); Tom Candiotti, Concord (Dodgers); and the star of all, Joseph Dimaggio, Martinez (Yankees). Jolting Joe lives in San Francisco but has relatives in Martinez and occasionally will be seen driving around Contra Costa County.

San Ramon Valley Little Leaguers won the national pennant in 1991.

The Swift & Agile

Speedy Contra Costans: Swimmers Donna deVarona, Lafayette, John Hencken, Kensington, and Matt Biondi, Moraga; and runner Eddie Hart, Pittsburg. All won Olympic gold medals. Tom Gloy, Lafayette, and Fred Agabashian, Alamo, Indy drivers; Brad Lackey, Walnut Creek, World Motorcross champion; Dick Mann, Richmond, Grand National champ, motorcycles. Limber Contra Costans: gymnasts Julianne McNamara, San Ramon, Olympic gold medalist; Tracee Talavera, Walnut Creek, silver medal winner.

2/School Rankings

Contra Costa County Public Schools — Reading, Writing, Math, Science & History

ALTHOUGH MANY CONTRA COSTA schools score well over the 50th percentile, the question — how good are the schools — is difficult to answer because scores are greatly influenced by parents and background.

If your mother and father attended college and drummed into you that you should attend college, well, chances are good — many studies strongly indicate — that you're going to score high on tests that try to determine the minimum you should know. That's what the CAP tests attempted to do: they tested basic knowledge. The tests are now history, shot down in the political wars that regularly sweep the state. The last CAP test was confined to eighth graders and given in early 1992. New tests will be introduced starting in 1993.

In the meantime the CAP tests results are among the best we have for determining not how individual students or classes did, but for how the school is made up demographically. High scores generally identify well-to-do or educated neighborhoods, middling scores middle-class neighborhoods, low, poor neighborhoods. For a discussion see Chapter 7 on public schools.

These rankings, issued by the California Department of Education, are slightly weighted to allow for enrollment differences but are very close to unalloyed percentiles.

What Percentiles Mean

If a school scores in the 91st percentile, it has done better than 91 percent of the other public schools in the state. If it scores in the 51st percentile, it has done better than 51 percent of the others; the 40th rank, better than 40 percent of the others. If a school scores in the first percentile (some have), 99 percent of the other schools have scored higher.

CONTRA COSTA SCHOOL RANKINGS 27

These rankings are drawn from state tests given over three years, 1988, 1989, 1990, and from the 1992 eighth-grade test. For the most part, the rankings will follow a pattern. High one year will be high the next, low will be low.

When the numbers fluctuate wildly, the number of children who took the tests will often be low. In a small class, one or two kids having a bad or good day will cause wide swings. Sometimes the children fail to understand instructions and this lowers their grade. Sometimes they just have an off day.

A Cautionary Note

Ranking systems don't recognize overall gains or losses. If every school in California raised raw scores 20 percent, some schools would still be ranked at the bottom, a few at the top. The same if every raw score dropped. A ranking system shows how one school did against all other schools.

ACALANES UNIFIED HIGH SCHOOL DISTRICT
(Lafayette, Moraga, Orinda)
Districtwide

12th Grade	1988	1989	1990	1992
Reading	98	98	98	—
Writing	—	98	96	—
Math	98	97	97	—
No. Tested	1,211	1,132	1,034	—

Acalanes High

12th Grade	1988	1989	1990	1992
Reading	98	98	96	—
Writing	—	97	95	—
Math	97	96	95	—
No. Tested	341	285	267	—

Campolindo High

12th Grade	1988	1989	1990	1992
Reading	96	98	96	—

CORPORATE & INDIVIDUAL RELOCATION SPECIALIST

Coldwell Banker
Residential Real Estate Services
1909 Mt. Diablo Blvd. Walnut Creek, CA 94596

(510) 942-3512
Voice Mail (24 Hr.)

HEIDI SLOCOMB
GRI, CRS

Contra Costa Resident Since 1966
— Serving Central Contra Costa County —

Walnut Creek	Orinda	Blackhawk
Pleasant Hill	Lafayette	Diablo
Concord	Moraga	Danville
Martinez	Alamo	San Ramon

CALL FOR A COMPLIMENTARY RELOCATION PACKET

28 CONTRA COSTA SCHOOL RANKINGS

ACALANES UNIFIED (Continued)
Campolindo High

12th Grade	1988	1989	1990	1992
Writing	—	96	89	—
Math	97	97	95	—
No. Tested	298	276	234	—

Los Lomas High

12th Grade	1988	1989	1990	1992
Reading	90	85	95	—
Writing	—	88	90	—
Math	92	93	92	—
No. Tested	286	307	255	—

Miramonte High

12th Grade	1988	1989	1990	1992
Reading	98	98	98	—
Writing	—	98	98	—
Math	98	98	98	—
No. Tested	268	244	262	—

ANTIOCH UNIFIED SCHOOL DISTRICT
Districtwide

3rd Grade	1988	1989	1990	1992
Reading	59	60	51	—
Writing	56	60	56	—
Math	50	54	48	—
No. Tested	892	989	992	—
6th Grade	1988	1989	1990	1992
Reading	68	68	54	—
Writing	55	67	65	—
Math	54	65	53	—
No. Tested	735	909	928	—
8th Grade	1988	1989	1990	1992
Reading	58	56	60	55
Writing	55	—	—	48
Math	48	50	54	50
History	60	59	58	57
Science	50	50	64	64
No. Tested	707	750	741	896
12th Grade	1988	1989	1990	1992
Reading	62	56	44	—
Writing	—	50	59	—
Math	53	47	46	—
No. Tested	632	601	564	—

Antioch High

12th Grade	1988	1989	1990	1992
Reading	64	55	47	—
Writing	—	51	60	—
Math	59	45	45	—
No. Tested	594	588	541	—

Antioch Jr. High

8th Grade	1988	1989	1990	1992
Reading	50	58	55	45
Writing	44	—	—	33
Math	43	49	54	46
History	50	55	50	50

8th Grade	1988	1989	1990	1992
Science	44	56	60	59
No. Tested	370	360	399	422

Belshaw El.

3rd Grade	1988	1989	1990	1992
Reading	52	67	65	—
Writing	53	69	65	—
Math	46	47	67	—
No. Tested	109	103	114	—
6th Grade	1988	1989	1990	1992
Reading	82	77	89	—
Writing	72	81	78	—
Math	75	78	84	—
No. Tested	92	115	114	—

Bidwell El.

3rd Grade	1988	1989	1990	1992
Reading	35	70	62	—
Writing	37	64	60	—
Math	36	76	65	—
No. Tested	137	130	111	—
6th Grade	1988	1989	1990	1992
Reading	66	64	43	—
Writing	40	67	55	—
Math	50	74	54	—
No. Tested	99	111	130	—

Fremont El.

3rd Grade	1988	1989	1990	1992
Reading	49	46	51	—
Writing	60	49	44	—
Math	69	51	54	—
No. Tested	89	120	142	—
6th Grade	1988	1989	1990	1992
Reading	45	38	38	—
Writing	36	44	44	—
Math	24	35	28	—
No. Tested	56	99	95	—

Kimball El.

3rd Grade	1988	1989	1990	1992
Reading	64	77	55	—
Writing	53	69	63	—
Math	41	66	46	—
No. Tested	106	138	116	—
6th Grade	1988	1989	1990	1992
Reading	66	67	59	—
Writing	67	69	82	—
Math	61	67	56	—
No. Tested	117	112	121	—

Marsh El.

3rd Grade	1988	1989	1990	1992
Reading	54	16	21	—
Writing	51	25	26	—
Math	43	22	25	—
No. Tested	110	103	112	—
6th Grade	1988	1989	1990	1992
Reading	48	19	37	—
Writing	35	32	50	—

Moving? Get A Head Start.

With the CENTURY 21® VIP® Referral Network, you can start looking for a new home, in a new area, even before you move there.

As part of the largest real estate sales organization, we have access to thousands of CENTURY 21 offices nationwide. That means we can help sell your house here, and then refer you to a trained CENTURY 21 Sales Associate who can help you find a new house there.

JUST TELL US WHAT YOU WANT... IT'S AS GOOD AS DONE.™

©1992 Century 21 Real Estate Corporation as trustee for the NAF. ® and ™ trademarks of Century 21 Real Estate Corporation. Equal Housing Opportunity. EACH OFFICE IS INDEPENDENTLY OWNED AND OPERATED.

ANTIOCH UNIFIED (Continued)
Marsh El.

6th Grade	1988	1989	1990	1992
Math	44	34	54	—
No. Tested	94	93	100	—

Mission El.

3rd Grade	1988	1989	1990	1992
Reading	62	54	54	—
Writing	70	54	57	—
Math	64	36	34	—
No. Tested	103	129	125	—
6th Grade	1988	1989	1990	1992
Reading	74	82	50	—
Writing	75	86	73	—
Math	66	74	36	—
No. Tested	196	127	98	—

Park Jr. High

8th Grade	1988	1989	1990	1992
Reading	60	49	61	67
Writing	62	—	—	62
Math	55	51	61	54
History	70	53	65	64
Science	61	45	73	67
No. Tested	329	380	342	462

Sutter El.

3rd Grade	1988	1989	1990	1992
Reading	50	68	51	—
Writing	65	68	59	—
Math	46	45	39	—
No. Tested	125	141	154	—
6th Grade	1988	1989	1990	1992
Reading	61	69	59	—
Writing	45	61	65	—
Math	51	45	63	—
No. Tested	90	141	142	—

Turner El.

3rd Grade	1988	1989	1990	1992
Reading	83	71	62	—
Writing	74	67	68	—
Math	59	69	64	—
No. Tested	113	125	118	—
6th Grade	1988	1989	1990	1992
Reading	50	78	41	—
Writing	40	69	50	—
Math	45	72	40	—
No. Tested	91	111	128	—

BRENTWOOD UNIFIED ELEMENTARY DISTRICT
Districtwide

3rd Grade	1988	1989	1990	1992
Reading	54	71	47	—
Writing	61	64	58	—
Math	84	91	72	—
No. Tested	147	159	190	—
6th Grade	1988	1989	1990	1992
Reading	56	34	22	—
Writing	76	33	50	—

6th Grade	1988	1989	1990	1992
Math	41	28	38	—
No. Tested	156	168	156	—
8th Grade	1988	1989	1990	1992
Reading	77	50	63	70
Writing	62	—	—	89
Math	40	50	54	51
History	78	63	74	85
Science	61	53	63	63
No. Tested	151	135	167	173

Brentwood El.

3rd Grade	1988	1989	1990	1992
Reading	62	68	46	—
Writing	71	63	62	—
Math	89	72	70	—
No. Tested	71	79	81	—

Edna Hill El.

6th Grade	1988	1989	1990	1992
Reading	55	38	22	—
Writing	70	34	50	—
Math	44	28	41	—
No. Tested	156	168	156	—
8th Grade	1988	1989	1990	1992
Reading	73	51	61	70
Writing	60	—	—	87
Math	45	50	56	51
History	77	58	73	83
Science	61	53	65	62
No. Tested	151	135	167	173

Garin El.

3rd Grade	1988	1989	1990	1992
Reading	41	65	49	—
Writing	50	60	52	—
Math	59	91	64	—
No. Tested	76	80	109	—

BYRON UNION ELEM. DISTRICT
Districtwide

3rd Grade	1988	1989	1990	1992
Reading	69	90	74	—
Writing	79	82	64	—
Math	38	78	59	—
No. Tested	49	61	72	—
6th Grade	1988	1989	1990	1992
Reading	83	57	69	—
Writing	84	63	61	—
Math	61	58	79	—
No. Tested	49	47	68	—
8th Grade	1988	1989	1990	1992
Reading	88	68	68	71
Writing	48	—	—	86
Math	55	61	70	68
History	48	61	53	70
Science	57	66	70	86
No. Tested	51	51	52	83

…

CENTURY 21® Offices
Serving Contra Costa County

ANTIOCH
CENTURY 21 Rounsaville Real Estate
2901 Lone Tree Way
Antioch, CA 94509
(510) 754-4242

BYRON
CENTURY 21 Realty Advantage
1555 Riverlake Road, Suite N
Byron, CA 94514
(510) 634-5800

CONCORD
CENTURY 21 Aamerica West
2924 Clayton Road
Concord, CA 94519
(510) 686-4700

CENTURY 21 Diablo Valley Realty
4415 Cowell Road, Suite 1020
Concord, CA 94518
(510) 682-4663

CENTURY 21 Harmony
4425-J Treat Blvd.
Concord, CA 94521
(510) 687-9900

CENTURY 21 Kropa Realty
2975 Treat Blvd., Suite A-1
Concord, CA 94518
(510) 676-8300

CENTURY 21 Lee Parker Realty
3108 Willow Pass Road
Concord, CA 94519
(510) 687-1750

HERCULES
CENTURY 21 Greenhills Realty, Inc.
1500 Sycamore Ave., Suite A-2
Hercules, CA 94547
(510) 799-1242

MARTINEZ
CENTURY 21 Landmark
6635 Alhambra Ave., Suite 201
Martinez, CA 94553
(510) 930-6688

MORAGA
CENTURY 21 Beaubelle & Associates, Inc.
432 Center St.
Moraga, CA 94556
(510) 254-1212

OAKLEY
CENTURY 21 Delta
2567 Main St.
Oakley, CA 94561
(510) 625-7000

ORINDA
CENTURY 21 Beaubelle & Associates, Inc.
232 Brookwood
Orinda, CA 94563
(510) 254-1212

PINOLE
CENTURY 21 Award Realty, Inc.
2669 Appian Way
Pinole, CA 94564
(510) 222-1244

PITTSBURG
CENTURY 21 Bedford & Associates
440 Railroad Ave.
Pittsburg, CA 94565
(510) 439-2711

PLEASANT HILL
CENTURY 21 Prestige Homes
1600 Contra Costa Blvd., Ste. D
Pleasant Hill, CA 94523
(510) 689-5660

SAN RAMON
CENTURY 21 Results
2355 San Ramon Valley Blvd., #204
San Ramon, CA 94583
(510) 831-6810

WALNUT CREEK
CENTURY 21 Broadway
1575 Treat Blvd., Suite 201
Walnut Creek, CA 94598
(510) 937-4040

CENTURY 21 Elite Realty
2270 C. Oak Grove Road
Walnut Creek, CA 94598
(510) 945-8585

CENTURY 21 Hosking Associates
877 Ygnacio Valley Blvd.
Walnut Creek, CA 94596
(510) 932-6161

Each Office Is Independently Owned & Operated

32 CONTRA COSTA SCHOOL RANKINGS

BYRON UNION (Continued)
Byron El.

6th Grade	1988	1989	1990	1992
Reading	76	53	62	—
Writing	76	62	61	—
Math	58	58	73	—
No. Tested	49	47	68	—
8th Grade	1988	1989	1990	1992
Reading	84	67	68	71
Writing	48	—	—	84
Math	55	59	34	65
History	47	58	53	71
Science	55	66	70	83
No. Tested	51	51	52	83

Discovery Bay El.

3rd Grade	1988	1989	1990	1992
Reading	64	83	71	—
Writing	74	76	62	—
Math	40	70	59	—
No. Tested	49	61	72	—

CANYON ELEM. SCHOOL DISTRICT
(Moraga)
Districtwide

3rd Grade	1988	1989	1990	1992
Reading	98	73	18	—
Writing	77	90	1	—
Math	91	97	1	—
No. Tested	3	8	2	—
6th Grade	1988	1989	1990	1992
Reading	99	98	49	—
Writing	57	53	39	—
Math	93	38	50	—
No. Tested	3	7	8	—

Canyon El.

3rd Grade	1988	1989	1990	1992
Reading	96	70	23	—
Writing	71	83	9	—
Math	85	93	11	—
No. Tested	3	8	2	—
6th Grade	1988	1989	1990	1992
Reading	99	97	50	—
Writing	54	33	39	—
Math	89	39	50	—
No. Tested	3	7	8	—

JOHN SWETT UNIFIED
(Crockett, Rodeo)
Districtwide

3rd Grade	1988	1989	1990	1992
Reading	67	61	49	—
Writing	48	56	50	—
Math	54	50	44	—
No. Tested	147	164	166	—
6th Grade	1988	1989	1990	1992
Reading	80	69	55	—
Writing	64	52	45	—
Math	52	65	50	—

6th Grade	1988	1989	1990	1992
No. Tested	132	140	146	—
8th Grade	1988	1989	1990	1992
Reading	66	89	77	74
Writing	59	—	—	93
Math	37	77	50	41
History	60	70	64	62
Science	69	90	80	50
No. Tested	129	109	139	137

Carquinez Middle

6th Grade	1988	1989	1990	1992
Reading	74	65	53	—
Writing	61	52	44	—
Math	51	60	51	—
No. Tested	132	140	146	—
8th Grade	1988	1989	1990	1992
Reading	63	86	76	73
Writing	56	—	—	91
Math	41	75	51	42
History	57	66	64	64
Science	67	88	79	50
No. Tested	129	109	139	137

Hillcrest El.

3rd Grade	1988	1989	1990	1992
Reading	62	61	50	—
Writing	47	56	50	—
Math	54	50	46	—
No. Tested	147	164	166	—

John Swett High

12th Grade	1988	1989	1990	1992
Reading	68	59	65	—
Writing	—	67	81	—
Math	49	44	41	—
No. Tested	103	101	93	—

KNIGHTSEN ELEM. DISTRICT
Districtwide

3rd Grade	1988	1989	1990	1992
Reading	47	31	28	—
Writing	90	29	3	—
Math	89	40	28	—
No. Tested	30	23	24	—
6th Grade	1988	1989	1990	1992
Reading	25	31	28	—
Writing	33	54	22	—
Math	45	55	22	—
No. Tested	19	27	23	—
8th Grade	1988	1989	1990	1992
Reading	82	25	56	50
Writing	21	—	—	68
Math	37	61	40	85
History	62	32	75	50
Science	39	34	78	79
No. Tested	28	22	23	23

Knightsen El.

3rd Grade	1988	1989	1990	1992
Reading	47	34	30	—

CONTRA COSTA SCHOOL RANKINGS 33

3rd Grade	1988	1989	1990	1992
Writing	84	30	14	—
Math	81	42	32	—
No. Tested	30	23	24	—
6th Grade	1988	1989	1990	1992
Reading	27	32	28	—
Writing	32	53	24	—
Math	48	55	24	—
No. Tested	19	27	23	—
8th Grade	1988	1989	1990	1992
Reading	79	29	54	50
Writing	23	—	—	68
Math	40	59	43	81
History	63	31	74	50
Science	38	36	77	78
No. Tested	28	22	23	23

LAFAYETTE ELEMENTARY DISTRICT
Districtwide

3rd Grade	1988	1989	1990	1992
Reading	99	98	98	—
Writing	97	98	99	—
Math	97	98	97	—
No. Tested	260	303	277	—
6th Grade	1988	1989	1990	1992
Reading	99	99	98	—
Writing	99	99	99	—
Math	99	99	99	—
No. Tested	256	271	302	—
8th Grade	1988	1989	1990	1992
Reading	99	98	99	99
Writing	98	—	—	98
Math	97	98	98	96
History	99	99	99	99
Science	99	98	99	98
No. Tested	272	277	289	320

Burton Valley El.

3rd Grade	1988	1989	1990	1992
Reading	98	96	98	—
Writing	88	85	98	—
Math	86	92	95	—
No. Tested	92	113	100	—
6th Grade	1988	1989	1990	1992
Reading	99	99	98	—
Writing	99	99	98	—
Math	99	99	98	—
No. Tested	101	98	104	—

Happy Valley El.

3rd Grade	1988	1989	1990	1992
Reading	98	99	98	—
Writing	99	99	97	—
Math	97	98	97	—
No. Tested	70	69	61	—
6th Grade	1988	1989	1990	1992
Reading	94	99	98	—
Writing	85	98	98	—
Math	93	99	99	—
No. Tested	54	62	66	—

Lafayette El.

3rd Grade	1988	1989	1990	1992
Reading	95	97	96	—
Writing	78	98	97	—
Math	92	94	93	—
No. Tested	47	46	43	—
6th Grade	1988	1989	1990	1992
Reading	99	97	91	—
Writing	98	97	97	—
Math	99	98	96	—
No. Tested	40	59	70	—

M.H. Stanley Int.

8th Grade	1988	1989	1990	1992
Reading	98	97	99	98
Writing	97	—	—	98
Math	96	98	97	95
History	98	98	98	98
Science	98	97	98	98
No. Tested	272	277	289	320

Springhill El.

3rd Grade	1988	1989	1990	1992
Reading	96	89	94	—
Writing	96	86	93	—
Math	98	94	91	—
No. Tested	51	75	67	—
6th Grade	1988	1989	1990	1992
Reading	97	99	97	—
Writing	91	98	95	—
Math	95	97	94	—
No. Tested	61	52	62	—

LIBERTY UNION HIGH DISTRICT
(Brentwood)
Districtwide

12th Grade	1988	1989	1990	1992
Reading	48	30	26	—
Writing	—	50	65	—
Math	35	25	43	—
No. Tested	301	282	225	—

Liberty High

12th Grade	1988	1989	1990	1992
Reading	49	35	41	—
Writing	—	50	71	—
Math	41	29	46	—
No. Tested	276	272	206	—

MARTINEZ UNIFIED
SCHOOL DISTRICT
Districtwide

3rd Grade	1988	1989	1990	1992
Reading	83	77	81	—
Writing	85	75	85	—
Math	80	76	65	—
No. Tested	232	237	261	—
6th Grade	1988	1989	1990	1992
Reading	86	76	81	—
Writing	76	77	66	—

MARTINEZ UNIFIED (Continued)
Districtwide

6th Grade	1988	1989	1990	1992
Math	66	69	66	—
No. Tested	226	229	237	—
8th Grade	1988	1989	1990	1992
Reading	81	90	66	75
Writing	86	—	—	90
Math	63	61	74	77
History	80	71	79	71
Science	86	91	76	86
No. Tested	231	208	221	228
12th Grade	1988	1989	1990	1992
Reading	50	48	66	—
Writing	—	57	74	—
Math	53	55	53	—
No. Tested	202	222	204	—

Alhambra High

12th Grade	1988	1989	1990	1992
Reading	50	48	65	—
Writing	—	60	72	—
Math	55	53	54	—
No. Tested	202	222	204	—

John Swett El.

3rd Grade	1988	1989	1990	1992
Reading	89	87	92	—
Writing	75	86	88	—
Math	73	81	84	—
No. Tested	73	83	88	—

Las Juntas El.

3rd Grade	1988	1989	1990	1992
Reading	79	28	65	—
Writing	91	29	75	—
Math	91	39	52	—
No. Tested	57	55	76	—

Martinez El.

3rd Grade	1988	1989	1990	1992
Reading	62	79	59	—
Writing	74	78	67	—
Math	55	74	44	—
No. Tested	102	99	97	—

Martinez Jr. High

6th Grade	1988	1989	1990	1992
Reading	80	71	75	—
Writing	70	71	65	—
Math	61	65	63	—
No. Tested	226	229	237	—
8th Grade	1988	1989	1990	1992
Reading	77	87	67	74
Writing	82	—	—	88
Math	65	62	73	74
History	79	68	77	72
Science	81	89	76	83
No. Tested	231	208	221	228

MORAGA ELEMENTARY SCHOOL DISTRICT
Districtwide

3rd Grade	1988	1989	1990	1992
Reading	99	97	98	—
Writing	98	97	98	—
Math	97	97	99	—
No. Tested	157	155	156	—
6th Grade	1988	1989	1990	1992
Reading	99	99	98	—
Writing	99	98	95	—
Math	98	99	98	—
No. Tested	165	186	162	—
8th Grade	1988	1989	1990	1992
Reading	98	99	99	98
Writing	99	—	—	99
Math	98	98	99	98
History	99	97	98	98
Science	98	95	99	98
No. Tested	196	199	183	178

Camino Pablo El.

3rd Grade	1988	1989	1990	1992
Reading	99	96	96	—
Writing	98	97	95	—
Math	92	97	97	—
No. Tested	64	73	80	—

Donald L. Rheem El.

3rd Grade	1988	1989	1990	1992
Reading	97	93	98	—
Writing	91	86	93	—
Math	94	90	98	—
No. Tested	93	82	76	—

Joaquin Moraga Int.

6th Grade	1988	1989	1990	1992
Reading	99	98	96	—
Writing	97	96	91	—
Math	97	98	98	—
No. Tested	165	186	162	—
8th Grade	1988	1989	1990	1992
Reading	97	98	98	97
Writing	98	—	—	99
Math	97	97	99	97
History	98	97	97	98
Science	97	95	99	97
No. Tested	196	199	183	178

MT. DIABLO UNIFIED SCHOOL DISTRICT
(Concord, Pleasant Hill, Martinez, Walnut Creek)
Districtwide

3rd Grade	1988	1989	1990	1992
Reading	85	85	85	—
Writing	79	81	85	—
Math	73	78	77	—
No. Tested	2,321	2,460	2,360	—

CONTRA COSTA SCHOOL RANKINGS 35

6th Grade	1988	1989	1990	1992
Reading	91	87	86	—
Writing	80	82	78	—
Math	84	84	79	—
No. Tested	2,055	2,168	2,148	—
8th Grade	1988	1989	1990	1992
Reading	87	87	84	86
Writing	84	—	—	80
Math	88	87	85	80
History	86	85	82	83
Science	86	84	80	82
No. Tested	2,076	1,923	2,070	2,015
12th Grade	1988	1989	1990	1992
Reading	90	83	73	—
Writing	—	79	81	—
Math	89	87	83	—
No. Tested	1,945	1,843	1,722	—

Ayers El., Con.

3rd Grade	1988	1989	1990	1992
Reading	53	64	65	—
Writing	50	60	82	—
Math	45	77	58	—
No. Tested	77	74	79	—
6th Grade	1988	1989	1990	1992
Reading	87	81	72	—
Writing	52	58	65	—
Math	55	67	74	—
No. Tested	81	83	61	—

Bancroft El., Wal. Cr.

3rd Grade	1988	1989	1990	1992
Reading	93	93	97	—
Writing	92	97	98	—
Math	91	97	99	—
No. Tested	89	92	89	—

Bel Air El., Pitt.

3rd Grade	1988	1989	1990	1992
Reading	—	44	51	—
Writing	—	37	67	—
Math	—	42	37	—
No. Tested	—	81	76	—

Clayton Valley High, Concord

12th Grade	1988	1989	1990	1992
Reading	80	79	76	—
Writing	—	78	75	—
Math	82	75	75	—
No. Tested	433	425	383	—

College Park High, Pl. Hill

12th Grade	1988	1989	1990	1992
Reading	95	89	82	—
Writing	—	90	86	—
Math	91	91	90	—
No. Tested	290	277	269	—

Concord High

12th Grade	1988	1989	1990	1992
Reading	89	76	52	—
Writing	—	76	79	—

12th Grade	1988	1989	1990	1992
Math	81	58	62	—
No. Tested	267	282	252	—

El Dorado Int., Concord

8th Grade	1988	1989	1990	1992
Reading	79	72	85	65
Writing	76	—	—	47
Math	78	79	79	73
History	78	64	76	72
Science	72	76	78	69
No. Tested	315	326	329	287

El Monte El., Concord

3rd Grade	1988	1989	1990	1992
Reading	55	79	64	—
Writing	54	56	53	—
Math	38	61	31	—
No. Tested	91	90	87	—
6th Grade	1988	1989	1990	1992
Reading	88	89	85	—
Writing	66	81	76	—
Math	73	72	65	—
No. Tested	91	98	80	—

Fair Oaks El., Pl. Hill

3rd Grade	1988	1989	1990	1992
Reading	70	65	50	—
Writing	47	50	58	—
Math	45	66	38	—
No. Tested	83	58	80	—

Foothill Int., Wal. Cr.

6th Grade	1988	1989	1990	1992
Reading	98	98	97	—
Writing	93	95	93	—
Math	97	95	93	—
No. Tested	276	312	295	—
8th Grade	1988	1989	1990	1992
Reading	96	98	96	96
Writing	95	—	—	87
Math	96	98	97	94
History	95	98	98	95
Science	94	97	96	95
No. Tested	310	272	317	310

Glenbrook Int., Concord

6th Grade	1988	1989	1990	1992
Reading	53	49	40	—
Writing	40	39	35	—
Math	41	43	51	—
No. Tested	225	207	190	—
8th Grade	1988	1989	1990	1992
Reading	50	58	50	49
Writing	50	—	—	42
Math	39	62	38	39
History	53	44	42	32
Science	53	57	57	38
No. Tested	185	202	213	173

Hidden Valley El., Martinez

3rd Grade	1988	1989	1990	1992
Reading	64	59	82	—

MT. DIABLO UNIFIED (Continued)

Hidden Valley El., Martinez

3rd Grade	1988	1989	1990	1992
Writing	68	63	78	—
Math	45	38	75	—
No. Tested	124	147	142	—

Highlands El., Concord

3rd Grade	1988	1989	1990	1992
Reading	81	73	81	—
Writing	86	67	72	—
Math	89	77	55	—
No. Tested	108	105	120	—
6th Grade	1988	1989	1990	1992
Reading	81	77	78	—
Writing	84	59	78	—
Math	79	81	80	—
No. Tested	79	81	68	—

Holbrook El., Concord

3rd Grade	1988	1989	1990	1992
Reading	75	57	60	—
Writing	62	48	46	—
Math	75	76	50	—
No. Tested	87	104	105	—

Meadow Homes El., Concord

3rd Grade	1988	1989	1990	1992
Reading	44	34	41	—
Writing	35	25	48	—
Math	33	21	40	—
No. Tested	98	98	83	—

Monte Gardens El., Concord

3rd Grade	1988	1989	1990	1992
Reading	97	97	99	—
Writing	97	98	99	—
Math	91	97	98	—
No. Tested	87	93	82	—

Mountain View El., Concord

3rd Grade	1988	1989	1990	1992
Reading	67	84	81	—
Writing	68	85	87	—
Math	65	75	80	—
No. Tested	107	91	97	—
6th Grade	1988	1989	1990	1992
Reading	96	77	70	—
Writing	91	86	84	—
Math	87	69	72	—
No. Tested	94	92	101	—

Mt. Diablo El., Clayton

3rd Grade	1988	1989	1990	1992
Reading	94	90	88	—
Writing	85	78	72	—
Math	69	69	63	—
No. Tested	126	142	108	—
6th Grade	1988	1989	1990	1992
Reading	95	92	97	—
Writing	90	96	91	—

6th Grade	1988	1989	1990	1992
Math	90	95	90	—
No. Tested	114	134	135	—

Mt. Diablo High, Concord

12th Grade	1988	1989	1990	1992
Reading	57	47	43	—
Writing	—	46	48	—
Math	53	41	58	—
No. Tested	199	230	183	—

Northgate, Walnut Creek

12th Grade	1988	1989	1990	1992
Reading	98	93	96	—
Writing	—	95	98	—
Math	96	97	97	—
No. Tested	350	311	254	—

Oak Grove Int., Concord

6th Grade	1988	1989	1990	1992
Reading	79	74	83	—
Writing	59	69	76	—
Math	74	84	76	—
No. Tested	206	237	240	—
8th Grade	1988	1989	1990	1992
Reading	83	73	75	82
Writing	80	—	—	86
Math	87	86	83	77
History	80	83	70	74
Science	75	80	71	80
No. Tested	234	196	224	194

Pine Hollow Int., Concord

8th Grade	1988	1989	1990	1992
Reading	85	82	77	89
Writing	84	—	—	71
Math	87	84	89	84
History	85	86	81	87
Science	83	83	83	89
No. Tested	384	345	330	334

Pleasant Hill El.

3rd Grade	1988	1989	1990	1992
Reading	83	88	65	—
Writing	79	72	62	—
Math	76	68	73	—
No. Tested	107	120	92	—

Rio Vista Elem., Pittsburg

3rd Grade	1988	1989	1990	1992
Reading	—	45	39	—
Writing	—	46	32	—
Math	—	26	61	—
No. Tested	—	83	80	—

Riverview Int., W. Pittsburg

6th Grade	1988	1989	1990	1992
Reading	39	52	33	—
Writing	45	49	25	—
Math	26	35	26	—
No. Tested	153	150	180	—

CONTRA COSTA SCHOOL RANKINGS 37

8th Grade	1988	1989	1990	1992
Reading	48	58	56	42
Writing	32	—	—	74
Math	35	39	34	28
History	59	42	40	55
Science	49	50	55	34
No. Tested	137	149	157	146

Sequoia El., Pleasant Hill

3rd Grade	1988	1989	1990	1992
Reading	95	99	96	—
Writing	95	99	91	—
Math	79	94	88	—
No. Tested	91	85	81	—

Sequoia Int., Pl. Hill

6th Grade	1988	1989	1990	1992
Reading	93	90	83	—
Writing	86	79	73	—
Math	88	82	80	—
No. Tested	248	285	278	—
8th Grade	1988	1989	1990	1992
Reading	85	94	86	94
Writing	91	—	—	79
Math	85	88	92	92
History	93	91	94	95
Science	93	92	86	95
No. Tested	227	211	219	236

Shore Acres El., Pittsburg

3rd Grade	1988	1989	1990	1992
Reading	31	26	16	—
Writing	26	31	14	—
Math	23	24	26	—
No. Tested	89	84	75	—

Silverwood El., Concord

3rd Grade	1988	1989	1990	1992
Reading	55	88	81	—
Writing	48	85	85	—
Math	60	70	77	—
No. Tested	74	66	81	—
6th Grade	1988	1989	1990	1992
Reading	89	67	90	—
Writing	82	81	91	—
Math	73	48	75	—
No. Tested	56	44	66	—

Strandwood El., Pl. Hill

3rd Grade	1988	1989	1990	1992
Reading	88	90	84	—
Writing	86	84	90	—
Math	87	81	89	—
No. Tested	93	106	112	—

Sun Terrace El., Concord

3rd Grade	1988	1989	1990	1992
Reading	38	55	54	—
Writing	32	68	46	—
Math	38	46	38	—
No. Tested	105	103	89	—

RELIABILITY, INTEGRITY, EXPERIENCE

MARY ANN PATISON, CRS, GRI

Serving Buyers & Sellers in the Communities of

Walnut Creek, Lafayette, Orinda, Moraga, Alamo, Danville, Diablo, Blackhawk, San Ramon, Pleasant Hill, Concord, Clayton, Martinez

CALL FOR YOUR COMPLIMENTARY RELOCATION PACKET

A MEMBER OF THE SEARS FINANCIAL NETWORK

COLDWELL BANKER

RESIDENTIAL REAL ESTATE SERVICES

1909 Mt. Diablo Blvd.
Walnut Creek, CA 94596
Bus: 510-942-3508
Res: 510-933-3116

For the Last 13 Years, One of Coldwell Banker's Leading Agents

MT. DIABLO UNIFIED (Continued)

Valhalla El., Pl. Hill

3rd Grade	1988	1989	1990	1992
Reading	80	68	96	—
Writing	64	74	94	—
Math	50	66	90	—
No. Tested	91	116	100	—

Valle Verde El., Wal. Cr.

3rd Grade	1988	1989	1990	1992
Reading	93	93	85	—
Writing	84	91	94	—
Math	90	94	93	—
No. Tested	60	54	49	—

Valley View Int., Pl. Hill

6th Grade	1988	1989	1990	1992
Reading	80	78	72	—
Writing	58	71	66	—
Math	70	64	61	—
No. Tested	274	298	317	—
8th Grade	1988	1989	1990	1992
Reading	76	85	77	81
Writing	68	—	—	94
Math	77	82	76	65
History	81	85	75	80
Science	82	81	74	70
No. Tested	278	222	273	335

Walnut Acres El., Walnut Creek

3rd Grade	1988	1989	1990	1992
Reading	97	96	97	—
Writing	96	98	95	—
Math	91	93	88	—
No. Tested	144	122	131	—

Westwood El., Concord

3rd Grade	1988	1989	1990	1992
Reading	75	58	57	—
Writing	73	66	63	—
Math	60	41	56	—
No. Tested	63	62	72	—
6th Grade	1988	1989	1990	1992
Reading	74	66	76	—
Writing	80	70	66	—
Math	74	83	78	—
No. Tested	78	83	66	—

Woodside El., Concord

3rd Grade	1988	1989	1990	1992
Reading	94	93	86	—
Writing	96	91	91	—
Math	89	96	94	—
No. Tested	74	91	88	—

Wren Ave. El., Concord

3rd Grade	1988	1989	1990	1992
Reading	75	71	71	—
Writing	68	74	50	—
Math	50	60	64	—
No. Tested	88	88	83	—

6th Grade	1988	1989	1990	1992
Reading	42	60	55	—
Writing	45	81	59	—
Math	43	56	68	—
No. Tested	72	81	66	—

Ygnacio Valley El., Concord

3rd Grade	1988	1989	1990	1992
Reading	83	59	55	—
Writing	72	65	59	—
Math	84	55	68	—
No. Tested	65	85	66	—

Ygnacio Valley High, Concord

12th Grade	1988	1989	1990	1992
Reading	74	77	63	—
Writing	—	80	81	—
Math	81	84	74	—
No. Tested	376	341	336	—

OAKLEY ELEM. DISTRICT
Districtwide

3rd Grade	1988	1989	1990	1992
Reading	63	57	56	—
Writing	55	62	69	—
Math	56	48	56	—
No. Tested	213	243	281	—
6th Grade	1988	1989	1990	1992
Reading	41	55	49	—
Writing	45	49	50	—
Math	39	46	49	—
No. Tested	156	203	238	—
8th Grade	1988	1989	1990	1992
Reading	77	86	49	73
Writing	75	—	—	73
Math	32	28	28	50
History	64	77	60	79
Science	76	82	57	76
No. Tested	127	166	190	252

Gehringer Primary

3rd Grade	1988	1989	1990	1992
Reading	61	57	65	—
Writing	57	60	74	—
Math	56	49	62	—
No. Tested	213	243	138	—

Oakley School

3rd Grade	1988	1989	1990	1992
Reading	—	—	50	—
Writing	—	—	53	—
Math	—	—	51	—
No. Tested	—	—	143	—

O'Hara School

6th Grade	1988	1989	1990	1992
Reading	—	—	49	—
Writing	—	—	49	—
Math	—	—	48	—
No. Tested	—	—	238	—
8th Grade	1988	1989	1990	1992
Reading	—	—	48	72

CONTRA COSTA SCHOOL RANKINGS 39

8th Grade	1988	1989	1990	1992
Writing	—	—	—	73
Math	—	—	31	50
History	—	—	59	77
Science	—	—	57	74
No. Tested	—	—	190	252

ORINDA ELEMENTARY DISTRICT
Districtwide

3rd Grade	1988	1989	1990	1992
Reading	99	99	99	—
Writing	99	99	99	—
Math	99	99	99	—
No. Tested	212	178	204	—
6th Grade	1988	1989	1990	1992
Reading	97	99	98	—
Writing	99	99	98	—
Math	99	99	98	—
No. Tested	165	194	173	—
8th Grade	1988	1989	1990	1992
Reading	94	98	97	96
Writing	94	—	—	98
Math	97	98	98	96
History	93	98	98	95
Science	96	98	98	95
No. Tested	183	165	181	172

Del Rey El.

3rd Grade	1988	1989	1990	1992
Reading	97	96	99	—
Writing	98	97	98	—
Math	98	97	96	—
No. Tested	59	53	65	—

Glorietta El.

3rd Grade	1988	1989	1990	1992
Reading	96	99	98	—
Writing	97	98	99	—
Math	97	99	99	—
No. Tested	73	63	62	—

Orinda Int.

6th Grade	1988	1989	1990	1992
Reading	94	98	95	—
Writing	97	98	97	—

6th Grade	1988	1989	1990	1992
Math	98	98	97	—
No. Tested	165	194	173	—
8th Grade	1988	1989	1990	1992
Reading	91	97	96	95
Writing	92	—	—	97
Math	97	98	98	95
History	91	98	96	94
Science	96	97	97	94
No. Tested	183	165	181	172

Sleepy Hollow El.

3rd Grade	1988	1989	1990	1992
Reading	99	99	99	—
Writing	99	99	98	—
Math	99	99	98	—
No. Tested	80	62	77	—

PITTSBURG UNIFIED SCHOOL DISTRICT
Districtwide

3rd Grade	1988	1989	1990	1992
Reading	54	38	39	—
Writing	55	49	50	—
Math	55	45	55	—
No. Tested	615	561	647	—
6th Grade	1988	1989	1990	1992
Reading	41	7	24	—
Writing	55	33	37	—
Math	48	24	22	—
No. Tested	476	466	504	—
8th Grade	1988	1989	1990	1992
Reading	42	33	50	37
Writing	47	—	—	50
Math	46	31	31	34
History	39	29	40	32
Science	50	39	44	28
No. Tested	389	370	434	434
12th Grade	1988	1989	1990	1992
Reading	22	61	37	—
Writing	—	82	71	—
Math	21	33	30	—
No. Tested	268	227	260	—

Professional, Caring & Experienced

For assistance in real estate & relocation and for information about schools call a relocation specialist...

JEANNE PENNELL

A Contra Costa resident since 1952

(510) 210-6100

Mason-McDuffie Real Estate, Inc.
51 Moraga Way, Suite #1, Orinda, CA 94563

PITTSBURG UNIFIED (Continued)
Central Jr. High

6th Grade	1988	1989	1990	1992
Reading	28	7	14	—
Writing	41	17	25	—
Math	31	10	16	—
No. Tested	217	218	268	—
8th Grade	1988	1989	1990	1992
Reading	13	18	40	24
Writing	13	—	—	28
Math	14	21	25	18
History	16	16	27	20
Science	22	25	30	16
No. Tested	157	170	201	221

Foothill El.

3rd Grade	1988	1989	1990	1992
Reading	58	41	57	—
Writing	56	53	49	—
Math	73	52	76	—
No. Tested	95	87	86	—

Heights El.

3rd Grade	1988	1989	1990	1992
Reading	80	83	62	—
Writing	84	89	63	—
Math	87	88	64	—
No. Tested	118	89	123	—

Highlands El.

3rd Grade	1988	1989	1990	1992
Reading	52	29	31	—
Writing	55	37	30	—
Math	50	27	40	—
No. Tested	108	114	121	—

Hillview Jr. High

6th Grade	1988	1989	1990	1992
Reading	55	37	39	—
Writing	62	53	51	—
Math	63	37	32	—
No. Tested	259	248	236	—
8th Grade	1988	1989	1990	1992
Reading	67	52	58	53
Writing	74	—	—	74
Math	72	45	43	63
History	59	44	53	51
Science	69	53	60	43
No. Tested	232	200	233	213

Los Medanos El.

3rd Grade	1988	1989	1990	1992
Reading	27	35	35	—
Writing	35	42	67	—
Math	16	68	59	—
No. Tested	79	79	114	—

Parkside El.

3rd Grade	1988	1989	1990	1992
Reading	44	18	30	—
Writing	54	27	62	—

3rd Grade	1988	1989	1990	1992
Math	54	20	58	—
No. Tested	118	121	109	—

Pittsburg High

12th Grade	1988	1989	1990	1992
Reading	29	60	47	—
Writing	—	82	77	—
Math	29	32	38	—
No. Tested	251	227	235	—

Village El.

3rd Grade	1988	1989	1990	1992
Reading	37	30	24	—
Writing	40	32	26	—
Math	26	29	30	—
No. Tested	97	71	94	—

RICHMOND UNIFIED SCHOOL DISTRICT
(El Cerrito, El Sobrante, Hercules, Kensington, Pinole, Richmond, San Pablo)

Districtwide

3rd Grade	1988	1989	1990	1992
Reading	35	38	35	—
Writing	37	39	39	—
Math	30	35	29	—
No. Tested	2,127	2,291	2,362	—
6th Grade	1988	1989	1990	1992
Reading	35	39	47	—
Writing	35	41	47	—
Math	32	34	45	—
No. Tested	1,814	1,954	2,162	—
8th Grade	1988	1989	1990	1992
Reading	35	30	34	37
Writing	32	—	—	32
Math	37	31	29	37
History	36	35	34	35
Science	25	23	31	30
No. Tested	1,535	1,668	1,643	1,756
12th Grade	1988	1989	1990	1992
Reading	38	38	26	—
Writing	—	54	40	—
Math	35	34	27	—
No. Tested	1,449	1,434	1,389	—

Adams Middle,

6th Grade	1988	1989	1990	1992
Reading	—	68	84	—
Writing	—	70	89	—
Math	—	66	81	—
No. Tested	—	351	249	—
8th Grade	1988	1989	1990	1992
Reading	—	—	81	87
Writing	—	—	—	68
Math	—	—	70	85
History	—	—	73	82
Science	—	—	76	70
No. Tested	—	—	303	240

CONTRA COSTA SCHOOL RANKINGS 41

Bayview El., San Pablo				
3rd Grade	1988	1989	1990	1992
Reading	38	22	19	—
Writing	30	16	25	—
Math	23	23	14	—
No. Tested	775	99	105	—
6th Grade	1988	1989	1990	1992
Reading	16	16	25	—
Writing	40	21	44	—
Math	21	26	20	—
No. Tested	762	68	82	—

Castro El., El Cerrito				
3rd Grade	1988	1989	1990	1992
Reading	87	42	65	—
Writing	81	53	53	—
Math	56	55	60	—
No. Tested	47	49	63	—
6th Grade	1988	1989	1990	1992
Reading	71	32	50	—
Writing	57	32	42	—
Math	74	44	51	—
No. Tested	31	28	30	—

Collins El., Pinole				
3rd Grade	1988	1989	1990	1992
Reading	61	70	40	—
Writing	67	78	63	—
Math	78	55	63	—
No. Tested	56	72	70	—
6th Grade	1988	1989	1990	1992
Reading	41	72	47	—
Writing	58	85	45	—
Math	51	71	32	—
No. Tested	59	52	75	—

Coronado El., Richmond				
3rd Grade	1988	1989	1990	1992
Reading	5	1	2	—
Writing	12	1	3	—
Math	11	1	1	—
No. Tested	56	69	65	—

6th Grade	1988	1989	1990	1992
Reading	3	9	11	—
Writing	3	2	5	—
Math	17	10	8	—
No. Tested	52	49	59	—

Crespi Jr. High, El Sobrante				
8th Grade	1988	1989	1990	1992
Reading	48	52	42	23
Writing	48	—	—	11
Math	50	50	40	29
History	48	50	36	28
Science	33	40	39	26
No. Tested	481	483	396	446

DeAnza, El Sobrante				
12th Grade	1988	1989	1990	1992
Reading	29	49	35	—
Writing	—	45	30	—
Math	27	30	26	—
No. Tested	256	264	229	—

Dover El., San Pablo				
3rd Grade	1988	1989	1990	1992
Reading	17	11	11	—
Writing	10	8	4	—
Math	31	21	8	—
No. Tested	71	95	75	—
6th Grade	1988	1989	1990	1992
Reading	2	16	7	—
Writing	4	17	7	—
Math	14	8	15	—
No. Tested	58	33	51	—

Downer El., Richmond				
3rd Grade	1988	1989	1990	1992
Reading	11	8	8	—
Writing	10	6	5	—
Math	17	21	21	—
No. Tested	110	94	113	—
6th Grade	1988	1989	1990	1992
Reading	7	25	8	—

HEAR YE!

Alone among cities west of the Mississippi, Martinez has its own town crier, a fellow by the name of Redmond O'Colonies. He shows up at Fourth of July festivities and other events, and says, "Oh ye! Oh ye! Oh ye! Kind hearts and gentle people. Let it be known to all present ...." His dress includes a tricorn hat, white wig, velvet leggings and frogged jacket.

O'Colonies, originally from England, traveled the world, then settled in Martinez. He says he wants to revive the practice of town crying, the way events were announced in the old days. The city council, amused and noting no dollars were demanded, named him official crier. O'Colonies says he hopes to attract town criers from England and the East Coast to Martinez for a "cry off."

RICHMOND UNIFIED (Continued)

Downer El., Richmond

6th Grade	1988	1989	1990	1992
Writing	5	18	13	—
Math	9	18	18	—
No. Tested	88	85	89	—

El Cerrito High

12th Grade	1988	1989	1990	1992
Reading	61	56	56	—
Writing	—	85	69	—
Math	59	66	66	—
No. Tested	337	337	336	—

El Portal El., San Pablo

3rd Grade	1988	1989	1990	1992
Reading	10	13	8	—
Writing	15	20	9	—
Math	8	33	9	—
No. Tested	93	79	79	—
6th Grade	1988	1989	1990	1992
Reading	135	13	36	—
Writing	32	9	22	—
Math	18	8	38	—
No. Tested	64	55	82	—

El Sobrante El.

3rd Grade	1988	1989	1990	1992
Reading	46	54	64	—
Writing	33	74	77	—
Math	50	82	77	—
No. Tested	34	40	40	—
6th Grade	1988	1989	1990	1992
Reading	59	62	85	—
Writing	29	35	59	—
Math	49	46	77	—
No. Tested	40	47	55	—

Ellerhorst El., Pinole

3rd Grade	1988	1989	1990	1992
Reading	89	91	84	—
Writing	84	93	90	—
Math	88	89	76	—
No. Tested	44	56	59	—

Ellerhorst El., Pinole

6th Grade	1988	1989	1990	1992
Reading	85	86	91	—
Writing	91	86	70	—
Math	76	69	83	—
No. Tested	50	53	40	—

Fairmont El., Richmond

3rd Grade	1988	1989	1990	1992
Reading	28	35	64	—
Writing	35	33	59	—
Math	22	37	81	—
No. Tested	50	43	64	—
6th Grade	1988	1989	1990	1992
Reading	38	41	25	—
Writing	24	31	35	—

6th Grade	1988	1989	1990	1992
Math	42	39	51	—
No. Tested	46	52	61	—

Ford El., Richmond

3rd Grade	1988	1989	1990	1992
Reading	34	24	21	—
Writing	50	24	19	—
Math	23	22	29	—
No. Tested	59	59	56	—
6th Grade	1988	1989	1990	1992
Reading	17	3	11	—
Writing	15	9	4	—
Math	15	5	6	—
No. Tested	60	60	49	—

Grant El., Richmond

3rd Grade	1988	1989	1990	1992
Reading	12	7	8	—
Writing	11	17	5	—
Math	17	13	6	—
No. Tested	97	87	89	—
6th Grade	1988	1989	1990	1992
Reading	27	22	10	—
Writing	17	9	13	—
Math	10	7	13	—
No. Tested	81	59	77	—

Harding El., El Cerrito

3rd Grade	1988	1989	1990	1992
Reading	50	73	59	—
Writing	48	80	72	—
Math	64	70	67	—
No. Tested	57	77	57	—
6th Grade	1988	1989	1990	1992
Reading	71	26	77	—
Writing	53	29	78	—
Math	64	53	60	—
No. Tested	48	26	59	—

Helms Jr. High, San Pablo

8th Grade	1988	1989	1990	1992
Reading	3	3	3	4
Writing	3	—	—	18
Math	5	4	4	8
History	4	6	6	9
Science	3	4	5	5
No. Tested	308	376	305	222

Hercules El.

3rd Grade	1988	1989	1990	1992
Reading	59	82	77	—
Writing	72	92	82	—
Math	83	84	80	—
No. Tested	57	83	93	—
6th Grade	1988	1989	1990	1992
Reading	59	80	91	—
Writing	53	84	90	—
Math	64	74	82	—
No. Tested	72	70	70	—

CONTRA COSTA SCHOOL RANKINGS

John F. Kennedy, Richmond

12th Grade	1988	1989	1990	1992
Reading	19	27	12	—
Writing	—	64	17	—
Math	15	17	6	—
No. Tested	216	241	213	—

Kensington El.

3rd Grade	1988	1989	1990	1992
Reading	91	95	93	—
Writing	83	94	95	—
Math	87	98	91	—
No. Tested	54	77	85	—

6th Grade	1988	1989	1990	1992
Reading	92	79	97	—
Writing	95	72	95	—
Math	98	82	98	—
No. Tested	42	16	58	—

King El., Richmond

3rd Grade	1988	1989	1990	1992
Reading	1	4	15	—
Writing	13	4	25	—
Math	14	3	4	—
No. Tested	73	67	59	—

6th Grade	1988	1989	1990	1992
Reading	8	5	9	—
Writing	16	14	22	—
Math	1	5	8	—
No. Tested	47	64	44	—

Lake El., San Pablo

3rd Grade	1988	1989	1990	1992
Reading	22	4	8	—
Writing	23	12	10	—
Math	14	17	12	—
No. Tested	40	45	35	—

6th Grade	1988	1989	1990	1992
Reading	28	2	9	—
Writing	39	9	3	—
Math	5	1	3	—
No. Tested	43	43	38	—

Lincoln El., Richmond

3rd Grade	1988	1989	1990	1992
Reading	12	3	1	—
Writing	2	1	1	—
Math	4	4	1	—
No. Tested	49	55	63	—

6th Grade	1988	1989	1990	1992
Reading	2	8	5	—
Writing	2	3	3	—
Math	3	4	4	—
No. Tested	40	34	50	—

Madera El., El Cerrito

3rd Grade	1988	1989	1990	1992
Reading	87	77	68	—
Writing	86	86	47	—
Math	66	61	42	—
No. Tested	45	45	29	—

6th Grade	1988	1989	1990	1992
Reading	85	26	26	—
Writing	80	76	76	—
Math	90	52	52	—
No. Tested	47	13	13	—

Mira Vista El., Richmond

3rd Grade	1988	1989	1990	1992
Reading	68	73	39	—
Writing	63	57	52	—
Math	63	53	29	—
No. Tested	60	67	78	—

6th Grade	1988	1989	1990	1992
Reading	49	55	57	—
Writing	24	42	44	—
Math	49	55	70	—
No. Tested	58	12	32	—

Montalvin Man. El., San Pablo

3rd Grade	1988	1989	1990	1992
Reading	10	15	15	—
Writing	23	13	10	—
Math	24	21	11	—
No. Tested	40	38	41	—

FIRST OF HER CLASS

Worried about declining enrollment, Salesian High School in Richmond in 1989 admitted girls, a first for the Catholic boys' institution.

Janet Rosete of Pinole transferred in, as a sophomore. The following year she was elected vice president of the student body, the first of her sex, and the following year, president, another first.

On the merit of her grades (perfect grade point average) she was named valedictorian of the 1992 graduating class. And she played on the school's basketball and volleyball teams.

"People in this school aren't very tall, so they have to make do with what they have," she said, before taking off for UC-Berkeley to study engineering.

RICHMOND UNIFIED (Contnued)

Montalvin Manor El., San Pablo

6th Grade	1988	1989	1990	1992
Reading	24	12	3	—
Writing	11	17	2	—
Math	12	6	11	—
No. Tested	38	27	27	—

Murphy El., El Sobrante

3rd Grade	1988	1989	1990	1992
Reading	21	40	63	—
Writing	16	46	67	—
Math	15	55	56	—
No. Tested	45	57	49	—
6th Grade	1988	1989	1990	1992
Reading	29	35	23	—
Writing	25	50	55	—
Math	31	33	66	—
No. Tested	35	25	37	—

Nystrom El., Richmond

3rd Grade	1988	1989	1990	1992
Reading	1	1	2	—
Writing	2	1	3	—
Math	1	1	3	—
No. Tested	65	71	74	—
6th Grade	1988	1989	1990	1992
Reading	1	1	11	—
Writing	4	1	7	—
Math	1	1	19	—
No. Tested	65	45	52	—

Ohlone El., Hercules

3rd Grade	1988	1989	1990	1992
Reading	73	83	86	—
Writing	64	78	80	—
Math	48	73	79	—
No. Tested	89	98	122	—
6th Grade	1988	1989	1990	1992
Reading	67	86	84	—
Writing	69	72	84	—
Math	63	72	77	—
No. Tested	71	84	123	—

Olinda El., El Sobrante

3rd Grade	1988	1989	1990	1992
Reading	71	89	82	—
Writing	76	76	73	—
Math	75	90	79	—
No. Tested	42	46	45	—
6th Grade	1988	1989	1990	1992
Reading	76	56	80	—
Writing	44	57	45	—
Math	59	45	78	—
No. Tested	22	43	39	—

Peres El., Richmond

3rd Grade	1988	1989	1990	1992
Reading	3	20	4	—
Writing	7	42	2	—
Math	3	20	3	—
No. Tested	71	67	57	—

6th Grade	1988	1989	1990	1992
Reading	1	13	6	—
Writing	2	9	2	—
Math	1	4	2	—
No. Tested	34	39	32	—

Pinole Jr. High

8th Grade	1988	1989	1990	1992
Reading	50	58	50	60
Writing	41	—	—	67
Math	46	62	50	70
History	51	63	50	57
Science	38	49	40	43
No. Tested	363	394	385	461

Pinole Valley High

12th Grade	1988	1989	1990	1992
Reading	58	53	50	—
Writing	—	59	62	—
Math	48	44	47	—
No. Tested	444	406	415	—

Portola Jr. High, El Cerrito

8th Grade	1988	1989	1990	1992
Reading	46	35	11	25
Writing	50	—	—	27
Math	59	28	10	20
History	49	28	17	26
Science	36	24	17	16
No. Tested	383	415	251	366

Richmond High

12th Grade	1988	1989	1990	1992
Reading	9	5	3	—
Writing	—	6	2	—
Math	13	5	2	—
No. Tested	185	179	176	—

Riverside El., Richmond

3rd Grade	1988	1989	1990	1992
Reading	30	20	35	—
Writing	30	33	23	—
Math	61	22	23	—
No. Tested	39	48	51	—
6th Grade	1988	1989	1990	1992
Reading	32	31	34	—
Writing	23	35	43	—
Math	14	35	40	—
No. Tested	32	21	42	—

Seaview El., San Pablo

3rd Grade	1988	1989	1990	1992
Reading	73	80	50	—
Writing	85	76	51	—
Math	82	63	59	—
No. Tested	27	30	44	—
6th Grade	1988	1989	1990	1992
Reading	67	88	55	—
Writing	47	95	87	—
Math	66	85	57	—
No. Tested	21	22	29	—

CONTRA COSTA SCHOOL RANKINGS 45

Shannon El., Pinole

3rd Grade	1988	1989	1990	1992
Reading	43	36	49	—
Writing	60	39	35	—
Math	38	20	42	—
No. Tested	36	34	48	—
6th Grade	1988	1989	1990	1992
Reading	40	52	39	—
Writing	35	58	51	—
Math	24	49	47	—
No. Tested	38	49	44	—

Sheldon El., El Sobrante

3rd Grade	1988	1989	1990	1992
Reading	94	78	90	—
Writing	88	84	92	—
Math	81	76	78	—
No. Tested	58	61	75	—
6th Grade	1988	1989	1990	1992
Reading	80	62	70	—
Writing	93	84	51	—
Math	89	71	66	—
No. Tested	63	61	74	—

Stege El., Richmond

3rd Grade	1988	1989	1990	1992
Reading	19	3	9	—
Writing	15	4	2	—
Math	4	1	2	—
No. Tested	80	63	63	—
6th Grade	1988	1989	1990	1992
Reading	9	1	1	—
Writing	16	4	13	—
Math	3	1	1	—
No. Tested	59	50	46	—

Stewart El., Pinole

3rd Grade	1988	1989	1990	1992
Reading	80	78	79	—
Writing	60	88	90	—
Math	54	68	85	—
No. Tested	61	60	60	—
6th Grade	1988	1989	1990	1992
Reading	91	84	70	—
Writing	83	91	83	—
Math	69	87	81	—
No. Tested	50	57	67	—

Tara Hills El., Pinole

3rd Grade	1988	1989	1990	1992
Reading	73	96	50	—
Writing	81	82	66	—
Math	71	50	43	—
No. Tested	56	62	57	—
6th Grade	1988	1989	1990	1992
Reading	82	86	64	—
Writing	60	66	81	—
Math	62	71	61	—
No. Tested	45	51	65	—

Valley View El., Richmond

3rd Grade	1988	1989	1990	1992
Reading	97	94	90	—
Writing	98	86	92	—
Math	95	82	90	—
No. Tested	52	50	57	—
6th Grade	1988	1989	1990	1992
Reading	97	96	87	—
Writing	85	88	83	—
Math	89	79	91	—
No. Tested	32	35	38	—

Verde El., Richmond

3rd Grade	1988	1989	1990	1992
Reading	5	4	1	—
Writing	15	8	1	—
Math	7	2	1	—
No. Tested	36	39	37	—
6th Grade	1988	1989	1990	1992
Reading	4	20	1	—
Writing	20	19	2	—
Math	5	6	2	—
No. Tested	27	21	23	—

Washington El., Richmond

3rd Grade	1988	1989	1990	1992
Reading	40	19	19	—
Writing	39	10	10	—
Math	14	13	11	—
No. Tested	28	35	38	—
6th Grade	1988	1989	1990	1992
Reading	48	10	27	—
Writing	26	15	16	—
Math	26	8	6	—
No. Tested	26	22	28	—

Wilson El., Richmond

3rd Grade	1988	1989	1990	1992
Reading	47	10	12	—
Writing	39	18	24	—
Math	23	17	19	—
No. Tested	75	74	67	—
6th Grade	1988	1989	1990	1992
Reading	50	33	37	—
Writing	73	53	30	—
Math	51	17	30	—
No. Tested	68	32	46	—

SAN RAMON VALLEY UNIFIED SCHOOL DISTRICT
(Alamo, Danville, San Ramon)
Districtwide

3rd Grade	1988	1989	1990	1992
Reading	97	98	97	—
Writing	98	96	97	—
Math	96	93	96	—
No. Tested	1,001	1,078	1,137	—

46 CONTRA COSTA SCHOOL RANKINGS

SAN RAMON UNIFIED (Continued)
Districtwide

6th Grade	1988	1989	1990	1992
Reading	97	96	95	—
Writing	94	89	93	—
Math	95	94	95	—
No. Tested	988	1,184	1,140	—
8th Grade	1988	1989	1990	1992
Reading	99	98	97	96
Writing	98	—	—	98
Math	96	95	95	97
History	96	96	96	96
Science	98	98	98	98
No. Tested	1,097	1,161	1,134	1,178
12th Grade	1988	1989	1990	1992
Reading	94	94	93	—
Writing	—	92	96	—
Math	93	91	91	—
No. Tested	250	1195	1,159	—

Alamo El.

3rd Grade	1988	1989	1990	1992
Reading	93	97	98	—
Writing	94	89	97	—
Math	93	92	97	—
No. Tested	57	56	48	—

Armstrong El. San Ramon

3rd Grade	1988	1989	1990	1992
Reading	95	96	93	—
Writing	88	92	92	—
Math	84	87	93	—
No. Tested	76	74	73	—
6th Grade	1988	1989	1990	1992
Reading	96	76	91	—
Writing	81	82	69	—
Math	92	77	73	—
No. Tested	65	62	53	—

Baldwin El., Danville

3rd Grade	1988	1989	1990	1992
Reading	96	89	92	—
Writing	96	90	90	—
Math	84	78	96	—
No. Tested	85	81	94	—
6th Grade	1988	1989	1990	1992
Reading	97	98	97	—
Writing	96	94	96	—
Math	96	96	97	—
No. Tested	68	97	91	—

Bollinger Can. El., San Ramon

3rd Grade	1988	1989	1990	1992
Reading	84	96	96	—
Writing	91	91	96	—
Math	87	81	97	—
No. Tested	73	90	94	—
6th Grade	1988	1989	1990	1992
Reading	94	95	89	—
Writing	88	92	89	—

6th Grade	1988	1989	1990	1992
Math	86	93	93	—
No. Tested	66	68	62	—

California High, San Ramon

12th Grade	1988	1989	1990	1992
Reading	94	85	93	—
Writing	—	69	97	—
Math	88	70	78	—
No. Tested	411	415	365	—

Charlotte Wood Int., Danville

8th Grade	1988	1989	1990	1992
Reading	98	97	97	97
Writing	98	—	—	98
Math	96	91	95	95
History	97	96	96	97
Science	97	97	94	96
No. Tested	320	345	306	318

Country Club El., San Ramon

3rd Grade	1988	1989	1990	1992
Reading	88	77	65	—
Writing	86	68	44	—
Math	90	63	67	—
No. Tested	70	66	57	—
6th Grade	1988	1989	1990	1992
Reading	81	77	90	—
Writing	79	75	62	—
Math	84	83	64	—
No. Tested	77	101	69	—

Golden View Elem.,

3rd Grade	1988	1989	1990	1992
Reading	—	—	91	—
Writing	—	—	90	—
Math	—	—	91	—
No. Tested	—	—	83	—
6th Grade	1988	1989	1990	1992
Reading	—	—	88	—
Writing	—	—	87	—
Math	—	—	83	—
No. Tested	—	—	56	—

Green Valley El., Danville

3rd Grade	1988	1989	1990	1992
Reading	98	90	93	—
Writing	98	97	93	—
Math	98	93	97	—
No. Tested	117	111	121	—

Greenbrook El., Danville

3rd Grade	1988	1989	1990	1992
Reading	77	96	95	—
Writing	87	97	97	—
Math	63	79	90	—
No. Tested	77	92	96	—
6th Grade	1988	1989	1990	1992
Reading	97	96	96	—
Writing	90	84	91	—
Math	91	93	91	—
No. Tested	78	109	96	—

Los Cerros Int., Danville

6th Grade	1988	1989	1990	1992
Reading	94	90	93	—
Writing	90	88	92	—
Math	90	87	94	—
No. Tested	222	284	247	—
8th Grade	1988	1989	1990	1992
Reading	97	97	95	96
Writing	97	—	—	98
Math	94	94	90	96
History	95	91	92	96
Science	97	97	95	98
No. Tested	295	265	264	306

Montair El., Danville

3rd Grade	1988	1989	1990	1992
Reading	96	96	93	—
Writing	94	96	96	—
Math	93	96	97	—
No. Tested	55	85	64	—
6th Grade	1988	1989	1990	1992
Reading	89	93	83	—
Writing	93	84	87	—
Math	80	83	65	—
No. Tested	77	79	95	—

Monte Vista, Danville

12th Grade	1988	1989	1990	1992
Reading	96	95	97	—
Writing	—	98	95	—
Math	95	95	94	—
No. Tested	377	334	389	—

Montevideo El., San Ramon

3rd Grade	1988	1989	1990	1992
Reading	80	96	96	—
Writing	90	90	88	—
Math	78	95	89	—
No. Tested	73	73	74	—
6th Grade	1988	1989	1990	1992
Reading	93	89	68	—
Writing	88	67	64	—
Math	92	80	81	—
No. Tested	87	80	80	—

Pine Valley Int., San Ramon

8th Grade	1988	1989	1990	1992
Reading	96	93	94	92
Writing	94	—	—	94
Math	92	91	93	95
History	91	92	93	93
Science	96	95	97	94
No. Tested	363	425	428	391

Rancho Romero El., Alamo

3rd Grade	1988	1989	1990	1992
Reading	96	99	94	—
Writing	98	98	92	—
Math	95	93	77	—
No. Tested	57	69	90	—

FRIENDLY, KNOWLEDGEABLE, EXPERIENCED RELOCATION EXPERTS

We have done it 12 times ourselves

Bob, Sandy and Kelly

THE McDOUGALL TEAM

Custom-build to suit, new homes, sales of existing homes in Contra Costa County

Call for **free** brochure and complimentary relocation package or answers to specific area questions.

Bus: (510) 837-3414, ext. 139
Home: (510) 672-2499
Fax: (510) 672-1666

The Prudential
California Realty

SAN RAMON UNIFIED (Continued)

San Ramon Valley High, Danville

12th Grade	1988	1989	1990	1992
Reading	89	94	72	—
Writing	—	94	86	—
Math	91	90	84	—
No. Tested	419	418	378	—

Stone Valley School, Alamo

6th Grade	1988	1989	1990	1992
Reading	95	95	92	—
Writing	94	87	98	—
Math	89	95	96	—
No. Tested	112	140	140	—
8th Grade	1988	1989	1990	1992
Reading	99	99	98	97
Writing	98	—	—	94
Math	98	99	97	98
History	97	98	97	96
Science	98	99	99	99
No. Tested	119	126	136	146

Twin Creeks El., San Ramon

3rd Grade	1988	1989	1990	1992
Reading	96	86	90	—
Writing	97	67	93	—
Math	76	68	86	—
No. Tested	62	64	58	—
6th Grade	1988	1989	1990	1992
Reading	98	97	92	—
Writing	90	74	87	—
Math	92	88	94	—
No. Tested	51	66	54	—

Vista Grande El., Danville

3rd Grade	1988	1989	1990	1992
Reading	96	98	96	—
Writing	97	94	97	—
Math	96	89	94	—
No. Tested	107	121	122	—

Walt Disney El., San Ramon

3rd Grade	1988	1989	1990	1992
Reading	88	89	87	—
Writing	92	89	78	—
Math	77	89	78	—
No. Tested	92	96	63	—
6th Grade	1988	1989	1990	1992
Reading	80	70	84	—
Writing	71	65	62	—
Math	81	88	81	—
No. Tested	85	98	97	—

WALNUT CREEK ELEM. SCHOOL DISTRICT

Districtwide

3rd Grade	1988	1989	1990	1992
Reading	98	96	97	—
Writing	98	97	96	—
Math	98	98	97	—
No. Tested	263	277	285	—

6th Grade	1988	1989	1990	1992
Reading	96	96	97	—
Writing	88	93	98	—
Math	96	96	97	—
No. Tested	268	275	236	—
8th Grade	1988	1989	1990	1992
Reading	96	97	96	97
Writing	93	—	—	98
Math	96	97	96	97
History	96	99	98	97
Science	95	97	96	96
No. Tested	241	235	273	233

Buena Vista El.

3rd Grade	1988	1989	1990	1992
Reading	93	96	95	—
Writing	96	96	88	—
Math	96	97	95	—
No. Tested	72	76	54	—

Indian Valley El.

3rd Grade	1988	1989	1990	1992
Reading	96	96	94	—
Writing	94	97	86	—
Math	98	97	93	—
No. Tested	45	56	47	—

Murwood El.

3rd Grade	1988	1989	1990	1992
Reading	98	88	95	—
Writing	98	84	95	—
Math	95	91	84	—
No. Tested	68	72	36	—

Parkmead El.

3rd Grade	1988	1989	1990	1992
Reading	—	99	87	—
Writing	—	81	94	—
Math	—	98	98	—
No. Tested	—	6	62	—

Walnut Creek Int.

6th Grade	1988	1989	1990	1992
Reading	93	92	95	—
Writing	82	89	94	—
Math	92	93	94	—
No. Tested	268	275	236	—
8th Grade	1988	1989	1990	1992
Reading	95	96	96	96
Writing	91	—	—	97
Math	94	96	95	97
History	95	98	97	96
Science	94	96	95	94
No. Tested	241	235	273	233

Walnut Heights El.

3rd Grade	1988	1989	1990	1992
Reading	98	93	96	—
Writing	95	91	91	—
Math	92	92	91	—
No. Tested	78	67	86	—

ROGER STUMBO

SPECIALIZING IN CORPORATE RELOCATION

18 YEARS OF DEDICATED AND COMMITED SERVICE TO FAMILIES RELOCATING INTO THE BAY AREA

What some of Roger's clients have to say about his service:

On top of finding the right location, price and amenities, your help in securing the financing and title company saved me considerable time. These along with connecting me with great people at the insurance end made the entire transaction seem effortless. I am extremely grateful for all of your help. Call me anytime for a recommendation.
David Lasser, Vice-President, Levi Strauss & Co.

Your personal contact in advance of our visit to determine our needs, your unlimited time & energy in showing us homes, squeezing in unplanned second appointments, forthright information on how best to proceed in preparing our house for market, and negotiating effectively with our seller from the time our offer was tendered to the close of escrow all speak to the high level of service you provided us. Barbara & I regard you very highly & would happily recommend you as one who represents your client's interests and needs in the best possible way.
Dan Steben, Vice-President, Bank of America

Your marketing plan, salesmanship, follow-up and knowledge of the local market conditions separate you from the rest. If you'll excuse the analogy, you're like a good mechanic who is worth his weight in gold.
Arthur Fabsits, Vice-President, Bank of America

Join Roger's family of satisified relocation buyers and sellers today.

SPECIALIZING IN THESE CONTRA COSTA CITIES:
Walnut Creek, Lafayette, Orinda, Moraga, Alamo, Danville, Diablo, Blackhawk, San Ramon, Pleasant Hill, Concord, Clayton, & Martinez

CONTACT ROGER STUMBO AT:
510-937-4880 OFFICE
510-918-9444 CELLULAR
800-766-7589 TOLL FREE

BETTER HOMES REALTY
300 Ygnacio Valley Road
Walnut Creek, CA. 94596

**ROGER STUMBO
BROKER - OWNER**

3/Contra Costa City Profiles

Communities Here Come in All Sizes, Shapes and Life-styles — Rich & Poor, Rural & Urban

WHERE DO YOU WANT to live? What can you afford? What are the choices? The following profiles of Contra Costa cities and towns may help.

Alamo

Located just south of Walnut Creek, Alamo is home to top and rising executives.

Small businesses, some offices along Danville Boulevard, the main drag, and at Stone Valley Road, but Alamo is not interested in attracting many businesses. Stately, quiet, country-like — the qualities Alamo admires.

Unincorporated, which means it's governed from Martinez by the Board of Supervisors and county bureaucrats. This leads to grumbling about "What is Martinez doing to us now?" and occasional talk about incorporating as a city with its own council. But a 1989 phone poll suggested most residents would vote against incorporation.

Alamo is not helpless. If a developer proposed something outrageous, someone or some group would sue and tie the project up in court.

Some modest homes near freeway and Danville Boulevard and in hills but this is big-money country. Nice large homes and estates hide behind hedges. The Roundhill Country Club homes east of the freeway set the pace for that section. Views from hills.

The 1990 census counted 297 occupied rental units and 3,921 owner-occupied homes. Another way of stating this, 93 percent of the residents are homeowners, a good indication of stability. A few more homes are added yearly. Occasionally, Alamo is referred to as "Alamo-Blackhawk." The hills east of the freeway are steadily being developed, and the communities of

Alamo and Blackhawk have started to blend into one another.

No neighborhood parks. The county does not have a parks department. But plenty to do. Residents can afford own tennis courts, pools. School grounds substitute for playgrounds, playing fields. Regional parks nearby and Mt. Diablo State Park. Golf course. An abandoned rail right-of-way is popular for hiking and jogging. Department stores at Walnut Creek and Pleasanton, restaurants at Danville.

Low crime. Patrolled by sheriff's department. School scores very high. Served by San Ramon Valley School District. Voters passed $40 million bond in 1991 to build and improve schools.

Short hop to BART in downtown Walnut Creek. Drivers have to navigate I-680-Highway 24 junction at Walnut Creek and congestion to Bay Bridge.

Antioch

On the Delta. One of the fastest-growing cities in Contra Costa. Added 19,152 people in the last decade, an increase of 46 percent.

Good place to find playmates for the kiddies. Children under age 18 make up 31 percent of population, as compared to 25 percent countywide.

Good place also to shop for new homes. Antioch is one of the few towns in the county that has been building homes by the thousands. More homes coming, including mansions (up to $1 million) and condos near waterfront.

Why the boom? The Concords and Walnut Creeks have almost run out of land. Antioch has plenty or through annexations will have plenty. The freeway has made East Contra Costa more accessible. The new office complexes in the Central County have created thousands of jobs with a much closer commute.

You can buy new three- and four-bedroom homes in Antioch for well under $200,000. You can't in the Central County. (These prices, however, may not include special taxes or fees levied for schools and other improvements.)

State tally (Jan. 1992) showed 24,286 residences of which 17,321 were single homes, 1,087 single homes attached, 5,513 multiples, 365 mobile homes. Antioch added about 7,000 housing units in the last decade. If you want to see the new Antioch, take a ride out Lone Tree Way or Hillcrest Avenue.

Academic rankings middling. Schools are scrambling to find seats for the thousands of new children. Several new schools built. Some schools are now going year-round. Neighborhood schools may not have space for some children. If moving in, contact local school as soon as possible.

High school and junior high offer seven periods, but last is optional. If your kids are on academic track, kick them into seventh period.

Much belt-tightening, a reflection of the underfunding of California schools. Counselors eliminated at high school, class sizes increased, busing fees imposed. New high school planned for new neighborhoods (Lone Tree Way and Deer Valley Road); and school district is searching for money to upgrade Antioch High.

Los Medanos Community College is located just over city limits. Over 350 courses a semester.

Antioch sings its song of "Delta Pride." Plays up its waterfront, recently decked out with a promenade, a nice place for an evening stroll. New marina. Fishing pier. Restaurants. Downtown, near the water, has been spruced up with old-fashioned lights and brick sidewalks, and new civic buildings.

The downtown pleases, and gives the city some cohesion, a point of reference, which it needs. The new developments have pushed city limits way out into the countryside and, probably, weakened the small town, everyone-knows-everyone feeling that Antioch cultivates.

Commute improved but still a pain. But BART is coming to the East County in a few years (to West Pittsburg) and work continues to widen and improve the freeway. All this will help. Tri Delta Transit runs buses along fixed routes throughout East County. Express buses to Central Contra Costa.

The FBI reported six homicides in 1991, six in 1990, five in 1989, three in 1988, two in 1987, four in 1986. Although in the range of what is common for suburban towns, crime worries residents, especially parents. Some shooting incidents involved teens. In some troublesome sections in the downtown, police have switched to foot patrols. New police station also built.

Shopping opportunities include County East Mall, overhauled and expanded — Gottschalks, Mervyn's, Sears, J.C. Penney.

Over five dozen clubs, civic, sports and cultural groups, from Boy Scouts to Weight Watchers. Five parks, 18 playgrounds. Big park, swim center on way. Seniors Center.

Roller skating rink. Bowling alley. Community theater. Close to big regional park and, of course, the Delta. Much fishing, water skiing, and boating. Fast way to Tahoe, Yosemite and snow country. Highway 4 and Antioch Bridge beats the traffic to Sierra. Amtrak stop.

Rivertown Jamboree and County Fair, annual events, draw thousands.

Antioch used to have one of the few drive-in movies left in the county. Closed in 1992. On the plus side, post office opened a philatelic center for stamp collectors. Part-time hours. A money-maker.

Delta Hospital provides care. The in-thing is to get behind the annual benefit, which in past has featured Tony Bennett and Bob Hope. Kaiser clinic-medical offices expanded in 1992.

Garbage dump east of freeway closed in 1992, pleasing residents. A long fight over that one.

Antioch is a pretty town in a suburban-country way. Water soothes the nerves, and Antioch has plenty of that. The new tracts border miles of open country and command views of Mt. Diablo.

Bethel Island
Small Delta town that might get much bigger if developments go ahead.

Located just east of Antioch and Oakley. Covers 3,500 acres, access through one bridge. Levees keep the water out.

Fishing, boating, houseboating, water skiing, swimming. Bait shops, marinas and saloons. Golf course. The easy life. Many people retire here or visit on weekends. About 40 percent of population is over age 55 (1990 census). Total residents, about 2,200.

For home buyers price depends on proximity to water. Some nice homes.

Many Delta islands were artificially created. Early farmers built levees, pumped out the water, and presto, islands. But islands only as strong as their levees. In recent decades, some levees have buckled, causing flooding.

Developers wanted to build about 2,300 homes on Bethel Island and the nearby Hotchkiss Island. But environmental groups see far fewer. Arguments continue with movement toward compromise.

Tri Delta buses to Antioch and Pittsburg, connection to Concord BART.

Blackhawk

Rich village, condos and custom homes, in Mt. Diablo foothills, near Danville. Census (1990) counted 6,199 residents, about 28 percent of them under age 18, only 11 percent over age 55 - which gives Blackhawk a youngish cast.

Developed by Ken Behring, owner of the Seattle Seahawks, Blackhawk has been written up in countless magazines for its architecture and way of life, which can be summed up, you only go around once, so why not the best.

Blackhawk, by reputation, draws entrepreneurs, people who made their own bucks. It also draws sports types. Residents have included Billy Martin, John Madden, and Jose Canseco. The neighborhood has a certain brashness; no apologies for wealth.

Of the neighborhood's 1,824 housing units, about 1,500 or 82 percent were valued over $500,000 by the 1990 census. About half the homes have nine or more rooms, the census reported.

Two 18-hole golf courses, a country club, 20 lighted tennis courts, a 25-acre sports complex that includes playing fields and a pool, and many homes that have individual pools. A picturesque location. Rolling hills. Mt. Diablo in the background. Many clubs and social activities.

Kids attend Vista Grande Elementary, Los Cerros Intermediate and Monte Vista High — schools that score usually in the top 10th percentile. There's an association of Blackhawk children and the usual games, soccer, baseball, etc.

Blackhawk Plaza, shops and restaurants, a supermarket. Nearby, a big Safeway. Also nearby, Behring Museum, over $100 million in vintage cars, and a movie complex, seven screens. The University of California in 1991 opened a natural history museum. All are part of plan to draw people to plaza.

FBI doesn't track unincorporated communities but Blackhawk crime is quite low. Security gates surround town. Private patrols.

Median & Average Prices of Owner-Occupied Homes

City or Town	Units	Median	Average
Alamo	3,639	*$500,001	$499,986
Antioch	12,602	156,900	163,681
Bayview-Montalvin	824	135,700	139,939
Bethel Island	329	195,800	217,789
Blackhawk	1,824	*500,001	566,626
Brentwood	1,416	159,500	160,474
Clayton	2,070	302,300	303,306
Concord	21,429	195,300	207,182
Crockett	700	173,100	185,036
Danville	9,085	359,200	372,176
Discovery Bay	1,758	320,800	332,431
East Richmond Heights	961	193,000	193,584
El Cerrito	5,752	253,400	267,730
El Sobrante	2,297	172,500	192,063
Hercules	3,941	224,100	227,756
Kensington	1,730	327,400	340,348
Lafayette	6,317	393,200	412,889
Martinez	7,593	203,700	215,919
Moraga	4,163	404,700	406,163
Oakley	4,294	164,000	179,739
Orinda	5,366	432,200	442,339
Pacheco	485	166,700	171,021
Pinole	4,293	193,400	202,671
Pittsburg	8,460	138,900	139,64
Pleasant Hill	7,322	229,400	245,097
Richmond	15,671	144,300	161,403
Rodeo	1,577	180,500	181,692
San Pablo	3,054	117,900	121,127
San Ramon	8,097	316,500	324,453
Tara Hills	1,193	168,200	165,266
Vine Hill	705	141,900	146,177
Walnut Creek	12,887	291,500	298,034
West Pittsburg	2,858	122,100	125,720
Remainer	9,681	269,291	293,376
Countywide	174,376	219,400	254,100

Source: 1990 Census. Asterisk (*) prices were the maximum reported by census. Actual prices may have been higher. Median means half way. In 100 homes, the 50th is the median.

The only cloud hovering over Blackhawk: all roads lead to Interstate 680 and the freeway mess, which proves you cannot buy complete happiness. But Blackhawk comes close.

Brentwood

Farm town turning to bedroom community. Increased its population by 46 percent in 1980s.

Plans envision continual annexations and possibly — sit down for this — a population of 107,000 within 30 years. Lots of talk about planning, development. One plan even has a new city — 7,000 homes on 4,900 acres — going up near Brentwood (but it will probably be included in Brentwood).

Close to Delta and boating, fishing and water sports. Mt. Diablo stands tall to the west, a delight to the eye.

New tract homes and apartments sit beside orchards and bountiful fields — peaches, pears, nuts, apricots, tomatoes, cherries, eggs, corn, asparagus, almonds, walnuts, pistachios, black-eyed peas. Commuters on their way home stop for fresh fruit and vegetables at farmers' stands, and in summer many from the Central County come out to Brentwood and Knightsen to pick their own.

Hot in summer, cool in winter. But the heat is dry, rarely humid, the cool is rarely cold — a Delta pattern. Winter fog.

Downtown clean, shows care. Village square, gazebo, Masonic hall, small

---

AMERICAN TITLE
INSURANCE COMPANY

**Providing you the service you need
is our number one priority.**

County Headquarters
101 Ygnacio Valley Road, #100
Walnut Creek, CA 94596
510-934-4221

Concord
1868 Clayton Road, #126
Concord, CA 94520
510-798-8731

Walnut Creek
1331 N. California Blvd., #110
Walnut Creek, CA 94596
510-939-9143

Danville
146 Diablo Road
Danville, CA 94526
510-838-1098

"Serving the American Dream"

stores. A 24-hour Safeway and shopping center opened in 1990, a great convenience to residents. City completed a detour that shunts many of the trucks around the downtown.

To its credit, the city recognizes that it must plan for development, has allocated money for landscaping and to improve its sewers and water supply. Some people worrying that the fields and rural charm will fade.

Home prices fall in the category of affordable suburban but like many towns Brentwood hungers for the upscale. One development, Apple Hill, is decidedly mansion class.

Utilities undergrounded in the new subdivisions. The new look vies with the old, and sometimes the old — the town square with its gazebo — softens the dazzle of the new.

Annual state tally (Jan. 1992) showed 2,993 residences: 2,097 single homes, 202 single-family attached, 463 multiples, 231 mobile homes.

Home prices will greatly influence how Brentwood turns out ethnically. If homes stay affordable, the town should have a good ethnic mix.

Work is to begin in mid-1990s on a Delta Expressway, which will widen Highway 4, between Antioch and Brentwood, to four lanes. As a condition for construction, developers already are widening portions of the road.

If you work in Central Contra Costa or in Livermore, Pleasanton or Dublin, the commute is not bad. If San Francisco, it's a long haul. To make way for a reservoir, the county is rerouting Vasco, the road to Interstate 580 (comes in at Livermore). Tri Delta buses to Antioch and Pittsburg shopping centers, connection to Concord BART.

FBI doesn't carry crime stats for cities under 10,000 but Brentwood cops reported one homicide in 1987, one in 1988, none in 1989, two in 1990, zero in 1991.

Academic rankings are down one year, up the next, but the basic pattern is middling plus. Liberty High School, which serves kids in Brentwood, Oakley, Byron, Discovery Bay, Knightsen, was recently renovated. New money lowered class sizes for freshmen.

New elementary, Nunn, opened in 1991, a year-round school. Renovation of middle school started in late 1992; new computer, science labs, library.

Summer Harvest Festival draws 5,000. Two parks, museum, swimming pool, library, baseball, basketball, football, soccer. New developments to include golf courses. Community theater stages plays at high school.

Still a lot of small-town flavor. For homecoming, football team and high school students parade through downtown, an event that attracts thousands.

Byron

Tiny town in East Contra Costa, on the verge of going big time.

Buchanan, county's main airport in Concord, is cramped for space and Byron is being expanded to take the overflow. In 20 years you could see jets

Number & Value of Owner-Occupied Dwellings

City or Area	< $100K -199K	$200K -299K	$300K -399K	$400K -499K	$500K -plus
Alamo	74	215	488	889	1,973
Antioch	9,625	2,816	131	19	13
Bayview-Montalvin	779	43	1	1	0
Bethel Island	170	102	42	7	8
Blackhawk	14	12	47	255	1,496
Brentwood	1,160	224	30	0	2
Clayton	244	770	927	90	39
Concord	11,438	8,203	1,525	185	78
Crockett	454	192	44	5	4
Danville	640	2,040	3,146	1,976	1,283
Discovery Bay	188	557	644	234	135
East Richmond Heights	520	392	43	3	3
El Cerrito	1,421	2,620	1,172	344	195
El Sobrante	1,507	547	183	40	20
Hercules	1,535	1,864	490	46	6
Kensington	138	553	635	259	145
Lafayette	275	1,280	1,721	1,258	1,783
Martinez	3,662	2,920	808	130	73
Moraga	263	532	1,224	1,324	820
Oakley	3,316	706	150	82	40
Orinda	133	596	1,527	1,325	1,785
Pacheco	398	79	6	1	1
Pinole	2,391	1,639	208	43	12
Pittsburg	7,955	470	19	10	6
Pleasant Hill	2,538	3,269	1,123	333	59
Richmond	12,117	2,363	950	146	98
Rodeo	1,041	491	36	6	3
San Pablo	2,940	99	9	0	6
San Ramon	768	2,823	2,768	1,493	245
Tara Hills	1,093	97	3	0	0
Vine Hill	633	69	2	0	1
Walnut Creek	2,417	4,451	4,181	1,309	529
West Pittsburg	2,776	69	5	3	5
Remainder	2,998	2,738	1,945	828	1,172
Countywide	77,620	45,841	26,233	12,644	12,038

Source: 1990 Census. The chart shows the number of owner-occupied dwellings within a set price range. Data for some towns or residential areas are grouped with those covering a larger geographic area.

taking off from Byron. County has purchased 1,300 acres at the airport. Feds approved grant of $3.5 million for improvements.

Byron used to be famous for its hot springs and a grand resort, long gone to ruin.

Byron schools serve Discovery Bay. School rankings and the number of children considered gifted (I.Q. 132 plus) have risen dramatically in the last few years. No revolution here although the district may be doing an excellent job. The demographics are changing, more middle and upper-middle class. At high school, kids move to Liberty in Brentwood (see Brentwood).

Lots of business and residential development coming.

Clayton

Small town, quaint, in 1990s bustling with construction. Located just east of Concord, at base of Mt. Diablo.

After years of dithering whether to develop, Clayton bit in a big way, about 1,500 homes, duets and townhouses, Oakhurst Country Club, which will increase city's housing by 60 percent and bring the population to 12,000.

State tally (Jan. 1992) showed 2,590 residences: 2,344 single family homes, 242 single family attached, 3 multiples, 1 mobile.

Streets have been overhauled. New routes shunt traffic away from old downtown, which caused grumbling among merchants but efforts were made to work things out. Build-out is scheduled for 1996 but a sluggish housing market may stretch this further.

As for rest of Clayton, generally quite nice. For decades, the town has favored homes a cut above the going market, tract but slightly larger, with more amenities. Clayton attracts professionals, managerial types.

Family town. About 30 percent of 7,317 residents (1990 census) are under age 18. Lots of activities for kids, soccer, baseball, etc.

Farmers' market in summer. Parade on the Fourth of July. Restaurants, few shops. Close to Concord Pavilion. Nearby are a bowling alley, shopping plazas (supermarkets) and a fitness club. State university campus opened in Concord in 1992, less than five miles away.

Mt. Diablo visually dominates most of Contra Costa County but in Clayton its presence is overwhelming — in a pleasurable way. Real country feeling.

Horsy town, with stables on the outskirts. Hiking and equestrian trails.

Clayton started out as a hamlet and in the Fifties woke up horrified to see Concord galloping down the road with heaps of subdivisions. Not for us, said Clayton, which then incorporated as a city.

Residents didn't want growth, but they wanted amenities — roads, sewers, parks — and didn't want to boost taxes. For years town councils would be tempted by developments then throw their hands up when opposition surfaced.

Oakhurst offered an enticing package: golf course, shopping plaza, parks, money for middle school (to open in 1993), upscale housing.

Mt. Diablo Unified School District. School scores in top 25th percentile. Day care at many schools. All schools in district are or have been recently renovated, thanks to passage of bond.

FBI does not track crime in cities under 10,000, but Clayton, secluded, upper-middle class, probably runs same as Orinda — very low.

Commuters to San Fran and Oakland have to brave Ygnacio Valley or Clayton Valley roads, then freeways, formidable obstacles during peak periods. But BART stations are in Pleasant Hill and Concord, County Connection buses are available and if you work in the central county, you're within 10 to 30 minutes. Fast shot over Kirker Pass Road to East County.

Concord

A bustling, argumentative city, Contra Costa's largest, excellent sports and community programs, site of a new college campus.

In the 1950s and 1960s, Concord added residents by the tens of thousands. Now almost built out. Population increased by 8,000 in the last decade.

The big event for 1992: the opening of a satellite campus of California State University, Hayward. Called the Contra Costa Center, it offers upper division (junior and senior) classes and master's courses.

If you ask the Cal State bureaucrats, the center will remain a satellite until well into the next century. But some influential locals have been pushing for years to make the campus independent.

Either way, the campus, located off Ygnacio Valley Road near Alberta Way, is a plus for Concord.

Compared to other cities, Concord's a good commute but the freeways are congested at peak hours. BART station, end of the line, which means first dibs on seats in the morning. A second station is located just outside city limits. Two freeways, one of which was recently widened. County Connection buses.

Freeway bottleneck at Walnut Creek — the I-680-Highway 24 interchange. It is now being rebuilt.

Buchanan Airport is located just outside Concord city limits, near Highway 4 and I-680.

Concord is loaded with activities for adults and kids — one of the advantages of having a good tax base. Nineteen parks, 12 playgrounds, golf courses, community center, several fitness clubs, and one of best miniature golf courses on the West Coast. Blue Devils Marching Band among best in nation. Concord, in many ways, including scholarships, has always gotten behind music. Local boy who made good: Dave Brubeck.

Concord Pavilion. First-class entertainment: country, rock, jazz, pop and classical. Also several small theaters. Many restaurants. City plans to build a cinema complex, 2,500 seats, in the downtown but lawsuits are flying.

School scores bounce all over but many in the top 40th percentile. Served by Mt. Diablo Unified School District. Day care at most elementaries. Bond was passed several years ago to renovate every school in the district. Much of the work was done in 1992.

A few years ago, Concord placed among top 12 cities nationwide for "City Livability Awards." In 1991, Zero Population Growth, rating for environmental health, named Concord as one of the best places to live.

Concord was built out from its downtown in three waves. Between 1950 and 1960 the population went from 7,000 to 36,000, in the next decade to 85,164 and by 1980 to 103,00.

In the downtown and immediate neighborhoods, you'll find some heritage homes, the old Concord, homes built in the Fifties, and apartment complexes. One neighborhood is built around a lake.

As you move out, the homes generally become larger and more modern, the designs varying by tract but almost all middle-class suburban. More apartments can be found on Clayton Road. A new tract, upscale, is going in near the university but the heyday of rapid growth has passed.

State tally (1992) showed 44,326 residences, of which 25,873 were single homes, 2,783 single-family attached, 14,235 multiples, 1,435 mobile homes.

Biggest employer is the Bank of America, which dominates the downtown, thousands of white collar workers. Chevron, located on Diamond Boulevard near Interstate 680, also employs thousands. Concord has a Sheraton, a Hilton and a Holiday Inn. New auto center in downtown. North Concord, in a quiet way, is booming: warehouses, light industry, a discount warehouse store. Two other discount warehouses opened in 1992 off Concord Boulevard.

SunValley, the giant shopping mall, is located in west Concord — Sears, Penney's, Macy's, Emporium. Good shopping town. All these stores generate sales tax revenue that helps pay for city services.

Crime low-average for large suburban city. Three homicides in 1991, three in 1990, three in 1989, five in 1988, three each the preceding two years. Homeless shelter in north section, warehouse zone.

Cops worked with residents to clean up drug problems in some apartment complexes. Cleverly planned and executed effort, appears to have worked. Speaks well for intelligence of cops.

Concord finds itself frequently in the headlines. The Naval Weapons Station (bombs, some believed to be nuclear) is located on the northern border. Year-round pickets, accepted as everyday routine, camp near one of the gates.

In the late 1980s, the city council passed one of those ordinances that asks us all to live in peace and harmony. Race and creed and color — no problem. Sexual preference — ka-boom!

After a long, bitter battle, the city in 1991 voted, by 42 votes, against recognizing rights of homosexuals. In 1992 judge threw out the election results. Outside of court, arguments continue.

Is Concord prejudiced? If you asked gays, yes. The city is certainly no San Francisco. Many residents say gays should not be harassed but neither should

CONTRA COSTA CITY PROFILES 61

they be accorded special privileges — one way the civil rights ordinance was interpreted. Gays say they want equal, not special rights.

In other important ways Concord and Central Contra Costa are changing with little fuss: More Asians, Blacks and other minorities. A majority of the city council favored rights for gays, and city leaders and many residents are tired of the fights and headlines. This dispute, however, is going to drag on.

City manager (woman) quit in 1992 and sued city, alleging sexual harassment by a council member, who declared, not me, folks.

Crockett

Village at entrance to Carquinez Strait, 3,228 residents (1990 census). Also known as Sugar City, after C&H Sugar refinery that dominates waterfront.

Crockett used to be a company town. C&H funded almost everything and almost everyone worked for the refinery, but years ago C&H pulled back. When the freeway came, many workers moved out of Crockett, further diluting the Sugar City image.

Crockett in many parts is drab, C&H bewitchingly ugly. But the views are great and residents love the burg and fight to make it better or keep it from getting worse. Antique stores, marina, some restaurants add charm.

Seasonally windy on hills. Newer homes on hills, older units below. Some crime but usually confined to saloon bozos. Three teens recently killed in traffic accident.

Freeway splits town. About 15 minutes to Bay Bridge when traffic moves, much longer at peak hours. Regional park going in east of Crockett.

School scores middling plus. Elementary kids go to school in Rodeo, which shares district with Crockett.

C & H has been pushing to add a cogeneration plant that might block some views of the Strait. Ask Realtor about project.

Danville

Prestige town in the middle of the San Ramon Valley. Increased its population 18 percent in the last decade, from 26,446 to 31,306 residents, a misleading statistic.

When people say Danville, they often include the tracts going up outside the city limits. These developments look to Danville (and San Ramon) for shopping and civic leadership for the San Ramon Valley. Both are legal cities with directly elected city councils. The unincorporated neighborhoods are governed from Martinez by Board of Supervisors.

Danville homes rise from the valley floor up the Las Trampas Ridge to the west and the foothills of Mt. Diablo to the east.

Eugene O'Neill wrote some of his finest plays — "Long Day's Journey into Night," "The Iceman Cometh" — while looking down from a West

Danville hill. Home now a national monument.

An upscale address, Danville nonetheless has many apartments and homes that look plain old suburban. The town is attracting the new professionals coming into the valley, the Pac Bell and Chevron folks.

Served by San Ramon Valley School District, which also includes San Ramon and Alamo. School rankings in the 90th percentile, among the tops in the state. Voters passed $40 million bond in 1991 to build and improve schools.

Old school torn down, new middle school opened in 1991. Includes a multipurpose room and gym.

Interstate 680 through the San Ramon Valley is a lovely wide freeway but at Walnut Creek it joins Highway 24, the freeway to Oakland and San Francisco, and runs into traffic from Concord, Pittsburg, Solano County, etc.

Interstate 680, at Pleasanton, also connects to Interstate 580, another freeway to Oakland and San Francisco. If Highway 24 is jammed, take I-580 or vice versa. But both lead to the Bay Bridge toll plaza, a mess.

In a few years, traffic flows should improve. The Walnut Creek interchange is being rebuilt and I-680 from Martinez to Milpitas has been widened.

But with California and the Bay Area growing in population, no one is predicting an end to jams, congestion and delays. Alternatives are out there: BART, County Connection, car pooling (See commuting chapter). Estimated drive time to San Fran is 55 minutes.

Danville is trying to make sense out of its downtown roads, which were built for skinny horses. Railroad Avenue has been revamped and pressed into service as an arterial. Traffic aside, the downtown, with its old-west motif, is a plus. It gives Danville what so many new suburban cities lack: charm, a genuine connection with the past. The city has added to the flavor with old-fashioned lamps, pear trees, and brick and cobblestone paving.

Quality restaurants, some with outdoor seating. Also specialty shops, an ice cream parlor, delicatessens. On Sundays, the main street is sometimes closed for arts and crafts fairs.

Among cultural offerings: theater, melodrama, jazz, chamber orchestra, symphony concerts and art and photo exhibits. For arts and crafts classes, call San Ramon Valley Community Services, (510) 837-8235.

Baseball team, representing San Ramon Valley, won '91 Little League title, lost to Taiwan in World Series.

At Christmas, thousands stroll with lighted candles to a large oak in the downtown for a tree-lighting ceremony. Major shopping malls are located in Walnut Creek, Concord and Pleasanton, short drives.

Crime low. No homicides in 1991, two in 1990, none in 1989, 1988, one in 1987, none in 1986.

Two regional parks, Mt. Diablo and Las Trampas, thousands of acres, border the town. Five community parks. Tennis courts, soccer fields, play areas. Danville is playing catch-up on parks but is making progress.

Median & Average Rents of Renter-Occupied Dwellings

City or Area	Units	Median	Average
Alamo	281	$936	$931
Antioch	7,544	565	578
Bayview-Montalvin	288	695	674
Bethel Island	163	504	495
Blackhawk	76	1,001	1,213
Brentwood	773	524	507
Clayton	161	1,001	1,046
Concord	16,237	618	652
Crockett	588	459	482
Danville	1,318	999	994
Discovery Bay	223	971	1,010
East Richmond Heights	255	684	689
El Cerrito	3,656	645	689
El Sobrante	1,349	601	659
Hercules	664	880	920
Kensington	310	986	956
Lafayette	2,105	714	767
Martinez	4,104	603	617
Moraga	877	833	883
Oakley	987	563	574
Orinda	527	946	872
Pacheco	246	666	679
Pinole	1,411	655	690
Pittsburg	5,971	566	541
Pleasant Hill	4,872	696	743
Richmond	14,688	506	514
Rodeo	969	459	470
San Pablo	4,538	503	503
San Ramon	3,925	861	905
Tara Hills	502	698	722
Vine Hill	354	576	589
Walnut Creek	9,064	675	740
West Pittsburg	2,180	523	502
Remainder	4,756	620	648
Countywide	95,962	613	642

Source: 1990 Census. Units are total number of renter-occupied dwellings. Rents are stated as monthly payments. Median means halfway. In 100 homes, the 50th is the median.

Schools are used for playgrounds and recreation centers. Many of the new developments have swimming pools and rec. centers. Soccer is popular. One league is drawing 3,000 players. Annual Devil Mountain Run attracts thousands.

Iron Horse Trail, an abandoned rail route, is used for walking, jogging, horseback riding, cycling.

State tally (1992) showed 12,041 residences: 9,246 single homes, 2,081 single-family attached, 707 apartments, 7 mobile homes.

For the townhouses and homes going up outside borders of Danville and San Ramon, drive east on Diablo Road or Sycamore Valley Road or Crow Canyon Road or Tassajara Road. Ask Realtors about coming developments.

Diablo

Old-money neighborhood in the hills above Danville. About 1,200 residents. Little turnover in homes. Own security force. Golf course. Diablo Country Club. Reagan spoke there on one of his visits to Contra Costa. Horseback riding. "A tranquil island of money," one newspaper called Diablo.

Discovery Bay

A water-oriented community on eastern border of Contra Costa, near Byron. Nice homes, many luxurious. One section with deep anchorages is called "Millionaires' Row."

Discovery Bay started out in the 1970s as a retirement or second-home village, designed to tap into Delta recreation. Homes generally back up to the water or onto the golf course.

By and by, families and working adults bought in and the majority today use Discovery Bay as permanent home. Sales coincided with the office boom in Central Contra Costa, the San Ramon Valley and Pleasanton. The residential buck just went a helluva lot farther in Discovery Bay and the commute was not that long. But even when it was long — San Jose — people bought the homes.

The 1990 census counted 5,351 residents, about 20 percent under age 18.

About 3,700 homes, condos and duets have been constructed. In the planning or talking stage for the vicinity are about 4,100 more.

Some residents want Discovery Bay to incorporate as a city but without a stronger tax base (more stores) this idea might not fly. Municipal Advisory Council serves as community watchdog, sounding board. Crime low. Patrolled by sheriff's deputies. Roads are winding but flat and an invitation to speed.

Scores are generally well above the 50th percentile in Discovery Bay Elementary. From there, kids go to Liberty High in Brentwood.

Fishing, boating, water skiing, tennis, the outdoor life, small parks put in by developers. Many residents own rec. vehicles and boats. RV parking lot off Highway 4. Country club. Small shopping plaza. Baseball and soccer for the kids. Mt. Diablo in the background. Cocktails on the deck, quiet strolls, a round of golf in the evening. Short drive to Stockton and skiing and gambling in the Sierra. Lot of farm country, tomatoes and asparagus and fruit trees.

The drawbacks: You have to like country life. If you want theater and choice of fine restaurants, you have to drive. Many residents shop for groceries, necessities in other towns.

Second, the commute: It's not bad to Livermore, Pleasanton, or San Ramon. It can be wearying to San Jose, Oakland, San Francisco. Buses to Antioch and Pittsburg, connection to Concord BART.

Third, the prices. House for house, amenity for amenity, Discovery Bay is much cheaper than Central Contra Costa. New three- and four-bedroom homes in mid-1992 were selling for under $200,000. But many homes sell for much higher. For some people, a dig-deep town.

El Cerrito

West County city, rising about 1,000 feet from flats to hills. A bedroom community with a business strip that runs down San Pablo Avenue.

Built out. Expected to add no more than 1,000 residents in the next 20 years. A good address in a quiet way. Views from the hills. Nice homes. Popular with University of California professionals, especially hill homes.

Excellent commute, as commutes go along the shore. Two BART stations. Bay Bridge toll plaza is seven miles away via Interstate 80 — a slow seven at peak hours — but El Cerritans are watching the evening news while others are creeping along the freeways.

Close to Berkeley, another plus. Berkeley prices and rent controls make it impossible for many to live in that city, but Berkeley is so full of arts and fun that people want to live nearby.

Added 138 residents in last decade. Population hit 25,500 in 1960, dropped to 22,731 in 1980 and since has crept up to about 23,000. About 32 percent of population is over age 55, an indication of many retired people. Widowed and divorced, mostly women, make up about 18 percent of residents.

School scores middling but deceptive. El Cerrito draws many students from low-scoring flatlands but also sends many to top-notch colleges. Served by Richmond Unified School District, which has money problems (see schools). Two Catholic schools, one Jewish, which is expanding to 300 students, and a few others.

El Cerrito has spent much time and money reviving San Pablo Avenue, the city's main thoroughfare. Target Department Store opened recently, Home Depot on the way. A lot of work around Del Norte BART station.

Annual fees are levied on homes and apartments to pay for landscaping, park maintenance, street sweeping and street lights.

One of the first towns in nation with recycling center. El Cerrito does a good job in parks and rec and has an excellent community theater. Mira Vista Golf and Country Club rolls over the El Cerrito hills. Residential volunteer funding is keeping pool open year-round. Community Center. Regional parks nearby. City sponsors tiny tot programs. Exercise classes.

Zero homicides in 1991, 1990 and 1989, one in 1988, none in preceding three years. Thefts push crime rate up.

Good housing mix, 7,311 single homes, 325 single-family attached, 2,638 multiples, 74 mobile homes (1992 state tally).

Summing up: stable, reasonably safe, good commute, close to delights of Berkeley and San Fran.

El Sobrante

Scenic valley east of San Pablo, site of much residential building in recent years. Great views from the hills.

Governed by two entities, the City of Richmond and the county board of supervisors. Richmond has been annexing parcels in the valley for decades. Almost all the new developments are in Richmond.

Sheriff's deputies patrol unincorporated section, Richmond police the rest. Richmond Unified School District, which has money problems (see schools) serves all. School scores bounce around the middle but, with influx of middle class, should be coming up.

Census counted 9,852 residents in unincorporated El Sobrante, the "county" part.

Despite traffic congestion, a reasonably good commute compared to ones from Vallejo, Pittsburg and Antioch. El Sobrante is only 14 miles from the Bay Bridge toll plaza, and San Pablo Dam Road — affectionately, sometimes not, called the Dam Road — leads directly to Central Contra Costa.

Many fights over development. Residents, citing traffic and hillside protection, want fewer new homes; developers, noting location, want more.

Much to do in the way of recreation, notably at nearby regional parks and San Pablo Reservoir, which is open for hiking and fishing. Close to Tilden, one of the best regional parks in the Bay Area. Library.

Newer neighborhoods are decidedly middle class, in a nice way. Older neighborhoods generally a mix of blue- and white-collar. Business district tatty, but Hilltop Mall only a few miles away.

Hercules

Bedroom town, now catching its breath after 15 years of rapid development. Just about tripled its population in the 1980s, rising from 5,963 to about 17,000 residents.

Not too long ago, the town was almost all homes. Now shops and supermarkets have arrived to make life easier.

Hercules has also attracted some high tech, notably Bio-Rad, located down on the waterfront.

Until the mid-seventies, Hercules was a company town with a few hundred workers living in homes owned by Hercules Powder Co. Then company closed plant and sold most of land. Up went a modern suburb, the first tracts going in east of Interstate 80. Hercules is a planned town, one of its quiet strengths, and it's a modern town.

In recent years, developers have been filling in parcels west of freeway and near waterfront and Hercules is now debating about expanding into the Franklin Canyon Golf Course area. But residents in 1992 voted down one development plan.

Integrated community. Filipinos make up about a fourth of population; Asians, 17 percent; Blacks, 13; Hispanic, 10; Whites, 35. Town makes a strong effort to help people get along harmoniously.

Middle class. Crime low but residents concerned about troublesome youths and burglaries. No homicides in 1991, 1990, 1989, 1988 or 1987.

In initial years, an oil refinery on town's outskirts filled city coffers with sales tax revenues, allowing Hercules to put a lot of money into parks and activities. Refinery makes news occasionally with complaints about pollution but the wind blows odors toward downtown Rodeo. Refinery mprovements promised which might add almost $2 million annually to Hercules treasury, a lot of money for a small city.

Hercules runs day-care programs at schools. Town served by Richmond School District, which has money woes (see schools). School scores up there. About 30 percent of Hercules, census showed, is under age 18 — a family town. Interest high in kid activities.

Seniors center, community center, swimming complex. Bond was passed to improve and expand the town's parks.

From the freeway Hercules looks boring: all those tract homes marching over the hills. But the hill homes give good views of San Pablo Bay.

The state in 1992 tally counted 3,651 single homes, 1,665 single-family attached, 679 multiples (including condos), 7 mobile homes.

Fair commute, 17 miles to Bay Bridge but I-80 often clogs. Hercules is divided by Highway 4, the road-freeway to the Central County. An easy commute in that direction but in rush hours the central freeways jam. BART stations in El Cerrito. WestCAT buses. Also Dial-a-Ride.

Kensington

Prestigious village in hills between El Cerrito and Berkeley. Favorite of University of California families. "I like Kensington because you can watch Berkeley without feeling responsible for it," said one resident.

Lot of old-timers. About 35 percent of residents are over age 55; only 16 percent under age 18, the last census reported. Total population is about 5,000.

Great views. Some stately homes but many just modest and nice. Good police, fire protection. Few crimes, mostly burglaries and even those are few. Some slide problems near El Cerrito border. Ask Realtors.

Unincorporated, meaning it's governed by the county from Martinez but through local organizations Kensington controls its own affairs.

The one elementary school scores generally in the 90th percentile. Town is within Richmond Unified School District, which has money troubles. Kids usually go to El Cerrito High.

Kensington, 900 acres, is built out, about 2,250 housings units, 85 percent of them owner-occupied single homes, another indication of social stability.

Freeway and BART stations about a mile away.

Lafayette

Prestige town that does some hand wringing over amenities and sprucing up its main drag but is considered one of the best addresses in the county.

School rankings very high, crime low, restaurants top notch, views pretty (many hills), commute better than most. Lafayette straddles Highway 24, the freeway to San Fran. BART station in downtown. Buses to and from station.

Residents upper-middle class or rich, well educated, suburban, traveled, managerial or professional. One Nobel laureate.

A little in-filling here and there but the days of big growth are over. Lafayette added 2,622 residents in the last decade and may, according to regional planners, add about 1,500 people in the next 20 years — peanuts by the standards of the county. Tight planning controls.

The La in Lamorinda (Moraga and Orinda). Although the towns differ, they share many interests: dining in Lafayette, basketball at St. Mary's College in Moraga, Shakespeare at Orinda (outdoor theater), football and classical music at UC Berkeley, just over the hills. One high school district serves all but each town has its own high school and its own elementary schools.

Some apartments and condos in downtown but mostly single homes, many of them custom homes, more than a few opulent. Also many quite modest. When you buy in Lafayette, you pay for the schools, the safety, the address.

State count in 1992 showed 9,324 residences: 7,441 single homes, 302 single-family attached, 1,576 multiples, 5 mobile homes.

For years the city has been sprucing up Mt. Diablo Boulevard, its main drag, in the hope of attracting more businesses.

But many stores are empty, thanks to the recession and probably local attitudes. Residents are not anti-business but prizing the low-key life and beauty and not wanting more traffic, they are not aggressively for business.

For shopping, many residents head for Walnut Creek (Nordstrom, Emporium).

School rankings among the tops in the state. Acalanes students regularly win admission to top colleges in nation: Harvard, Yale, etc.

Parents of school children are quietly asked to kick in a few bucks for education programs — in effect, a kid tax. Bond measure passed in 1988 to renovate all high schools; much of the work was done recently. Voters in 1991 and 1992 passed parcel taxes to maintain academic programs at the schools.

Low crime. One homicide in 1991, no homicides in previous six years, reports FBI.

Many kid activities, a lot of them organized by parents. The most popular seem to be soccer and swimming and, for girls, dancing; for boys, Little League.

Lafayette Reservoir. Boating and fishing, favorite of joggers. Another regional park nearby. St. Mary's College and UC-Berkeley; culture and sports. Many trails in region.

Some traffic congestion. Streets south of the freeway narrow and meander, and feed into Orinda and Moraga streets. If buying in Lafayette, drive the neighborhood at rush hour.

Another irritant to a few residents: Morehouse, a small "college" that prizes love and started in the hippie era. It's on the outskirts of the city. Nothing, it is generally agreed, is more nauseating than open affection among the middle-aged.

Martinez

County seat. A mix of old town and new suburbs. Martinez starts at the Carquinez Strait and ends almost at Taylor Boulevard in Pleasant Hill.

A town noted for its oil refineries (Shell and Tosco) and spin-off industries, one of which blew up in 1992, killing one worker, maiming another and delighting half the residents. They were sorry for the men, but as they had been fighting the plant for years over its intention to burn toxics, they were happy to see it fall flat on its kisser.

Shortly after, the toxics proposal

No More Wild Goose Chases

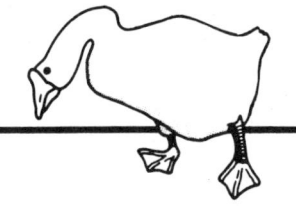

Looking for a new home? *The Home Buyer's Checkbook* can help you find your new home faster, easier, and at the best possible price.

Skip the wild goose chases - call and ask about *The Home Buyer's Checkbook!*

Call us at: (510) 935-9100

"Nobody knows Contra Costa County Better!"

SOLD

HERITAGE REAL ESTATE, INC.

Better Homes and Gardens®

Each firm independently owned and operated.
© Copyright Meredith Corporation 1986

Number of Units Available at Selected Rents

City or Area	<$100 -249	$250 -499	$500 -749	$750 -999	$1,000 -plus
Alamo	3	30	49	64	113
Antioch	538	1,912	3,716	1,168	116
Bayview-Montalvin	17	26	149	88	3
Bethel Island	22	51	62	12	1
Blackhawk	0	1	2	1	59
Brentwood	150	193	280	123	5
Clayton	2	4	13	50	89
Concord	623	2,054	9,110	3,343	721
Crockett	47	292	188	31	9
Danville	4	31	284	324	641
Discovery Bay	1	5	17	99	99
East Richmond Heights	7	52	98	75	19
El Cerrito	137	525	1,783	787	350
El Sobrante	29	214	727	250	96
Hercules	5	8	136	335	162
Kensington	0	28	66	55	143
Lafayette	68	258	822	518	379
Martinez	315	872	1,940	717	198
Moraga	2	65	277	249	260
Oakley	131	283	226	293	15
Orinda	30	95	73	62	233
Pacheco	6	47	87	87	10
Pinole	27	154	771	352	73
Pittsburg	831	1,349	2,855	814	36
Pleasant Hill	184	338	2,243	1,445	604
Richmond	1,991	5,079	5,550	1,633	230
Rodeo	274	249	296	118	20
San Pablo	612	1,591	1,940	242	100
San Ramon	11	27	1,144	1,711	988
Tara Hills	4	16	307	169	3
Vine Hill	13	102	171	50	9
Walnut Creek	161	691	4,973	1,881	1,209
West Pittsburg	332	638	966	193	5
Remainder	400	803	1,997	956	419
Countywide	6,977	18,083	43,319	18,295	7,417

Source: 1990 Census. The chart shows the number of rental units counted within a set range of rates.

was withdrawn, and peace descended on one of the oldest towns in the county.

The refineries and industries straddle I-680 and when motorists cross the Benicia Bridge they see large tankers docked at Shell. From this, they conclude that Martinez is an industrial town, coated with oil and grimed with smoke.

Just not the case. All but a small part of the Martinez area is suburban residential, and some of it — Alhambra Valley — opulent. Oil and industry are not the main employers. Governments and institutions are.

Thousands work for the sheriff's department or the county hospital (Merrithew Memorial) or the courts or miscellaneous county agencies or Kaiser Hospital or the Veterans Clinic or the college district, which is headquartered in Martinez, or the Highway Patrol.

As for the refineries and industries, Shell has been in Martinez since 1913 and for most of the refinery's existence it could do no wrong, even when it did wrong — spilled oil, belched smoke. Tosco is about three miles east of the downtown and not as much a presence as Shell.

Then came the environmental revolution, which opened eyes, and brought changes.

Like many big industries, Shell plays the role of good corporate citizen. It has upgraded the plant, installed pollution controls, and when things go boom-bang-boom, as they occasionally do, Shell apologizes, performs some civic penance (marsh restoration, park improvement), and things settle down.

When the schools or a charity needs a few bucks, Shell often kicks in. Shell and Tosco workers are neighbors; jobs are jobs. That counts a lot in a small town. Finally, whatever pollution there may be generally blows somewhere else. No grime, no coat of oil.

Forewarned, forearmed. If the simple presence of industry offends you, don't move to Martinez. If the town is acceptable but industrial proximity is not, drive the neighborhoods south of Highway 4. Plenty of choices.

Over a dozen parks, many activities — fishing, boating, soccer, cycling and jogging along the shore, baseball, movies, softball, hiking, football, swimming and more. Boys Club. Yacht Club. Annual art exhibit. Opera sing-off. Farmers market. Regional park on waterfront, and big one in the

---

A 'RESIDENT' OF CONTRA COSTA SINCE 1913...

A GREAT PLACE TO LIVE AND WORK!

Shell Oil Company
MARTINEZ MFG. COMPLEX

Briones hills. Comedy club in the Morello shopping center.

Martinez Museum, photos, memorabilia, Martinez as it used to be. Shell also has a museum.

John Muir, conservationist hero, lived in Martinez. His home is a national park. Perhaps because of Muir, a fair number of Martinez residents are active in conservation, parks and preserving hills and shore.

Bocce is very popular. Exercise nil. But food, wine, cheers, jeers, beers, good times ... yes!

Residents divide the town into two sections: north of the Santa Fe trestle (or Highway 4) and south of trestle. Old-town, north of the trestle, exudes a faint charm that appeals to people who want a little history in their lives. City has installed decorative brick in Main Street sidewalks along with old-time street lights. Many restaurants, antique shops, two bookstores, on or near Main Street.

When suburbia arrived in the 1950s, many of the homes went up south of the trestle. They are still going up, although in far fewer numbers. Martinez has also spread to the east, toward Morello and Pacheco Boulevard.

Population rose 41 percent in the last decade, a combination of migration and annexations.

Two freeways (Highway 4 and I-680), about a half-hour to Oakland when traffic is light, 45 minutes to San Francisco. When heavy, an exhausting haul. Amtrak. Buses to BART at Concord, SunValley Mall, about five miles away.

Martinez School District serves the downtown, Morello Avenue north, and south of Highway 4 near Alhambra Avenue. Mt. Diablo District serves Hidden Lakes area. After Hidden Valley Elementary, students move up to Valley View Intermediate and College Park High in Pleasant Hill.

Thanks to voter approval of bonds, every public school in the city has been renovated or improved, Alhambra High getting the most work —new gym, playing fields, tennis courts, pool, classrooms, labs, large main building that looks traditional but inside is quite modern.

College Park High scores in the 90th percentile, Alhambra about the 50th. Elementary and junior high rankings are coming in well above the 50th percentile.

Day-care has been installed at all Martinez district elementaries. YMCA runs program for Hidden Valley at nearby building.

Crime about average for suburban town, but Martinez enjoys high police visibility — police, sheriff's deputies, CHP officers.

No homicides in 1991, one in 1990, one in 1989, four in 1988, two in 1987, none in 1986, 1985, reports FBI.

Highway 4 area booming with two shopping centers, a movie complex and discount warehouses that attract thousands.

Breezes from the Carquinez Strait. Weather generally balmy, even in summer heat. Fog in winter.

In 1992, the state counted 13,137 units: 7,770 single homes, 2,199 single-family attached, 3,154 multiples, 14 mobile homes. Seniors center and several housing complexes for elderly; hotel for seniors to open in 1993.

Moraga

Secluded town, crime rate among lowest in the state, school scores among highest. Home to many professionals and managers.

According to crime rates, one of the safest towns in California. One homicide in 1991, none in previous six years, reports FBI.

The MOR in Lamorinda (Lafayette, Moraga, Orinda) and much like sister cities. Upscale, nice homes. Tree-lined streets. Country feeling. Rolling hills. Deer prance across lawns, nibble at the gardens. Utility wires were recently undergrounded along Moraga Way, the main drag.

Close to freeway (Highway 24) and BART stations, but far enough away to be "hidden," one reason for low crime. Many crimes are crimes of opportunity. Thieves and thugs can't find Moraga and the few roads into the town are easily monitored. Moraga has its own police force.

According to census, Moraga added only 838 residents in the last decade, and regional planners predict the town will add only 1,000 residents in the next 20 years. By the standards of most cities, Moraga is essentially built out.

State tally in 1992 showed 5,721 residences, of which 3,870 were single homes, 985 single-family attached, 861 multiples, 5 mobile homes.

MUIR WEST
R E A L T Y

We provide you with personal service to suit your individual needs.

We specialize in residential/commercial & investment properties throughout Contra Costa County with membership on 3 Boards and our own in-house property management service.

Dave Silva
BROKER
1734 Alhambra Ave., Martinez, CA 94553
Office: (510) 229-1400 & Home: (510) 228-8652

Home Price Sampler from Classified Ads

Alamo
3-bedroom, 2.5-bath ranch home, formal dining, family, bonus room, pool, $448,000.
4-bedroom, 3.5-bath, 4,500 sq. ft., 3/4 acre, 3 fireplaces, huge rooms, giant master w/ spa, view family room, $799,000.

Antioch
3-bedroom, 2-bath, deck, court location, garden window, ceiling fan, $139,500.
5-bedroom, 3-bath, 2,100+ sq. ft., family room, fireplace, upgrades, 6 yrs. old, $204,940.

Blackhawk
4-bedroom, 3-bath, custom 3,300 sq,. ft., cul-de-sac, on golf course, 2 fireplaces, 3-car garage, view of Mt. Diablo, $519,000.
5-bedroom, 3.5-bath, home on big level culde-sac lot, $654,500.

Brentwood
3-bedroom, 2.5-bath, 3.6 acres, l0-car garage, $425,000.
4-bedroom, 2.5-bath, 2,300 sq. ft., remodeled, shop barn, $399,500.

Clayton
3-bedroom, 2-bath, yard w/pool & spa, $269,950.
4-bedroom, 2.5-bath, family room, formal dining, solar-heated pool, spa, large RV parking, private garden area, $299,950.
4-bedroom w/gourmet kitchen, 3 yrs. old, upgrades, Regency Meadows, $349,950.

Concord
4-bedroom, 2-bath, automatic landscaping, close to everything, $183,000.
4-bedroom, 2.5-bath, country views, tile roof, large yard, walk to schools, new college, upgrades, $287,000.

Crockett
3-bedroom, 1-bath, large lot, basement could become apartment, $168,000.
3-bedroom, 2-bath, 1,850 sq. ft., sunset & water views, large living room, $285,000.

Danville
3-bedroom, 2,000 sq. ft., pool, family room, 4+car garage, remodeled, $309,000.
4-bedroom, 2.5-bath, 2,200 sq. ft., cul-de-sac, automatic sprinklers, inside laundry, pool & clubhouse facilities, $329,950.

Diablo
4-bedroom, 3-bath, footbridge & creek, separate guest cottage, $1,029,000.
5-bedroom, 5-bath, 5,200 sq. ft., private bridge, pool, spa, huge oaks, $1,250,000.

Discovery Bay
3-bedroom, 2-bath, on 8th fairway, move-in condition, $189,000.
4-bedroom, 2-bath, 2,500 sq. ft., on 18th tee, view, extras, $239,500.

El Cerrito
3-bedroom, 1-bath, corner lot, newly remodeled, $245,000.
3-bedroom, 3-bath, in-law unit, fireplace, vaulted ceiling, BART, shopping, $189,900.
5-bedroom, 3-bath, on 1/4 acre, Bay views, custom finishes, amenities, $439,500.

El Sobrante
3-bedroom, 2-bath, large family room, separate workshop, hot tub, $225,000.
3-bedroom, 2-bath, 2-car asttached garage, $168,000.
4-bedroom, 2-bath, Carriage Hills home, landscaped, $245,000.

Hercules
3-bedroom condo, carefree, convenient, cost effective, $148,000.
3-bedroom, 1,600 sq. ft., view of the bay, $189,950.
3-bedroom, 2.5-bath, lush garden, walk to BART express, $197,000.

Kensington
2-bedroom Tudor, heart of Kensington, ideal for young family or couple, $259,000.
Victorian Village, view, $239,900.

Lafayette
3-bedroom, 2.5-bath, 3/4 acre, wooded, custom, Mt. Diablo view, bonus room, $334,950.
5-bedroom, 3-bath, 3,500 sq. ft., 1/2 acre, huge garage, RV & boat parking, 3 blocks from freeway, $575,000.

Martinez
3-bedroom, 2-bath, 2-story, concrete-block detached building w/1/2-bath, central location, good condition, $153,500.
3-bedroom, 2-bath, deep lot, custom built, views, near county offices, $255,000.
3-bedroom, 2-bath, atrium, family room, patios, near freeway, parks, shops, $272,500.

Moraga
4-bedroom, 2-bath, pool, spa, 2 fireplaces, large rooms, family room, $420,000.
5-bedroom, 3-bath, 2-story colonial, formal dining , family room, $469,00.

Oakley
3-bedroom, 2-bath, nice backyard, community pool, 2 parks, $143,900.
3-bedroom, 2-bath, 1,500 sq. ft., 1 yr. old, many upgrades, $168,000.

Orinda
2-bedroom, 1.5-bath, bonus room, deck, new kitchen & baths, $267,500.
3-bedroom, 2-bath + separate guest house, 1+ acre, country club area, $675,000.
4-bedroom, 3-bath, 1/3 acre lot, den, new kitchen, near schools, BART bus, $453,500.

Home Price Sampler from Classified Ads

Pacheco
3-bedroom, 2.5-bath, den/bonus room, Oak Tree Villas, $242,950.
3-bedroom, 2.5-bath townhouse, spacious, secluded, 2-car garage, $161,000.

Pinole
2-bedroom, remodeled kitchen & bath, den, deck, dog run, country-sized lot, $149,950.
3-bedroom, 2-bath, new kitchen, big backyard, fruit trees, patio, double garage, fireplace, $167,000.

Pittsburg
2-bedroom, family room, new carpet, large yard, $108,000.
3-bedroom, 3-bath, remodeled, RV parking, $155,500.

Pleasant Hill
3-bedroom, 2-bath, pool, spa, alarms, deck, fireplace, hardwood floors, $249,950.
4-bedroom, gourmet kitchen, family room, vaulted ceilings, walk-in closets, large lot, RV parking & spa, $339,950.

Richmond
2-bedroom, formal dining, sun rooms, nice yard, new paint, $185,000.
5-bedroom, 2-bath, 2-car garage, remodeled, view of Bay, $217,900.

Rodeo
4-bedroom, 2-bath, new carpets, linoleum and appliances, solar heating, $164,950.
3-bedroom, 2.5-bath, 2,200+ sq. ft., spa, formal dining, family room, $239,000.

Rossmoor
Wood-shingle condo duplex, facing east, golf course, spacious, $475,000.

San Pablo
3-bedroom, 1-bath, fruit trees, garage-loft, good area, $115,000.
4-bedroom, 2-bath, in Tara Hills, $165,000.

San Ramon
3-bedroom, 3-bath, vaulted ceilings, wet bar, pool, deck, RV parking, $299,500.
Golf course villa, formal dining, living room, gourmet kitchen, master suite, $319,500.
4-bedroom, 3-bath, 4 yrs. old, new paint, new kitchen, remodeled bathroom, $227,950.

Walnut Creek
3-bedroom, 2-bath, ranch home, corner lot, remodeled kitchen, baths, $299,996.
6-bedroom, 5-bath, 4,700+ sq. ft., older home, 1 acre, view, marble, oak, $795,000.

Source: Survey of local classified advertising in summer and fall, 1992.

Schools score quite high, many kids go on to the best colleges and much parental energy goes into education. Voters in 1991 passed a $42 parcel tax to maintain programs at the high school (Acalanes District), and Miramonte High School, thanks to a bond, is being renovated and upgraded with new equipment. In 1992, a parcel tax, ($75 annually) was passed to avoid teacher layoffs and to buy school supplies.

Miramonte in 1991 was named a Blue Ribbon School, one of only 222 honored nationally. White House presentation.

Country club. No shortage of tennis courts. Swimming is big with kids. Matt Biondi, the Olympic gold medal winner, is from Moraga.

Scenic trails wind through gently rolling hills. On summer evenings and weekends, hundreds will be found strolling, chatting, jogging. Little in the way of neighborhood parks, the main exception being 20 acres, the commons, in the center of town. Summer concerts. School grounds are used for soccer, baseball, basketball. Large regional parks located just outside town. Also on edge of town, a redwood grove, remnant of the giants that used to grow there.

St. Mary's College. Pretty campus. Football and basketball games, many cultural events that attract residents.

Lots of socializing. In California it's pretty near impossible to use the word society without someone snickering but Lamorinda prizes "Society" and throws the teens debutante balls. Boutiques, stores, market, restaurants in small shopping area. For big-ticket items, Moragans head to Walnut Creek or San Francisco.

Hacienda Las Flores, an old mansion built by oil magnate, was purchased by city for a community center. Many people take their entertainment in Berkeley, Oakland or San Fran. New Shakespeare Festival recently opened outside Orinda, near the freeway. To cut down on hay fever, the town plants trees that rarely make people wheeze, sneeze or cough.

Moraga's major drawback: traffic. The roads are narrow, winding and at peak hours congested.

Once through the roads, the commute picture brightens. BART stations at Lafayette and Orinda. Highway 24 to the Bay Bridge is generally stop-and-go during rush hours but Lamorinda residents, being close to the Caldecott Tunnel, avoid the freeway jams found toward Walnut Creek.

Oakley

In 1992, Oakley opened two elementary schools, symbols for what is happening to the once-sleepy farm hamlet. In the last decade the population shot up by about 600 percent, from 2,844 residents to 18,374. The homes are still going up, and in 1993 a McDonald's will open.

Many young families. About a third of the residents are under age 18, the census revealed.

The main attraction: housing prices. A home costing $300,000 in Walnut Creek would probably sell for less than $200,000 in Oakley.

Other factors: Contra Costa is running out of flatland suitable for building. Oakley, situated on the Delta, is flat, and thanks to Highway 4, accessible, although the commute for many is nerve-wracking.

Located off Highway 4, south of the Antioch Bridge. Open fields remain but Oakley is now a bedroom community. New subdivisions to the left and right of Highway 4. Homes nice, lawns well-kept.

The new Oakley is symbolized by the Cypress Square Shopping Center — Raley's, fast-food restaurants, shops — opened in 1989, and followed by another supermarket.

Fishing, boating, water sports. Wine festival. Almond Festival. Quick ride up to the Sierra. The town has several ball fields, located at the schools, and a small library in the old town. Homeowners pay a tax of about $30 a year for park and recreation. YMCA has opened a club-activities center.

As new tracts come in, developers are required to set aside land for parks.

Holy Ghost Festival, held since 1926, draws 5,000, celebrates Portuguese legend of a ship bringing meat and bread to the starving of the Azores Islands.

Kids attend schools in Oakley district, then move up to Liberty High in Brentwood. Liberty district has purchased 60 acres for a high school in Oakley and commissioned architectural plans but construction is years off. Scores are bouncing all over, some below the 50th percentile, many well above. To handle all the kids, schools are switching to a year-round system.

Oakley is unincorporated, meaning it's governed from Martinez by the county board of supervisors, which may or may not listen to advice from local groups. Several civic leaders are pushing to have Oakley incorporate as a city but so far the effort has not jelled. Crime not tracked by FBI but rural-suburban towns usually come in on the low side.

At Antioch, Highway 4 veers south and turns into a two-lane road. It is now being widened to four lanes.

The highway at peak hours often jams, usually near Concord, but a bottleneck at Willow Pass is being eliminated and BART, which is being extended to the East County, will take some traffic off.

For people who work in Livermore-Pleasanton, Vasco Road, the shortcut to I-580, is going to be rerouted. Tri Delta buses to Antioch and Pittsburg, connection to Concord BART.

Orinda

Located just over the hill from University of California. Probably the most prestigious town in Contra Costa. Home to bosses, professionals, professors. The INDA in Lamorinda (Lafayette, Moraga, Orinda).

Crime low, school rankings among highest in state. Voters in 1991 passed a $70 parcel tax to avoid cutting elementary school programs and personnel. Also passed in 1991 was a $42 parcel tax to maintain programs at the local high school (Acalanes District). Thanks to taxpayers support, all high schools in Lamorinda are now being renovated and upgraded with new equipment.

Homes nice, some opulent, many modest, most custom, upscale but not ostentatious. Orinda does not like the showy. City council in 1990 restricted size of homes — nothing over 4,200 sq. feet on a half-acre lot.

One of best commutes in the county but many complain about street traffic. If buying home, check the traffic at rush hours. BART station in the downtown, right next to freeway.

Republican country, sort of. In 1992, George Bush paid Orinda a visit, a fundraiser, $10,000 per couple. He got the money, but on election day, et tu, Orinda. Clinton carried the town.

Second-lowest crime rate in county, one of lowest in state. No homicides in 1991, 1990, 1989, 1988, one in 1987.

Orinda backs up to a large regional park, Tilden, one of the biggest and best equipped in Bay Area, (trails, merry-go-round, playing fields, lake, golf course, botanical garden).

The town has 6,560 residences: 6,151 single homes, 142 single-family attached, 263 multiples, 4 mobile homes (1992 state figures).

Very little new construction. Orinda has open land but much of it is slide prone or too steep to build on. Population dropped by 183 in 1980s.

Residents a bit on the mature side. About 29 percent over age 55, compared to 22 percent under age 18.

Between Orinda and the Caldecott Tunnel is a scenic valley, called Gateway. Although served by freeway access, it has not been developed. Now builders are knocking at the door— 338 homes, conference center, golf course. Over 100 meetings, many arguments. Home buyers should ask Realtors to point out the Gateway location.

Upscale markets, shops in the downtown, also a large single movie theater, beautifully renovated. The theater is the centerpiece in an office-store complex that may succeed but for years has struggled. The developer had hoped to build in four years; after 10 he allowed the $24 million project to slide into foreclosure. The place opened in 1991 and seems to be attracting tenants.

The reasons for the delays are many and diverse but they boil down to the character of Orinda. The town is loaded with critics, all ready to fight what they dislike. This said, when Orinda gets behind a project, it moves. A Shakespearean festival and theater opened in 1991, near the Gateway freeway exit. By all accounts, a roaring success.

Although UC-Davis, not UC-Berkeley, is the preferred university for Lamorinda high school seniors, Berkeley greatly influences Lamorinda, especially Orinda. Berkeley used to be a bastion for progressive Republicans. Many of them moved to Orinda. The educational push is strong, the environmental-good government foundation solid.

Book Fair in 1992 raised $16,000 for library and Friends of Library sponsored a writing contest for local students — small things but they signal a big interest in education and learning.

One small park next to Community Center, one other park recently purchased. Orinda is an old town but, having incorporated only seven years ago, a new city, and is only now building a park system.

Still plenty to do — at Tilden and UC-Berkeley, which is loaded with activities open to public (sports, plays, concerts, recitals, top names).

Kids use schools for ball field and swim meets. Swimming popular in Lamorinda. Community Center runs academic classes.

Community Center sponsors kindergym, seniors' activities, soccer, dance, art classes, much more. Call (510) 254-2445 for catalog. Also located in Orinda, John F. Kennedy University. Runs interesting programs.

Clubs many, society lively, people interesting, often accomplished. Orinda costs a lot, but its fans say it's worth a lot. (See also Lafayette and Moraga.)

Pinole

Bedroom town in West County. Quiet, middle class, school rankings high, crime low, commute fair. Pinole starts at San Pablo Bay then moves back in a rectangular shape into the hills. Many good views. Nice neighborhoods. City has reputation for being well-run.

The state in its 1992 tally counted 6,700 residences: 4,926 single homes, 453 single-family attached, 1,072 multiples., 249 mobile homes.

Bowling alley, nice library, fairly new sports fields on Pinole Valley Road, movie complex (nine screens), small theater. Many activities for kids, seasonal swimming, Tiny Tots program. Pinole has a small waterfront, nice for an evening stroll. Some shopping in downtown, much shopping in a plaza at intersection of Appian Way and I-80. In the works, a Target and a Mervyn's. Hilltop, the regional mall in Richmond, is one freeway exit away.

Local hospital, Doctors, is near freeway and Appian Way.

West of the freeway and south of Pinole are unincorporated neighborhoods, Tara Hills and Seaview. Middle class, much like Pinole.

Scores generally above the 50-60th percentile, many in the 80s. Schools are in Richmond Unified School District, which has severe money problems (see schools). Catholic elementary in downtown.

Traffic on I-80 is often congested but compared to other towns, a good commute. Pinole straddles the freeway, 14 miles to Bay Bridge. Buses to BART stations. Highway 4 to East and Central County is a mile away.

Crime middling, mostly thefts. No homicides in 1991 and preceding six years. In 1992, a high school student, off campus, shot and wounded another student. Combined with other West County incidents involving teenagers, the shooting called attention to teen violence, the struggling school district, and gave parents the jitters. Still, Pinole has to be considered suburban safe.

Pinole has an old town, which the city is improving. Once you leave Pinole going east it's almost all country— pretty.

Local kid who made good: Gino Toretta, winner of the 1992 Heisman trophy. For the football ignorant, this is a Big Deal.

Pittsburg

Another changing city. Used to be known more for its problems (crime in old town) than its promise, but location, new demographics and aggressive civic action have fleshed out the promise. First city over the Willow Pass, the opening in the hills that divides Central and East Contra Costa.

Rising prices have made it impossible for many middle-class people to buy homes in the Central County. Pittsburg is getting many of these buyers, and the arrival of BART at West Pittsburg in a few years will spur the migration.

More middle class means lower crime, higher school rankings.

Pittsburg has doubled its population in the last two decades and is still building. Many housing choices. One of the largest marinas in northern California (718 berths).

Pittsburg used to be solidly blue collar, many Italians, many Blacks, a small but significant number of Hispanics. Thousands of residents were employed in local industries. During World War II, a camp was built and used as a staging area for troops destined for the Pacific.

After the Korean War, the camp was dismantled and Pittsburg returned to its self-contained existence, but not for long. The freeway, Highway 4, was extended out to East County, opening the land for suburban growth.

About the same time, major firms — Chevron, Pac Bell, Bank of America — built large office complexes in the Central County, bringing thousands of jobs within short driving distance of the East County. In poured the newcomers, many of them white collars, ethnically diverse.

When the freeway came, it bypassed and just about killed Pittsburg's downtown. Some industries remained but, because of automation and foreign competition, thousands of factory jobs were lost. Several downtown neighborhoods went into decline. Crime rose sharply and Pittsburg won a reputation for being unsafe. Since that time, much has changed.

The new neighborhoods, many of them built south of the freeway, are more middle class — school rankings higher, crime lower. In the downtown, Pittsburg bulldozed some of crime blocks (which had also served as housing for the poor.) 1993 will see the start of residential construction in this section.

The marina, heavily subsidized, reintroduced middle class into the downtown. Other improvements have also upgraded the downtown. Nonetheless, some neighborhoods in the downtown still demand extra wariness.

The Pittsburg crime rating is about suburban average but includes many burglaries and crimes of violence. Four homicides in 1991, three in 1990, four in 1989, six in 1988, four in 1987, six in 1986.

Highway 4 through Willow Pass is being widened, which will remove a bottleneck. The BART extension follows the freeway and includes more freeway improvements.

Kirker Pass, a four-lane expressway, scoots you down to Walnut Creek. The Concord BART is within 10 miles. Tri Delta Transit runs buses throughout the East County. County Connection runs express buses to the Walnut Creek and Concord BART stations.

Los Medanos Community College is located in Pittsburg; over 350 academic and vocational classes each semester.

The 1990 census revealed a sharp rise in children, now about 31 percent of population. The school district recently opened a new elementary and in 1994 may start year-round sessions at some schools. Call the district — (510) 432-4705 — to find out what schools your children will attend. School rankings are rising but many are still low. Parents should understand that they need to give the kids a strong push at home. Two large private schools in town.

Fourteen parks, baseball, soccer, softball, football, fishing, boating, water sports, bocce, new Boys and Girls Club, YWCA. Bowling alley.

Swim center, seniors center, community center, Los Medanos Community Hospital. The college runs a child development program with many classes on rearing kids. New movie complex, 12 theaters. Also new roller skating rink. Small World Park chugs kids around in a miniature train. Concord Pavilion is just over the hill. Annual Seafood Festival draws over 80,000. Pittsburg also celebrates Juneteenth Days and Columbus Day.

Diverse population. Pittsburg has its share of ethnic disputes but there's a lot of get along, go along. School superintendent is black, college president Chinese descent, city manager Italian descent, assistant city managers are women, one Hispanic, one Black. Mixed city council.

Walmart and Target stores opened in recent years. In 1992, Burlington Coat Factory opened an outlet and Pace opened a giant store, which, citing no business, it then closed. Regional mall just over the border in Antioch.

BART cars to be built in Pittsburg, a boost to local employment.

The state in 1992 tallied 17,094 residences:10,084 single homes, 991 single-family attached, 4,660 multiples, 639 mobile homes.

Landfill opened in 1992 in the hills. Most of the garbage is dumped at Martinez and then taken by truck to the landfill, called Keller Canyon. Neighboring residents don't like the landfill, others say it's not obtrusive. Take Bailey Road south off the freeway and form your own opinion.

PG&E towers range across Pittsburg. Big industry (Dow and U.S. Steel-Posco) still a major presence and a lot of Pittsburg is just plain suburban.

But Mt. Diablo is in the background, the town is on the water. Pittsburg's close, it's affordable, a lot of people are finding it attractive.

Pleasant Hill

Quiet town, school scores high, activities many. In 1991, it opened a new city hall that civic leaders hope will give the city a surer sense of itself.

Bedroom community, with education and services provided by a variety of agencies. Residents shop in other towns and pay little attention to who provides the services as long as they are provided — a common situation in suburbia. SunValley, the regional mall, is just outside city limits.

Site of main county library, scads of books. And Diablo Valley College, largest community college in county. Many offerings, activities, a plus for town. Also in Pleasant Hill, YMCA club and pool, private gym facilities.

Park district has good reputation: soccer, tennis, softball, swimming (public pool), bowling, dance, mushball, softball, track, basketball, excursions and more. Many more classes at adult school. Active programs for seniors, including afternoon dances.

A canal trail winds through the town; popular with hikers and cyclists. Eleven city parks. Bridge center. Community center. Briones Regional Park. Summer farmers' market near main library.

Many restaurants in the category of Chevy's and Velvet Turtle, good food, nothing fancy, reasonably priced.

The state in 1992 counted 8,155 single homes, 1,461 single-family attached, 4,019 multiples (many near Diablo Valley College and BART station), 58 mobile homes.

Although Pleasant Hill has many new homes, most residential construction took place in the 1950s and 1960s, tract homes, generally well kept. The city increased population by 26 percent in last decade.

Much construction going on at unincorporated land near Pleasant Hill BART station. Plans call for 892 residential units, three hotels, two 10-story office buildings, a day-care center, underground parking for 1,175 vehicles. Pac Tel and Levi Strauss have moved some of their operations to buildings at this location. New parking garage for BART opened in 1992.

Offices, stores, restaurants, near freeway, along Contra Costa Boulevard. City is working on redevelopment to spruce up downtown near I-680 and Gregory Lane. Bank of America employs hundreds in four office buildings in Ellinwood complex, near the freeway.

Mt. Diablo District schools. Sequoia Elementary and Junior, two of the first basic schools in county, enjoy high parental support and high scores. College Park High rankings are landing in the 80th and 90th percentiles and the school is winning a reputation for academics. Local paper reported that students in other high schools are trying to transfer to College Park for its prep courses. Day care at many elementaries. All schools in Mt. Diablo District have been renovated, thanks to bond passed several years ago.

Crime low-middling, pushed up by thefts at stores. One homicide in 1991, none in 1990, two in 1989, two in 1988, one in 1987, none in 1986, one in 1985, reports FBI.

Some complaints about noise from planes taking off and landing at Buchanan Airport in Concord. If buying home, check with neighbors.

One BART station, second station at Lafayette, a short drive. City served by County Connection (buses). One freeway, I-680, congested at rush hours but recently widened and still being improved.

Back roads will take you around freeway bottleneck at Walnut Creek. Short drive to Highway 4, the main road to East and West Contra Costa.

Richmond

A dynamic city, second most populous in the county, beset with problems, foremost crime in downtown neighborhoods, yet successful in attracting businesses and new residents.

Interesting, diverse, racially mixed, rapidly changing, distinct neighborhoods. Population increased by 17 percent in last decade.

Many home buyers and business people turn up their noses at Richmond because its reputation is not just bad, but heavy-duty bad.

Richmond, however, is like Oakland or New York or San Francisco. It has its safe and unsafe neighborhoods. The city stretches from El Cerrito to Pinole and out into the El Sobrante Valley. Away from the downtown, many sections are typical suburban.

Richmond has advantages that time has improved. The city is a few miles up the road from Berkeley, Oakland and the Bay Bridge. The great days of home building along the east shore are just about over. The population keeps rising. Any reasonable city close in is going to get a second look.

Richmond has two freeways, I-80 and, recently completed, I-580. It has a bridge to San Rafael and Marin County, which at times seems to be doing its best to drive out business. Richmond has BART and Amtrak and bus service and Santa Fe. The city has a UPS terminal and a seaport. I-80 is often congested but for commuters and shippers Richmond offers a lot.

Richmond has the Chevron refinery, which catches flak over pollution but provides jobs and tax revenues. Hilltop Mall, one of the largest in the East Bay, is located in the northern sector of Richmond.

The south section has Bay frontage, and great views of San Francisco and, for some, the Golden Gate. In the 1980s, builders took a chance on the south, built Marina Bay (1,500 residential units) and offices.

Industry also discovered the south area and other parts of Richmond. In 1992, a software company moved to Pt. Richmond, and a bio-tech firm located near Hilltop. Kaiser is building a new hospital in the downtown.

The city in 1992 got a favorable write-up in the N.Y. Times and not a few boosters were thinking, well, at long last, Richmond's good points are being recognized. But granting Richmond does much better than its reputation, it has serious problems impossible to gloss over.

Modern Richmond was born on Dec. 7, 1941, when the bombs fell on Pearl Harbor. Henry Kaiser months earlier had won a contract to build tramp steamers for the beleaguered British — Liberty ships.

With the war, the U.S. poured millions into the shipyards. Richmond in 1940 had 23,642 residents, almost everyone White. Many were employed by Chevron, the town's biggest industry, and crucial to the war. Kaiser had nobody to build ships. He dispatched recruiters throughout the South and lured thousands of poor Blacks and poor Whites to Richmond. The population zoomed to over 100,000, and tensions simmered.

After the war, the national economy took off, suburbia galloped into Contra Costa, freeways came, and Blacks demanded civil rights.

In Richmond, many Whites fled to places like San Pablo, El Sobrante and Concord and the population dropped below 75,000.

The Blacks stayed put initially then grew a middle class that spread to the new Richmond. In the Fifties and Sixties, Richmond jumped over its borders and annexed like crazy, thousands of acres. Left behind were thousands of poor people, many of them residing in and around the old downtown. Much has changed but not some of the basic elements: School scores are very low in these sections. Crime is high and drugs and a multitude of shootings have made things worse.

Two police officers were killed in late 1992 while investigating a family dispute. Shocked and saddened Richmond.

Homicides numbered 61 in 1991, 36 in 1990, 38 in 1989, 31 in 1988, 16 the year previous, 21 the year before that, and before that, 19, the FBI reports.

Many of the victims are teenagers and this has made parents jittery, not only about the city but about the schools, which have severe money problems (see schools). The newer neighborhoods are not crime free but have much less, and as the schools move out from the downtown, the scores rise.

Blacks have made it into the power structure — not as much as they would like, but enough to make them establishment. The Whites, for the most part, are in the Berkeley and labor tradition, liberal or progressive.

Richmond school district, thanks to the middle-class migration, is generally well integrated. The district stretches to Hercules and includes almost every city in the West County. Finally, Whites and Blacks have had over 50 years to work out differences. Racial animosity remains a problem. But many Whites and Blacks are friends and get along, and so do the kids.

If all this doesn't sound complicated enough, the ethnic picture is changing: more Hispanics, Filipinos and Asians.

Here's a rundown on the neighborhoods.

• The downtown and adjoining neighborhoods. BART, Amtrak, the Social Security Payment Center (1,300 employees), the city hall complex, large library, biggest indoor auditorium in the county, a museum, an arts center, a Kaiser Medical Center, and new housing.

The downtown has run-down housing but also housing that looks good and has been well kept, which underscores an important point. In talking about crime, it's easy to indict an entire neighborhood or an entire people and lump the good with the bad. But many law-abiding people live in the downtown. Still, a place to be extra wary.

• Flatlands two. Near Interstate 80, north of Barrett, south of Potrero (Richmond annex) crime drops and neighborhoods become more stabilized.

• Marina Bay, Brickyard Landing, Point Richmond, also known as SoKnox. Close to downtown, these neighborhoods are separated from the poor neighborhoods by an industrial belt and by the Knox freeway (Interstate 580).

Point Richmond is old Richmond, the city's first neighborhood, with a main street laid out about the turn of the century. Educated, politically savvy, liberal, the Point and its residents exercise great influence. Several nice restaurants and sandwich shops, a library, churches, tennis courts and the Richmond Plunge, a large indoor pool. Brickyard Cove and Marina Bay are upscale developments along the south shore. Security gates at Marina Bay. Hiking trails. Shoreline park. Boating. Marina. Mostly elderly retired, empty-nesters and young professionals.

• Richmond Hills, East Richmond. Hillside neighborhoods that back up against a regional park. Middle class. Great views. Older homes that have held their value. Generally unincorporated, which means they're governed from Martinez and patrolled by sheriff's deputies.

- El Sobrante Valley, east of Interstate 80. About half the valley is unincorporated, the other half in Richmond. Almost all the new homes in the valley are in Richmond. Low in crime. Policed by Richmond. Scores middling to 90 percentiles. Middle class.

Well-kept streets and lawns. Views from hills. Congestion at freeway approaches. Oriented somewhat to Central County job market. Many commuters take the Dam Road to Highway 24.

- Hilltop. Site of mall and many new apartments, condos, paired homes, light industry, and offices. Major expressway scheduled for the area, which will move cars faster to the San Rafael Bridge. Macy's, Emporium, Penney's, Sears in mall. Movies. YMCA opened a new gym, health facility in late 1992.

- North Richmond. Unincorporated neighborhood west of San Pablo. High in crime but in 1992 sheriff's deputies and civic leaders did a cleanup that supposedly discouraged some crime. Site of new jail.

- Oil-Chemical-Industrial-Warehouse neighborhoods. Generally the shoreline, from the southern border up to and around the bridge, then up to Point San Pablo, and around Point Pinole. Skirts around Marina Bay and Point Richmond.

The biggest player, the Chevron refinery, parts of which blow up from time to time. Protests and pressure from regional agencies have raised Chevron's consciousness about pollution, and improvements are being made. But accidents happen.

Despite complaints from environmentalists, the place has a strong constituency. Chevron refinery and other Chevron businesses employ thousands in Richmond and account for about 27 percent of the city's tax income. The company is a major supporter of charities and benevolent groups.

Recreation, community activities? Good selection. Museum, boating, clubs, three regional parks, 26 city parks, swimming, baseball (Willie McGee's hometown), football, basketball, etc. Richmond has always had a strong interest in art, symbolized by its support of the Richmond Art Center.

Excellent choice of housing. Some older homes for under $100,000. The 1992 state tally showed 35,736 residences, of which single homes numbered 20,215; single attached, 2,495; multiples, 12,968; mobile homes, 58.

Other points: close to UC-Berkeley and Contra Costa Community College (San Pablo). More BART stations in nearby El Cerrito. Chamber of commerce puts out an unusually good information packet, (510) 234-3512.

Summing up, watch the crime and schools but keep an open mind. Many pluses.

Rodeo

A two-neighborhood town: old town west of the freeway, Viewpointe subdivision, built in 1970s, east of the freeway. Old town faded in the Fifties when freeway bypassed it.

Rodeo's center is gradually moving toward the freeway. A big Safeway located about a half-mile west of the freeway is town's commercial center.

The 1990 census counted 7,586 residents, a drop of 700 over the previous decade. Under 18-year-olds make up 29 percent of town — high percentage.

Marina lends some charm to old town. Union Oil refinery, in Rodeo since 1903, takes some away but coexistence prevails. Pacific Refinery, located in adjoining Hercules, occasionally wafts odors into downtown Rodeo. Pressure is being applied, and refinery promises to clean up.

Bayo Vista, small county housing tract, introduces some crime into the downtown. But most of Rodeo is quiet, suburban.

Viewpointe is a nice subdivision built on hillside. Good views. Park. Homeowners association. Gradually, the new people have taken over from the old towners. Old town, blue collar; Viewpointe, a mixture of white and blue.

Rodeo, unincorporated, is governed from Martinez by board of supervisors and patrolled by sheriff's deputies. Civic groups exercise a fair amount of government control.

John Swett School District serves Crockett and Rodeo. The one high school, John Swett, is in Crockett. Catholic elementary school in downtown Rodeo. Boys-Girls Club. Basketball, arts and crafts. Baseball and swimming are popular in Rodeo.

Right off Interstate 80 and Highway 4. Usual complaints about traffic on 80 but a better commute than most. Park 'n' ride lot near the freeway.

San Pablo

Small West Contra Costa city, straddles the freeway, good commute, nice city hall, site of community college, low school scores, high crime.

When Richmond moved north after World War II, San Pablo, a village, incorporated as a city to avoid Richmond's grasp. San Pablo boomed after the war because it built a lot of housing for veterans and newcomers.

But as Richmond surrounds San Pablo, the city was destined to remain small. While other county towns turned suburban, San Pablo, beset with crime problems, faded. The population hit 21,500 about 1970, then slipped to 19,500. The 1980s saw a revival. In 1990, the census counted 25,158 residents, 30 percent under age 18. New demographics: more Asians, Filipinos, Hispanics, Blacks. Integrated town.

To revive, San Pablo embraced redevelopment, a tax approach that among other things spruces up streets and neighborhoods to make them more presentable to businesses and developers. The city is showing some sparkle but in 1994 will lose a department store, one of the major business attractions.

Interstate 80 congestion is infuriating but San Pablo, because it is close to urban centers, is a much better commute than many towns in the East Bay.

Crime has depressed residential prices, making homes and rentals more affordable.

CONTRA COSTA CITY PROFILES 87

The FBI reported seven homicides in 1991, eight in 1990, five in 1989, four in 1988, two in 1987, zero in 1986 and six in 1985. Some neighborhoods suffer more than others. Just by driving the town, you can get a feel for the hot spots.

Served by Richmond Unified School District, which has money problems. See chapter on public schools.

Home to Brookside Hospital and the most influential cultural institution in the West County, Contra Costa College. Many activities at the college, which has a performing arts center and an innovative program that educates high school kids.

Picturesque city hall and historic buildings that recall old days of San Pablo. El Portal Shopping Plaza, hospital and college are close to freeway.

State count in 1992 showed 9,562 residences — 4,239 single homes, 713 single-family attached, 3,795 multiples, 815 mobile homes. City hall reports influx of young couples and singles. Home prices vary. Over 400 homes were built before World War II. Cheap. New homes get up in price but not as high as other Contra Costa towns. Good place, if you lack money, to get into home ownership.

San Ramon

A bedroom town with the largest office complexes in the county, over 15,000 white-collar jobs.

Middle- to upper-middle-class burg and inching higher but too middle class to be considered ritzy. Professional and managerial.

School rankings high, crime low. Commute good-to-awful but will get better this decade when freeway improvements are finished, and BART comes to Dublin. Added 12,947 residents in the 1980s, an increase of 58 percent.

Dougherty Valley, 6,000 acres east of San Ramon, is slated for development, up to 12,000 housing units, and the anti- and pro-growthers are whacking away at each other. In November, 1992, voters elected an anti-growther for county supervisor.

San Ramon is located just south of Danville and is the last Contra Costa city before Alameda County. Although the character and development of each differ, the communities of the San Ramon Valley — Alamo, Danville, San Ramon — flow into one another, and into Dublin and Pleasanton.

San Ramon is home to Bishop Ranch, a 600-acre office park. Where cows grazed and orchards grew, Pac Bell, Chevron and other firms erected office buildings, some quite large (5,000-plus workers). Recent arrivals include biotech.

The town started out with middle-income tracts, nice but not overwhelming, and has pretty much stayed in this vein. The closeness of the highly desirable jobs and the prettiness of the region — Mt. Diablo rises a few miles to the east — have elevated housing prices beyond the ordinary.

Incorporated as city in 1983, San Ramon has worked to build a cohesive community with services to match the demands of citizens — not an easy task. The city has annexed Bishop Ranch and Canyon Lakes, an apartment-home development.

San Ramon has a new hotel and in 1990 a major hospital opened, the San Ramon Regional Medical Center. More offices are planned for Bishop Ranch. Many local streets have been improved and widened.

San Ramon has been steadily adding shops, restaurants, banks, insurance firms, and retail centers, and in convenience of shopping and choices available does very well. For big ticket items, shoppers head for Stoneridge Mall (Nordstrom, Macy's, etc.) in Pleasanton. Alcosta Mall, one of the original shopping areas, was demolished to make way for improvements.

No homicides in 1991, 1990, 1989, 1988, 1987, 1986, 1985, reports FBI.

Served by San Ramon Valley School District. School scores high. Schools take bow and credit curriculum that stresses academics. But scores often reflect demographics, and the valley has been attracting more upper-middle-income families, traditionally high scorers. Voters passed a $40 million bond in 1991 to build and improve schools. Enrollment up. Several elementary schools opened in recent years.

Many tutors are setting up shop in the Valley and finding a market in parents who want to give their kids the extra push.

Sports appear to be booming. Besides school sports, activities include baseball (Pee Wee, Little League, American Legion), roller and ice skating, basketball, tennis, youth wrestling, swimming, biking, soccer (youth and adult), softball, including girls league, football, ice hockey, golf. Two regional parks. Mt. Diablo State Park looks down upon all, and has so much open space that, even with the new development, San Ramon retains its country flavor.

In 1992, the state tallied 13,931 residences: 8,942 single homes, 1,491 single attached, 3,490 multiples. Older tracts are just east of freeway but entering the east hills, homes become spanking new.

City council is following suburban trend on parks: hook them to schools. Parks are to be or have been built at Twin Creeks, Walt Disney, Montevideo and Country Club schools.

Community center includes auditorium, teen center, ballet studio and club rooms. New library. Senior center.

California State University-Hayward, Diablo Valley College and UC-Berkeley joined forces to open the Center for Higher Education, which in 1991 moved into a larger building and installed new computers and equipment. Many classes. Call (510) 866-1822.

If you work in Bishop Ranch or Walnut Creek, you'll be home for the 5:30 news. If you work in Oakland, it's still possible to keep your sanity. You can grab I-580 at Dublin or Crow Canyon Road and most days swoop into the downtown.

If you work in San Francisco, it's a wearying haul. The Bay Bridge and its approaches can be awful. No matter how much the freeways are improved, that bridge can absorb only a limited number of vehicles.

This is probably the only big drawback to San Ramon. Try alternatives: BART, car pooling, staggered work hours.

Walnut Creek

One of the older suburban towns in Contra Costa, Walnut Creek grew rapidly after World War II, fell out of love with development in the 1980s, set growth limits and channeled its energy into making the city more enjoyable.

The Chronicle, ranking cities in amenities, schools and low crime, placed Walnut Creek first in the East Bay and 18th overall in the Bay Region.

The U.S. Conference of Mayors in 1989 named Walnut Creek "the most livable small city in the nation."

Although a bedroom town, Walnut Creek rounded itself out with stores, restaurants, office complexes employing thousands, theaters, museums, and cultural ornaments. Walnut Creek has a night life.

Most of the town's stores are small and clustered in the downtown. For heavy-duty shopping, there's Nordstrom and Emporium.

In 1990, the city opened the Regional Center for the Arts, $20 million, two theaters, an art gallery; symphonies, chamber music, plays, musicals. The center attracted 250,000 patrons last year to 450 events.

Walnut Creek funds an animal shelter-museum and an historic ranch.

FROM CONDOS TO CASTLES...
I'll help find the perfect California home for you!

MARIANNA BOTTARI
(510) 746-2085
(510) 930-8967

Serving Buyers & Sellers in the communities of Walnut Creek, Concord, Clayton, Lafayette, Moraga, Orinda, Alamo, Danville and San Ramon

#1 Listing Agent — Grubb & Ellis 1992, Mt. Diablo and San Ramon Valley.

It has 15 open-space areas or parks, including one added in 1992, 2 community pools, 18 tennis courts, an equestrian center, 2 golf courses, 2 libraries, garden center, model railroad center. The activities offered through recreation department are unusually numerous and diverse, including sports, culture and art classes, and crafts, for adults and children.

The town has adopted an unusual sport: synchronized swimming. Two sisters on the Aquanauts won gold at the Barcelona Olympics.

On the way: a community gym at Foothill School, and a replacement museum.

Churches, clubs, social events — they're all there. Kaiser Hospital, recently expanded. So, too, did John Muir Hospital.

Rossmoor, a retirement community, is located in Walnut Creek. The oldtimers, most of them Republicans, give politics a conservative, preservationist cast. Residents over age 55 make up a third of the population. City leaders are sensitive to needs and interests of elderly.

Although conservative, Walnut Creek, educated and genteel, increasingly is a sophisticated town, tolerant of diverse lifestyles. The general feeling is that as long as what's done is done privately and discreetly — which it is — then it's nobody's business.

City council in 1991 toughened smoking ordinance: no puffing in restaurants, offices and stores. Exempted were bars and cocktail lounges.

School rankings are among the tops in the state. Served by Mt. Diablo School District, Walnut Creek Elementary District and Acalanes High School District. Call a school district to find out which school your child will attend.

Mt. Diablo District, several years ago, passed a construction bond. Every school in the district was renovated or improved.

In 1992, a university campus, affiliated with Cal State Hayward, opened just over the hill in Concord, about 5 minutes from Walnut Creek.

Crime is not negligible but it's low. Three homicides in 1991, zero in 1990, two in 1989, one in 1988, none in 1987, three in 1986, none in 1985, FBI reports.

In a suburban way, a pretty town. Tree-lined streets, well-kept lawns. Mt. Diablo, just east of the city, is close enough to be a real and pleasant presence, and the peak is surrounded by thousands of acres of park land.

Downtown has two freeways and a BART station and the Pleasant Hill BART station is so close that it might as well be in Walnut Creek.

Many apartments are located near BART stations. For thousands of renters, BART is a short walk or bus ride.

But BART and the freeways skirt the western border; most people live in the east and center. To get to mass transit, they have to drive across town on city streets — congestion.

Highway 24 and Interstate 680 come together at Walnut Creek at an interchange that was inadequate the day it was built. Almost every commute evening, and many weekends, the freeways jam at the interchange. In a few years, all this will be much improved. The interchange and the freeway connectors are being rebuilt.

Even with the jams, Walnut Creek does better than many other local cities. It's only 18 miles from the Bay Bridge (but these can be slow miles).

Annual state count (1992) showed 30,495 residences: 11,346 single homes, 4,732 single attached, 14,401 multiples (many in downtown and Rossmoor), 16 mobiles. Walnut Creek expects to add 6,000 residents this decade, 6,000 the next.

Dow Chemical shut a research center in 1992, a loss of about 200 jobs, and some blamed the city's anti-development policies. The city has been arguing about growth for decades.

In the town's building boom years, prices were aimed at middle and upper-middle people. Many ranch homes, well kept. Two-story and four and five bedrooms are common.

The town also has older, smaller homes, many of them near the downtown. Good singles town: the apartments and townhouses.

West Pittsburg

Changing neighborhood, governed by county supervisors, patrolled by sheriff's deputies, scheduled to get a BART station in a few years.

Freeway is now being improved and interchange at Willow Pass is to be rebuilt. BART, 2,100 parking spaces, will possibly improve West Pittsburg, which suffers prostitution, excess crime in some sections. Several police crackdowns in 1992.

Many new homes. West Pitt started 1980s with 8,773 residents, finished with 17,453. Lot of kids, about 31 percent of the residents. Mobile homes popular with elderly.

Served by Ambrose Park and Recreation District, which runs community center, parks, swimming pool.

Ethnically diverse: Whites, Hispanics, Asians, Blacks. Schools are trying to balance attendance by ethnicity.

School rankings bounce between the 30th and 50th percentile, a cause for concern but if the town turns more middle class, scores should come up. Served by Mt. Diablo School District. Teens attend Mt. Diablo High in Concord.

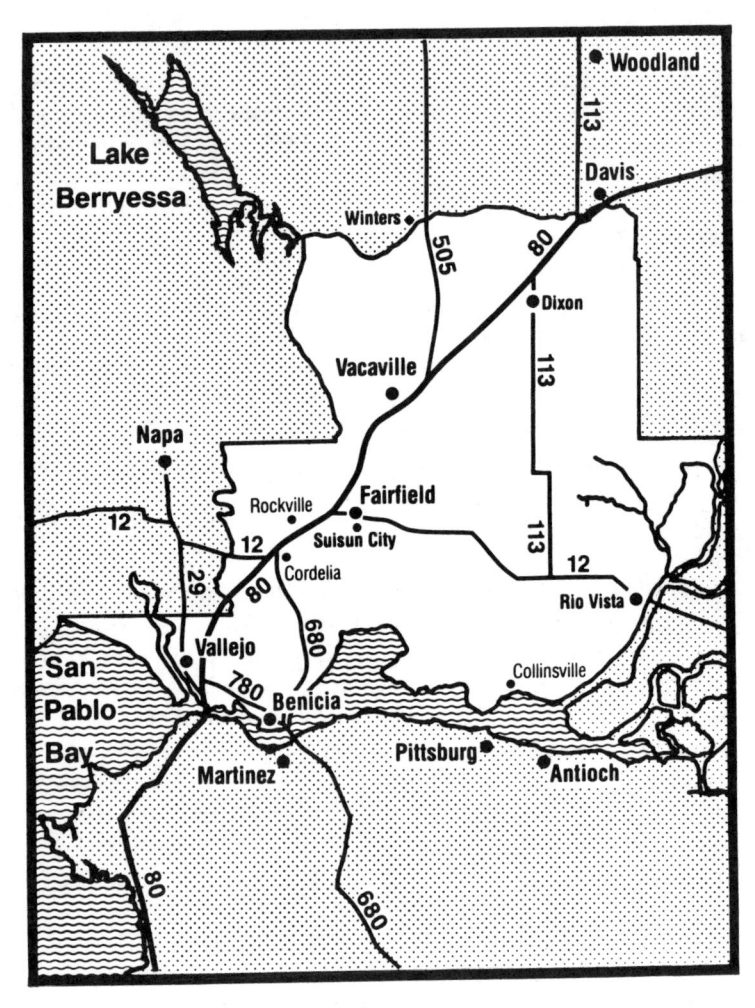

Solano County

4/Solano County at a Glance

Middle America — Ethnically Diverse, Fast Growing, Tough Commute, Low Home Prices

NOTED NOT TOO LONG AGO FOR ITS FARM PRODUCTS, Solano now is one of the fastest-growing suburban counties in the Bay Area, especially popular with families.

In the 1980s the county, named after an Indian chief, increased its population by 45 percent. The great majority of the new arrivals were middle-class parents, attracted to the county by what they considered low home prices.

In the Bay Area, children under age 18 make up 23 percent of the population and adults over 55 years 19 percent (1990 census). In Solano County, about 29 percent of the residents are under 18 and 15 percent over 55 — a young county.

Freeway's Offspring

Excepting Benicia, all the cities in Solano County are children of Interstate 80. Once this freeway was opened and key bridges constructed, Solano became accessible to the suburban migration that poured out of Oakland and San Francisco following World War II.

Solano's time came later because it had to wait for the migration to move through Contra Costa County. In the 1970s developable land became scarce in Central and West Contra Costa, and homebuilders moved across the Carquinez Strait. They also moved out from Sacramento. Vacaville and Dixon travel in the Sacramento orbit and draw many workers from the capital.

Jobs followed the migration. Chevron, Pac Bell, Bank of America and others moved thousands of jobs to Contra Costa County, cutting the commute time to Solano. Solano itself is now attracting many firms. Bank of America is to move thousands to Vacaville this decade.

94 SOLANO COUNTY AT A GLANCE

Solano County Population

City or Area	Male	Female	Total	*Total
Benicia	12,055	12,382	24,437	26,350
Davis**	22,526	23,683	46,209	49,600
Dixon	5,240	5,161	10,401	11,500
Fairfield	38,849	38,362	77,211	85,600
Rio Vista	1,637	1,679	3,316	3,600
Suisun City	11,417	11,269	22,686	23,550
Vacaville	39,478	32,001	71,479	78,300
Vallejo	54,444	54,755	109,199	112,100
Remainder	11,226	10,466	21,692	NA
Countywide	174,346	166,075	340,421	353,300

Source: 1990 Census and Demographic Research Unit of the California Dept. of Finance. Key: NA (not available). *Population estimates by Dept. of Finance., Jan. 1, 1992. **Yolo County city.

Average Household Income

City	1990	*1995	*2000
Benicia	$57,852	$60,200	$64,000
Dixon	45,584	47,800	50,100
Fairfield	46,004	49,900	53,300
Rio Vista	40,641	41,700	43,600
Suisun City	44,823	46,200	48,700
Vacaville	48,411	50,100	55,500
Vallejo	43,598	46,400	50,900
Remainder	55,068	58,200	63,900
Countywide	46,868	49,600	53,900

Source: Association of Bay Area Governments, "Projections 92." Average income per household includes wages and salaries, dividends, interest, rent and transfer payments such as Social Security or public assistance. Based on 1990 Census data, income is stated in 1990 dollars. *Projections.

Lastly, Solano is a pleasing place. The weather is balmy, crime generally low, school rankings middling to high (although crowding is a problem.)

Little League, football, baseball, swimming, gymnastics — the delights of childhood abound. Marine World, a large theme park, is located at Vallejo. Softball, golf, hiking, fishing, cycling, water sports, duck hunting, wining (Napa County is next door and Solano has its own wineries), dining, craft pursuits, art, history and cultural pursuits — adults need not be bored. In winter, the Sierra snow is within a two-hour drive.

Education Level of Population Age 18 & Over

City or Town	HS	SC	AA	BA	Grad
Benicia	23	27	10	20	10
Davis*	10	36	6	25	20
Dixon	27	27	6	11	5
Fairfield	30	32	8	9	4
Rio Vista	38	22	5	7	3
Suisun City	28	31	9	9	3
Vacaville	29	28	8	11	4
Vallejo	28	27	9	13	4
Solano County	28	29	9	12	5

Source: 1990 Census. **Key**: HS (adults with high school diploma or GED only); SC (adults with some college education, no degree); AA (adults with an associate degree); BA (adults with a bachelor's degree only); Grad (adults with a master's or higher degree). Figures are percent of population age 18 and older, rounded to the nearest whole number. Not shown are adults with less than a 9th grade education or with some high school education but no diploma or GED. *Yolo County city.

Although the biggest problem, traffic congestion does not afflict all. Many residents work in Sacramento, an easier commute. The Mare Island Naval Shipyard, Travis Air Force Base, and the University of California, Davis (just over the county line) employ thousands.

Some History

Spanish expeditions explored the East Bay in 1772 and 1776. The dates tell an important story. Although first to the New World and in "possession" of California since the 1500s, Spain did little to secure its northern jewel. Fierce Indians and the northern Mexican desert made the overland trip hazardous. Feeble sea explorations left the wealth of California unknown. San Francisco Bay was not discovered until 1769 and little was done to colonize the land.

Mexico overthrew Spain in 1821 but the neglect continued. Historian Alan Hynding estimated that in 1845, on the eve of the American invasion, California had fewer than 7,000 Hispanic colonialists and of the 7,000 about half were adult males.

When gold was discovered and the Yankees poured over mountains or sailed 'round the horn or crossed the Isthmus of Panama, they didn't really conquer the Californios so much as overwhelm them by sheer numbers.

The Spanish-Mexican-Yankee legacy? Place names, an inclination toward Spanish architecture, the extermination of Indians, mostly by disease, a sorry chapter in the state's history and only in recent decades recognized as a tragedy.

Coming & Going
(Driver's License Address Changes)

County	Moved to Solano from	Moved Out of Solano to	Net
Alameda	1,940	1,187	753
Alpine	4	1	3
Amador	20	31	-11
Butte	124	179	-55
Calaveras	14	34	-20
Colusa	15	27	-12
Contra Costa	3,042	1,999	1,043
Del Norte	13	35	-22
El Dorado	83	141	-58
Fresno	127	172	-45
Glenn	17	22	-5
Humboldt	58	69	-11
Imperial	19	22	-3
Inyo	0	1	-1
Kern	123	126	-3
Kings	33	39	-6
Lake	68	121	-53
Lassen	13	26	-13
Los Angeles	961	618	343
Madera	25	38	-13
Marin	392	163	229
Mariposa	0	8	-8
Mendocino	53	48	5
Merced	70	58	12
Modoc	6	9	-3
Mono	4	7	-3
Monterey	140	95	45
Napa	864	1,168	-304
Nevada	60	79	-19
Orange	263	206	57
Placer	99	128	-29
Plumas	13	25	-12
Riverside	144	134	10
Sacramento	1,096	1,489	-393
San Benito	9	8	1
San Bernardino	249	195	54
San Diego	587	528	59

Note: Data covers fiscal year July 1, 1991-June 30, 1992.

Coming & Going
(Driver's License Address Changes)

County	Moved to Solano from	Moved Out of Solano to	Net
San Francisco	1,335	645	690
San Joaquin	250	263	-13
San Luis Obispo	76	75	1
San Mateo	1,023	466	557
Santa Barbara	69	94	-25
Santa Clara	641	410	231
Santa Cruz	91	48	43
Shasta	80	147	-67
Sierra	3	5	-2
Siskiyou	28	34	-6
Sonoma	383	401	-18
Stanislaus	92	115	-23
Sutter	49	65	-16
Tehama	39	69	-30
Trinity	2	15	-13
Tulare	60	61	-1
Tuolumne	21	24	-3
Ventura	94	85	9
Yolo	552	563	-11
Yuba	28	66	-38
All Counties	15,664	12,887	2,777
Out of State	4,874	4,703	171
Total	20,538	17,590	2,948

Source: California Department of Finance. Data covers fiscal year July 1, 1991-June 30, 1992. Out-of-state counts have been adjusted for non-compliers.

Although one of the original 21 counties of California when it entered the union in 1850, Solano soon faded into obscurity because its population was small, its resources few. Outside of military activity at bases at Vallejo and Benicia, the county spent the latter half of the 19th century and much of the 20th mowing wheat, raising sheep and cattle, reeling in fish and shooting ducks.

Historical highlights
• County name. Chief Sem Yeto, his tribe defeated by the Spanish in 1817, became friends with Commandante Mariano Vallejo and a Christian. Baptized, he was given the name "Solano" after St. Francisco Solano.

• State capital. First it was Vallejo, about 1850, then Benicia, 1853-54, and

Religion in Solano County

Denomination	No.	Members	Total
African Methodist Episcopal Zion	1	350	475
American Baptist	10	4,511	5,888
Assemblies of God	11	1,766	4,092
Baptist General Conference	1	370	483
Baptist Missionary Association	1	39	51
Catholic	11	NA	56,833
Christian & Missionary Alliance	2	110	245
Church of Christ	3	226	295
Disciples of Christ	2	220	273
Christian Reformed	1	67	101
Church of Christ, Scientist	3	NR	NR
Church of God (Anderson, Ind.)	2	121	121
Church of God (Cleveland, Tenn.)	2	295	385
Church of God (Prophecy)	2	62	81
Latter-day Saints	16	NA	8,924
Church of the Nazarene	5	633	840
Church of Christ	7	981	1,207
Church of God (General Convention)	1	19	25
Conservative Baptist	2	NR	NR
Episcopal	4	1,121	1,837
Evangelical Free	1	249	551
Evangelical Lutheran	4	1,435	2,172
Free Will Baptist	1	97	127
Greek Orthodox	1	NR	NR
Independent Fundamental	2	NR	NR
Foursquare Gospel	5	169	221
Lutheran-Missouri Synod	4	1,224	1,903
Open Bible Standard	1	NR	NR
Pentecostal Church of God	2	104	330
Pentecostal Holiness	2	92	120
Presbyterian (USA)	6	2,112	2,757
Salvation Army	2	99	109
Seventh-Day Adventist	5	959	1,252
Southern Baptist	16	7,080	9,241
Unitarian-Universalist	1	41	47
United Church of Christ	4	345	450
United Methodist	6	2,012	2,626
Jewish*	1	NA	1,200
Independent, Charismatic*	1	NA	300
Independent, Non-Charismatic*	3	NA	1,150
Countywide	155	36,712	119,508

Source: Glenmary Research Center, Atlanta, Ga. **Key**: No. (number of churches in the county); Members (communicant, confirmed, full members); Total (all adherents); NA (not applicable); NR (not reported). *Estimates.

Voter Registration

City	Democrat	Republican	NP
Benicia	7,616	5,053	1,744
Dixon	2,349	2,023	501
Fairfield	18,707	11,960	4,219
Rio Vista	950	793	191
Suisun City	4,874	2,892	1,220
Vacaville	14,986	12,779	4,114
Vallejo	35,561	11,251	4,756
Unincorporated Areas	4,874	4,123	982
Countywide	89,917	50,874	17,727

Source: Secretary of State of California & Solano County Registrar of Voters, November, 1992. Key: NP (Voters who declined to state any political party affiliation.)

Presidential Voting in Solano Couty

Year	Democrat	D-Votes	Republican	R-Votes
1948	Truman*	23,257	Dewey	12,345
1952	Stevenson	25,569	Eisenhower*	18,456
1956	Stevenson	24,903	Eisenhower*	17,865
1960	Kennedy*	26,977	Nixon	18,751
1964	Johnson*	34,930	Goldwater	15,263
1968	Humphrey	27,271	Nixon*	17,683
1972	McGovern	23,742	Nixon*	29,210
1976	Carter*	33,682	Ford	26,136
1980	Carter	30,952	Reagan*	40,919
1984	Mondale	41,982	Reagan*	51,678
1988	Dukakis	54,344	Bush*	50,314
1992**	Clinton*	62,051	Bush	37,113

Source: Solano County Registrar of Voters and Secretary of State of California.
*Election winner nationally. **Ross Perot (26,772).

Benicia even built a capitol, which stands today.

• Mare Island. Purchased by U.S. government in 1852. Its first commandant was David Farragut, who years later at the battle of Mobile Bay shouted, "Damn the torpedoes, full speed ahead."

• Benicia Arsenal. Opened in 1852. Closed in 1964, deeded to Benicia. A young Ulysses Grant served there and supposedly was jailed for drunkenness.

Many of the original buildings still stand, including commandant's residence and camel barns. For a few years, army experimented with camels to carry troops throughout California. Didn't pan out, beasts sold at auction.

Population Profile by Occupation

City or Town	EX	PF	TC	SA	CL	SV	AG	MF
Benicia	17	19	4	15	16	10	1	19
Davis*	14	33	9	9	15	11	2	8
Dixon	13	10	5	11	16	12	5	28
Fairfield	11	11	4	13	17	15	1	28
Rio Vista	8	8	1	14	14	17	2	37
Suisun City	10	10	4	11	16	16	3	30
Vacaville	12	11	4	13	15	14	1	29
Vallejo	12	12	5	11	20	16	1	24
Solano County	12	12	4	12	17	14	2	16

Source: 1990 Census. **Key**: EX (executive and managerial); PF (professional specialty); TC (technicians); SA (sales); CL (clerical and administrative support); SV (service occupations, including household, protective and other services); AG (agricultural including farming, fishing, forestry); MF (manufacturing including precision production, craft, repair; also machine operators, assemblers, inspectors, equipment cleaners and handlers, helpers and laborers). Figures are percent of population, rounded to the nearest whole number. *Yolo County city.

• Transcontinental Rail. The Southern Pacific came down Solano County in 1879 and crossed the strait at Benicia, using what were then the largest ferries in the world. One measured 425 feet. The depot still stands. In 1929 Southern Pacific built a bridge over the strait at Benicia, ending the ferry service, and clearing trains out of downtown Benicia. Car ferries continued until the 1960s.

• Decline-revival of the marshes. The Sacramento and San Joaquin rivers have created some of the finest habitats in this country for the nourishment of ducks and coots and all sorts of aquatic life.

Unfortunately, where environmentalists later saw gold, early farmers saw muck to be drained and land reclaimed. Nature fought back with rising salinity. Many of the lands have gone back to muck, and the state has become much more protective.

• Travis. Mare Island. In 1942, to fight the Pacific war, the Army paved flat lands at Fairfield into one of the largest military air fields in the world. Now called Travis, it employs 11,000 and is a mainstay of the nation's defense. Mare Island in Vallejo was turned into a submarine base. Many subs were built there.

• Bridges. The Carquinez Strait and Suisun Bay separate Solano County from the Bay Area. All the freeways in the world would have done the county little good unless bridges were built and improved. Going into the 1950s, only the Crockett-Vallejo bridge carried cars.

A second bridge was built at Vallejo in 1958. In 1962, construction was finished on the Martinez-Benicia Bridge, dooming the ferries that formerly tied the two towns together.

Solano County Ethnic Makeup

City, Town or Area	White	Af.Am.	Hisp.	Asn./PI	N. Am.
Benicia	19,341	1,284	1,808	1,839	142
Davis*	35,159	1,311	3,425	5,955	291
Dixon	6,978	130	2,958	238	76
Fairfield	48,343	10,237	10,208	7,608	630
Rio Vista	2,965	3	264	57	25
Suisun City	13,095	3,106	3,645	3,594	185
Vacaville	51,494	5,486	11,366	2,471	584
Vallejo	50,399	22,599	11,777	23,550	670
Countywide	207,476	43,858	45,517	40,494	2,469

Source: 1990 Census. **Key**: Af.Am. (African-American); Hisp. (Hispanic); Asn./PI (Asian/Pacific Islander); N. Am. (Native American including American Indian, Eskimo and Aleut). Not included, a small number identified by census as "other race." *Davis is in Yolo County.

• The new Solano. Middle class, suburban, ethnically mixed. Many military and retired military. A county proud to fly the flag on the Fourth. To a large extent family and school oriented. Just about every city is adding or recently has added parks and schools and other amenities.

5/Solano School Rankings

Solano County Public Schools —
Reading, Writing, Math, Science & History Tests

THESE RANKINGS ARE drawn from state tests given over three years, 1988, 1989, 1990, and an eighth grade test given in 1992. For the most part, they will follow a pattern. High one year will be high the next, low will be low.

When the numbers fluctuate wildly, the number of children who took the tests will often be low. In a small class, one or two kids having a bad or good day will cause wide swings. Sometimes the children fail to understand instructions and this lowers their grade. Sometimes they just have an off day.

A Cautionary Note

Ranking systems don't recognize overall gains or losses. If every school in California raised raw scores 20 percent, some schools would still be ranked at the bottom, a few at the top. The same if every raw score dropped. A ranking system shows how one school did against all other schools. There is no one perfect method of testing.

Family background, particularly education of parents, greatly influences how children will score in schools. See introduction to Contra Costa scores (Chapter 2) and Chapter 7 on How Public Schools Work.

BENICIA UNIFIED DISTRICT
Districtwide

3rd Grade	1988	1989	1990	1992
Reading	94	97	92	—
Writing	93	97	93	—
Math	81	94	88	—
No. Tested	245	310	333	—
6th Grade	1988	1989	1990	1992
Reading	78	89	65	—
Writing	91	95	86	—

6th Grade	1988	1989	1990	1992
Math	81	90	80	—
No. Tested	241	305	305	—
8th Grade	1988	1989	1990	1992
Reading	64	67	83	87
Writing	69	—	—	86
Math	78	81	87	83
History	80	90	86	93
Science	86	81	89	87
No. Tested	285	281	268	335

CENTURY 21® Offices Serving Solano County

BENICIA

CENTURY 21 Action Realty
78 Solano Square
Benicia, CA 94510
(707) 745-5544

CENTURY 21 Egidio Realty, Inc.
439 First St.
Benicia, CA 94510
(707) 746-7921

CENTURY 21 Fulton Realty
2000 Columbus Parkway
P.O. Box 319
Benicia, CA 94510
(707) 745-8822

DIXON

CENTURY 21 ACE Realty
1115 Stratford Ave., Suite F
Dixon, CA 95620
(916) 678-9292

FAIRFIELD

CENTURY 21 Alamo Realty & Investment
1955 W. Texas St., Suite 1
Fairfield, CA 94533
(707) 422-7100

CENTURY 21 American Properties, Inc.
1377 Oliver Road
Fairfield, CA 94533
(707) 422-2866

CENTURY 21 Egidio Realty, Inc.
1313 Travis Blvd., Suite A
Fairfield, CA 94533
(707) 429-2121

CENTURY 21 Fairfield Realty, Inc.
1935 N. Texas St.
Fairfield, CA 94533
(707) 429-4800

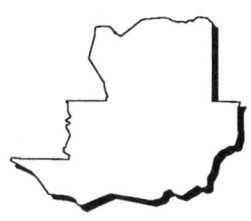

SUISUN CITY

CENTURY 21 Enterprise
288 Sunset Ave.
Suisun City, CA 94585
(707) 421-2100

VACAVILLE

CENTURY 21 Alamo Realty & Investment Co.
1241 Alamo Drive, Suite 1
Vacaville, CA 95687
(707) 446-2121

CENTURY 21 Cardosi Real Estate
779 E. Monte Vista Ave.
Vacaville, CA 95688
(707) 447-1900

CENTURY 21 Creekside Realty
190 S. Orchard Ave., #A105
Vacaville, CA 95668
(707) 449-1970

CENTURY 21 Orange Tree Realty, Inc.
601 D Orange Drive
Vacaville, CA 95687
(707) 447-2200

VALLEJO

CENTURY 21 Cole & Cole Realty
330 Broadway, Suite 2
Vallejo, CA 94590
(707) 643-0314

CENTURY 21 Davis & Associates
1209 Tennessee St.
Vallejo, CA 94590
(707) 554-3455

CENTURY 21 Egidio Realty, Inc.
2801 Redwood Parkway
Vallejo, CA 94591
(707) 553-9340

CENTURY 21 Egidio Realty, Inc.
95 Flemingtowne Center
Vallejo, CA 94589
(707) 552-5421

CENTURY 21 Friend, Inc.
1826 Springs Road
Vallejo, CA 94590
(707) 553-8000

CENTURY 21 Schutjer Realty, Inc.
2255 Tennessee St.
Vallejo, CA 94591
(707) 644-4076

WINTERS

CENTURY 21 ABC Tortosa Realty
600 Railroad Ave.
Winters, CA 95694
(916) 795-3224

Each Office Is Independently Owned & Operated

BENICIA UNIFIED (Continued)
Districtwide

12th Grade	1988	1989	1990	1992
Reading	62	40	85	—
Writing	—	63	92	—
Math	53	59	85	—
No.Tested	258	248	239	—

Benicia High

12th Grade	1988	1989	1990	1992
Reading	69	47	85	—
Writing	—	72	91	—
Math	61	63	87	—
No. Tested	240	225	223	—

Benicia Middle

6th Grade	1988	1989	1990	1992
Reading	73	84	59	—
Writing	85	92	81	—
Math	73	86	74	—
No. Tested	241	305	305	—
8th Grade	1988	1989	1990	1992
Reading	61	64	80	85
Writing	66	—	—	84
Math	75	78	85	80
History	79	86	83	92
Science	81	80	86	84
No. Tested	285	281	268	335

Farmar El.

3rd Grade	1988	1989	1990	1992
Reading	93	95	82	—
Writing	93	95	82	—
Math	68	82	72	—
No. Tested	65	67	89	—

Henderson El.

3rd Grade	1988	1989	1990	1992
Reading	94	98	96	—
Writing	94	98	97	—
Math	94	95	91	—
No. Tested	68	86	117	—

Mills El.

3rd Grade	1988	1989	1990	1992
Reading	84	95	69	—
Writing	75	91	65	—
Math	49	86	66	—
No. Tested	45	75	63	—

Semple El.

3rd Grade	1988	1989	1990	1992
Reading	78	80	83	—
Writing	79	80	82	—
Math	62	81	78	—
No. Tested	67	87	64	—

DIXON UNIFIED DISTRICT
Districtwide

3rd Grade	1988	1989	1990	1992
Reading	56	27	54	—
Writing	46	29	46	—
Math	27	29	56	—
No. Tested	208	219	210	—
6th Grade	1988	1989	1990	1992
Reading	42	46	49	—
Writing	38	65	56	—
Math	45	49	46	—
No. Tested	181	206	216	—
8th Grade	1988	1989	1990	1992
Reading	41	61	56	65
Writing	55	—	—	64
Math	60	50	64	66
History	68	51	66	81
Science	61	50	68	91
No. Tested	185	187	178	185
12th Grade	1988	1989	1990	1992
Reading	41	49	41	—
Writing	—	59	57	—
Math	36	48	53	—
No. Tested	155	172	159	—

Anderson El.

3rd Grade	1988	1989	1990	1992
Reading	54	30	55	—
Writing	45	30	45	—
Math	28	33	56	—
No. Tested	208	219	210	—

Dixon High

12th Grade	1988	1989	1990	1992
Reading	39	59	44	—
Writing	—	61	52	—
Math	40	50	58	—
No. Tested	38	157	145	—

Jacobs Intermediate

6th Grade	1988	1989	1990	1992
Reading	44	47	49	—
Writing	36	64	57	—
Math	48	48	46	—
No. Tested	181	206	216	—
8th Grade	1988	1989	1990	1992
Reading	41	59	53	65
Writing	52	—	—	64
Math	59	50	64	65
History	68	51	66	80
Science	61	52	69	87
No. Tested	185	187	178	185

FAIRFIELD-SUISUN UNIFIED
Districtwide

3rd Grade	1988	1989	1990	1992
Reading	74	75	78	—
Writing	71	73	77	—
Math	55	68	62	—
No. Tested	1,360	1,384	1,558	—
6th Grade	1988	1989	1990	1992
Reading	83	82	82	—
Writing	85	80	80	—
Math	79	77	79	—
No. Tested	1,092	1,284	1,316	—

SOLANO SCHOOL RANKINGS 105

8th Grade	1988	1989	1990	1992
Reading	60	58	58	68
Writing	59	—	—	78
Math	50	53	47	57
History	62	66	65	66
Science	60	60	57	62
No. Tested	1,154	1,136	1,151	1,230
12th Grade	1988	1989	1990	1992
Reading	63	50	54	—
Writing	—	46	50	—
Math	52	61	51	—
No. Tested	722	772	766	—

Armijo High

12th Grade	1988	1989	1990	1992
Reading	68	53	50	—
Writing	—	41	39	—
Math	57	54	47	—
No. Tested	376	382	348	—

Blanc El.

3rd Grade	1988	1989	1990	1992
Reading	75	75	71	—
Writing	86	75	71	—
Math	72	65	55	—
No. Tested	135	130	140	—
6th Grade	1988	1989	1990	1992
Reading	74	82	74	—
Writing	83	86	79	—
Math	73	82	76	—
No. Tested	95	121	141	—

Bransford El.

3rd Grade	1988	1989	1990	1992
Reading	61	74	57	—
Writing	66	79	64	—
Math	58	82	46	—
No. Tested	68	75	92	—
6th Grade	1988	1989	1990	1992
Reading	82	51	28	—
Writing	49	81	61	—
Math	41	35	46	—
No. Tested	49	62	53	—

Crescent El.

3rd Grade	1988	1989	1990	1992
Reading	40	53	44	—
Writing	37	53	35	—
Math	26	43	37	—
No. Tested	190	189	202	—

Crystal El.

6th Grade	1988	1989	1990	1992
Reading	68	71	66	—
Writing	77	57	60	—
Math	70	62	57	—
No. Tested	260	290	287	—

Dover El.

3rd Grade	1988	1989	1990	1992
Reading	50	59	68	—
Writing	52	56	66	—

3rd Grade	1988	1989	1990	1992
Math	43	50	62	—
No. Tested	62	59	95	—
6th Grade	1988	1989	1990	1992
Reading	81	89	78	—
Writing	72	58	76	—
Math	69	55	70	—
No. Tested	61	86	85	—

Fairfield High

12th Grade	1988	1989	1990	1992
Reading	64	50	57	—
Writing	—	56	63	—
Math	53	67	57	—
No. Tested	334	373	399	—

Fairview El.

3rd Grade	1988	1989	1990	1992
Reading	62	53	71	—
Writing	62	66	60	—
Math	83	55	72	—
No. Tested	70	76	91	—
6th Grade	1988	1989	1990	1992
Reading	63	37	75	—
Writing	80	50	55	—
Math	70	54	48	—
No. Tested	51	57	51	—

Falls El.

3rd Grade	1988	1989	1990	1992
Reading	98	95	82	—
Writing	98	95	93	—
Math	98	76	94	—
No. Tested	24	35	21	—
6th Grade	1988	1989	1990	1992
Reading	86	93	78	—
Writing	92	93	85	—
Math	80	80	62	—
No. Tested	31	32	29	—

Gordon El.

3rd Grade	1988	1989	1990	1992
Reading	50	47	86	—
Writing	38	56	61	—
Math	41	60	62	—
No. Tested	84	59	74	—
6th Grade	1988	1989	1990	1992
Reading	77	72	66	—
Writing	57	70	68	—
Math	50	43	84	—
No. Tested	73	84	95	—

Grange Intermediate

8th Grade	1988	1989	1990	1992
Reading	61	46	52	57
Writing	48	—	—	76
Math	51	49	45	50
History	60	50	56	64
Science	64	56	47	52
No. Tested	341	473	450	465

FAIRFIELD-SUISUN UNIFIED (Continued)

Green Valley Intermediate

8th Grade	1988	1989	1990	1992
Reading	63	64	66	75
Writing	64	—	—	80
Math	59	66	54	61
History	62	79	77	64
Science	64	61	69	64
No. Tested	298	235	293	318

Jones El.

3rd Grade	1988	1989	1990	1992
Reading	88	95	95	—
Writing	87	91	97	—
Math	58	88	89	—
No. Tested	109	127	124	—
6th Grade	1988	1989	1990	1992
Reading	95	93	95	—
Writing	90	89	98	—
Math	93	94	92	—
No. Tested	198	118	128	—

Kyle El.

3rd Grade	1988	1989	1990	1992
Reading	62	53	65	—
Writing	68	56	52	—
Math	57	22	44	—
No. Tested	88	58	82	—
6th Grade	1988	1989	1990	1992
Reading	76	72	52	—
Writing	87	57	49	—
Math	72	52	39	—
No. Tested	62	67	61	—

Oakbrook El.

3rd Grade	1988	1989	1990	1992
Reading	87	79	90	—
Writing	80	74	95	—
Math	90	71	88	—
No. Tested	40	61	70	—
6th Grade	1988	1989	1990	1992
Reading	58	97	98	—
Writing	60	94	97	—
Math	67	95	94	—
No. Tested	23	42	33	—

Richardson El.

3rd Grade	1988	1989	1990	1992
Reading	55	60	54	—
Writing	54	49	52	—
Math	31	36	39	—
No. Tested	109	120	149	—
6th Grade	1988	1989	1990	1992
Reading	50	63	70	—
Writing	65	60	57	—
Math	39	53	70	—
No. Tested	84	109	107	—

Sheldon El.

3rd Grade	1988	1989	1990	1992
Reading	56	49	71	—

3rd Grade	1988	1989	1990	1992
Writing	4	59	69	—
Math	42	54	63	—
No. Tested	73	70	86	—
6th Grade	1988	1989	1990	1992
Reading	69	57	53	—
Writing	64	53	69	—
Math	51	55	60	—
No. Tested	42	50	65	—

Suisun El.

3rd Grade	1988	1989	1990	1992
Reading	71	76	69	—
Writing	61	74	79	—
Math	51	61	58	—
No. Tested	148	155	148	—

Suisun Valley El.

3rd Grade	1988	1989	1990	1992
Reading	77	68	78	—
Writing	88	70	80	—
Math	64	82	58	—
No. Tested	27	37	31	—
6th Grade	1988	1989	1990	1992
Reading	96	86	93	—
Writing	92	85	66	—
Math	95	94	86	—
No. Tested	25	19	33	—
8th Grade	1988	1989	1990	1992
Reading	—	—	—	94
Writing	—	—	—	93
Math	—	—	—	82
History	—	—	—	94
Science	—	—	—	89
No. Tested	—	—	—	20

Sullivan Intermediate

8th Grade	1988	1989	1990	1992
Reading	48	61	52	72
Writing	48	—	—	69
Math	43	54	48	68
History	62	64	64	74
Science	51	63	57	69
No. Tested	406	428	396	366

Tolenas El.

3rd Grade	1988	1989	1990	1992
Reading	92	89	83	—
Writing	85	89	84	—
Math	75	92	70	—
No. Tested	53	53	55	—
6th Grade	1988	1989	1990	1992
Reading	91	72	69	—
Writing	88	95	91	—
Math	93	92	85	—
No. Tested	63	57	52	—

Weir El.

3rd Grade	1988	1989	1990	1992
Reading	89	73	93	—

SOLANO SCHOOL RANKINGS

3rd Grade	1988	1989	1990	1992
Writing	82	73	91	—
Math	66	66	84	—
No. Tested	80	80	98	—
6th Grade	1988	1989	1990	1992
Reading	66	86	89	—
Writing	76	89	79	—
Math	58	88	86	—
No. Tested	75	90	96	—

TRAVIS UNIFIED SCHOOL DISTRICT
Districtwide

3rd Grade	1988	1989	1990	1992
Reading	97	85	90	—
Writing	98	93	93	—
Math	97	90	94	—
No. Tested	257	274	301	—
6th Grade	1988	1989	1990	1992
Reading	76	63	71	—
Writing	65	71	73	—
Math	79	71	56	—
No. Tested	216	217	237	—
8th Grade	1988	1989	1990	1992
Reading	67	78	80	75
Writing	79	—	—	52
Math	83	84	67	66
History	78	86	73	72
Science	86	84	88	88
No. Tested	275	199	221	236
12th Grade	1988	1989	1990	1992
Reading	56	81	85	—
Writing	—	54	67	—
Math	61	66	50	—
No. Tested	155	158	149	—

Cambridge El.

3rd Grade	1988	1989	1990	1992
Reading	90	50	82	—
Writing	96	70	89	—
Math	94	79	91	—
No. Tested	67	70	68	—

Center El.

3rd Grade	1988	1989	1990	1992
Reading	94	72	88	—
Writing	93	89	88	—
Math	93	88	90	—
No. Tested	87	72	77	—

Golden West Intermediate

6th Grade	1988	1989	1990	1992
Reading	71	60	64	—
Writing	62	66	69	—
Math	72	66	55	—
No. Tested	216	217	237	—
8th Grade	1988	1989	1990	1992
Reading	64	77	77	74
Writing	74	—	—	52
Math	79	80	66	65
History	77	82	72	73

8th Grade	1988	1989	1990	1992
Science	81	83	86	85
No. Tested	275	199	221	236

Scandia El.

3rd Grade	1988	1989	1990	1992
Reading	94	97	94	—
Writing	92	98	87	—
Math	93	91	81	—
No. Tested	53	67	63	—

Travis El.

3rd Grade	1988	1989	1990	1992
Reading	95	72	74	—
Writing	96	82	85	—
Math	93	72	89	—
No. Tested	50	65	93	—

Vanden High

12th Grade	1988	1989	1990	1992
Reading	60	81	87	—
Writing	—	68	64	—
Math	62	68	60	—
No. Tested	144	147	135	—

VACAVILLE UNIFIED SCHOOL DISTRICT
Districtwide

3rd Grade	1988	1989	1990	1992
Reading	70	65	68	—
Writing	77	72	70	—
Math	81	75	68	—
No. Tested	717	909	953	—
6th Grade	1988	1989	1990	1992
Reading	72	77	78	—
Writing	64	62	78	—
Math	71	76	78	—
No. Tested	716	764	853	—
8th Grade	1988	1989	1990	1992
Reading	63	60	56	64
Writing	58	—	—	50
Math	74	64	67	74
History	66	71	67	80
Science	59	58	60	66
No. Tested	696	761	774	836
12th Grade	1988	1989	1990	1992
Reading	36	47	42	—
Writing	—	61	63	—
Math	36	52	51	—
No. Tested	556	611	526	—

Alamo El.

3rd Grade	1988	1989	1990	1992
Reading	90	87	69	—
Writing	87	84	74	—
Math	90	91	68	—
No. Tested	101	94	97	—
6th Grade	1988	1989	1990	1992
Reading	96	79	84	—
Writing	88	81	90	—
Math	94	86	87	—
No. Tested	62	63	64	—

VACAVILLE UNIFIED (Continued)

Elm El.
3rd Grade	1988	1989	1990	1992
Reading	44	40	50	—
Writing	41	53	55	—
Math	57	49	50	—
No. Tested	65	68	60	—
6th Grade	1988	1989	1990	1992
Reading	72	62	50	—
Writing	54	36	53	—
Math	71	59	70	—
No. Tested	47	78	66	—

Elmira El.
3rd Grade	1988	1989	1990	1992
Reading	59	83	78	—
Writing	78	80	76	—
Math	72	84	72	—
No. Tested	78	123	180	—

Fairmont El.
3rd Grade	1988	1989	1990	1992
Reading	29	39	43	—
Writing	60	56	36	—
Math	54	58	52	—
No. Tested	105	121	118	—

Hemlock El.
3rd Grade	1988	1989	1990	1992
Reading	65	55	73	—
Writing	76	80	77	—
Math	84	66	72	—
No. Tested	68	75	70	—
6th Grade	1988	1989	1990	1992
Reading	64	82	47	—
Writing	24	67	60	—
Math	46	58	52	—
No. Tested	64	59	62	—

Jepson Jr. High
8th Grade	1988	1989	1990	1992
Reading	65	67	71	75
Writing	51	—	—	67
Math	71	78	69	71
History	66	68	74	82
Science	54	57	66	65
No. Tested	241	348	335	347

Markham El.
3rd Grade	1988	1989	1990	1992
Reading	82	48	73	—
Writing	80	52	75	—
Math	85	55	70	—
No. Tested	89	100	116	—
6th Grade	1988	1989	1990	1992
Reading	53	55	67	—
Writing	64	50	76	—
Math	45	56	67	—
No. Tested	85	102	113	—

Orchard El.
3rd Grade	1988	1989	1990	1992
Reading	88	76	88	—
Writing	78	91	84	—
Math	89	90	77	—
No. Tested	43	48	37	—
6th Grade	1988	1989	1990	1992
Reading	95	79	97	—
Writing	84	74	88	—
Math	83	78	93	—
No. Tested	47	49	56	—

Padan El.
3rd Grade	1988	1989	1990	1992
Reading	63	73	70	—
Writing	78	81	75	—
Math	75	80	70	—
No. Tested	123	130	136	—
6th Grade	1988	1989	1990	1992
Reading	66	63	56	—
Writing	67	51	61	—
Math	72	68	73	—
No. Tested	118	114	121	—

Sierra Vista El.
3rd Grade	1988	1989	1990	1992
Reading	62	58	58	—
Writing	50	50	54	—
Math	54	44	37	—
No. Tested	121	123	111	—

Ulatis El.
3rd Grade	1988	1989	1990	1992
Reading	76	21	13	—
Writing	76	27	31	—
Math	87	14	77	—
No. Tested	24	27	28	—
6th Grade	1988	1989	1990	1992
Reading	43	65	67	—
Writing	67	54	91	—
Math	68	84	79	—
No. Tested	16	25	26	—

Vaca Pena Intermediate
6th Grade	1988	1989	1990	1992
Reading	51	78	74	—
Writing	58	71	68	—
Math	55	74	67	—
No. Tested	277	274	345	—
8th Grade	1988	1989	1990	1992
Reading	—	—	—	58
Writing	—	—	—	41
Math	—	—	—	73
History	—	—	—	74
Science	—	—	—	67
No. Tested	—	—	—	489

Vacaville High
12th Grade	1988	1989	1990	1992
Reading	37	48	45	—
Writing	—	65	64	—

SOLANO SCHOOL RANKINGS

12th Grade	1988	1989	1990	1992
Math	40	52	52	—
No. Tested	546	597	511	—

Wood Jr. High

8th Grade	1988	1989	1990	1992
Reading	54	52	41	—
Writing	56	—	—	—
Math	71	51	62	—
History	64	68	60	—
Science	61	55	54	—
No. Tested	355	413	439	—

VALLEJO CITY UNIFIED
Districtwide

3rd Grade	1988	1989	1990	1992
Reading	47	51	48	—
Writing	40	41	41	—
Math	45	38	36	—
No. Tested	1,258	1,397	1,526	—
6th Grade	1988	1989	1990	1992
Reading	75	61	57	—
Writing	57	43	43	—
Math	61	54	48	—
No. Tested	1,190	1,312	1,290	—
8th Grade	1988	1989	1990	1992
Reading	63	40	60	47
Writing	61	—	—	50
Math	50	56	47	36
History	48	50	49	37
Science	47	49	44	41
No. Tested	1,058	1,076	1,172	1,208
12th Grade	1988	1989	1990	1992
Reading	30	41	42	—
Writing	—	56	64	—
Math	31	29	34	—
No. Tested	832	810	812	—

Bev. Hills El.

3rd Grade	1988	1989	1990	1992
Reading	54	45	32	—
Writing	54	14	18	—
Math	39	24	17	—
No. Tested	54	36	60	—
6th Grade	1988	1989	1990	1992
Reading	37	72	70	—
Writing	23	49	46	—
Math	25	74	43	—
No. Tested	48	54	48	—

Cave (Elmer) El.

3rd Grade	1988	1989	1990	1992
Reading	57	75	81	—
Writing	68	67	74	—
Math	72	55	75	—
No. Tested	112	103	131	—
6th Grade	1988	1989	1990	1992
Reading	76	66	63	—
Writing	89	52	45	—
Math	72	69	57	—
No. Tested	106	127	112	—

Cooper (Johnston) El.

3rd Grade	1988	1989	1990	1992
Reading	50	49	35	—
Writing	47	39	25	—
Math	47	29	23	—
No. Tested	103	124	105	—
6th Grade	1988	1989	1990	1992
Reading	75	50	62	—
Writing	71	34	34	—
Math	72	41	44	—
No. Tested	81	124	86	—

Dan Mini El.

3rd Grade	1988	1989	1990	1992
Reading	39	53	60	—
Writing	37	48	44	—
Math	41	50	61	—
No. Tested	144	140	133	—
6th Grade	1988	1989	1990	1992
Reading	61	53	55	—
Writing	59	49	44	—
Math	59	55	47	—
No. Tested	130	136	149	—

Davidson (John) El.

3rd Grade	1988	1989	1990	1992
Reading	52	33	23	—
Writing	31	16	16	—
Math	44	41	31	—
No. Tested	40	35	36	—
6th Grade	1988	1989	1990	1992
Reading	67	58	22	—
Writing	48	46	24	—
Math	72	55	16	—
No. Tested	49	38	33	—

Farragut El.

3rd Grade	1988	1989	1990	1992
Reading	7	27	11	—
Writing	14	18	8	—
Math	17	11	12	—
No. Tested	42	50	56	—
6th Grade	1988	1989	1990	1992
Reading	25	26	49	—
Writing	17	11	46	—
Math	7	31	31	—
No. Tested	42	29	29	—

Federal Terrace El.

3rd Grade	1988	1989	1990	1992
Reading	40	57	40	—
Writing	36	54	30	—
Math	37	34	28	—
No. Tested	68	73	80	—
6th Grade	1988	1989	1990	1992
Reading	95	67	61	—
Writing	72	70	64	—
Math	84	56	74	—
No. Tested	89	57	82	—

VALLEJO CITY UNIFIED (Continued)

Franklin Jr. High

8th Grade	1988	1989	1990	1992
Reading	41	43	45	41
Writing	31	—	—	50
Math	30	41	35	31
History	26	30	33	30
Science	26	42	25	31
No. Tested	216	216	249	250

Glen Cove Ellimentary

3rd Grade	1988	1989	1990	1992
Reading	—	78	56	—
Writing	—	56	63	—
Math	—	63	59	—
No. Tested	—	71	113	—
6th Grade	1988	1989	1990	1992
Reading	—	79	64	—
Writing	—	66	48	—
Math	—	76	59	—
No. Tested	—	60	69	—

Highland El.

3rd Grade	1988	1989	1990	1992
Reading	46	49	49	—
Writing	39	33	40	—
Math	43	50	28	—
No. Tested	119	106	94	—
6th Grade	1988	1989	1990	1992
Reading	66	64	29	—
Writing	68	56	24	—
Math	61	54	21	—
No. Tested	66	87	91	—

Hogan Senior High

12th Grade	1988	1989	1990	1992
Reading	40	49	55	—
Writing	—	68	61	—
Math	36	35	50	—
No. Tested	367	380	365	—

Lincoln El.

3rd Grade	1988	1989	1990	1992
Reading	31	44	31	—
Writing	25	33	34	—
Math	29	18	16	—
No. Tested	45	42	40	—
6th Grade	1988	1989	1990	1992
Reading	78	60	60	—
Writing	70	43	60	—
Math	61	37	51	—
No. Tested	33	43	35	—

Loma Vista El.

3rd Grade	1988	1989	1990	1992
Reading	37	23	42	—
Writing	30	23	30	—
Math	27	14	19	—
No. Tested	56	72	77	—

6th Grade	1988	1989	1990	1992
Reading	64	39	53	—
Writing	41	37	35	—
Math	43	49	51	—
No. Tested	82	90	79	—

Mare Island El.

3rd Grade	1988	1989	1990	1992
Reading	66	85	84	—
Writing	40	79	64	—
Math	58	78	74	—
No. Tested	62	59	81	—
6th Grade	1988	1989	1990	1992
Reading	89	83	69	—
Writing	83	66	73	—
Math	83	76	64	—
No. Tested	38	49	46	—

Patterson (Grace) El.

3rd Grade	1988	1989	1990	1992
Reading	13	18	9	—
Writing	13	9	6	—
Math	11	10	6	—
No. Tested	59	81	93	—
6th Grade	1988	1989	1990	1992
Reading	48	17	24	—
Writing	20	17	12	—
Math	32	12	9	—
No. Tested	82	66	83	—

Pennycook El.

3rd Grade	1988	1989	1990	1992
Reading	86	78	72	—
Writing	71	64	63	—
Math	82	77	61	—
No. Tested	162	175	199	—
6th Grade	1988	1989	1990	1992
Reading	76	82	72	—
Writing	56	48	70	—
Math	74	67	68	—
No. Tested	133	150	181	—

Solano Jr. High

8th Grade	1988	1989	1990	1992
Reading	67	18	60	35
Writing	79	—	—	29
Math	55	54	50	38
History	59	50	50	39
Science	48	28	52	23
No. Tested	272	306	328	316

Springstowne Jr. High

8th Grade	1988	1989	1990	1992
Reading	72	52	69	51
Writing	68	—	—	61
Math	50	57	53	44
History	52	54	52	35
Science	53	55	54	47
No. Tested	298	295	322	356

SOLANO SCHOOL RANKINGS

Steffan Manor El.

3rd Grade	1988	1989	1990	1992
Reading	34	49	49	—
Writing	37	46	32	—
Math	33	38	43	—
No. Tested	102	116	129	—
6th Grade	1988	1989	1990	1992
Reading	58	48	47	—
Writing	52	43	50	—
Math	66	62	56	—
No. Tested	126	103	87	—

Vallejo Jr. High

8th Grade	1988	1989	1990	1992
Reading	52	54	50	54
Writing	45	—	—	59
Math	64	71	47	45
History	53	60	52	61
Science	51	73	48	48
No. Tested	272	259	273	286

Vallejo Senior High

12th Grade	1988	1989	1990	1992
Reading	27	37	40	—
Writing	—	50	61	—
Math	29	25	26	—
No. Tested	455	421	432	—

Widenmann (Elsa) El.

3rd Grade	1988	1989	1990	1992
Reading	29	15	17	—
Writing	15	12	8	—
Math	14	13	5	—
No. Tested	90	114	99	—
6th Grade	1988	1989	1990	1992
Reading	53	36	39	—
Writing	24	25	24	—
Math	38	31	26	—
No. Tested	85	99	80	—

6/Solano City Profiles

A Capsule Look at Towns and Cities — Trends, Schools, Recreation, Pace of Development

A FAST-GROWING COUNTY, Solano has both old and new, small and large in homes and towns. Where to live? What's available? The following profiles of cities and towns may help.

Benicia

Pretty, historic town. Crime low, academic rankings are generally in the top 20th percentile in the state.

Every few years, the Chronicle, the largest-selling newspaper in Northern California, ranks local cities according to schools, crime, recreation, home prices, commuting, and other aspects. Benicia, in 1991, got the Chronicle's nod for best family town in the Bay Region. Activities abound for kiddies (but Benicia doesn't have movies; Vallejo, however, does.)

Up until 1991, miserable was perhaps the best word to describe the commute. Most Benicians work in Contra Costa, Alameda or San Francisco counties, all requiring the crossing of the Carquinez Strait. The four-lane bridge at Benicia clogged morning and evening, and on Friday afternoons, when many people were heading for the Sierra, the bridge was often backed up for miles.

Now the commute has improved and can be classified as merely bad. Two lanes have been added to the bridge and, on the Contra Costa side, to Interstate 680. Traffic still jams at Walnut Creek but the bottleneck interchange is being rebuilt.

The real sufferers: San Francisco commuters; the Bay Bridge hasn't been up to the job for years. Still, the freeway improvements are helping. BART stations in Concord and Pleasant Hill; park and ride. In the vague future, the state wants to build a second bridge, but don't hold your breath waiting.

Named after Dona Benicia Vallejo, wife of the Californio commandante.

Benicia had the great sense or the great luck to elect people who did not tear down the city's history. The town used to be the state capital. The Capitol still stands, along with many homes built in the last century and early in this century.

The army built an arsenal at Benicia, stayed there for over 100 years, then deeded the land to the city. You can see the commandant's residence and the officers' quarters.

When Southern Pacific straightened out its transcontinental line, it ran the tracks over a bridge just east of the Benicia auto bridge, leaving much of the Benicia waterfront open to public access.

Benicia is built on hills, and the town is angled so it looks down the Carquinez Strait and into the setting sun. Glorious views. Many artists — some of national fame — have set up studios in the old arsenal.

Two homicides in 1991, none in 1990, one in 1989, none in 1988, 1987, 1986, reports FBI. Overall crime rate one of the lowest in the Bay Area.

A lot of activities for the kids, including soccer, Little League, swimming, ballet, gymnastics, sailing and windsurfing in the strait, and skateboarding on the hills (discouraged) or in a small skateboard park. Fire museum. New park, 30 acres, to open in Southampton subdivision. Tucked behind the hills is a lake surrounded by park and open space.

Good mix of restaurants, fast-food to everyday Chinese, Mexican and American fare, to a few top-notch places. The kind of town where you can stroll after dinner. A state park is located at the west end of town, on the water. Many residents jog from that park along the shore into the downtown and back.

Yacht harbor and club. New library. A fishing pier angles off First Street, and Dillon Point, in the state park, is popular with fishermen. Although voters in 1991 turned down an improvement tax for the downtown, the city is sprucing up what it can and adding a promenade and trails. Public art getting a start; first sculpture, a bench, unveiled in 1991. Good party town. St. Patrick's Day. Annual Peddlers Fair. Handicraft Fair. Opening Day on the Strait (parties, blessing of fleet, games). Waterfront Festival. Annual jazz festival.

Despite improvements, Benicia is disappointed that more tourists have not discovered its downtown.

Curbside recycling. Disposal center for motor oil, paint and car batteries. Annual volunteer cleanup of shore.

A town with many new homes and apartments. Up until the 1970s, Benicia was a quaint village, with almost all homes concentrated in the old section south of Highway 780. The Martinez bridge had introduced commuters into Benicia but little was done to house them until Southampton came along.

Southampton jumped over the north side of Highway 780 and marched the homes up the hill. The homes are nice, the views great, but the mix of new and old jars some senses. Benicia is half history, half suburbia.

To strengthen its tax base, Benicia in the 1960s welcomed the Exxon

Median & Average Prices of Owner-Occupied Dwellings

City or Area	Units	Median	Average
Benicia	5,640	$202,500	$209,638
Davis*	6,444	191,300	205,040
Dixon	2,099	139,500	148,513
Fairfield	12,621	139,900	148,402
Rio Vista	713	109,000	123,983
Suisun City	4,121	140,300	143,050
Vacaville	12,700	147,900	157,144
Vallejo	20,178	140,600	152,638
Remainder	3,745	253,076	259,697
Countywide	61,817	147,300	163,275

Source: 1990 Census. Median means half way. In 100 homes, the 50th is the median.
*Yolo County city.

refinery, somewhat hidden behind hills to the east. If you don't like refineries, you're not going to like this part of Benicia but in fairness to Exxon, many residents don't see it as a disruptive force. Benicia is a distribution port for car importers. The land just west of the bridge looks like a vast parking lot. Tankers and cargo ships sail up the strait and do some fancy maneuvering to dock at Benicia.

Despite this industrial base, Benicia may still be tax poor. After Proposition 13, the property tax declined as a source of revenue for cities and the sales tax ascended. To generate sales taxes, a city usually needs stores that sell taxable items at a fast rate — something like the Solano Mall or SunValley Shopping Plaza.

Benicia has the Southampton Shopping Center. Also First Street, a little shopping plaza at the top of First, a little plaza at the west end of town, and hidden in the industrial park, a few businesses. That's about it.

The city council voted in 1989 to impose a 4 percent tax on gas, electric, cable TV and in-state phone bills.

After losing once, parents and schools in 1991 won a two-thirds vote on a $29.5 million bond to renovate the town's schools. A new elementary school is on the way. Benicia has been blowing hot and cold on year-round schools.

State count in 1992 showed 9,990 residences, of which 6,387 were single homes, 998 clustered homes, 2,263 apartments, 252 mobile homes.

The old town has custom homes and the more interesting homes. Some nice townhouses can be found down on the water, just east of First Street, and more townhouses are to be built.

Southampton and small subdivisions have larger view homes. City council in mid-1989 approved 1,000 more homes for Southampton. Lot more homes

Number & Value of Owner-Occupied Dwellings

City or Area	< $100K -199K	$200K -299K	$300K -399K	$400K -499K	$500K -plus
Benicia	2,744	2,397	414	49	36
Davis*	3,571	2,278	437	112	46
Dixon	1,834	220	35	7	3
Fairfield	10,854	220	35	7	3
Rio Vista	756	37	12	5	2
Suisun City	3,971	133	12	3	2
Vacaville	10,820	1,620	179	49	32
Vallejo	16,389	3,227	487	48	27
Remainder	1,297	1,224	792	260	172
Countywide	48,566	10,459	2,058	447	287

Source: 1990 Census. The chart shows the number of owner-occupied dwellings within a designated price range. Data for some towns or residential areas are grouped with those covering a larger geographic area. *Yolo County city.

planned for Sky Valley, 5,000 acres northeast of Lake Herman but this project is still at the arguing stage.

Also in the arguing stage is a proposal to build 30,000-seat amphitheater for rock and music shows. Location: I-680 and Lake Herman Road, industrial-commercial section, removed from homes.

Some homes on Rose Drive were found to have been built on a dump. Ask questions.

Traffic is the strongest, possibly the only drawback to Benicia. It's a lovely place but the coming and going frays the nerves.

Cordelia

Where freeways meet, development inevitably follows. Just west of Fairfield proper, Interstate 80 splits off a branch called Interstate 680, the main road to Benicia and to Central Contra Costa.

Cordelia is approximately at this junction. There is a hamlet of Cordelia at an old Southern Pacific whistle stop about a mile away.

The junction itself is about what you would expect: service stations, fast foods, a deli, hotels, Scandia (a little amusement park). But a short distance away, subdivisions are going up. They seem nice, middle class and suburban. This is the new Cordelia which, properly speaking, is not a town but a neighborhood. To secure municipal services, Cordelia annexed to Fairfield.

Fairfield has taken some flak for annexing the countryside but if you are going to build subdivisions, they are best placed within a city, where they can get police protection, parks and recreation and other services.

Cordelia has a new elementary school and park. A high school is supposed to be built in the mid-1990s.

Statistics on crime have been folded into the Fairfield total but new subdivisions, being middle class and full of homeowners, generally have few crime problems.

As commutes go in Solano County, not bad. Less than 10 minutes to the Martinez-Benicia Bridge.

Solano Community College is located nearby, a campus full of activities and classes (academic and vocational), a gymnasium and other goodies.

The freeway interchange is to be rebuilt, which has brought some grumbling from residents.

Davis

University town, located just over the border in Yolo County, but part of the Interstate 80 family and influential in Solano County. About 13 miles from downtown Sacramento. Added about 10,000 residents in the last decade.

Academic scores high, crime low. Middle class, innovative. Crisscrossed with bike trails, suburban in look. Take away the university and Davis would pass as a quaint, well-kept California town that divides between the provincial and the cosmopolitan.

Bookstores. Latest movies. Sidewalk cafes. Quality restaurants. Bakeries. Many art galleries. New art center. Little theater.

Plus all the University of California offers: lectures, musical events, extension classes, and, by no means the least of pleasures, sporting events. Books are great, but it's nice to break for the Friday basketball game or Saturday football.

University is the biggest employer, about 16,000 people, a good chunk of them working in downtown Sacramento at the medical center.

Ten parks, four swimming complexes, a municipal golf course, tennis courts, country club, softball fields, a seniors complex, many activities for kids. New teen center.

Davis calls itself "The Bicycle Capital of the World." Bikes all over the place, by one count, 45,000, about one per person.

Also bike thieves. The Davis crime rate, a little high for a suburban town, owes its ascendency to simple theft. No homicides in 1991, 1990, 1989, 1988, 1987, 1986, reports FBI. In 1992, a teenage boy was killed in incident; shocked town.

School rankings among the highest in the state. Much attention to schools. Parcel taxes have been passed to lower class sizes, guarantee a seventh period at junior high and high schools. Many special programs. Science center. Child care at elementary schools.

Davis High School sends an unusually high number of students to the University of California, many of them to the Davis campus.

Liberal in politics but no Berkeley. Davis lacks the scruffiness and ethnic diversity of that town.

To make sure small shops would thrive, the city council limited the size of supermarkets. But then one supermarket chain wanted to build a giant jobber, loaded with goodies, the kind of store people love to shop. The solution: the supermarket was "divided" into "two" stores, each division fitting within the restrictions of the ordinance. If you buy turnips or potatoes or meat you pay at one register, if you buy booze, you pay at another register.

Politically correct but practical — Davis.

Constant fights over development — goes with territory in a college town. After a drawn-out battle that included a referendum, a builder got OK to build on 528 acres to the east of the city 1,000 homes and apartments, a commercial center, a light industrial park, several parks, a school, and a park-and-ride lot.

The university plans to add more buildings and move the stadium. If buying in Davis, ask Realtors about what is scheduled to be built and where. Also in the works, road and freeway-access changes to smooth the traffic.

Apartments plenty. Many students live on campus. Fairly good mix of housing, and recently, a shot of the new, some of it upscale. Most of the tracts went up in the Sixties and Seventies. Freeway divides the town. Housing tracts on both sides. Here and there remnants of the old orchards, the fruit still tasty.

State talley (Jan. 1992) showed 19,101 residences: 7,910 single-family homes, 2,116 single family attached, 8,673 multiples, 402 mobile homes.

Farm country. UC-Davis, enrollment about 23,000, is known as a university that has the knack to make plants and vines grow. There's a farmer's market Wednesday and Saturday in the downtown.

Kaiser outpatient facility. Sutter-Davis is the main community hospital. UC-Davis medical school in Sacramento.

All in all, a nice, civilized town that prizes education and getting along. A little hot; July temperatures average 74. But heat makes for solar energy, which Davis uses in abundance.

Dixon

In 1992, Dixon added a second supermarket (Safeway) and two banks, broke ground for more single-family homes, and began planning for a Wendy's.

Solano Community College announced plans for a satellite campus, to open this decade, and a new elementary school finished its first year of year-round education, a first for the town.

All of which is to say that this small farm city is turning suburb.

Located on I-80, Dixon is the last town going east before the county line. Increased its population by 38 percent in 1980s. Three of every 10 residents are kids (under 18), the 1990 census reported, an unusually high number.

First residents were Patwin Indians, who buried many of their dead in the flat land. Remains of two dozen were discovered in 1992.

Dixon's original name was Dickson, after the first settler, but California Pacific Railroad, which opened a depot in town, screwed up the spelling and the mistake stuck.

Dixon retains small town flavor: Little League season kicks off with a parade through the downtown, and when Tremont Elementary elects a student council, the story makes page one on the local paper.

To city slickers, this may suggest Hicksville, and Dixon, surrounded by open country, also comes across as sleepy.

But residents have choices. Dixon is located just down the freeway from the University of California at Davis — movies, theater, art shows, restaurants, and classes open to the public.

Limits have been set on residential construction but even with limits Dixon built over 1,000 units, mostly single homes, in the last decade. State tally (Jan. 1992) showed 3,831 residences: 2,909 single-family homes, 185 single-family attached, 699 multiples, 38 mobile homes.

School rankings are low to middling, and rising. Dixon is moving from rural to suburban, and attracting more middle-class families. This should raise the rankings. Town and parents make a fuss over kids — good sign. Over summer Tremont Elementary parents helped with landscaping, and painting.

Activities include T-ball, baseball, football, softball and soccer. Park recently landscaped for more ball fields. Four parks, two playgrounds. Library. Jazz festival. Community theater. A fairground, called Dixon May, hosts several events annually.

Town looks neat, well-cared-for. Some Victorians in downtown. Flat-top buildings here and there, housing popular just after World War II. Old but not run-down. Downtown utility lines being undergrounded.

No homicides in 1991, one in 1990, zero in 1989, one in 1988, one in 1987, reports FBI. Overall crime is low.

About 20 trains a day rumble through downtown, interrupting traffic and occasionally killing a person. The town is pushing for a separation of grade or undergrounding.

Solano County, local historians say, used to have more sheep than any other county in U.S. Dixon recalls ba-baa days with annual Lambtown Festival.

Fairfield

Military-family town, home to Travis Air Force Base. Second-largest city in Solano County. Added 19,112 residents in the last decade, up 33 percent.

Towns in the path of growth sometimes hunker down, curtail development, set themselves at odds with the builders. Other towns welcome growth but try to channel it and squeeze out its benefits, mostly money for parks and civic amenities.

Fairfield, under an innovative city manager, sought out projects it wanted, annexed aggressively to keep the countryside under its planning control and paid attention to quality of life and to dealing with problems.

The streets are clean, the median strips planted and maintained. Fairfield dings developers for a tree fee. When a new homeowner moves in, the city offers a choice of 40 trees that it will plant at no charge.

Named after home town of founding father. County seat. Travis Air Force Base, the mainstay of the local economy, employs over 11,000, and, according to newspaper, is the busiest military airport on the West Coast. About 70,000 landings and takeoffs a year.

Veterans Administration announced in 1992 that it will build hospital, 255 beds, next to Travis hospital.

Eight homicides in 1991, two in 1990, three in 1989, three in 1988, two in 1987, one in 1986, reports FBI. Crime rate a little high but Solano Mall and shopping centers attract light-fingered and this pushes up rate (Still, be careful, standard operating procedure in any American city). Fairfield girl kidnapped in late 1991; as of late 1992, not found.

Although overshadowed by the Solano Mall and the new subdivisions, the downtown still has enough vigor to be considered the heart of the city. Laid out in grids, and — the old-fashioned touch — the streets are named after presidents. Tall trees form avenues of shade.

Lot of sprucing up done on Texas Street, the main drag — decorative sidewalks, antique street lights, planters. Big library. Swim center. Adult school. Senior citizens center. New Center for the Performing Arts.

Big shopping mall, the Solano, just off the freeway. Several neighborhood shopping plazas. Shops in the downtown.

In 1992 "City Hall at the Mall" opened, a city office where residents can pay water bills and traffic citations, register for activities, and buy transit passes.

Target and Home Depot, and Price Club have opened stores in recent years.

Thirteen parks, over 40 tennis courts, including those at schools and at athletic club, three public or club pools, first public golf course opened in 1989, another one on the way, fishing in the nearby Delta or at Lake Berryessa, Air Force museum, skating rink, miniature golf, many clubs

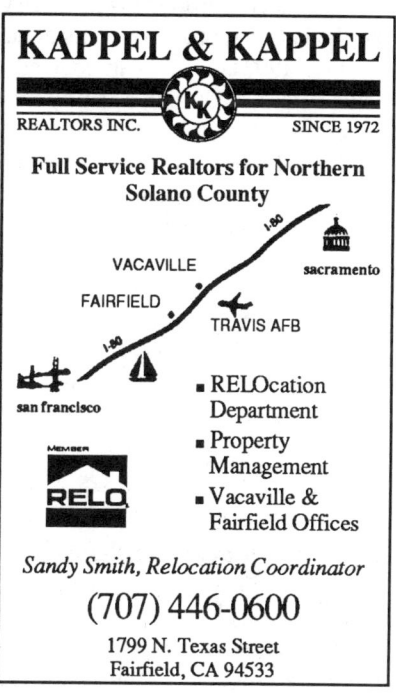

KAPPEL & KAPPEL

REALTORS INC. SINCE 1972

Full Service Realtors for Northern Solano County

- RELOcation Department
- Property Management
- Vacaville & Fairfield Offices

Sandy Smith, Relocation Coordinator

(707) 446-0600

1799 N. Texas Street
Fairfield, CA 94533

Median & Average Rents of Renter-Occupied Dwellings

City or Area	Units	Median	Average
Benicia	2,714	$599	$630
Davis*	10,578	547	590
Dixon	1,125	484	491
Fairfield	10,985	501	529
Rio Vista	472	404	424
Suisun City	2,274	521	554
Vacaville	7,946	561	578
Vallejo	14,081	511	513
Countywide	41,148	521	537

Source: 1990 Census. Units are total number of renter-occupied dwellings. Rents are stated as monthly payments. Median means half way. In 100 homes, the 50th is the median. *Yolo County city.

and activities. Softball popular, attracts about 8,000 players, men and women

Every year Travis puts on an air show, the highlight being the Thunderbirds, Air Force aerobatics team. Military means young men and women. Many apartments along the south side of Air Base Parkway.

New jail in the downtown. When you're the county seat, you get the courts and the jails and other government buildings.

In its 1992 tally, the state counted 28,843 residences, of which 18,394 were single homes, 1,230 single-family attached, 8,231 apartments, and 988 mobile homes.

In the 1980s, Fairfield built about 5,300 single homes, firmly anchoring the city as a middle-class suburb.

North of the freeway is blooming with new housing tracts, mostly middle class but a few, notably Rancho Solano, upscale.

A lot more homes are coming. City to make northeast Fairfield a residential base, the Cordelia area (west) a business base, and the center a mix of homes and jobs — double the population in 30 years.

Most of Fairfield is flat but some neighborhoods rise into the hills and where there are hills there are views — of the Delta and Mt. Diablo.

In between apartments, townhouses, the very new and the old, there are about a half dozen neighborhoods of single-family homes probably built in the Sixties, Seventies and early Eighties. Most of them are north of Travis Boulevard. Nice, well-kept, middle class, mostly three and four bedrooms.

Pac Bell in 1991 opened a $40 million computer center. Employs 150.

Highway 12, along the southern border, takes some pressure off Interstate 80, but ultimately feeds into 80, which carries on to Vallejo and by Interstate 680 to Benicia and Martinez. Both routes lead to San Fran and Oakland.

Number of Units Available at Selected Rents

City or Area	<$100 -249	$250 -499	$500 -749	$750 -999	$1,000 -plus
Benicia	194	565	1,172	567	162
Davis*	593	3,436	4,392	1,495	531
Dixon	107	514	410	67	1
Fairfield	855	4,198	3,918	1,112	78
Rio Vista	53	263	135	8	1
Suisun City	154	867	807	417	9
Vacaville	382	2,450	3,791	1,116	119
Vallejo	1,305	5,005	5,874	1,115	146
Remainder	214	583	381	89	53
Countywide	3,264	14,445	16,488	4,491	569

Source: 1990 Census. The chart shows the number of rental units counted within a designated range of rates. *Yolo County city.

This is the main drawback to Fairfield. If you work in San Francisco or Oakland, it's a wearying haul. The Benicia Bridge in 1991 added two lanes, which helps. More freeway improvements are being made. Many Solano County commuters pick up the BART train at Concord. Solano Commuter Information will help find you a car pool. Call (707) 447-POOL.

Two school districts, Fairfield-Suisun and Travis. Rankings middling to high.

Fairfield district is running year-round programs at several elementary schools.

Mello-Roos law is being used to tax new residents for new schools but the recession has cut money from this source, forcing slowdown in school construction.

Some grumbling about how money is being spent and some parents in 1992 tried unsuccessfully to recall school trustees. The real problem, however, is the state recession, which has forced severe cuts in government services.

Much attention to schools because there are a lot of kids. About 30 percent of residents are under age 18 (1990 census).

American Demographics, a magazine, identified Fairfield-Vacaville-Napa region as fifth most popular "baby-boomer magnet" in U.S. If you are looking for playmates for kiddies, this is it.

Solano Community College, many academic and vocational classes, is located in Cordelia neighborhood.

Jumbo jets fly out of Travis and pilots practice touching down and taking off. An editor has pulled to the side of the road, shut off the motor, and listened to a jumbo directly overhead. Very quiet. This is his opinion. If buying a home, take the time to listen. The Air Force has done a study on plane noise and where it might get worse. City hall has report.

Rio Vista

Rip Van Winkle of the county. Slept through the last decade. Started the 1980s with 3,142 residents, finished with 3,316. The 1990s promise to be much different. Developers have discovered Rio Vista.

The city in 1991 approved permits for a seniors complex much like Rossmoor in Contra Costa County, 4,000 homes, two golf courses, tennis courts, swimming pools, 25 acres for shops. Other developments, with thousands of residential units, are also in the works.

If all this pans out, the population could zoom to 20,000, say civic leaders.

Picturesque town. Right on the Sacramento River. You can launch your boat at the end of Main Street.

In 1980s, Rio Vista ran into money problems. Salaries were frozen, city staff reduced. Civic leaders, to strengthen tax base and diversify economy, went after development.

Meanwhile, the Bay Area had grown up and out, bringing Rio V within a reasonable commute of job centers. Its river location makes it quite attractive.

New airport, runway 4,600 feet, going up, replacing a smaller one that's being turned into a light-industry park. Also in the works, if all goes right, more parks, a civic center, a library, two fire stations and a senior center.

One obstacle: the bridge over the river. To handle more traffic, it needs to be replaced and its access roads improved.

If you visit Rio Vista before the carpenters and tractors do much changing, you'll find a small downtown that caters to fishermen and tourists, a little subdivision in the west hills, a few streets on the east side, an elementary school, a high school and a couple of parks.

A railroad museum, located about 12 miles out of town, draws many visitors. Railroad museum has over 30 cars, one dating to 1888, trolleys and an eight-mile track (but most rides are shorter). Phone (707) 374-2978.

Big annual event for the town: Bass Derby.

The FBI doesn't track towns with less than 10,000 people. But Rio Vista is a peaceful burg. By the last count (1992), Rio Vista had 1,517 single homes, 47 single-family attached, 304 apartments, and 129 mobile homes.

Suisun City

A waterfront city that did something drastic about the blight that was stifling its old town. It bought up blocks of apartment buildings, demolished them, absorbed some of the residents and said goodbye to the rest.

Results are not yet in but action should cut crime, raise school rankings, move neighborhood, called the Crescent, into middle class. The apartments are to be replaced by single homes.

Suisun City started the last decade with 3,655 residential units and 11,087 people and finished with 6,875 units and 22,686 residents — doubling itself.

Almost all the newcomers settled in single-home tracts removed from the old town. Many of the tracts hugger-mugger up to Fairfield and without "city limit" signs it would be impossible to distinguish one town from the other.

Old Suisun City, located just south of downtown Fairfield, has the makings of a nice town center. Suisun Slough, which bisects the downtown, meanders out to Suisun Bay and gives the city water access to the Delta.

With aggressive planning decades ago, a lot could have been made out of this: marinas, restaurants, fishing piers, a night life that attracted people from Fairfield, a sales tax base that could have funded parks and other amenities.

Suisun City staggered in this direction but for the most part the town was allowed to drift. The most noticeable feature of Main Street is not a marina nor restaurant but an oil transfer depot that parks its tanker trucks in full view.

Also debasing the old town were blocks of apartments that were allowed to sink into crack, crime and disrepair. But they were cheap housing, popular with poor and low income.

Suisun City crime is about suburban average. One homicide in 1991, one in 1990, two in 1989, two in 1988, three in 1987, zero in 1986, reports FBI. A lot of the crime was concentrated in four blocks in the Crescent.

Suisun City formed a redevelopment agency, raised money to buy these blocks and 40 apartment buildings, bulldozed the great majority of them, and relocated some of the residents to other parts of town or, mainly, Fairfield. Moving expenses were paid for and rents subsidized, if residents couldn't find comparable rents at new places.

Redevelopment millions are also being used to overhaul Main Street, improve marine access, and build a new marina (421 berths). The oil business is to be moved and the train depot renovated and used as a commute hub.

The state in 1992 counted 7,148 residences, of which 5,476 were single homes, 46 single attached, 1,251 multiples, and 87 mobile homes.

Away from the downtown, the town is almost pure suburb, blue- and white-collar middle class. Lawler Ranch is the latest tract and a study in modern California. On any evening, kids of all races can be found playing together in the streets. Plans call for a 25-acre sports park — soccer and softball fields, trails — near new subdivisions.

School rankings middling to high. The city is served by the Fairfield-Suisun School District.

A new elementary school was opened in 1990. Another is planned for Lawler Ranch in a few years. The school district runs many year-round schools.

Suisun City has a senior complex, a public swimming pool (at Crystal School) and at least three parks. City hall, a striking white building, is located on the slough. You can bait your hook and fish in the downtown. Or moor your boat. Or launch it, mud and tide permitting. Just outside the city, 2,000 acres of marsh have been placed in a preserve.

Or you can go to Fairfield for your fun. That city's parks and amusements, its downtown, are located a few minutes away. So are Solano Mall and shops. Suisun City has opened a neighborhood shopping center west of Sunset Avenue. Both towns celebrate Heritage Days, Suisun City's contribution a bathtub derby up the slough.

Vacaville

The third biggest city in the county. With development of its Lagoon Valley in the 1990s, about to grow much bigger. Plan calls for homes, offices, hospital, golf course and park.

Bank of America is supposed to move 2,000-3,000 employees to the valley, into a 600,000-square-foot complex. City officials, fingers crossed and watching the economy, will believe this when it happens.

A pleasant town in a suburban way. Crime low. Many school rankings above the 50th percentile.

Lot of kids. About 27 percent of population is under age 18 years, 1990 census reported, and if you set aside the 7,400 inmates at state prison, the percentage rises to about 30. The Chronicle placed it third in the Bay Region in towns congenial to family life.

Named after Manuel Vaca, who received a grant of 41,000 acres in 1841, a few years before the great Yankee migration. A Vacaville resident is called a "Vacan."

Although incorporated as a city 100 years ago, Vacaville is pretty much a "new" town, booming with residential and commercial construction. The city's population, 1,600 in 1940, doubled in a decade, rose to 10,898 by 1960, then to 26,435 by 1970, then to 43,367 by 1980. In the last decade, the count rose by 28,000, to 71,479 residents.

When you shop for homes, you get a mixture of the brand new and homes that were built in tracts throughout the Fifties, Sixties, Seventies and Eighties.

The state in 1992 tallied 25,235 housing units, of which 17,620 were single homes, 873 single attached, 5,573 apartments, 1,169 mobile homes.

Many tree-lined streets. Homes and streets generally well-kept. Rundown spots few. Custom homes hidden on side streets. Plenty of sparkle in the new tracts. Middle America.

Concerned about pace of development, city is restricting building permits annually, in the hope of catching up with parks, schools, amenities. Vaca Valley Hospital opened five years ago. Kaiser to open big medical center in 1996.

Vacaville's growth in the Fifties was fueled by nearby Travis Air Force Base and by the Vacaville Medical Facility, built in 1955, a state institution for screening the accused and the guilty. In effect, it's a psychiatric holding and treatment prison.

New homes, apartments and townhouses are going up on the outskirts, along with neighborhood shopping centers. All this makes sense, but it has greatly weakened the downtown as the "heart" of the city.

Vacaville has a famous restaurant, the Nut Tree, located just off the freeway. Right next to the Nut Tree is a small airport. People fly in just for lunch and dinner, and thousands of people driving to and from the Sierra and the gambling resorts have stopped at the restaurant.

A shopping plaza (over 100 factory outlets — furniture, dishes, clothes, bedding) has been constructed nearby. An auto mall, backed by city money, is settling in. Banks also.

The city is pumping money and energy into old Vacaville but faced with such competition the section may never revive as the true center.

Developers are required to pay city and school fees up front, and these costs are passed on to home buyers. Vacaville and many Solano towns are charging $10,000 to $30,000 per home.

Two school districts serve town, Vacaville, the larger, and Travis. Located southwest of city, Travis used to serve only children from air base. Now town has grown out to meet school district with the result that enrollment is on the rise. School rankings range from low-middle to high, many about the 50th percentile. Some concern about dropouts.

New schools are scheduled to be built in 1990s, which will change attendance boundaries. Call schools to find out which your children will attend. Some schools are starting after-class programs: music, sports, games, arts and crafts.

Studies indicate that Travis and Vacaville districts will attract an additional 9,000 students this decade. For years Vacaville turned down efforts to start year-round schools, now two are running this way, and no doubt more to come.

Solano College in mid-1990s is to open a satellite campus on 50-60 acres near Interstate 505 and Midway Road.

Crime suburban low-average. One homicide in 1991, zero in 1990 and 1989, two in 1988, four in 1987, none in 1986, FBI reports.

Twenty-two parks and playgrounds, three private pools, two public, golf course, movies, jogging courses, museum. New sports center

KAPPEL & KAPPEL

REALTORS INC. **SINCE 1972**

Full Service Realtors for Northern Solano County

- RELOcation Department
- Property Management
- Vacaville & Fairfield Offices

Sandy Smith, Relocation Coordinator

(707) 446-0600

355 Main Street
Vacaville, CA 95688

— basketball, volleyball courts — went up in 1989. New library, theater, community center to open in 1993. City rec department offers gymnastics, teen sock hops, preschool, Jazzercise, much more. Fiesta Days — annual hoo-hah when town celebrates its western and Hispanic heritage. Also Onion Festival. Chefs take field, try for tastiest dishes. Annual art show. Waterslide, miniature golf in Lagoon Valley. Pumpkin contest at Nut Tree.

Travis Air Force Base has done a study showing flight paths where noise is high. Fact of life: Travis is here to stay. If you want info, contact city hall. Noise doesn't seem to be a big issue in Fairfield or Vacaville.

One major difference between two towns: Fairfield, Realtors say, is oriented toward Bay Area jobs, Vacaville toward Sacramento jobs. The latter is straight shot on a wide freeway.

Vallejo

Waterfront town, most populous city in Solano County, and although recession has slowed growth, more homes and businesses are coming.

Started the 1980s with 80,303 residents, finished with 109,199, census reports, an increase of 36 percent or 28,896, more than the entire population of neighboring Benicia. Many of the new residents were attracted by low (relative to other cities) home prices.

School rankings above and below the 50th percentile, and rising. Crime a problem in some sections.

Site of Marine World Africa USA, a theme park that attracts hundreds of thousands of visitors annually and has made Vallejo a tourist center.

The best commute in Solano County to San Francisco and Oakland. Bisected by Interstate 80, which runs straight to the Bay Bridge but is often congested at peak hours. Highway 780 shunts over to the Martinez-Benicia Bridge and Central Contra Costa County. Freeway improvements near Marine World should eliminate what has been an irritating bottleneck.

Named after Mariano Vallejo, wily Californio who exerted great influence during the Mexican and early Yankee days.

Overlooks the Carquinez Strait and San Pablo Bay. Has a big naval shipyard, Mare Island, that specializes in submarines and until almost 1980 Vallejo was known as a military blue-collar town.

The Eighties brought new housing, Marine World, the collapse of Soviet empire and the end of the Cold War. Vallejo still loves the Navy but the military work force in recent years has shrunk from 9,400 workers to 6,500. Skaggs Island, a Naval intelligence station located west of Vallejo, is closing.

With the influx of white-collar commuters by the thousands, the town's orientation has gone suburban.

Neighborhoods in and near the old downtown suffer from drugs, violence and prostitution. Almost every American city suffers crime problems. The question here is one of degree: How bad? Not remotely as bad as parts of

Price Sampler from Classified Ads

Benicia
4-bedroom, 2.5-bath, beautifully decorated & landscaped, all upgrades, $249,900.
4-bedroom, 2.5-bath, water view, new paint, carpets, spa, gazebo, decks, $265,000.

Cordelia
3-bedroom, 2-bath, beautifully updated, new carpet & paint, spa, deck, $150,000.
4-bedroom, 3-bath, 2,100 sq. ft., Spanish-style roof, $194,950.

Dixon
4-bedroom, 2.5-bath, pool, spa, oversized garage, many extras, $227,500.
5-bedroom, 3.75-bath, pool, master suite, bar, private dining room, $260,000.

Fairfield
3-bedroom, 2-bath, 2,000 sq. ft., 2 fireplaces, family room, dining room, breakfast nook, pool, solar heat, $234,900.
4-bedroom, 3-bath, landscaped, deck, fruit trees, garden, under $200,000.
4-bedroom, 2-bath, fireplace, skylight, large kitchen, formal dining, new paint, $149,500.

Green Valley
4-bedroom w/den, custom, view of Mt. Diablo, $549,900.
Green Valley Lake homes up to 2,433 sq. ft. at 10-acre lake, $194,950 to $314,950.

Rio Vista
4-bedroom, 3-bath ranch home on 1/2 acre at Birds Landing, $229,500.

Vacaville
3-bedroom, 3-bath, new, 5 acres, 4-plus-car garage, $394,250.
4-bedroom, 2-bath, fruit trees, grapes, wine cellar, big family room & kitchen, $183,950.
4-bedroom, 2.5-bath, large lot, custom home, buy now & finish to your specs, $309,000.

Vallejo
4-bedroom, 2-bath, family room, fireplace, large corner lot, pool, 5 yrs. old, $188,000.
5-bedroom, 4-bath, 4,000 sq. ft., 2 master bedrooms, fireplaces, marble floor, tri-level, entry hall, Marine World view. $395,000.
3-bedroom, new paint, new bath, new roof, large yard, near school, $119,900.

Winters
1,600 sq. ft. w/master suite, custom brickwork, yard, $168,000.
3-bedroom, 2-bath, 1,906 sq. ft., Almond Orchard subdivision, $181,900.
4-bedroom, 2-bath, one story, like new, 3 yrs. old, $209,500

Source: Survey of local classified advertising in summer and fall, 1992.

Oakland, Richmond, San Francisco. Not as good as Concord, Fairfield or Vacaville. Vallejo is a suburban city with troublesome neighborhoods. You must be wary, lock doors, join Neighborhood Watch efforts, caution children.

Vallejo police have opened two substations to improve visibility and protection and will open another in 1993. Schools have stepped up efforts to help kids resist drugs.

FBI reports thirteen homicides in 1991, eight in 1990, sixteen in 1989. The counts for the preceding years were 13, 15, 6 and 6.

Crime does not appear to have infected the new subdivisions and, indeed, many parts of old Vallejo.

Activities are plentiful: baseball, basketball, soccer, softball. Many adult pursuits. New movie complex. Vallejo has a senior center and a seasonal farmers' market.

Museum, swim center open all year, Children's Wonderland, two community centers, a waterfront, a yacht harbor, a downtown that's no longer the true heart of the city but still has that old Main Street feel, a mix of government buildings and Victorians. Hills and sweeping views of the Bay and Strait. You can fish in Vallejo. The wine country starts a short distance off. Vallejo has a symphony orchestra.

Vallejo is home to the Solano County Fair, which draws about 180,000 annually. Horse racing, rides, top name bands and singers, a lot of fun.

Shopping good and getting better. Besides Wal-Mart, a warehouse retail-food store recently opened.

Two events are believed to have tipped the town into a desirable address: Glen Cove succeeded. Marine World in 1984 bet its bundle on Vallejo.

Glen Cove is a housing development or group of developments on the Carquinez Strait to the east of the bridge. Without being gushy, Glen Cove, the first "new" subdivision, looks nice: New school, marina, shopping center, views of strait and empty hills of Contra Costa, a lot of tender, loving care to the homes and landscaping. And, yes, safe, or more precisely as safe as many neighborhoods in Concord, Fairfield, Hercules — middle-suburbia safe.

Glen Cove announced to the world that Vallejo was a good place to shop for a home. The other subdivisions sprang up to satisfy the boom.

Marine World, in a different way, did the same thing. Just by setting up in the town the amusement complex said we trust Vallejo and we are going to back our trust with millions. And the unwritten message, which sinks in imperceptibly, was, you, too, can trust Vallejo.

Vallejo mixes poor and middle-class kids. School rankings reflect demographics; poor neighborhoods often score low, middle class, much higher. With Vallejo turning more middle class, the rankings are coming up.

Two elementary schools, a high school and possibly a middle school are planned for the 1990s, the cost to be paid by a parcel tax on new developments, a favorite revenue raiser these days. It means the new residents are picking up the bill. Many of Vallejo's elementary schools are run year-round. Schedules vary. Check with school district. For choice, Vallejo has a Catholic high school.

Vallejo is an integrated town, and the schools are paying a lot of attention to helping kids get along socially.

Good housing and price mix, one of the advantages of a town that has built homes probably in every decade of its existence. You can buy a Victorian in Vallejo, or tract homes built in the Fifties, Sixties and Seventies.

In its 1992 tally, the state counted 40,575 residences: 26,6524 single homes, 1,639 single attached, 11,078 multiples, and 1,334 mobile homes.

Recession has slowed residential construction.

California Maritime Academy, a public college that trains men and women for the merchant marine, is located down on the water, just west of the bridge. Each year, the midshipmen sail the Pacific, practicing what they have learned in class. Big to-do when they return.

American Canyon, a large subdivision-community that blends in with Vallejo, is not located in Vallejo. It's in Napa County. Town recently voted to incorporate as a city.

You live in Vallejo, you work in San Fran, you don't want to drive. Vallejo has an alternative: a ferry.

7/How Public Schools Work

SAT Scores, the UCs Local Grads Prefer, Getting the Most Out of Your Child's School

SCORES MEASURE ACADEMIC success but they have their shortcomings. Some students know the material but are not adept at taking tests and some tests are so poorly designed that they fail to assess what has been taught. The rankings in the chapters on school rankings do not break out students as individuals. A basic exam tests the least the children should know, not the most. There are other legitimate criticisms of the California Assessment Program test and indeed most tests.

Nonetheless, CAP scores do correlate to SAT scores, to other measures and with teacher observations. Schools that score high on CAP tests usually score high on the SAT and send, proportionally, a greater number of their students on to college.

When your children attend a school with high scores, they are not assured of success. These schools have their failures. Neither can you be certain that your children will get the best teachers or right programs. Other schools with lower scores might do better on these points. What you can be certain of is that your children are entering a setting that has proven successful for many students. The main problem with making sense out of scores concerns what is called socioeconomics, a theory educators love, hate and widely believe.

Socioeconomics

In its crudest form, socioeconomics means rich kids score high, middle-class kids score about the middle and poor kids score low. Not all the time, not predictably by individual. Many children from poor and middle-class homes succeed in school and attend the best colleges. But as a general rule socioeconomics enjoys much statistical support.

Contra Costa Scholastic Aptitude Test (SAT) Scores

High School	*Enrollment	No. Tested	Verbal	Math
Acalanes	236	189	483	556
Alhambra	213	58	424	479
Antioch	591	203	399	467
California	341	160	430	512
Campolindo	230	195	484	558
Clayton Valley	328	127	437	512
College Park	302	142	449	505
Concord	295	112	421	472
De Anza	278	104	405	472
El Cerrito	293	182	405	479
John Swett	100	31	427	515
Kennedy	170	57	413	464
Las Lomas	242	142	475	533
Liberty	365	71	411	481
Miramonte	204	166	502	583
Monte Vista	416	316	473	535
Mt. Diablo	227	64	386	460
Northgate	307	249	478	555
Pinole Valley	443	187	395	484
Pittsburg	343	101	369	430
Richmond	228	43	273	338
San Ramon Valley	379	245	472	534
Ygnacio Valley	388	176	438	531
Contra Costa Avg.	—	—	442	513

Source: California Department of Education, 1992 tests. Scholastic Aptitude Test scores are greatly influenced by who and how many take the test. A school that has more marginal students taking the test will, by one line of reasoning, be doing a good job, but the scores are likely to be lower. *The enrollment of the senior class at the time of the test.

Compare the rankings in the preceding chapter with income by cities. Orinda, rich, high scores; San Pablo, poor, low; Antioch and Martinez, middle class towns, middling scores. The SAT scores also show this pattern.

Similar divisions can be found in Solano County. The middle-income neighborhoods of Vallejo score higher than the lower-income neighborhoods.

In Alameda County, schools in Oakland's poorer areas score low; well-to-do Piedmont scores high. The pattern shows up around the Bay Area, the country and in other countries. The federal study, "Japanese Education Today," notes a "solid correlation between poverty and poor school performance ...."

Solano Scholastic Aptitude Test (SAT) Scores

High School	*Enrollment	No. Tested	Verbal	Math
Armijo	474	142	429	469
Benicia	255	128	425	503
Davis*	341	274	475	543
Dixon	190	62	398	445
Fairfield	516	192	390	465
Hogan	478	174	379	446
Vacaville	311	132	415	478
Vallejo	443	156	381	437
Vanden	161	52	438	491
Winters*	99	12	427	517
Solano County Avg.	—	—	403	465

Source: California Department of Education, 1992 tests. See remarks for Contra Costa SAT scores on page 130. *Enrollment at time of test. **Yolo County schools.

Family and Culture

In its refined form, socioeconomics moves away from the buck and toward culture and family influence. Note the charts on Pages 16 and 97. The towns with the highest number of college educated are generally also the towns with the highest scores. If your mom or dad attended college, chances are you will attend college or do well at school because in a thousand ways while you were growing up they and their milieu pushed you in this direction. Emphasis on "chances are." Nothing is certain when dealing with human beings.

What if mom and dad never got beyond the third grade? Or can't even speak English? Historically, many poor and immigrant children have succeeded at school because their parents badgered, bullied and encouraged them every step of the way and made sacrifices so they would succeed. Asian kids are the latest example of poor kids succeeding but earlier generations could point to the children of peasant Europeans.

Does it make a difference if the child is English proficient? Or the parents rich? Individual differences will always count. Immigrant children unfamiliar with English will have more difficulties with literature and language-proficient courses than native-born children. Nonetheless, the home-school correlation retains much validity: the stronger the educational support the child receives at home, the better he or she will do at school.

So thoroughly does the California Department of Education believe in socioeconomics that it worked the theory into a mathematical model. Teachers collect data on almost all students: are they on welfare, do they have language problems (immigrants), how educated are their parents? The information is fed to computers and used to predict how students will score on tests.

Role of Schools

If you carry the logic of socioeconomics too far, you come to the conclusion that schools and teachers or teaching methods don't matter: Students succeed or fail according to their family or societal backgrounds.

Nonsense. No matter how dedicated or well-intentioned the parent, if the teacher is grossly inept the child probably will learn little. If material or textbooks are out-of-date or inaccurate, what the student learns will be useless or damaging. Conversely, if the teacher is dedicated and knowledgeable, if the material is well presented and appropriate, what the child comes away with will be helpful and, to society, more likely to be beneficial.

Almost every one of us can recall a favorite teacher who worked with us and influenced our lives.

Where the Confusion Enters

When scores rise or fall, frequently the blame or credit goes to the school or the scores are treated as a reflection solely of school life. Scores in School A go up. The principal thanks the teachers and the students for their hard work and says, we're on the right track. Scores in School B drop. The principal blames cuts in funding or a program that needs to be reworked.

In late 1992, CAP scores for eighth graders were released showing drops from recent years. Educational leaders blamed funding cuts and difficulties of educating immigrant students. The immigrant aspect was also given a money shading: if schools had more money, they could do a better job.

All of this is true. If the schools are adequately funded, if class sizes are kept manageable, teachers can do a better job.

But to get a rounded picture of why scores are dropping or rising or are low or high, family background and social values have to be included.

Scores in east Contra Costa are rising. Better teachers, better teaching methods? Perhaps. But the demographics of the region are changing. Priced out of other markets, more middle-class people are moving to the East County.

Richmond Unified has some of the lowest scoring schools in the state and some of the highest. All teachers are paid the same, all are recruited by the same agency and all, presumably, meet the standards of the district.

Why the difference in scores? The backgrounds of the children are different. El Cerrito and Kensington are home to many professionals affiliated with the University of California. Academic culture strong. Scores high.

Richmond flatlands have many poor students, many welfare families. Academic push weak. Scores very low.

The flatlands also have many minority children but to define achievement solely by ethnicity distorts the picture. Many middle-class towns or neighborhoods, especially in the West County, have high numbers of students from the same ethnic groups. Scores are much higher, sometimes very high. The difference: probably family stability and a host of other social influences.

California College Admissions of Public School Graduates
Contra Costa County

High School	UC	CSU	Com	Total	Enroll
Acalanes	53	17	74	144	246
Alhambra	13	4	92	109	177
Antioch	26	35	262	323	559
California	30	58	155	243	353
Campolindo	59	17	59	135	222
Clayton Valley	23	43	202	268	340
College Park	18	22	177	217	269
Concord	13	20	138	171	263
De Anza	18	25	113	156	281
El Cerrito	50	34	88	172	285
John Swett	3	7	45	55	89
Kennedy	6	28	52	86	162
Las Lomas	36	28	132	196	256
Liberty	12	18	119	149	312
Miramonte	35	20	39	94	178
Monte Vista	61	48	99	208	346
Mt. Diablo	8	3	107	118	205
Northgate	53	36	131	220	273
Pinole Valley	39	37	224	300	413
Pittsburg	10	3	116	129	288
Richmond	7	13	53	73	173
San Ramon Val.	56	66	167	289	402
Ygnacio Valley	28	34	171	233	314

Solano County

High School	UC	CSU	Com	Total	Enroll
Armijo	21	25	152	198	389
Benicia	12	38	54	104	265
Davis*	128	55	63	246	382
Dixon	7	11	39	57	146
Fairfield	23	23	176	222	427
Hogan	15	35	128	178	362
Vacaville	28	38	244	310	590
Vallejo	11	28	150	189	438
Vanden	6	8	51	65	140

Source: California Department of Education, fall, 1991. The chart shows which California colleges 1991 public high school graduates selected for freshmen enrollment. The state does not track graduates enrolling in private or out-of-state colleges. Continuation schools not included in list. **Key:** UC (University of California system); CSU (Cal State system); Com (Community Colleges); Total (total number of graduates attending California colleges); Enroll (total enrollment of 1991 senior class at time of graduation). *Yolo County school.

UCs Chosen by Solano Public School Graduates

School	Berk	Davis	Irv	UCLA	SD	SB	River	SC	Total
Armijo	0	7	0	0	1	1	0	0	9
Benicia	1	4	0	1	1	1	0	3	11
Davis*	13	67	0	5	4	7	0	7	103
Dixon	0	15	1	0	0	0	0	0	16
Fairfield	5	15	0	1	0	1	0	2	24
Hogan	2	10	0	0	0	0	1	0	13
Vacaville	2	17	0	1	1	3	0	1	25
Vallejo	0	3	0	1	0	0	0	3	7
Vanden	0	7	0	1	0	1	0	0	9

Source: California Dept. of Education. See Contra Costa chart. *Yolo County school.

Which is more important?

Background or school? Educators argue about this, many contending that regardless of socioeconomics, schools should be able to educate all students. Some schools and teachers, to their great credit, do succeed with students from academically impoverished backgrounds.

Many others, however, fail. The harsh truth seems to be that without a home or social life that nourishes academics — or without large scale social programs — success in school is difficult.

Back to Scores

If a school's scores are middling, it may still be capable of doing an excellent job, if it has dedicated teachers and sound programs. The middling scores may reflect socioeconomics, not instructional quality.

Don't judge us by our overall scores, many schools say. Judge us by our ability to deliver for your son or daughter.

This gets tricky because the children do influence one another and high-income parents often interact differently with schools than low-income parents. To some extent, the school must structure its programs to ability of the students. But schools with middling and middling-plus grades can point to many successes.

Basic Instruction-Ability Grouping

California and American schools attempt to meet the needs of students by providing a good basic education and by addressing individual and subgroup needs by special classes and ability grouping.

In the first six years in an average school, children receive some special help according to ability but for the most part they share the same class experiences and get the same instruction.

UCs Chosen by Contra Costa Public School Graduates

School	Berk	Davis	Irv	UCLA	SD	SB	River	SC	Total
Acalanes	12	35	2	7	7	6	1	4	74
Alhambra	1	0	0	0	1	1	0	2	5
Antioch	1	13	1	3	2	0	1	1	22
California	7	15	1	1	2	4	1	5	36
Campolindo	14	24	4	5	9	7	1	4	68
Clayton Valley	5	6	2	1	4	1	1	2	22
College Park	5	12	1	3	1	4	1	0	27
Concord	6	5	2	0	2	3	0	1	19
De Anza	4	7	0	0	0	0	0	0	11
El Cerrito	11	18	0	7	6	5	0	11	58
John Swett	1	5	0	0	0	0	0	1	7
Kennedy	5	10	0	2	0	0	0	2	19
Las Lomas	5	12	1	4	4	2	1	1	30
Liberty	2	3	0	0	0	1	0	0	6
Miramonte	26	13	1	11	9	10	1	7	78
Monte Vista	13	20	5	20	10	22	4	1	95
Mt. Diablo	2	11	0	1	0	0	0	0	14
Northgate	12	35	2	7	7	6	1	4	74
Pinole Valley	10	16	1	3	1	1	1	1	34
Pittsburg	4	1	0	2	0	2	0	1	10
Pleasant Hill	0	1	0	0	0	0	0	0	1
Richmond	0	1	0	0	0	2	1	3	7
San Ramon	8	9	1	9	6	11	2	0	46
Ygnacio Valley	3	7	2	4	0	5	2	2	25

Source: California Department of Education. The chart shows which University of California that a 1990 public high school graduate selected for freshmen enrollment. **Key**: Berk (Berkeley), Irv (Irvine), River (Riverside), SD (San Diego), SB (Santa Barbara), SC (Santa Cruz).

About the seventh grade, until recently, students were divided into classes for low achievers, middling students and high achievers, or low-middle and advanced — tracking. Texts, homework and expectations were different for each group. The high achievers were on the college track, the low, the vocational.

Pressured by the state, schools are curtailing this practice, but many schools retain accelerated English and math classes for advanced seventh and eighth graders. Parents can always request a transfer from one group to another (whether they can get it is another matter). The reality often is, however, that remedial and middle children can't keep pace with the high achievers.

In the last 30 years or so schools introduced into the early grades special programs aimed at low achievers or children with learning difficulties. Although they vary greatly, these programs typically pull the children out of class for instruction in small groups then return them to the regular class.

Many schools also pull out gifted (high I.Q.) students and a few cluster them in their own classes.

College Influence

The junior high divisions sharpen at high school. Colleges exercise great influence over what students are taught in high school. So many students attend the University of California and California State University schools that public and private high schools must of necessity teach classes demanded by these institutions.

So the typical high school will have a prep program that meets University of California requirements. The school will also offer general education classes in math and English but these will not be as tough as the prep courses and will not be recognized by the state universities. Usually the school will teach some trades so those inclined can secure jobs.

How "Mediocre" Schools Succeed — College Admissions

The state traces public college freshmen, age 19 and under, to their high schools. The data can mislead but it shows the strengths of the middling schools (See Chart on Page 133).

If a student attends a California State University, a community college or a University of California (Berkeley, Los Angeles, San Diego, Davis, etc.), the state generally will know where he or she attended high school in California. The chart, using data from fall 1991, tracks freshmen in California public colleges back to their high schools. The UCs generally restrict themselves to the top 13 percent in the state. The Cal States take the top third.

Notice El Cerrito High. In basic score rankings, it places low to the middle. Yet it sent 50 kids to the University of California. Or Kennedy High School in Richmond, even lower scores, yet 6 went to the University of California, 28 to Cal States, 52 to community colleges.

These schools have a prep program in place that prepares the kids for college, even the top colleges. So if your local rankings are mediocre, even low, there's hope. Get the kids into the college-track classes.

Where does the chart mislead? For starters, the Cal States and UCs run on academics, the community colleges run on academics and vocational classes. Just because a student attends a community college does not mean he or she is pursuing a bachelor's degree.

Students who qualify for a Cal State or even a UC often take their freshman and sophomore years at a community college. It's cheaper and closer to home.

UC-Berkeley, the only UC in the Bay Area, in recent years has aggres-

Dropout Rates — High School Districts
Contra Costa County

District	1986	1990	1991	*No.
Acalanes	4%	3%	2%	24
Antioch	8%	11%	3%	22
John Swett	25%	21%	18%	19
Liberty	14%	18%	5%	19
Martinez	13%	4%	3%	7
Mt. Diablo	21%	13%	13%	290
Pittsburg	7%	14%	11%	52
Richmond	15%	17%	17%	331
San Ramon	5%	9%	4%	50
Contra Costa County	13%	12%	10%	814

Solano County

District	1986	1990	1991	*No.
Benicia	5%	4%	7%	19
Dixon	20%	10%	6%	14
Fairfield-Suisun	23%	14%	14%	169
Travis	1%	5%	4%	7
Vacaville	25%	22%	17%	133
Vallejo	7%	12%	10%	115
Solano County	16%	13%	12%	457

Source: California Department of Education. Percentages cover dropouts in a class that would have graduated in the year shown. *No. is actual number of dropouts in 1991.

sively pursued ethnic diversity. The other UC and Cal States have done the same. To attract minority students, the universities, in many instances, have modified their admission policies. The numbers mentioned above and listed in the accompanying chart may not reflect, according to the standard admissions policy, the top 13 and 33 percent.

The chart does not track private colleges. It doesn't tell us how many local students went to St. Mary's or the University of San Francisco or Stanford or Harvard, or public colleges out of the state.

The chart does confirm the influence of socioeconomics: the rich towns send more kids to the UCs than the poorer ones. But socioeconomics does not sweep the field. Not every student from a high-scoring school goes on to college. Many students from low- and middle-income towns come through.

Dissatisfaction

If high schools can deliver on college education and train students for vocations, why are so many people dissatisfied with public schools? These schools can also cite other accomplishments: textbooks and curriculums have been improved, the dropout rate has been cut, and proficiency tests have been adopted to force high school students to meet minimum academic standards.

Yet for the last 15 years or so, the California public, despite many pleas, has refused to rally round the schools and provide funding even close to what is needed. In 1992 a measure to fund education through vouchers — a private school initiative — barely missed qualifying for the ballot.

Many children are still failing and dropping out, and the system is expensive, about $28 billion annually for kindergarten-through-12 schools. Scores are stagnant or up one year, down the next, and remain very low in many urban districts. In the latest tests, California SAT math rose two points and came in 8 points above the national average of 476. Verbal SAT rose 1 point to 416 but this is 7 points below the national average. The CAP (basic) scores for eighth graders dropped slightly in math, and in reading (over two years) erased almost all the gains made in the last decade.

Employers report that many high school grads are unable to understand instructions or write competently. Low-skills jobs are disappearing. Colleges complain that honor high school students often need remedial math and English. It is not the intention of this book to dwell on controversies, but to explain how schools work it is necessary to look at some of the disputes.

Major Disputes
• Not enough money. Many school districts in the county have cut instructional time and staff and increased class sizes, even as enrollments rise.

Almost every year bitter fights break out in Sacramento over funding for schools. With the recession, which has decreased state revenues, the battles have become more vitriolic.

Democrats generally favor more money for schools, but few in Sacramento seem to favor another tax increase, which would probably be necessary for higher funding. Republicans contend that additional money would go for salaries, not to relieve crowding or restore programs.

• Private vs. public. A complex battle, it boils down to one side saying public schools are the best and fairest way to educate all children versus the other side saying public education is inefficient and will never reform until it has meaningful competition. In 1992, Sacramento approved funding to allow 100 schools statewide to restructure their programs according to local needs — an effort at eliminating unnecessary rules.

• Teachers' pay and influence. Although school funding has not kept pace with growth or need, salaries, in large measure, have remained competitive. California teachers rank usually fourth to sixth in the nation in pay. Many teachers, however, believe the entire profession is underpaid and is not keeping pace with inflation.

District Enrollments & Key '93 Dates
Contra Costa Schools

District	Enrollment	Spring Break	Last Day
Acalanes	4,020	4/05-4/09	June 11
Antioch	13,580	4/09-4/16	June 18
Brentwood	2,150	4/12-4/16	June 10
Byron	764	4/12-4/16	June 17
Canyon	59	4/05-4/09	June 11
John Swett	2,079	4/12-4/16	June 10
Knightsen	250	4/12-4/16	June 10
Lafayette	2,914	4/05-4/09	June 10
Liberty	2,080	4/12-4/16	June 10
Martinez	3,385	4/12-4/16	June 18
Moraga	1,603	4/05-4/09	June 11
Mt. Diablo	33,238	4/12-4/16	June 17
Oakley	2,950	4/09-4/16	June 17
Orinda	2,012	4/05-4/09	June 11
Pittsburg	8,136	4/09-4/16	June 10
Richmond	31,375	4/12-4/16	June 16
San Ramon	16,386	4/12-4/16	June 17
Walnut Creek	2,918	4/05-4/09	June 11

Solano County Schools

District	Enrollment	Spring Break	Last Day
Benicia	4,446	4/9-4/16	June 11
Dixon	2,972	4/9-4/16	June 11
Fairfield-Suisun	20,877	4/9-4/16	June 10
Travis	3,802	4/9-4/16	June 11
Vacaville	12,974	4/9-4/16	June 18
Vallejo	19,884	4/9-4/16	June 18

Source: County offices of education. Enrollment totals are for the 1991-92 school year. Some districts take a ski week off, some schools run year-round and will not follow this schedule.

Through their union, teachers exert great influence over school legislation and, often, over local school boards.

• Programs inadequately funded. Washington and Sacramento have legislated certain programs into existence and underfunded them or left their funding to local jurisdictions. Proposition 13 and other measures, however, restrict the ability of school districts to raise taxes. As a result, districts are biting into regular programs to sustain the special programs.

• Class size and teaching days. Many teachers argue that class sizes, often above 30 in California, are too large. The typical California school year runs 175 teaching days. The Japanese school year is over 230 days.

• Teacher competency. Once tenured, teachers are almost impossible to fire, which opens schools to accusations of coddling incompetents.

• Educational methods. Furious arguments rage over what will work. One simmering pot: how to educate children who can't speak English. Bilingual teachers are in short supply.

• Minorities and integration. One of the touchiest topics in the state. California minorities are growing rapidly and will soon be a majority in the state. Hispanics are scoring low; many Black students are also scoring low but an impressive number have made solid advances. Asians score high and, for college admissions, are often not considered a "minority."

Some educators argue that what is taught in public schools fails to instill pride in the accomplishments of various cultures and ethnic groups, that too much attention is paid to European civilization, too little to Asian and African. The state is now introducing textbooks that emphasize the accomplishments of minorities and women and approach history from diverse perspectives.

Ability clustering in many school districts breaks the students out along ethnic lines, and calls attention to how the system seems to work for some groups and not for others.

More money is needed for language instruction.

• Clustering children by ability or problems. Opponents argue that children labeled "low achievers" will fulfill that prophecy. The sad fact is that many programs aimed at low achievers have not worked or work poorly.

California is curtailing tracking, which might seem a reform, but it raises other questions. Many children are entering kindergarten months, sometimes years behind "average" students and in need of immediate remedial work. The state is arguing that children widely ranging in academic ability can be educated in the same classroom and no one will suffer. There are doubters.

• Parental influence. Almost everyone agrees that schools would work better, students would score higher, if parents did a better job at home. This is a major but often muted complaint among teachers: society (family, television, social influences) is failing the schools, not the schools failing the society. The problem: how to get parents to do a better job, how to influence home life.

• Many of the above problems are tied together. If funding was adequate, pull-out programs might work better, class sizes could be lowered allowing teachers to work better with mixed groups, and so on.

The Parent's Role

What's a parent to do? You would be foolish to ignore the socioeconomic message: To succeed in school, children need strong support from the home. Bookstores and libraries are full of books with advice on how you can work

Ethnic Enrollments by School District
Contra Costa Schools

District	White	Af.Am.	Asian	Filipino	Hisp.	Nat.
Acalanes	83	1	11	1	4	1
Antioch	73	4	3	3	17	1
Brentwood	63	*0	*0	1	35	*0
Byron	86	1	2	*0	10	1
Canyon	80	7	10	*0	3	*0
John Swett	55	15	7	10	13	*0
Knightsen	76	*0	*0	1	23	*0
Lafayette	88	1	8	*0	1	*0
Liberty	69	1	1	1	26	1
Martinez	75	4	3	2	13	3
Moraga	83	1	14	*0	2	*0
Mt. Diablo	74	4	7	2	11	*0
Oakley	74	2	2	1	20	1
Orinda	86	1	10	1	2	*0
Pittsburg	32	25	5	8	29	*0
Richmond	29	35	13	6	17	1
San Ramon	83	2	9	2	4	*0
Walnut Creek	84	2	6	1	6	1

Solano County Schools

District	White	Af.Am.	Asian	Filipino	Hisp.	Nat.
Benicia	77	6	4	4	8	*0
Dixon	59	1	1	*0	38	*0
Fairfield-Suisun	53	16	7	6	15	1
Travis	63	17	3	7	10	1
Vacaville	75	7	2	1	13	1
Vallejo	31	30	3	21	12	*0

Source: California Dept. of Education, 1991. *Less than .5 percent. Note: Figures are percentages, rounded to the nearest whole number. Total may not add up to 100 percent. Key: Af.Am. (African-American); Asian (includes Pacific Islanders); Hisp. (Hispanics); Nat. (Native American Indians & Alaskans).

with your child. You as a parent, with a little work and discipline, can make a real difference in the quality of your child's education.

You should probably look for outside help even if your child is doing well.

This is a hard call because many children are doing well. The belief seems almost universal, however, that the schools are underfunded, that programs and instruction are being weakened, and that large infusions of money will not be forthcoming.

In well-to-do neighborhoods and rich towns, parents are informally taxing themselves to raise money for schools. Poor and middle-class parents find it hard, if not impossible, to duplicate the efforts of the richer towns.

Shop for Bargains

This dumps the burden on financially struggling families who have high educational ambitions for their children. Shop for bargains: reading classes in the summer, local tutors who might work with small groups, day schools that have afternoon programs. Perhaps a private school.

The editors, as a matter of policy, do not endorse private schools over public or vice versa, but private schools, having more flexibility than public institutions, clearly have a place in the educational picture.

Choosing the Right School

Almost all public schools have attendance zones, usually the immediate neighborhood. The school comes with the neighborhood; often you have no choice. If you don't know your school, call the school district office.

Many parents mix private day care with public education. The day-care center takes the kid to the school in the morning and picks him up in the afternoon. Many public schools have installed day-care programs.

If you don't like your neighborhood school, you can request a transfer to another school in the district or to a school outside the district. But the school won't provide transportation.

Transfers to schools inside the district are easier to get than transfers outside the district. A relatively new law supposedly makes it easier for parents to get a transfer to towns where they work. If your child has a special problem that may demand your attention — say a medical condition — speak to the school administrators about a transfer to a school close to your job.

School districts dislike outside transfers because they lose funds. For every student enrolled, the state allots a district a certain amount of money. When a student transfers out, the allotment goes with him or her.

The Low-Scoring School

Should you place your child in a low-scoring school? Often the teachers in these schools are quite dedicated and the buildings funded as well as any public school. But the teacher may be forced to move at a pace well below your child's capability.

In a class of 30 where 22 score low, 5 in the middle and 3 high, the teacher would be derelict if she didn't pace the class to the low end. Educators often scorn the idea that students influence one another academically but, when trying to get pupils to shun sex and drugs, schools sing the praises of peer influence.

Richmond Schools

ALTHOUGH RICHMOND UNIFIED School District began 1993 on a positive note, serious money problems remain. In 1991, the district went bankrupt. Teachers have been forced to take a pay reduction, programs have been cut, the instructional day, for many students, has been shortened. The deficit is estimated at $30 million plus.

In early 1993 Democrats and Republicans worked out a compromise that will lessen the pain. Among other things, the district will be allowed to sell surplus property. In 1992, a new superintendent was hired and he seems to be winning back some of the respect the district lost.

Richmond district, second largest in the county, serves Kensington, El Cerrito, Richmond, El Sobrante, San Pablo, Tara Hills, Pinole and Hercules. Poor neighborhoods in Richmond score among the lowest in the state. Middle- and high-income towns such as Pinole, Hercules and Kensington score in the 70th, 80th and 90th percentiles.

For decades the district balanced its books but did little outside the ordinary to boost scores in the flatlands. Then the school board brought in Walter Marks, a great public speaker who delighted in the novel. He raised salaries, installed a system of choice: certain schools were to offer special programs — art, music, classical studies and so on. Students bored at one school could transfer to another. Sounded great and even those who criticize Marks will often grant that his ideas have merit.

But Marks was financially erratic, borrowing from one categorical fund to replenish another, betting on grants that never appeared, buying equipment in excess of what could be afforded. After he was forced out, a state conservator stepped in and deep cuts were made.

Can your child get a good education in Richmond schools? The question is beyond the scope of this book. It can safely be said, however, that Richmond district will continue to send many kids to college. To get them there, however, parents might have to pay for enrichment classes and give them a much stronger push at home. Ask plenty of questions.

High school students should get the schedule of classes from Contra Costa Community College. They are eligible to attend some classes at the college. Phone (510) 235-7800.

Does Remedial Help Work?

This is a minefield of conflicting studies. Nothing would seem more logical than to give a child special attention when he or she falters in class. Some children clearly do benefit.

But, critics argue, singling a child out for this attention often implants the idea that he is inferior, that he can't do the work without special help. Also, the teacher may lower her expectations for the pull-out group, may move them at a pace slower than they are capable of.

If your child is pulled out for remedial education, don't assume that the problem is solved. The kid may need extra help at home.

Gifted Programs

The labeling accusation, in different form, surfaces when schools implement gifted programs for very young children. By labeling one group extra smart, the rest of the children may conclude they are dumb, the argument runs. Where the gifted are clustered in their own classes (magnet programs), the fault is supposedly accentuated. On the other side, parents of these children argue that they should be allowed to learn as fast as they can.

Here's how the Gifted and Talented Education (GATE) program usually works. About the third grade, usually at the teacher's recommendation, the advanced children are given an I.Q. or achievement test. Those who score about I.Q. 132 or in the top 2 percent will be admitted to the program. This generally means they spend about three hours a week on special projects or in activities with other gifted children. Programs vary from district to district.

Tips for Parents: Tap Into the School's Gossip

Schools never release evaluations of teachers, but parents informally work out their own rankings. Join the PTA. Get to know other parents.

Although teachers are rarely dismissed, it doesn't follow that many deserve to be fired. Don't approach the schools with a chip on your shoulder. They will resent you. Schools, like private businesses, have their lackluster people but most teachers are diligent and greater efforts are being made to improve teacher quality.

If your kid gets an incompetent, request a transfer to another class. For that matter, ask for a particular teacher before the teaching assignments are made. Schools try to cooperate with parents. If you can't get your first choice, you might get your second.

The Official Rhetoric

School officials cannot say anything public against individual teachers. To do so would violate the union contract and expose the district to a lawsuit for slander.

Even when a teacher is grossly incompetent, the school district will not say anything. When asked, most administrators will say teachers are "wonderful," "underpaid" and "the salt of the earth."

If the teacher is screwing up royally, get the principal behind a closed door and tell her. If she doesn't take action, union contracts usually spell out the procedure for confronting a teacher.

Grade Level

If your child falls behind and is put in a remedial class, it often doesn't mean the school will bring him up to grade level. It may mean that the teacher will try to keep him from falling further behind.

Year-Round Schools

Year-round schools are becoming increasingly popular as a way to handle rapidly increasing enrollments. Schedules, called "tracks," vary from district to district but all students attend a full academic year (175-180 teaching days). Traditional holidays are observed. One group may start in summer, one in late summer and so on. A typical pattern is 12 weeks on, four weeks off. One track is always off, allowing another track to use its class space.

So far, year-round education has been confined to elementary and junior high schools. For more information, call the school districts.

Busing

School districts can charge, and several do. Fees range from $125 to about $400. Some low-income and special-education kids ride free.

New Tests

The California Dept. of Education is working on them now and will introduce them over the next few years. Instead of testing grades 3,6,8 and 12, the new exams will be given to grades 4,5,8 and 10. The old (CAP) tests used multiple choice and, critics contended, did not assess thinking skills. The new ones supposedly will.

The CAP tests focused on classes and schools, not individual students. Other tests — still in use — were used to test individuals and the results were sent home to parents. The new tests will break out students individually.

Register Early

It helps the schools with their planning and in some instances it may help win your children a more favorable situation. Some schools districts, short of space, have to shunt kids away from their neighborhood schools. When new schools open or schools close, attendance boundaries have to be shifted.

Repeating a Grade

Between 1986 and 1989, about 6 percent of all California kindergartners repeated the grade, and about 4 percent of all first graders. After that, retention rates dropped, less than 1 percent of all fourth-graders repeating a grade.

Good idea or bad? Bad, the state says now, after reviewing 60 studies.

Compared to similar students, retained children, the studies revealed, performed less effectively in "achievement, personal adjustment, self-concept, and attitude toward school."

8/Private Schools & Colleges

Directory of Contra Costa, Solano Private Schools

AFTER LOSING ENROLLMENT for several years, private schools in California are making a comeback, a reflection in large measure of the troubles afflicting public schools. In recent years, many public schools have reduced instructional hours and programs. Some have severe discipline problems that defy easy solutions. Violence plagues some schools. Academic rankings are low at many inner-city schools and mediocre at many suburban schools.

Private schools are not free of problems. The typical private or parochial school is funded way below its public school counterpart. In size, facilities and playing fields, and in programs, public schools usually far outstrip private schools. Private school teachers earn less than public school teachers.

By their nature, however, private schools enjoy certain advantages.

The Advantages

Public schools must accept all students, have almost no power to dismiss incompetent teachers and are at the mercy of their neighborhoods for the quality of students — the socioeconomic correlation. The unruly often can cannot be expelled or effectively disciplined.

Much has been said about the ability of private schools to rid themselves of problem children and screen them out in the first place. But tuition probably does more than anything else to assure private schools quality students.

Parents who pay extra for their child's education and often agree to work closely with the school are, usually, demanding parents. The result: fewer discipline problems with the students, fewer distractions in the class, more of a willingness to learn.

When you place your child in a good private school, you are, to a large

California College Admissions of Private School Graduates
Contra Costa County

High School	UC	CSU	Com	Total
Athenian	7	3	NA	NA
Berean	2	1	3	6
Carondolet	35	28	59	122
Christian Heritage	NA	NA	76	NA
CC Christian	0	4	3	7
DeLaSalle	32	32	73	137
Salesian	5	10	12	27
Total*	81	83	229	393

Solano County

High School	UC	CSU	Com	Total
Calvary Baptist	0	0	1	1
St. Patrick	14	18	28	60
St. Vincent Ferrer	1	6	1	8
VacaValley Christian	0	0	1	1
Total	15	24	31	70

Source: California Dept. of Education, fall, 1990. First-time freshmen. **Key**: UC (University of California system); CSU (Cal State system); Com (Community Colleges). *Total includes students from small or home schools not listed in the chart.

extent, buying him or her scholastic classmates. They may not be the smartest children — many private schools accept children of varying ability — but generally they will have someone at home breathing down their necks to succeed in academics.

The same attitude, a reflection of family values, is found in the high-achieving public schools. When a child in one of these schools or a private school turns to his left and right, he will see and later talk to children who read books and newspapers. A child in a low-achieving school, public or private, will talk to classmates who watch a lot of television and rarely read.

(These are, necessarily, broad generalizations. Much depends on whom the children pick for friends. High-achieving students certainly watch television but, studies show, much less than low-achieving students. Many critics contend that even high-scoring schools are graduating students poorly prepared for college.)

The Quality of Teaching

Do private schools have better teachers than public schools? Impossible to tell. Both sectors sing the praises of their teachers. Private schools have much

UCs Chosen by Private School Graduates
Contra Costa County

School	Berk	Davis	Irv	UCLA	SD	SB	River	SC	Total
Athenian	1	4	0	0	0	0	1	1	7
Berean	1	1	0	0	0	0	0	0	2
Carondelet	5	16	2	1	1	8	0	2	35
DeLaSalle	7	7	3	0	1	7	6	1	32
Salesian	2	2	0	1	0	0	0	0	5

Solano County

School	Berk	Davis	Irv	UCLA	SD	SB	River	SC	Total
St. Patrick	3	6	0	0	0	3	1	1	14
St. Vincent	1	0	0	0	0	0	0	0	1

Source: California Dept. of Education. The chart shows which UC a 1990 public high school graduate selected for freshmen enrollment. The state does not track graduates enrolling in private colleges or out-of-state colleges. **Key**: Berk (Berkeley), Irv (Irvine), River (Riverside), SD (San Diego), SB (Santa Barbara), SC (Santa Cruz).

more freedom to dismiss teachers but this can be abused. The private schools themselves advise parents to avoid schools with excessive teacher turnover.

Although most can't pay as much as public schools, private institutions claim to attract people fed up with the limitations of public schools, particularly the restrictions on disciplining and ejecting unruly children. Some proponents argue that private schools attract teachers "who really want to teach."

Religion and Private Schools

Private schools talk in depth about religion or ethics, and many teach a specific creed.

Until recently public schools almost never talked about religion or religious figures. They now teach the history of major religions and the basic tenets of each, and they try to inculcate in the children a respect for all religions.

It's hard, if not impossible, however, for public schools to talk about values within a framework of religion or a system of ethics. Often, it's difficult for them to talk about values. Some people argue that this is major failing.

Many religious schools, Catholic and Protestant, accept students of different religions or no religion. Some schools offer these students broad courses in religion — less dogma. Ask about the program.

Money

Private-school parents pay taxes for public schools and they pay tuition. Public-school parents pay taxes but not tuition. Big difference.

Ethnic Diversity

Many private schools are integrated and the great majority of private-school principals — the editor knows no exceptions — welcome minorities. Some principals fret over tuition, believing that it keeps many poor students out of private schools.

Money, the lack of it, weighs heavily on private schools. Scholarships, however, are awarded, adjustments made, family rates offered. Never hurts to ask.

What's in Contra Costa and Solano

Contra Costa County has more than 100 private schools and Solano County about a third as many. Here is a brief overview:

A surprising number are one-family schools, mother and father teaching their own children at home. A support network that supplies books and materials has grown up for these people.

Some regular private schools have low teacher-pupil ratios, fewer than 15 students per teacher, occasionally around 10 to 1. Public school classes usually go 25 to 30 per teacher, sometimes higher.

Class sizes in Catholic schools run close to the public-school ratio, and in some schools higher. (See Catholic schools profile.)

Catholic schools, nonetheless, are the most popular, a reflection in part of the high number of Catholics in Contra Costa and Solano counties. Some Catholic schools have waiting lists.

Private schools in both counties come in great variety, Christian, Jewish, Montessori, Carden (schools with different teaching approaches), prep schools, schools that emphasize language or music, boarding and day schools, schools that allow informal dress, schools that require uniforms.

Choosing a Private School

1. Inspect the grounds, the school's buildings, ask plenty of questions. "I would make myself a real pest," advised one private school official. The good schools welcome this kind of attention.

2. Choose a school with a philosophy congenial to your own, and your child's. Carden schools emphasize structure. Montessori schools, while somewhat structured, encourage individual initiative and independence.

Ask whether the school is accredited. Private schools are free to run almost any program they like, to set any standards they like, which sounds nice but in some aspects hurts the schools. A few bad ones spoil the reputation of the good ones. To remedy this an increasing number of private schools are submitting to inspections by independent agencies such as the Western Association of Schools and Colleges and the California Association of Independent Schools. These agencies try to make sure that schools meet their own goals.

(Continued on Page 152)

Profile of Catholic Schools

THE LARGEST PRIVATE school system in Contra Costa County, Catholic schools enroll 7,312 students — 5,208 elementary, 2,104 high school (1992 numbers).

In Solano County Catholic schools enroll, reports the diocese headquarters in Sacramento, 2,046 elementary students and 679 high school students (1992).

• Contra Costa: 18 elementary schools, kindergarten through eighth, three high schools. Solano: four elementaries, one high.

• All races, creeds welcome. Where schools are full, preference is given to Catholic children from families active in parish, and siblings. After that, to active Catholics unable to get into own parish schools.

• Alameda and Contra Costa are included in one school system. Here is ethnic breakdown for entire system:

Ethnic breakdown for entire system: elementary schools: American Indian, 85; Asian-Pacific Island, 3,204; Blacks, 5,710; Hispanics, 2,861; Whites, 7,205. For high schools: American Indian, 35; Asians-Pac Is., 1,008; Blacks, 947; Hispanics, 745; Whites, 5,876.

How Solano schools break out: Asian and Filipino, 38 percent; Blacks, 4; Hispanics, 11; Whites, 46.

• Contra Costa high schools: De La Salle High, boys, Carondelet High, girls, but schools are next to each other in Concord and mix classes at upper levels; Salesian High in Richmond used to be all boys but in fall, 1989, opened doors to girls. Solano: St. Patrick's High-St. Vincent's High in Vallejo, coed. High schools recruit regionally for students. They give admissions tests but accept average students. Standards vary by school.

• Why parents send kids to Catholic schools: academics, discipline, religion, safety, said a survey. Order changes by parish. What happens in public schools affects enrollment in Catholic schools, said one educator. "Parents are looking for safe, positive environment," said another.

• Curriculum. Elementary schools cover same basic subjects as public schools but weave in religious-moral viewpoint. "Philosophy based in Jesus Christ. Religious values are integral to learning experience." State textbooks often used. Each school picks texts.

High school instruction, although varied, is influenced by University of California requirements. Educators advise parents to approach high schools as they would any educational institution: ask about grades, what percentage of students go on to college, accreditation.

• Non-Catholics. Same instruction as Catholics, including history of church and scripture. Attend Mass but not required to take sacraments.

(Continued on Next Page)

(CATHOLIC SCHOOLS, Continued from Previous Page)
"We don't try to convert them," said one nun. Non-Catholics make up 8 percent of the Solano enrollment. In Alameda-Contra Costa, among secondary students, non-Catholics account for 31 percent of enrollment.

• Corporal punishment. Thing of past. More aware now of child abuse. Stress positive discipline, name on board, detention, probation.

• Few expulsions. Try to work with kid, parents to solve problems. Elementary expulsions usually have to be approved by diocese. Often parents withdraw child before expulsion.

• Class sizes. Maximum usually 35, minimum usually 25. Some higher and lower. Average, 30, though smaller for high schools because of special classes, e.g. French. Would like smaller but point out that with well-behaved students, teachers accomplish a lot. Also economics. If parents want smaller classes, they would have to pay more.

• Schedule. 180 teaching days, 8:30 a.m. to 3 p.m.

• Ability grouping. In elementary grades (Kinder-8th) not done by class. Some grouping within classes, advanced children working at one level, slower children at another. Tutoring after class.

All diocesan high schools run prep programs, tend to attract prep students, but will accept remedial students, if they have remedial instruction. Admission standards vary by high school.

Scores also vary by school — socioeconomics. Suburban Catholic schools tend to score higher than city schools.

• Report cards. At least four a year, plus results of state tests. Parents are expected to attend conferences, back-to-school nights.

• Teacher quality. Hired for competence and commitment to Catholic educational philosophy. No restriction in hiring non-Catholics but system seems to attract Catholic teachers. "No trouble in attracting high-quality applicants."

• Uniforms. Yes. Generally skirts, blouses for girls, collared shirts and trousers for boys. High schoolers have more sartorial discretion.

• Extended care. Many offer before- and after-school care. Ask.

• Drugs. "We're not immune to dangers of the larger society," said one educator. Schools try to work with kids.

• Extracurricular activities. Though small, schools try to offer variety of activities, sports, arts, music.

High schools offer good variety: music, band, arts, intramural sports, many club activities, cycling, golf. They usually field competitive football and basketball teams. "They help build school pride."

For more information, call school directly. For Oakland diocese education office, (510) 893-4711. For Solano schools, (916) 441-4841.

(Continued from Page 149)

To save money some good schools do not seek accreditation.

3. Have all details about tuition carefully explained. How is it to be paid? Are there extra fees? Book costs? Is there a refund if the student is withdrawn or dropped from the school?

4. Progress reports. Parent conferences. How often are they scheduled?

5. What are the entrance requirements? When must they be met? Although many schools use entrance tests, often they are employed to place the child in an academic program, not exclude him from the school.

6. For prep schools, what percentage of the students go on to college and to what colleges?

7. How are discipline problems handled?

8. What are the qualifications of the teachers? What is the teacher turnover rate?

9. How sound financially is the school? How long has it been in existence? There is nothing wrong per se with new schools. But you want a school that has the wherewithal to do the job.

10. Don't choose in haste but don't wait until the last minute. Some schools fill quickly, some fill certain classes quickly.

Lastly, don't assume that because your child attends a private school you can expect everything will go all right, that neither the school nor the student needs your attention.

The quality of private schools in California varies widely. The prudent parent will keep a watchful eye, and the good schools will welcome your interest.

Adult Schools

Although rarely in the headlines, adult schools serve thousands of Contra Costa and Solano residents. Upholstery, microwave cooking, ballroom dancing, computers, cardiopulmonary resuscitation, aerobics, investing in stocks, art, music, how to raise children — these and more are offered in the adult schools.

These schools and programs are run by school districts and by cities. Many schools also run adult sports programs, basketball, volleyball, tennis. Call your local school or city for a catalog.

Getting the Older Students

As the public's needs have changed, so have the colleges. The traditional college audience — high school seniors — is still thriving but increasingly colleges are attracting older students and working people.

Many colleges now offer evening and weekend programs, especially in business degrees and business-related subjects. Some programs — an MBA — can take years, some classes only a day.

PRIVATE SCHOOLS & COLLEGES 153

Here is a partial list of local colleges and specialty schools. As with any venture, the student should investigate before enrolling or paying a fee.

Community Colleges

Contra Costa, Los Medanos, Diablo Valley, collectively the most popular colleges in Contra Costa County, enrollment about 40,000. Run by the Contra Costa Community College District. In Solano County, Solano Community College. Although fees were recently increased and may again rise, they are still low: $30 to $50 per class. For college grads, $150 to $250 per class.

Many students attend these two-year public colleges then transfer to state universities or University of California schools, or other colleges.

Day and evening sessions. Many classes, academic and vocational. No entrance requirement but many students drop along the way. Special classes to ease women and minorities into college life. Many students take one or two classes a year, usually vocational, as needed.

Associate degrees, certificates, training for licenses (reg. nurse, medical technician, real estate, many others). Sports, activities. Phone for more info and catalogs or visit campuses.

• Contra Costa College, 2600 Mission Bell Drive, San Pablo, 94806. Phone (510) 235-7800.

• Diablo Valley College, 321 Golf Club Road, Pleasant Hill, 94523. Phone (510) 685-1230.

• Los Medanos College, 2700 E. Leland Road, Pittsburg, 94565. Phone (510) 439-2181.

• Solano Community College, 4000 Suisun Valley Road, Suisun, 94585. Phone (707) 864-7000.

Other Colleges and Schools

• University of California, Berkeley. Bachelor's, master's, doctorates. High admission standards. Sports, many activities, one of the great universities of the world. Call (510) 642-6000.

The university also runs a popular extension program, all sorts of classes, many vocational, for the general public. Phone (510) 642-4111. Ask for catalog.

• California State University, Hayward. Bachelor's and master's degrees. Day and evening classes. Cal State, Hayward, because of its proximity, draws many students from the San Ramon Valley and El Cerrito-Richmond.

The University of California schools take the top 13 percent or so of graduating high school seniors. The state university schools take the top one-third. The UC schools award doctorates, the Cal State schools stop at the master's level.

A complete college, Cal State has football, basketball, student activities, dorms. Open university at Cal State allows students to take classes without

Community College Transfers to UCs
Contra Costa County

College	Berk	Davis	Irv	UCLA	SD	SB	River	SC	Total
Con. Costa	22	6	0	0	1	2	0	2	33
Diablo Val.	134	50	4	34	20	34	5	29	310
Los Medanos	1	6	0	0	2	1	0	2	12

Solano County

College	Berk	Davis	Irv	UCLA	SD	SB	River	SC	Total
Solano	13	33	0	0	1	1	1	3	52

Source: California Dept. of Education. The chart shows which UCs community college transfers entered in fall, 1991. The state does not track transfers to private colleges or out-of-state colleges. **Key:** Berk (Berkeley), Irv (Irvine), River (Riverside), SD (San Diego), SB (Santa Barbara), SC (Santa Cruz).

Community College Transfers to CSUs
Contra Costa County

College	CPly	Chico	Fres	Hay	Sacto	SF	SJ	Son	Total
Con. Costa	0	0	2	36	10	21	12	7	96
Diablo Val.	30	69	8	163	147	104	36	20	673
Los Medanos	0	4	3	25	13	3	3	4	65

Solano County

College	CPly	Chico	Fres	Hay	Sacto	SF	SJ	Son	Total
Solano	3	13	4	10	111	14	7	17	190

Source: California Dept. of Education. The chart shows which California State Universities community college transfers entered in fall, 1991. The state does not track transfers to private colleges or out-of-state colleges. **Key:** CPly (Cal Poly San Luis Obispo), Chico (Chico State), Fres (Fresno), Hay (Hayward), Sacto (Sacramento), SF (San Francisco), SJ (San Jose), Son (Sonoma), Total (total Cal State transfers, including those not listed).

pursuing degree. Phone (510) 881-3000 for schedule, information.

• **Contra Costa Center.** Satellite campus of California State University, Hayward. In 1992 it moved from Pleasant Hill into new facilities off Ygnacio Valley Road in Concord.

Instruction starts at the junior year and goes through the master's degree. Day and evening classes. Enrolls many students from community colleges. Also, business people and homemakers trying to win new or better jobs. Bachelor's and master's in business. Education credentials, and degrees in English, liberal studies, psychology, computer science, others. Phone (510) 602-6700 for schedule, info. Both the Contra Costa Center and Cal State Hayward also offer extension classes. (510) 881-3605.

PRIVATE SCHOOLS & COLLEGES 155

• **St. Mary's College.** Loveliest campus in Contra Costa County. Run by the De La Salle Christian Brothers, St. Mary's is a full-fledged college, complete with sports teams, activities. Bachelor's degrees in liberal arts, economics, business administration, education.

St. Mary's also offers special programs, including master's in business, for working adults. Also, credentials in education and extension programs. Evening classes, flexible schedule. Phone (510) 631-4224.

• **Center for Higher Education,** 3150 Crow Canyon Place, San Ramon, 94583. Combined effort of Cal State Hayward, Diablo Valley College, University of California. Recently moved into newer, bigger building. Business, vocational, academic classes. Enrollment about 4,000. If you can't get classes you want at Diablo Valley College, try here. Phone: (510) 866-1822.

• **John F. Kennedy University,** headquartered in Orinda, with branches in Walnut Creek, Pleasant Hill, Oakland. Spirited college, private, tries to anticipate what the public wants. Popular with working adults. Offers bachelor's degrees in Management and Liberal and Professional arts. Graduate degrees in management, psychology, study of human consciousness. Also, law degrees. Phone (510) 253-2211.

• **University of San Francisco.** Jesuit University, based in San Francisco, but offers bachelor's and master's programs at its San Ramon Center in Bishop Ranch. Aimed at working adults. Bachelor's degrees in applied economics, information systems management, organizational behavior. Master's in human resources, organization management. (510) 867-2711.

• **University of Phoenix.** Classes in San Ramon. Phone (510) 820-7701.

• **Golden Gate University.** Based in San Francisco; Contra Costa branch in Walnut Creek. Bachelor's degrees in management and telecommunications. Master's in banking and finance, management, human resources management, information systems, marketing, taxation, telecommunications. (510) 945-7132. Solano County branch at Travis. Phone (707) 437-9402.

• **Chapman College.** Campus sites in Suisun, Travis AFB and Mare Island. For Suisun, 230 Link Road, Suite C-100, 94585, phone (707) 864-3356, for Travis (707) 437-3327 and Mare Island (707) 552-4646.

Directory of Private Schools

Schools provided the following directory information by responding to a phone survey. Many schools offer family rates. Religious schools often charge higher for non-members.

Contra Costa County
Alamo

Alamo Montessori, 971 Livorna Rd., Alamo, 94507. Ph: (510) 934-2669. Enroll: 12, Pre-3rd. Fee:$300-550/mo.

Creative Learning Center, 120 Hemme Ave., Alamo, 94507. Ph: (510) 837-4044. Enroll: 52, Pre & K. Fee: $362/mo.

Dorris-Eaton School, 1286 Stone Valley Rd., Alamo, 94507. Ph: (510) 933-5225. Enroll: NA, Pre-PreK. Fee: $2,200-$3,500/yr.

Antioch

Antioch Christian School, 415 W. 6th St., Antioch, 94509. Ph: (510) 778-1639. Enroll: 50, K-6th. Fee: $135/mo. Pentecostal.

Antioch Christian Tutorial School, 640 E. Tregallas Road, Antioch, 94509. Ph: (510) 757-1837. Enroll: 225, K-12th. Fee: $2,400/yr. Assemblies of God.

Child Day Schools, 112 E. Tregallas Road, Antioch, 94509. Ph: (510) 754-0144. Enroll: 120, Infants - 10 yrs. old. Fee: $390/mo.

Heritage Baptist Academy, 525 E. 18th St., Antioch, 94509. Ph: (510) 778-2234. Enroll: 70, K-12th. Fee: $199.50/mo. Baptist.

Hilltop Christian School, 320 Worrell Rd., Antioch, 94509. Ph: (510) 778-0214. Enroll: Pre-24; K-8th- 96, Pre-8th. Fee: $165-$185/mo. Seventh-day Adventist.

Holy Rosary School, 25 E. 15th St., Antioch, 94509. Ph: (510) 757-1270. Enroll: 364, PreKinder-8th. Fee: Call School. Cath. Extended day care available.

Brentwood

Dainty Center, 1265 Dainty Ave., Brentwood, 94513. Ph: (510) 634-4539. Enroll: 200, 4 mo.- gr. 4. Fee: $2,270- $3,025/yr.

Faith Christian Learning Centers, 50 Birch St., Brentwood, 94513. Ph: (510) 634-1415. Enroll: 20, K-12th. Fee: $180- $215/mo. Christian & Missionary Alliance.

Concord

Bianchi Elementary School, 4347 Cowell Road, Concord, 94518. Ph: (510) 680-8707 or 680-8600 (administration offices). Enroll: 12-Tod; 31-PreSch; 24-PreK, Pre & PreK. Fee: $458-498/mo.

Bianchi School, 480-A Sunvalley Mall, Concord, 94520. Ph: (510) 825-6671. Enroll: 25 max., Ages 2-12 yrs. Fee: $3.95 first hour, $.99-15 min. thereafter.

Carondelet High School, 1133 Winton Dr., Concord, 94518. Ph: (510) 686-5353. Enroll: 700, Ninth-12th Girls. Fee: $3,700- $3,900/yr. Catholic.

Christian Life Elementary School, 3950 Clayton Rd., Concord, 94521. Ph: (510) 676-6422. Enroll: 150, Pre-6th. Fee: $100-360/mo. Multidenominational Christian.

Concordia School, 2353 Fifth Ave., Concord, 94518. Ph: (510) 689-6910. Enroll: 90, Pre-6th. Fee: $390- $590/mo.

De La Salle High School, 1130 Winton Dr., Concord, 94518. Ph: (510) 686-3310. Enroll: 900, Ninth-12th Boys. Fee: $4,400/yr. Catholic.

Kinder Care Learning Center, 1551 Bailey Road, Concord, 94521. Ph: (510) 682-9560. Enroll: 140, Pre & K. Fee: $430/mo. K.

King's Valley Christian School, 4255 Clayton Rd., Concord, 94521. Ph: (510) 687-2020. Enroll: 350, K-8th. Fee: $2,340/yr. Concord Christian Center.

Melmed Learning Clinic, 1494 Washington Blvd., Concord, 94521. Ph: (510) 283-6777. Enroll: 250, PreK- 12, adults. Fee: $224/mo.

Queen of All Saints School, 2391 Grant St., Concord, 94520. Ph: (510) 685-8700. Enroll: 280, K-8th. Fee: $2,220-$2,700/yr. Catholic.

St. Agnes Elementary School, 3886 Chestnut Ave., Concord, 94519. Ph: (510) 689-3990. Enroll: 350, K-8th. Fee: $190- $300/mo.

St. Francis of Assisi School, 866 Oak Grove Rd., Concord, 94518. Ph: (510) 682-5414. Enroll: 330, K-8th . Fee: Call School.

Tabernacle Baptist School, 4380 Concord Blvd., Concord, 94521. Ph: (510) 685-9169. Enroll: 491, Pre-8th. Fee: $2,355/yr. Christian.

Ygnacio Valley Christian School, 4977 Concord Blvd., Concord, 94521. Ph: (510) 798-3131. Enroll: 175, K-8th. Fee: $226/mo. Christian.

Danville

Athenian School, 2100 Mt. Diablo Scenic

THE ACADEMY

Traditional - Academic - k-8

- SMALL CLASS SIZE
- EXTENDED DAY CARE
- AFTER SCHOOL ACTIVITIES
- SUMMER PROGRAM

EST. 1969

549-0605

2722 Benvenue Ave. • Berkeley

PRIVATE SCHOOLS & COLLEGES 157

Blvd., Danville, 94526. Ph: (510) 837-5375. Enroll: 252, Sixth-12th. Fee: $8,500-$10,028/yr. day program; $20,130/yr. boarding.
Bianchi School, 909 Camino Ramon, Danville, 94526. Ph: (510) 838-8541. Enroll: 46-Pre; 12-PreK; 13-K, Pre- K. Fee: $458-498/mo.
Das Montessori Kinderhaus, 101 Sonora Ave., Danville, 94526. Ph: (510) 831-6199. Enroll: 32, Pre & K. Fee: call school.
Fountainhead Montessori School, 939 El Pintado Road, Danville, 94526. Ph: (510) 820-1343. Enroll: 54, Pre & K. Fee: $570/mo. max all day. *See ad page 158.*
San Ramon Valley Christian Academy, 220 West El Pintado Rd., Danville, 94526. Ph: (510) 838-9622. Enroll: 225, K-8th. Fee: $3,060- $3,180/yr. Presbyterian.
St. Isidore Elem. School, 435 Lagonda Way, Danville, 94526. Ph: (510) 837-2977. Enroll: 340, K-8th. Fee: $2,370-$7,3100/yr. Catholic.

El Cerrito

Prospect School, 2060 Tapscott Ave., El Cerrito, 94530. Ph: (510) 232-4123. Enroll: 168, K-6th. Fee: $5,500/yr avg.
Sierra School, 960 Avis Drive, El Cerrito, 94530. Ph: (510) 527-4714. Enroll: 307, K-6th. Fee: $6,235/yr.
St. Jerome Elem. School, 320 San Carlos Ave., El Cerrito, 94530. Ph: (510) 525-9484. Enroll: 302, Kinder-8th. Fee: $2,300/yr. Catholic.
St. John The Baptist School, 11156 San Pablo Ave., El Cerrito, 94530. Ph: (510) 234-2244. Enroll: 312, K-8th. Fee: $163-$205/mo. Catholic.
Tehiyah Day School, 2603 Tassajara Ave., El Cerrito, 94530. Ph: (510) 233-3013. Enroll: 214, Kinder-8th. Fee: $5,100-$6,100/yr. Jewish day school.
Windrush School, 1800 Elm St., El Cerrito, 94530. Ph: (510) 970-7580. Enroll: 187, K-8th. Fee:$4,960-$5,560/yr.

El Sobrante

Bethel Christian Academy, 431 Rincon Ave., El Sobrante, 94803. Ph: (510) 223-9550. Enroll: 192, K-9th. Fee:$1,800/yr. Bethel Baptist Church.
Calvary Christian Academy & Preschool, 4892 San Pablo Dam Road, El Sobrante, 94803. Ph: (510) 222-3828. Enroll: 70—Pre./150— K-8, Pre-8th. Fee: $150-$250/mo. Calvary Christian Center.
El Sobrante Christian School, 5100 Argyle Rd., El Sobrante, 94803. Ph: (510) 223-2242. Enroll: 400, K-8th. Fee: $2,1500-$1,960/yr. Central Assembly of God.

Lafayette

Child Day School, 1049 Stuart St., Lafayette, 94549. Ph: (510) 284-7092. Enroll: 70, Pre & K. Fee: $420/mo.

DIABLO VALLEY MONTESSORI SCHOOL
Toddler (2, 3 and 5 day)
5-Day Preschool
Kindergarten Enrichment
Extended Day Care Programs
Child Care Programs
CALL: (510) 283-6036

THE HEAD-ROYCE SCHOOL

Independent Day School
Kindergarten through Grade 12

Full college preparatory program
including fine arts and athletics
Member of NAIS,
accredited by WASC

Students are admitted to the
School without regard to
race, color, religion
or national or ethnic origin

Director of Admissions
The HEAD-ROYCE SCHOOL
4315 Lincoln Avenue
Oakland, CA 94602
(510) 531-1300

Diablo Valley Montessori School, 3390 Deer Hill Rd., Lafayette, 94549. Ph: (510) 283-6036. Enroll: 150, Pre- K. Fee: K: $295/mo., ext. day $450/mo. *See ad page 157.*
Meher School, 999 Leland Dr., Lafayette, 94549. Ph: (510) 938-4826. Enroll: 375, Pre-5th. Fee: $230/mo.
Melmed Learning Clinic, 4581 Mt. Diablo Blvd. Suite 235, Lafayette, 94549. Ph: (510) 283-6777. Enroll: 250, PreK-12th & adults. Fee: $224/mo.
Montessori Children's House, 955A Moraga Road, Lafayette, 94549. Ph: (510) 284-9710. Enroll: 40, Pre & Kinder. Fee: $575/mo. full time.
St. Perpetua School, 3445 Hamlin Rd., Lafayette, 94549. Ph: (510) 284-1640. Enroll: 275, K-8th. Fee: $1,900- $2,100/yr. Catholic.
Temple Isaiah Religious School, 3800 Mt. Diablo Blvd., Lafayette, 94549. Ph: (510) 283-8575. Enroll: 406, Kinder-12th. Fee: Call school.
White Pony School, 999 Leland Dr., Lafayette, 94549. Ph: (510) 938-4826. Enroll: 350, Pre-5th. Fee: $240/mo.

Martinez

Agape Christian School, 444 Fig Tree Ln., Martinez, 94553. Ph: (510) 228-8155. Enroll: 120, Pre-4th. Fee: $180-$315/mo. Non-denominational Christian.
Bianchi School, 1285 Morello Ave., Martinez, 94553. Ph: (510) 372-7701. Enroll: 12 Toddler; 36 Pre; 12 PreK; 4 Inf., Pre & PreK. Fee:$458-508/mo.
Concordia School, 100 Church St., Martinez, 94553. Ph: (510) 689-6910. Enroll: 34, Pre & K. Fee: $390-$575/mo.
Higher Heights Christian Preschool, 245 Morello Ave., Martinez, 94553. Ph: (510) 372-7155. Enroll: 45, Pre & PreK. Fee: $160-365/mo. Non-denominational Christian.
Patchin's Preschool & Elementary School, 1200 Palm Ave., Martinez, 94553. Ph: (510) 228-1295. Enroll: 125, Pre-6th. Fee: $340/mo.
St. Catherine of Siena School, 604 Mellus St., Martinez, 94553. Ph: (510) 228-4140. Enroll: 230, K-8th. Fee: $2,200/yr. Catholic.

FOUNTAINHEAD MONTESSORI
AN ENVIRONMENT FOR DISCOVERY & LEARNING

TODDLER 1½-2½, PREP 2-4
PRESCHOOL 3-5, PRE-K/KINDERGARTEN 4-6
1ST, 2ND, 3RD GRADE 5½-9 YRS
CHILD CARE YEAR-ROUND 7 AM-6 PM
SUMMER SCHOOL AGES 1½-9

DANVILLE
939 El Pintado
(510) 820-6250

DUBLIN
6901 York Drive
(510) 829-2963

ORINDA
30 Santa Maria Way
(510) 254-7110

PLEASANT HILL
490 Golf Club Road
(510) 685-2949

ADMIN. OFFICE
115 Estates Dr., Danville 94526
(510) 820-1343

For Information, Call the Administration Office
(510) 820-1343

PRIVATE SCHOOLS & COLLEGES

Moraga
Saklan Valley School, 1678 School St., Moraga, 94556. Ph: (510) 376-7900. Enroll: 125, Pre-6th. Fee: $4,775-5,335/yr.

Orinda
Contra Costa Alternative School, 10 Irwin Way, Orinda, 94563. Ph: (510) 254-0199. Enroll: 40, Eighth-12th. Fee: Sliding Scale: $25- $750/mo.

Fountainhead Montessori School, 30 Santa Maria Way, Orinda, 94563. Ph: (510) 820-1343. Enroll: 100, Ages 2-6. Fee: $570/mo max. all day. *See ad page 158.*

North Bay Orinda School, 350 Camino Pablo, Orinda, 94563. Ph: (510) 254-7553. Enroll: 75, Seventh-12th. Fee: $6,200/yr.

Pacheco
Brighton Elementary, 106 Deodar Drive, Pacheco, 94553. Ph: (510) 798-1668. Enroll: 50, Pre-6th. Fee: $$450/mo. *See ad this page.*

Pinole
Happy Lion School, 2612 Appian Way, Pinole, 94564. Ph: (510) 222-2416. Enroll: 60-pre/12-K, Pre & K. Fee: $355/mo. includes day care.

St. Joseph School, 1961 Plum St., Pinole, 94564. Ph: (510) 724-0242. Enroll: 312, K-8th. Fee: $215-$408/mo. Catholic.

Pittsburg
Christian Center School, 1210 Stoneman Ave., Pittsburg, 94565. Ph: (510) 439-2552. Enroll: 425, K-12th. Fee:$2,190-2,400/yr. Non-denominational. *See ad this page.*

Concordia School, 195 Alvarado Ave., Pittsburg, 94565. Ph: (510) 689-6910. Enroll: 34, Pre & K. Fee: $390-$575/mo.

Kinder Care Learning Center, 150 East Leland Road, Pittsburg, 94565. Ph: (510) 432-8800. Enroll: 156, Infants- age 12. Fee: Call School.

Railroad Junction School, 2224 Railroad Ave., Pittsburg, 94565. Ph: (510) 427-2000. Enroll: 87, K. Fee: $350/mo.

Shore Acres Christian School, 500 Pacifica Ave., Pittsburg, 94565. Ph: (510) 458-2838. Enroll: 100, K- 12. Fee: $1650/yr. Non-denominational.

St. Peter Martyr School, 425 W. 4th St., Pittsburg, 94565. Ph: (510) 439-1014. Enroll: 290, PreK-8th. Fee: $180-$216/mo. Catholic.

Pleasant Hill
Anchor Intermediate Academy, 3161 Putnam Blvd., Pleasant Hill, 94523. Ph: (510) 256-8061. Enroll: 40, Sixth-9th. Fee: $5,950/yr. Christian.

Christ the King Elementary School, 195 Brandon Road, Pleasant Hill, 94523. Ph: (510) 685-1109. Enroll: 344, K-8th. Fee: $1,680- $1,940/yr. Catholic.

Fountainhead Montessori School, 490 Golf Club Road, Pleasant Hill, 94523. Ph: (510) 820-1343. Enroll: 96, Ages 18 mo.- 6 yr. Fee: $570/mo max. all day. *See ad page 158.*

La Cheim School, 1700 Oak Park Blvd., Pleasant Hill, 94523. Ph: (510) 930-7994. Enroll: 40, First-12th Special Ed. Fee: Contract with local schools. Specific learning disabled. Prog. for special ed., emotionally disturbed.

Mary Jane's Preschool and Kindergarten, 2902 Vessing Rd., Pleasant Hill, 94523. Ph: (510) 935-3084. Enroll: 41, Preschool & Kindergarten. Fee: Call. Non-demoninational.

Brighton Elementary

Grades 1 - 6 Small Class Sizes
Cross Curricular Studies
Art, Music, Drama, Computer Enrichment
Accredited Staff Childcare: 7 am - 6 pm

798-1668

Second Ave So. at Deodar Dr., Pacheco

CHRISTIAN CENTER SCHOOL & PRE-SCHOOL

Pre-School & Day Care
2 years 1 month-Kindergarten ready
6:30 a.m. to 6 p.m.

Kindergarten-12th Grade
• Advanced Christian Curriculum • Limited Class Size • Degreed Teachers • College Prep • Sports
1210 Stoneman, Pittsburg, CA
(510) 439-2552

New Vistas Christian School, 2073 Oak Park Blvd., Pleasant Hill, 94523. Ph: (510) 930-8894. Enroll: 70, K-6th. Fee: $5,900/yr.
Pleasant Hill Junior Academy, 796 Grayson Rd., Pleasant Hill, 94523. Ph: (510) 934-9261. Enroll: 130, K-10th. Fee: $1,300-$3,200/yr. Seventh-day Adventist.
Spectrum Center, 380 Civic Dr., Suite 300, Pleasant Hill, 94523. Ph: (510) 685-9702. Enroll: 50, Ungraded Special Ed. Fee: Referral by local school district.
Sunrise Montessori School, 1715 Oak Park Blvd., Pleasant Hill, 94523. Ph: (510) 946-0111. Enroll: 52, Pre & K. Fee: K: $460/mo.

Richmond
Canterbury Elementary School, 3120 Shane Dr., Richmond, 94806. Ph: (510) 222-5050. Enroll: 130, K-8th. Fee: $615/mo.
La Petite Academy, 3891 Lakeside Drive, Richmond, 94806. Ph: (510) 222-3070. Enroll: 150, Pre & Kinder. Fee: Call School.
Pacific Academy of Nomura School, 1615 Carlson Blvd., Richmond, 94804. Ph: (510) 528-1727. Enroll: 125, K-6th. Fee: $460/mo., day care extra.
Salesian High School, 2851 Salesian Ave., Richmond, 94804. Ph: (510) 234-4433. Enroll: 400, Ninth-12th. Fee: $2,800/yr. Catholic.
St. Cornelius School, 201 28th St., Richmond, 94804. Ph: (510) 232-3326. Enroll: 250, K-8th. Fee: $2,200/yr. Catholic.
St. David's Elem. School, 871 Sonoma St., Richmond, 94805. Ph: (510) 232-2283. Enroll: 367, Pre-8th. Fee: $1,840/yr. Catholic.
Via Center, 989 18th St., Richmond, 94801. Ph: (510) 234-7940. Enroll: 12, Ungraded Special Ed. Fee: Referrals from school districts.
Vista Christian School, 2354 Andrade Ave., Richmond, 94804. Ph: (510) 237-4981. Enroll: 143, K-8th. Fee: $2,150/yr. Non-denominational.
Western Regional Christian Academy, 3501 Macdonald Ave., Richmond, 94805. Ph: (510) 233-4661. Enroll: 40, Kinder-12th. Fee: Elem: $1,600/yr.; Jr. High: $1,700/yr.; High: $,1800/yr.

Rodeo
Spectrum Center, 545 Garretson Ave., Rodeo, 94572. Ph: (510) 245-7036. Enroll: 50, Ungraded Special Ed. Fee: Referral by local schools. *See ad this page*
St. Patrick's School, 907 7th St., Rodeo, 94572. Ph: (510) 799-2506. Enroll: 294, K-8th. Fee: $1,800-$3,560/yr. Catholic.

San Pablo
Calvary Church School, 1850 15th St., San Pablo, 94806. Ph: (510) 236-3590. Enroll: 13, Second-8th. Fee: None. Assembly of God.
St. Paul Elem. School, 1825 Church Ln., San Pablo, 94806. Ph: (510) 233-3080. Enroll: 315, K-8th. Fee: $1,950-$3,413/yr. Catholic.

San Ramon
Acorn Learning Center, 5075 Crow Canyon Road, San Ramon, 94583. Ph: (510) 735-7900. Enroll: 150, Pre & K. Fee: Call School.
Child Day Schools, 18868 Bollinger Canyon Road, San Ramon, 94583. Ph: (510) 820-2515. Enroll: Pre-115, K-20, In-

---

Special Education for Challenging Students

Spectrum Center

School Programs in
Marin, Alameda & Contra Costa Counties

Public School Funded
•
California Certified

Call 510-845-1321

Spectrum Center for Educational & Behavioral Development, Inc.
2855 Telegraph Ave., #312, Berkeley, 94705

PRIVATE SCHOOLS & COLLEGES

fants-12, Pre & K. Fee: $455/mo.
Diablo Hills Country School, 2701 Hooper Road, San Ramon, 94583. Ph: (510) 831-1210. Enroll: 59, Pre & K. Fee: $425- $490/mo.

Walnut Creek

Alice's Montessori, 3158 Putnam Blvd., Walnut Creek, 94596. Ph: (510) 947-0603. Enroll: 40, Pre & K. Fee: Kind: $415/mo.

Berean Christian High School, 245 El Divisadero Ave., Walnut Creek, 94598. Ph: (510) 945-6464. Enroll: 250, Ninth-12th. Fee: $3,575/yr. Interdenominational.

Bianchi School, 2521 Walnut Blvd., Walnut Creek, 94596. Ph: (510) 935-3276. Enroll: 41 PreSch; 13 PreK, Pre & PreK. Fee: $407-412/mo.

Bianchi School, 2850 Cherry Lane, Walnut Creek, 94598. Ph: (510) 943-6777. Enroll: 9-Tod; 31-Pre; 12-PreK, Pre & PreK. Fee: $458-508/mo.

Contra Costa Christian High, 2721 Larkey Ln., Walnut Creek, 94596. Ph: (510) 934-4964. Enroll: 250, Ninth-12th. Fee: $370/mo. Non-denominational. *See ad this page.*

Contra Costa Jewish Community Center, 2071 Tice Valley Blvd., Walnut Creek, 94596. Ph: (510) 938-7800. Enroll: 150, Infant-K. Fee: $65- $320/mo. Jewish, but open to all.

Dorris-Eaton School, 1847 Newell Ave., Walnut Creek, 94595. Ph: (510) 933-5225. Enroll: 400, K-8th. Fee: $6,300-$7,600/yr.

Morning Star Pre School, 2131 Olympic , Walnut Creek, 94595. Ph: (510) 947-2952. Enroll: 70, Pre & PreK. Fee: Call school.

Palmer School, 2740 Jones Road, Walnut Creek, 94596. Ph: (510) 934-4888. Enroll: 300, K-8th. Fee: $3,800-$4,800/yr.

Ronkin Education Group, 704A Bancroft Road, Walnut Creek, 94598. Ph: (510) 939-3200. Enroll: Call school, Seventh- Graduate work. Fee: $350- $695/mo.

Seven Hills School, 975 North San Carlos Dr. / PO Box 3300, Walnut Creek, 94598. Ph: (510) 933-0666. Enroll: 230, Pre-8th. Fee: $4,101-$6,915/yr.

Sprajngs Academy, 1903 Tice Valley Blvd., Walnut Creek, 94598. Ph: (510) 283-0200. Enroll: 60, Ungraded. Fee: Call school.

St. Mary's School, 1158 Bont Ln., Walnut Creek, 94596. Ph: (510) 935-5054. Enroll: 270, K-8th. Fee: Call school. Catholic.

Valley Lutheran School, 2317 Buena Vista Ave., Walnut Creek, 94596. Ph: (510) 932-2919. Enroll: 60, K-6th. Fee: $2550/yr.

Walnut Creek Christian Academy, 2336 Buena Vista Ave., Walnut Creek, 94596. Ph: (510) 935-1587. Enroll: 250, K-8th. Fee: $2,420/yr. Baptist.

Woodlands Christian School, 2721 Larkey Ln., Walnut Creek, 94596. Ph: (510) 945-6863. Enroll: 250, Pre-8th. Fee: $1,944- $3,432/yr. Christian. *See ad this page*

Yin Yang Seminary (Church of Divine Man), 2965-1/2 North Main, Walnut Creek, 94596. Ph: (510) 524-0436. Enroll: 20, Ungraded. Fee: Call seminary.

Solano County
Benicia

Children's Palace Montessori Traditional School, 525 Military East, Benicia, 94510. Ph: (707) 745-1220. Enroll: 60, Pre-2nd. Fee: $85/wk.

CONTRA COSTA CHRISTIAN HIGH
9TH-12TH GRADE
- COLLEGE PREP
- SPORTS • FINE ARTS
- COMPUTERS
- RESOURCE ROOM

934-4964

WOODLANDS CHRISTIAN
PRE-SCHOOL - 8TH GRADE
- DAY CARE
- MUSIC • COMPUTERS
- RESOURCE ROOM

945-6863

St. Dominic's School, 935 E. 5th St., Benicia, 94510. Ph: (707) 745-1266. Enroll: 325, Kinder-8th. Fee: $1,600/yr. avg. Catholic.

Davis

Montessori Country Day School, 1811 Renoir Ave., Davis, 95616. Ph: (916) 753-8373. Enroll: Pre: 35; K: 36, Pre & K. Fee: $396/mo. full day.

Redbud Montessori, 7 Patwin Rd.—PO Box 1562, Davis, 95616. Ph: (916) 753-2623. Enroll: 36, Pre- 1st. Fee: $375-$415/mo.

Russell Park Child Development Center, 400 Russell Park, Davis, 95616. Ph: (916) 753-2487. Enroll: 60, Pre & K. Fee: Call School.

St. James School, 1215 B Street, Davis, 95616. Ph: (916) 756-3946. Enroll: 265, K-8th. Fee: $2,100/yr.

Dixon

Neighborhood Christian School, 655 So. 1st Street, Dixon, 95620. Ph: (916) 678-9336. Enroll: 125, K-6th. Fee: $1850/yr. Christian.

Fairfield

Accolade Christian School, 844 Jackson St., Fairfield, 94533. Ph: (707) 422-3314. Enroll: 45, First-8th. Fee: $2,400/yr. Interdenominational.

Children's World, 3045 Rockville Rd., Fairfield, 94585. Ph: (707) 425-0518. Enroll: K: 24; 200 total, Pre-K. Fee: K only: $98/wk.

Little School House, 83 Tabor Ave., Fairfield, 94533. Ph: (707) 422-6225. Enroll: 80, Pre-3rd. Fee: $310/mo.

Noah's Ark, 1004 Utah, Fairfield, 94533. Ph: (707) 427-0210. Enroll: 50, Pre & K. Fee: $85/wk.

Solano Christian academy, 2200 Fairfield Ave., Fairfield, 94533. Ph: (707) 425-7715. Enroll: 190, Pre-8th. Fee: $1,700/yr. Church of Christ.

Vacaville

Bethany Lutheran Pre-School, 621 S. Orchard Ave., Vacaville, 95688. Ph: (707) 451-6675. Enroll: 130, Pre-K. Fee: K only: $160/mo. Bethany Lutheran Church.

La Petite Academy, 2501 Nut Tree Rd., Vacaville, 95687. Ph: (707) 447-5252. Enroll: 152, Age 2 through 12 yrs. Fee: $77- $101/wk.

Notre Dame Parochial School, 1781 Marshall Rd., Vacaville, 95687. Ph: (707) 447-1445 (or 1460). Enroll: 328, K-8th. Fee: $1,810/yr. Catholic.

Vacaville Christian Academy, 1117 Davis St., Vacaville, 95687. Ph: (707) 446-1776. Enroll: 65, Infants-9th. Fee: $165-$197/mo. Non-denominational.

Vallejo

Hilltop Christian School, 210 Locust Drive, Vallejo, 94591. Ph: (707) 643-1726. Enroll: 250, K-8th. Fee: $182- $202/mo. Interdenominational.

LaPetite Academy, 470 Avian Drive, Vallejo, 94591. Ph: (707) 642-7500. Enroll: K: 11; Preschool:152, Ages: Infant to 12 years. Fee: $77- $101/mo.

North Hills Christian School, 200 Admiral Callaghan Ln., Vallejo, 94591. Ph: (707) 644-5284. Enroll: 500, Pre-12th. Fee: $170- $190/mo.

Reignierd Schools, 380 Contra Costa St., Vallejo, 94590-6330. Ph: (707) 644-0447. Enroll: 160, PreK-12th. Fee: $1,950-2,050/yr.

St. Basil's School, 1230 Nebraska, Vallejo, 94590. Ph: (707) 642-7629. Enroll: 346, K-8th. Fee: $150/mo. Catholic.

St. Catherine's School, 3460 Tennessee, Vallejo, 94591. Ph: (707) 643-6691. Enroll: 320, K-8th. Fee: Call school. Catholic.

St. Patrick- St. Vincent High School, 1500 Benicia Rd., Vallejo, 94591. Ph: (707) 644-4425. Enroll: 670, Ninth-12th. Fee: $3,350- $3,470/yr. Catholic.

St. Vincent Ferrer School, 420 Florida St., Vallejo, 94590. Ph: (707) 642-4311. Enroll: 353, K-8th. Fee: $156- $257/mo. Catholic.

Vallejo Conservatory Learning Center, 1215 Georgia Street, Vallejo, 94590. Ph: (707) 552-1960. Enroll: 12, Pre-Kinder, day care. Fee: $2,750/yr. A multicultural approach.

9/Day Care

A List to Start You on Your Search for a Care Center in Contra Costa & Solano

DAY CARE OVER THE LAST 10-20 years has undergone a transformation in the Bay Region. As more mothers entered the work force, the demand for quality care rose and private enterprise moved to fill the need, followed, often begrudgingly, by public schools.

Yes, more can be done, especially in incorporating child care in work places. But compared to the 1970s, day care is much more accessible now and probably better managed. Community colleges train people who work in and run care centers. Because of well-publicized abuses in the past, many parents are more aware that day-care providers should be chosen carefully.

What Day-Care Directory Contains

Here is a list of day-care providers that serve the local towns. It is not an exhaustive list. The state licenses day-care providers according to the number of children served: over 12 children or under 12.

The following list, drawn from state sources and phone books, confines itself generally to the centers with 12 or more students.

This is not an endorsement list. McCormack's Guides does not inspect centers or in any way monitor their activities.

It is a list, as current as we could make it, to start you on your search for a day-care center.

Ask Questions

Ask plenty of questions, tour the facilities, check with other parents about the care of their children. Read a pamphlet or book on day-care centers and what to look for.

Contra Costa County
Alamo
Creative Learning, 120 Hemme Ave., Alamo, 94507. Ages: 2-6 yr. Ph: (510) 837-4044.
Dorris-Eaton School, 1286 Stone Valley Rd., Alamo, 94507. Ages: 2.9-6 yr. Ph: (510) 837-7248.
Methodist PreSch, 902 Danville Blvd., Alamo, 94507. Ages: 2.6-5 yr. Ph: (510) 837-2788.
Seaborn Country School, 1261 Laverock Lane, Alamo, 94507. Ages: 2 yr. & up. Ph: (510) 939-0779.

Antioch
Antioch Creative PreSch, 1800 Woodland Dr., Antioch, 94509. Ages: 2.9-5.10 yr. Ph: (510) 757-0305.
Child Day School, 112 Tregallas Rd., Antioch, 94509. Ages: 18 mo.-10 yr. Ph: (510) 754-0144.
Covenant Christian PreSch, 1919 Buchanan Rd., Antioch, 94509. Ages: 2.5-5 yr. Ph: (510) 757-5016.
East County Head Start, 10th & L St., Antioch, 94509. Ages: 3.4-5 yr. Ph: (510) 754-2560.
East County Head Start—Sunset, 3309 Sunset Lane, Antioch, 94509. Ages: 3.4-5 yr. Ph: (510) 778-2133.
Great Beginnings, 2800 Sunset Lane, Antioch, 94509. Ages: 4.9-12 yr. Ph: (510) 754-1422.
Great Beginnings, 512 West Texas, Antioch, 94509. Ages: 2-5 yr. Ph: (510) 778-5462.
Harbour Lights, 1020 E. Tregallas Rd., Antioch, 94509. Ages: 2-5 yr. Ph: (510) 757-3884.
Hilltop Christian PreSch, 320 Worrell Rd., Antioch, 94509. Ages: 2-6 yr. Ph: (510) 778-0214.
Holy Rosary School, 25 E. 15th St., Antioch, 94509. Ages: 4-6 yr. Ph: (510) 757-1270.
Kids Connection—Marsh, 2304 G St., Antioch, 95409. Ages: 4.9-12 yr. Ph: (510) 778-6371.
Kinder Care, 2300 Mahogany Way, Antioch, 94509. Ages: 0-12 yr. Ph: (510) 778-8888.
Kinder Care, 4308 Folsom Dr., Antioch, 94509. Ages: 0-12 yr. Ph: (510) 754-3137.
La Petite Academy, 1350 E. Tregallas Rd., Antioch, 94509. Ages: 4-12 yr. Ph: (510) 779-0110.
Little Lulu's, 2725 Minta Lane, Antioch, 94509. Ages: 2-6 yr. Ph: (510) 754-7771.
So Big Co-op PreSch, Antioch, 94509. Ages: 2-5 yr. Ph: (510) 757-6474.

Brentwood
Brentwood Sunshine House, 63 Chestnut St., Brentwood, 95413. Ages: 2-12 yr. Ph: (510) 634-5678.
Dainty Center, 1265 Dainty Ave., Brentwood, 94513. Ages: 2-12 yr. Ph: (510) 634-4539.
De Colores Children Ctr, 145 Orchard Dr., Brentwood, 94513. Ages: 2-5 yr. Ph: (510) 634-3477.
East County Headstart—La Palomita, 225 H Lone Tree Way, Brentwood, 94513. Ages: 2.5-4.9 yr. Ph: (510) 516-2060.
Raggedy Ann n' Andy, 25 Walnut Blvd., Brentwood, 94513. Ages: 3-6 yr. Ph: (510) 634-3498.

Clayton
Clayton Children's Ctr, 6760 Marsh Creek Rd., Clayton, 94517. Ages: 2-9 yr. Ph: (510) 672-0717.
Clayton Comm. School, 5880 Mt. Zion Dr., Clayton, 94517. Ages: 5-11 yr. Ph: (510) 672-0388.

Concord
All About Kids, 3033 Bonifacio St., Concord, 94522. Ages: 0-4.9 yr. Ph: (510) 689-5437.
Bianchi Drop-In CCCtr, 478 Sun Valley Mall, Concord, 94527. Ages: 2-4.9 yr. Ph: (510) 680-8600.
Bianchi School—Concord, 1850 Second St., Concord, 94521. Ages: 2-6 yr. Ph: (510) 825-6671.
Bianchi School—Cowell Rd, 4347 Cowell Rd., Concord, 94518. Ages: 2-6 yr. Ph: (510) 680-8707.
Calvary Baptist, 2140 Olivera Ct., Concord, 94520. Ages: 2-4.9 yr. Ph: (510) 685-1424.
Cambridge Comm. Ctr, 1135 Lacey Lane, Concord, 94520. Ages: 2-8 yr. Ph: (510) 827-4864.
Chautauqua Farms, 2140 Minert Rd., Concord, 94518. Ages: 2-12 yr. Ph: (510) 680-8164.
Clayton Valley Parent PreSch, 1645 West St., Concord, 94521. Ages: 2.9-6 yr. Ph: (510) 680-8770.
Clayton Valley Presbyterian, 1578 Kirker Pass Rd., Concord, 94521. Ages: 2-6 yr. Ph: (510) 672-0882.
Concord CCCtr, 1360 A Detroit Ave., Concord, 94520. Ages: 2-6 yr. Ph: (510) 689-8122.
Concord CCCtr, 1360 B Detroit Ave., Concord, 94520. Ages: 0-3 yr. Ph: (510) 689-8122.
Concord CCCtr, 1360 C Detroit Ave., Concord, 94520. Ages: 2-12 yr. Ph: (510) 689-5151.

DAY CARE

Concord Christian, 2120 Olivera Rd., Concord, 94520. Ages: 2-6 yr. Ph: (510) 825-1370.
Concordia Christian, 988 Oak Grove Rd., Concord, 94518. Ages: 2.5-5 yr. Ph: (510) 825-4170.
Concordia School, 2353 Fifth Ave., Concord, 94518. Ages: 2-7 yr. Ph: (510) 689-4535.
Family Stress Ctr—Respite Nursery, 20886 Commerce Ave., Concord, 94520. Ages: 0-6 yr. Ph: (510) 827-0212.
Family Stress Headstart Ctr—Cambridge, 1135 Lacey Lane, Concord, 94521. Ages: 2.9-5 yr. Ph: (510) 827-0212.
First Lutheran, 4006 Concord Blvd., Concord, 94519. Ages: 2-12 yr. Ph: (510) 798-5330.
First Presbyterian, 1965 Colfax St., Concord, 94520. Ages: 2.9-6 yr. Ph: (510) 676-7177.
George Miller Jr. Memorial Ctr, 3020 Grant St., Concord, 94520. Ages: 0-3 yr. dev. dis. Ph: (510) 646-5710.
Heather Acres, 1507 Heather Dr., Concord, 94521. Ages: 2.5-8 yr. Ph: (510) 676-5299.
Highland DCCtr, 1326 Pennsylvania Blvd., Concord, 94521. Ages: 4.9-12 yr. Ph: (510) 672-1942 main office; 672-6144 school.
Kiddie Kollege, 3950 Clayton Rd., Concord, 94521. Ages: 2.6-6 yr. Ph: (510) 676-4633.
Kids Connection—G. Miller East, 3020 Grant St., Concord, 94520. Ages: 2-5 yr. Ph: (510) 686-1789.
Kids Connection—Mountain View, 1705 Thornwood Dr., Concord, 94521. Ages: 4.9-12 yr. Ph: (510) 689-1170.
Kids Connection—Woodside, 761 San Simeon Dr., Concord, 94518. Ages: 5-11 yr. Ph: (510) 676-9534.
Kinder Care, 1551 Bailey Rd., Concord, 94521. Ages: 0-12 yr. Ph: (510) 682-9560.
King's Valley #3, 4255 Clayton Rd., Concord, 94521. Ages: 2-6 yr. Ph: (510) 687-2020.
La Petite Academy, 4304 Cowell Rd., Concord, 94518. Ages: 0-12 yr. Ph: (510) 676-4416.
Lads & Lassies, 1566 Bailey Rd., Concord, 94521. Ages: 2-6 yr. Ph: (510) 686-5621.
Lads & Lassies, 1649 Claycord Ave., Concord, 94520. Ages: 5-12 yr. Ph: (510) 687-4550.
MDCCCA—Baldwin Park, 2750 Parkside Circle, Concord, 94519. Ages: 2-5 yr. Ph: (510) 798-5021.
MDCCCA—Holbrook, 3333 A Ronald Way, Concord, 94520. Ages: 4.9-14 yr. Ph: (510) 685-7951.
Miss Nancy's Infant Day Care & Preschool, 1011 Oak Grove Rd., Concord, 94518. Ages: 0-2 yr. Ph: (510) 671-2979.
Miss Nancy's Infant Day Care & Preschool, 1015 Oak Grove Rd., Concord, 94518. Ages: 2-6 yr. Ph: (510) 671-9870.
Montessori School of Concord, 3039 Willow Pass Rd., Concord, 94519. Ages: 2-6 yr. Ph: (510) 682-8067.
Pam's Discovery Center, 3036 Clayton Rd., Concord, 94521. Ages: 2-5 yr. Ph: (510) 686-6168.
Pixie Play School, 1797 Ayers Rd., Concord, 94521. Ages: 2-6 yr. Ph: (510) 689-4030.
Railroad Junction, 2898 Concord Blvd., Concord, 94520. Ages: 0-12 yr. Ph: (510) 827-4450.
St. Michael's Episcopal, 2925 Bonifacio St., Concord, 94519. Ages: 2-6 yr. Ph: (510) 685-8859.
Sun Terrace PreSch, 3585 Port Chicago Hwy., Concord, 94520. Ages: 2-6 yr. Ph: (510) 676-4373.
Tabernacle Christian, 4380 Concord Blvd., Concord, 94521. Ages: 2-6 yr. Ph: (510) 685-9169.
Walnut Country PreSch, 4465 S. Larwin Dr., Concord, 94521. Ages: 2-6 yr. Ph: (510) 798-9686.
We Care, 2191 Kirker Pass Rd., Concord, 94521. Ages: 0-6 yr. dev. dis. Ph: (510) 671-0077.
World of Adventure, 3764 Clayton Rd., Concord, 94519. Ages: 2-12 yr. Ph: (510) 798-7364.
YWCA Shadelands, 1860 Silverwood Dr., Concord, 94519. Ages: 3-5.9 yr. Ph: (510) 685-3533.
Acorn School, 816 Diablo Rd., Danville, 94526. Ages: 2-10 yr. Ph: (510) 837-1145.

Danville

Bianchi School—Danville, 909 Camino Ramon, Danville, 94526. Ages: 2-6 yr. Ph: (510) 838-8541.
Community Presbyterian, 222 W. El Pintado Rd., Danville, 94526. Ages: 3-6 yr. Ph: (510) 837-3316.
Creative Learning, 2425 Camino Tassajara, Danville, 94526. Ages: 2-6 yr. Ph: (510) 736-3336.
Danville Children's Ctr, 989 San Ramon Valley Blvd., Danville, 94526. Ages: 2-6 yr. Ph: (510) 838-9511.
Das Montessori Kinderhaus, 101 Sonora Ave., Danville, 94526. Ages: 2 mo.-6 yr. Ph:

166 CONTRA COSTA & SOLANO

(510) 831-6199.
Diablo Hills, 1453 San Ramon Valley Blvd., Danville, 94526. Ages: 2-11 yr. Ph: (510) 820-8523.
Fountainhead Montessori, 939 El Pintado Rd., Danville, 04526. Ages: 2-6 yr. Ph: (510) 820-6250.
Garden Montessori, 495 Verona Ave., Danville, 94526. Ages: 3-5 yr. Ph: (510) 837-2969.
Kids Country—Green Valley, 1001 Diablo Rd., Danville, 94526. Ages: 5-11 yr. Ph: (510) 820-3646.
Kids Country—Greenbrook, 1475 Harlan Dr., Danville, 94526. Ages: 5-12 yr. Ph: (510) 831-8591.
Kids Country—J. Baldwin, 741 Brookside Dr., Danville, 94526. Ages: 5-12 yr. Ph: (510) 831-3530.
Kids Country—Montair, 300 Quinterra Lane, Danville, 94526. Ages: 5-12 yr. Ph: (510) 820-3131.
Kids Country—Vista Grande, 667 Diablo Rd., Danville, 94526. Ages: 5-12 yr. Ph: (510) 837-0330.
Larson's School, 920 Diablo Rd., Danville, 94526. Ages: 2-10 yr. Ph: (510) 837-4238.
Little Kids Corral, 432 La Gonda, Danville, 94526. Ages: 2-10 yr. Ph: (510) 820-6929.
Sycamore Valley, 1 Hartz Ct., Danville, 94526. Ages: 2-6 yr. Ph: (510) 736-2181.
Valley Parent's Nursery, 1550 Diablo Rd., Danville, 94526. Ages: 2.6-5.7 yr. Ph: (510) 837-5401.

El Cerrito

Bright Star Montessori, 7140 Gladys Ave., El Cerrito, 94530. Ages: 2-6 yr. Ph: (510) 233-5330.
Cerrito Vista Montessori, 1111 Navellier St., El Cerrito, 94530. Ages: 2-6 yr. Ph: (510) 527-6125.
Clubhouse Enrichment Ctr, 7230 Fairmount Ave., El Cerrito, 94530. Ages: 5-12 yr. Ph: (510) 528-2266.
El Cerrito City—Canyon Trail, 6757 Gatto Ave., El Cerrito, 94530. Ages: 5-12 yr. Ph: (510) 215-4393.
El Cerrito City—Castro, 1420 Norvell St., El Cerrito, 94530. Ages: 6-12 yr. Ph: (510) 620-9621.
El Cerrito City—Fairmont, 715 Lexington Rd., El Cerrito, 94530. Ages: 4.9-12 yr. Ph: (510) 215-4391.
El Cerrito City—Harding Park, 7115 C St., El Cerrito, 94530. Ages: 5-12 yr. Ph: (510) 215-4390.
El Cerrito Ctr Preschool Day Care, 7200 Moeser Lane, El Cerrito, 94530. Ages: 2-9 yr. Ph: (510) 526-1916.
Nomura PreSch, 522 Clayton Ave., El Cerrito, 94530. Ages: 2-5 yr. Ph: (510) 525-8300.
Peter Pan, 1422 Navellier, El Cerrito, 94530. Ages: 2.9-5 yr. Ph: (510) 234-5918.
Phoenix PreSch, 6830 Stockton Ave., El Cerrito, 94530. Ages: 2-6 yr. Ph: (510) 525-1785.
Yellow Brick Rd., 7075 Cutting Blvd., El Cerrito, 94530. Ages: 2.5-6 yr. Ph: (510) 235-4446.

El Sobrante

Calvary Christian School, 4892 San Pablo Dam Rd., El Sobrante, 94803. Ages: 2-6 yr. Ph: (510) 223-5960.
Canterbury PreSch, 4300 Santa Rita Rd., El Sobrante, 94803. Ages: 2-12 yr. Ph: (510) 222-5050.
Hansel & Gretel Parent Part. Nur., 5151 Argyle Rd., El Sobrante, 94803. Ages: 2.9-5 yr. Ph: (510) 223-7400.
Muppet DCCtr, 4410 San Pablo Dam Rd., El Sobrante, 94803. Ages: 18 mo.- 6 yr. Ph: (510) 222-7377.
Rainbow Valley, 4863 San Pablo Dam Rd., El Sobrante, 94803. Ages: 2.9-5 yr. Ph: (510) 235-7102.
Sherwood Forest, 5570 Olinda Rd., El Sobrante, 94803. Ages: 2 yr. & up. Ph: (510) 223-4417.
Sonshine DCCtr, 4333 Appian Way, El Sobrante, 94803. Ages: 2-9 yr. Ph: (510) 223-6146.
St. Timothy Lutheran, 5435 San Pablo Dam Rd., El Sobrante, 94803. Ages: 2-6 yr. Ph: (510) 222-2511.
WCC YM-Care Olinda, 5855 Olinda Rd., El Sobrante, 94803. Ages: 4.9-12 yr. Ph: (510) 222-9622.

Hercules

Hercules Before-After Program, 1919 Lupine Rd., Hercules, 94547. Ages: 5-12 yr. Ph: (510) 8259.
Ohlone Child Care Center, 1616 Pheasant Dr., Hercules, 94547. Ages: 5-12 yr. Ph: (510) 799-8224.
Pillow PreSch, 1702 Pheasant Dr., Hercules, 94547. Ages: 2-12 yr. Ph: (510) 799-5426.

Kensington

Arlington PreSch, 52 Arlington Ave., Kensington, 94707. Ages: 2-6 yr. Ph: (510) 524-8689.
Claremont Nursery, 1550 Oakview Ave., Kensington, 94707. Ages: 2-6 yr. Ph: (510) 526-1010.

Kensington Nursery, 52 Arlington Ave., Kensington, 94707. Ages: 2.5-6 yr. Ph: (510) 524-7963.
Montessori, 52 Arlington Blvd., Kensington, 94707. Ages: 2-6 yr. Ph: (510) 527-1278.
Neighborhood PreSch, 59 Arlington Ave., Kensington, 94707. Ages: 2-5 yr. Ph: (510) 524-8641.
Rainbow Hill, 90 Highland Blvd., Kensington, 94707. Ages: 4.9-12 yr. Ph: (510) 526-5749.
Skytown Parent Co-op, 1 Lawson Rd., Kensington, 94708. Ages: 0-6 yr. Ph: (510) 526-8481.

Lafayette

Burton Valley Co-op, 584 Glenside Dr., Lafayette, 94549. Ages: 2.9-5.9 yr. Ph: (510) 283-6170.
Child Day School, 1049 Stuart St., Lafayette, 94549. Ages: 2 yr. & up. Ph: (510) 284-7092.
Diablo Valley Montessori, 3390 Deerhill Rd., Lafayette, 94549. Ages: 2-6 yr. Ph: (510) 283-6036.
First Steps, 1000 Upper Happy Valley Rd., Lafayette, 94549. Ages: 0-12 yr. Ph: (510) 283-4048.
First Street, 961 First St., Lafayette, 94549. Ages: 4.9-12 yr. Ph: (510) 283-4500.
Growing Tree, 1000 Upper Happy Valley Dr., Lafayette, 94549. Ages: 2-5 yr. Ph: (510) 283-2101.
Happy Days, 3205 Stanley Blvd., Lafayette, 94549. Ages: 2 yr. & up. Ph: (510) 932-8088.
Lafayette Nursery, 979 First St., Lafayette, 94549. Ages: 2.6-6 yr. Ph: (510) 284-1639.
Lafayette-Orinda Presbyterian, 49 Knox Dr., Lafayette, 94549. Ages: 0-4 yr. Ph: (510) 283-8722.
Merriewood, 561 Merriewood Dr., Lafayette, 94549. Ages: 2.9-12 yr. Ph: (510) 284-2121.
Montessori Children's House, 955 Moraga Rd. #2, Lafayette, 94549. Ages: 2-6 yr. Ph: (510) 284-9710.
One Step at a Time, 984 Moraga Rd., Lafayette, 94549. Ages: 3 mo.-5.9 yr. Ph: (510) 283-4422.
White Pony & Maher School, 999 Leland Dr., Lafayette, 94549. Ages: 6 wk-6 yr. Ph: (510) 938-4826.

Martinez

Agape Christian, 444 Fig Tree Lane, Martinez, 94553. Ages: 2-6 yr. Ph: (510) 228-8155.
Bianchi School, 1285 Morello Ave., Martinez, 94553. Ages: 2-11 yr. Ph: (510) 372-7701.
Cherub Childcare, 853 Center Ave., Martinez, 94553. Ages: 6 wk-6 yr. Ph: (510) 228-5800.
Concordia School, 100 Church St., Martinez, 94553. Ages: 2-6 yr. Ph: (510) 228-1733.
First Step Learning Ctr, 4950 Pacheco Blvd., Martinez, 94553. Ages: 4 mo.-5 yr. Ph: (510) 283-4048.
Higher Heights Christian, 245 Morello Ave., Martinez, 94553. Ages: 2-6 yr. Ph: (510) 372-7155.
Little Acorns, 1121 Harbor View Dr., Martinez, 94553. Ages: 2.9-5 yr. Ph: (510) 228-2298.
Martinez Early Childhood, 615 Arch St., Martinez, 94553. Ages: 6 mo.-12 yr. Ph: (510) 229-2000.
Patchin's Play House, 831 Bella Vista, Martinez, 94553. Ages: 2.6-6 yr. Ph: (510) 228-1295.
Stepping Stones, 127 Midhill Rd., Martinez, 94553. Ages: 2-10 yr. Ph: (510) 933-6520.
Sunnybrook Learning Ctr, 6635 Alhambra Ave., Martinez, 94553. Ages: 0-10 yr. Ph: (510) 947-6800.
Woodbridge-Morello, 850 Jones St., Martinez, 94553. Ages: 5-11 yr. Ph: (510) 228-4166.
Woodbridge—John Muir, 205 Vista Way, Martinez, 94553. Ages: 5-11 yr. Ph: (510) 229-5767.
Woodbridge—John Swett, 4955 Alhambra Valley Rd., Martinez, 94553. Ages: 5-11 yr. Ph: (510) 228-7540.
Woodbridge—Las Juntas, 4105 Pacheco Blvd., Martinez, 94553. Ages: 5-11 yr. Ph: (510) 228-0672.

Moraga

Growing Tree, 22 Wakefield Dr., Moraga, 94556. Ages: 6 mo.-6 yr. Ph: (510) 376-8280.
Holy Cross Christian, 1695 Canyon Rd., Moraga, 94556. Ages: 2.6-6.6 yr. Ph: (510) 376-3458.
Montessori House, 22 Wakefield Dr., Moraga, 94556. Ages: 0-2 yr. Ph: (510) 376-8000.
Moraga Valley Nurtury, 30 Idlewood Ct., Moraga, 94556. Ages: 2-5 yr. Ph: (510) 376-4800.
Mulberry Tree PreSch, 1455 St. Mary's Rd., Moraga, 94556. Ages: 2.6-6 yr. Ph: (510) 376-1751.
Saklan School, 1678 School St., Moraga, 94556. Ages: 2-12 yr. Ph: (510) 376-7900.

Oakley

A Child's Place, 131 Main St., Oakley, 94561. Ages: 2-8 yr. Ph: (510) 625-9795.

Angela Guzman, Gehringer School, Bolton Rd., Oakley, 94561. Ages: 4.9-11 yr. Ph: (510) 625-3032.
Country Kids, 61 Delta Rd., Oakley, 94561. Ages: 2-6 yr. Ph: (510) 634-7979.

Orinda
Flagg's Happy Times School, 1 Ardor Dr., Orinda, 94563. Ages: 2.6-6 yr. Ph: (510) 254-2097.
Fountainhead Montessori, 24 Orinda Way, #11, Orinda, 94563. Ages: 2-6 yr. Ph: (510) 820-1343.
Orinda PreSch, 10 Irwin Way, Orinda, 94563. Ages: 2.9-5.9 yr. Ph: (510) 254-2551.
Shepherd of the Valley, 433 Moraga Way, Orinda, 94563. Ages: 2-5.10 yr. Ph: (510) 254-3422.
St. John PreSch, 501 Moraga Way, Orinda, 94563. Ages: 2-5 yr. Ph: (510) 254-3815.
St. Mark's Nursery, 451 Moraga Way, Orinda, 94563. Ages: 2.9-6 yr. Ph: (510) 254-5965.
St. Stephen's Nursery, 66 St. Stephen's Dr., Orinda, 94563. Ages: 2.5-5.5 yr. Ph: (510) 254-3770.
Village PreSch, 320 Camino Pablo, Orinda, 94563. Ages: 6 mo.-6 yr. Ph: (510) 254-6221.

Pacheco
Brighton Elementary, 106 Deodar Dr., Pacheco, 94553. Ages: NA. Ph: (510) 798-1668.
YWCA Pollywog, 106 Deodar Dr., Pacheco, 94553. Ages: 0-12 yr. Ph: (510) 827-9680.

Pinole
Deuel's, 2499 Simas Ave., Pinole, 94564. Ages: 2-5 yr. Ph: (510) 758-1355.
Happy Lion, 2612 Appian Way, Pinole, 94564. Ages: 2.5-6 yr. Ph: (510) 222-2416.
Our Savior, 3110 Avis Way, Pinole, 94564. Ages: 2.5-10 yr. Ph: (510) 758-1961.
Tweedle-Dee Nursery, 1839 Sarah Dr., Pinole, 94564. Ages: 2-6 yr. Ph: (510) 222-2102.
WCC YMCA Children's Ctr, 2040 Hoke Dr., Pinole, 94564. Ages: 2.9-11 yr. Ph: (510) 222-9622 main office, or 758-4917.
WCC YMCA—Ellerhorst, 3501 Pinole Valley Rd., Pinole, 94564. Ages: 5-12 yr. Ph: (510) 758-4949.

Pittsburg
Alves Lane Sunshine House, 15 Alves Lane, Pittsburg, 94565. Ages: 2-6 yr. Ph: (510) 458-3434.
Christian Ctr, 1210 Stoneman Ave., Pittsburg, 94565. Ages: 2-5 yr. Ph: (510) 432-3808.
Concordia School, 195 Alvarado Ave., Pittsburg, 94565. Ages: 2-6 yr. Ph: (510) 432-8585.
Family Stress Headstart Ctr—Ambrose Park, 125 Memorial Way, Pittsburg, 94565. Ages: 2-6 yr. Ph: (510) 458-6442.
First Baptist Church Headstart, 204 Odessa Ave., Pittsburg, 94565. Ages: 2-6 yr. Ph: (510) 432-7498.
First Baptist Church Headstart—Wee World, 2193 Knox Ave., Pittsburg, 94565. Ages: 3-5 yr. Ph: (510) 432-3909.
Kindercare, 150 E. Leland Rd., Pittsburg, 94565. Ages: 0-12 yr. Ph: (510) 432-8800.
Kings Kids Christian Ctr, 3801 Camino Andres, Pittsburg, 94565. Ages: 2-12 yr. Ph: (510) 458-1802.
La Petite Academy, 55 Castlewood St., Pittsburg, 94565. Ages: 6 wk-12 yr. Ph: (510) 427-1989.
Lido Square Headstart, 2131 Crestview Lane, Pittsburg, 94565. Ages: 2-6 yr. Ph: (510) 432-8191.
Lynn Day Treatment Ctr, 950 El Pueblo Dr., Pittsburg, 94565. Ages: 1 yr. & up. Ph: (510) 439-7516.
Martin Luther King Ctr, 950 El Pueblo Ave., Pittsburg, 94565. Ages: 2-5 yr. Ph: (510) 432-3568.
Pittsburg PreSch, 1760 Chester Dr., Pittsburg, 94565. Ages: 0-11 yr. Ph: (510) 439-2061.
Railroad Junction, 2224 Railroad Ave., Pittsburg, 94565. Ages: 2-12 yr. Ph: (510) 427-2000.
St. Peter Martyr., 425 West 4th St., Pittsburg, 94565. Ages: 3-5 yr. Ph: (510) 439-1014.
Tiny Tots, 60 Civic Dr., Pittsburg, 94565. Ages: 2.9-5 yr. Ph: (510) 439-9804.

Pleasant Hill
Creative Play, 2323 Pleasant Hill Rd., Pleasant Hill, 94523. Ages: 2.5-4.9 yr. Ph: (510) 932-3173.
Fair Oaks, 2400 Lisa Lane, Pleasant Hill, 94523. Ages: 4.9-12 yr. Ph: (510) 676-3174.
Fountainhead Montessori, 490 Golf club Rd., Pleasant Hill, 94523. Ages: 2-6 yr. Ph: (510) 685-2949.
Kids Connection—Strandwood, 416 Gladys Dr., Pleasant Hill, 94523. Ages: 5-12 yr. Ph: (510) 687-1004.
Kids Connection—Valhalla, 530 Kiki Dr., Pleasant Hill, 94523. Ages: 5-12 yr. Ph: (510) 827-4743.
Mary Jane's PreSch, 2902 Vessing Rd., Pleasant Hill, 94523. Ages: 2.6-6.11 yr. Ph:

(510) 935-3084.
Oak Park PreSch, 1649 Oak Park Blvd., Pleasant Hill, 94523. Ages: 2-6 yr. Ph: (510) 934-1422.
Peter Pan, 399 Gregory Lane, Pleasant Hill, 94523. Ages: 2-6 yr. Ph: (510) 685-2288 or 685-2289.
Play and Learn, 1898 Pleasant Hill Rd., Pleasant Hill, 94523. Ages: 2-9 yr. Ph: (510) 943-7007.
Pleasant Hill DC Ctr, 2097 Oak Park Blvd., Pleasant Hill, 94523. Ages: 4.9-12 yr. Ph: (510) 938-3043.
Pleasant Hill Discoveryland, 800 Grayson Rd., Pleasant Hill, 94523. Ages: 2-7 yr. Ph: (510) 935-3520.
Sequoia DC Ctr, 277 Boyd Rd., Pleasant Hill, 94523. Ages: 4.9-12 yr. Ph: (510) 939-6336.
St. Andrews CD Ctr, 1601 Mary Dr., Pleasant Hill, 94523. Ages: 2-10 yr. Ph: (510) 685-4720.
St. Mark's Christian, 3051 Putnam Blvd., Pleasant Hill, 94523. Ages: 2-6 yr. Ph: (510) 932-0700.
Stepping Stones, 2750 Pleasant Hill Rd., Pleasant Hill, 94523. Ages: 2-10 yr. Ph: (510) 933-6520.

Richmond

Annex Child Dev Ctr, 1738 Shasta St., Richmond, 94804. Ages: 2-5 yr. Ph: (510) 527-0993.
CCC Headstart—Belding, 989-18th St., Richmond, 94801. Ages: 3-5 yr. Ph: (510) 374-3732.
Crescent Park, 5050 Hartnett Ave., Richmond, 94804. Ages: 2-5 yr. Ph: (510) 374-3701.
Early Childhood Mental Hth Pro, 2801 Robert Miller Dr., Richmond, 94806. Ages: 2-6 yr. Ph: (510) 223-8926.
George Miller Jr. Memorial Ctr, West, 2801 Robert H. Miller Dr., Richmond, 94806. Ages: 0-3 yr. dev. dis. Ph: (510) 374-3981.
Greater Richmond Soc. Svcs. CCCtr, 1310-1350 Bissell Ave., Richmond, 94801. Ages: 0-5 yr. Ph: (510) 236-2581.
GRSSC Easter Hill, 660 Corto Square, Richmond, 94804. Ages: 2-5 yr. Ph: (510) 235-2142.
Jack in the Box, 777 Sonoma St., Richmond, 94805. Ages: 2-8 yr. Ph: (510) 232-7201.
Kathmandu CCCtr, 5622 Jefferson Ave., Richmond, 94804. Ages: 2-13 yr. Ph: (510) 236-5463.
Keystone Montessori, 801 Park Central, Richmond, 94803. Ages: 2-6 yr. Ph: (510) 223-4520.
Kiddie Tots, 543-21st St., Richmond, 94801. Ages: 2-4.9 yr. Ph: (510) 237-4575.
La Casita Bilingue Montessori, 2801 Robert Miller Dr., Richmond, 94806. Ages: 2-5 yr. Ph: (510) 223-7731.
La Petite Academy, 3891 Lakeside Dr., Richmond, 94806. Ages: 2-12 yr. Ph: (510) 222-3070.
Maloneys CCCtr, 3505 Morningside Dr., Richmond, 94803. Ages: 2-12 yr. Ph: (510) 527-7200.
Maritime Children's Ctr, 1014 Florida Ave., Richmond, 94804. Ages: 2-5 yr. Ph: (510) 374-3898.
New Destinies, 214 So. 11th St., Richmond, 94804. Ages: 2-12 yr. Ph: (510) 235-6347.
Odyssey School, 1605-1611 Coalinga Ave., Richmond, 94804. Ages: 2.9-10 yr. Ph: (510) 235-4825.
Opportunity Children's Ctr, 1350 Kelsey St., Richmond, 94801. Ages: 2-6 yr. Ph: (510) 237-4475.
Pacific Academy or Nomura School, 1615 Carlson Blvd., Richmond, 94804. Ages: 2-6 yr. Ph: (510) 528-1727.
Pullman Child Dev. Ctr, 2999 Pullman Ave., Richmond, 94804. Ages: 2-5 yr. Ph: (510) 234-6191.
Pullman Children's Ctr, 2730 Maine Ave., Richmond, 94804. Ages: 2-5 yr. Ph: (510) 374-3968.
St. David's Pre-K, 5613 Garvin Ave., Richmond, 94805. Ages: 3.9-5 yr. Ph: (510) 232-1736.
St. Timothy Lutheran, 3301 Morningside Dr., Richmond, 94803. Ages: 0-6 yr. Ph: (510) 222-9222.
Temple Beth Hillel, 801 Park Central, Richmond, 94804. Ages: 2-6 yr. Ph: (510) 223-2560.
WCC YM-Care Peres, 715 Fifth St., Richmond, 94801. Ages: 4.9-12 yr. Ph: (510) 237-0314.
WCC YM-Care Sheldon, 2601 May Rd., Richmond, 94803. Ages: 4.9-12 yr. Ph: (510) 222-6332.
WCC YM-Care Washington, 565 Wine St., Richmond, 94801. Ages: 4.9-12 yr. Ph: (510) 234-1358.
WCC YM-Care Wilson, 629-42nd St., Richmond, 94805. Ages: 4.9-12 yr. Ph: (510) 236-3699.
WCC YMCA CCCtr, 400 Lucas, Richmond, 94801. Ages: 0-17 yr. Ph: (510) 235-0271.
World of Children, 324-37th St., Richmond, 94804. Ages: 2-6 yr. Ph: (510) 237-6980.
YWCA Richmond Children's Ctr, 3230

MacDonald Ave., Richmond, 94804. Ages: 2 yr. & up. Ph: (510) 234-1270.

Rodeo

Bayo Vista Tiny Tots, 2 California St., Rodeo, 94572. Ages: 3-5 yr. Ph: (510) 799-4219.

Montessori Children's House, 734-3rd St., Rodeo, 94572. Ages: 2-6 ur. Ph: (510) 799-5233.

WCC YMCA Child Dev Ctr—Rodeo, 200 Lake Ave., Rodeo, 94572. Ages: 3-5 yr. Ph: (510) 799-3122.

San Pablo

ABC Christian Nursery, 2706-17th St., San Pablo, 94806. Ages: 2-6 yr. Ph: (510) 233-3792.

Child's Garden, 1860 Tyler St., San Pablo, 94806. Ages: 2-6.11 yr. Ph: (510) 232-5125.

Kinder Korner Nursery, 2984-19th St., San Pablo, 94806. Ages: 2.6-10 yr. Ph: (510) 232-4973.

Kindercare #1367, 3240 San Pablo Dam Rd., San Pablo, 94806. Ages: 0-12 yr. Ph: (510) 222-1144.

Roots & Wings Montessori Co-op, 2000 Southwood Dr., San Pablo, 94806. Ages: 2.9-6 yr. Ph: (510) 724-8858.

WCC YM-Care Bayview, 3001-16th St., San Pablo, 94806. Ages: 4.9-12 yr. Ph: (510) 237-8479.

San Ramon

Child Day School, 18868 Bollinger Canyon Rd., San Ramon, 94583. Ages: infant & up. Ph: (510) 820-2515.

Church of the Valley, 19001 San Ramon Valley Blvd., San Ramon, 94583. Ages: 2-5 yr. Ph: (510) 829-3368.

Diablo Hills Country, 2701 Hooper Dr., San Ramon, 94583. Ages: 2-11 yr. Ph: (510) 831-1210.

Happy Days, 20801 San Ramon Valley Blvd., San Ramon, 94583. Ages: 2.5-6 yr. Ph: (510) 828-8007.

Hobby Horse, 19801 San Ramon Valley Blvd., San Ramon, 94583. Ages: 2-6 yr. Ph: (510) 828-7605.

Joyful Noise, 19901 San Ramon Valley Blvd., San Ramon, 94583. Ages: 2.6-5 yr. Ph: (510) 828-8686.

Kids Country-Country Club, 7534 Blue Fox Way, San Ramon, 94583. Ages: 4.9-11 yr. Ph: (510) 829-4630.

Kids Country-Walt Disney, 3250 Pine Valley Rd., San Ramon, 94583. Ages: 5-12 yr. Ph: (510) 829-5221.

Kids Country—Bollinger Canyon, 2300 Talavera Dr., San Ramon, 94583. Ages: 5-12 yr. Ph: (510) 275-0574.

Kids Country—Montevideo, 13000 Broadmoor Dr., San Ramon, 94583. Ages: 4.9-11 yr. Ph: (510) 828-6717.

La Petite Academy, 1001 Market Pl., San Ramon, 94583. Ages: 1-12 yr. Ph: (510) 277-0626.

Stepping Stones, 2691 Crow Canyon Rd., San Ramon, 94583. Ages: 2-10 yr. Ph: (510) 820-8820.

Teddy Bears, 210 Porter Dr., San Ramon, 94583. Ages: 18 mo.-6 yr. Ph: (510) 838-4148.

Walnut Creek

A Child's World, 1985 Geary Rd., Walnut Creek, 94596. Ages: 2-5 yr. Ph: (510) 932-6660.

Alice's Montessori, 3158 Putnam Blvd., Walnut Creek, 9459. Ages: 2-6 yr. Ph: (510) 947-0603.

Bancroft DCCtr, 2200 Parish Dr., Walnut Creek, 94598. Ages: 4.5-12 yr. Ph: (510) 938-4063.

Bianchi School—Cherry Lane, 2850 Cherry Lane, Walnut Creek, 94596. Ages: 2-11 yr. Ph: (510) 943-6777.

Bianchi School—Walnut Creek, 2521 Walnut Blvd., Walnut Creek, 94596. Ages: 2-11 yr. Ph: (510) 935-3276.

Buena Vista School, 2355 San Juan Ave., Walnut Creek, 94596. Ages: 4.9-11 yr. Ph: (510) 934-0100.

Children's World, 2875 Mitchell Dr., Walnut Creek, 94598. Ages: 6 wk-13 yr. Ph: (510) 935-5562.

Church of Divine Man, 2965 1/2 North Main St., Walnut Creek, 94596. Ages: 2-12 yr. Ph: (510) 524-0436.

Concordia School, 1543 Sunnyvale Ave., Walnut Creek, 94596. Ages: 2-7 yr. Ph: (510) 689-6910.

Dorris-Eaton, 1847 Newell Ave., Walnut Creek, 94595. Ages: 2.9-5.9 yr. Ph: (510) 933-5225.

Evangelical Free Church PreSch, 2303 Ygnacio Valley Rd., Walnut Creek, 94598. Ages: 2.9-5 yr. Ph: (510) 934-1332.

First Baptist Preschool, 2336 Buena Vista Ave., Walnut Creek, 94596. Ages: 2-6 yr. Ph: (510) 935-1587.

Grace Co-Op, 2100 Tice Valley Blvd., Walnut Creek, 94595. Ages: 2-6 yr. Ph: (510) 935-2100.

His, Too, 2317 Buena Vista Ave., Walnut Creek, 94596. Ages: 2-6 yr. Ph: (510) 935-3360.

Indian Valley Kids Only Club, 551 Marshall

DAY CARE 171

Dr., Walnut Creek, 94598. Ages: 4.9-12 yr. Ph: (510) 943-7957.
Kid Time, 1547 Geary Rd., Walnut Creek, 94596. Ages: 2-6 yr. Ph: (510) 930-6550.
Morning Star PreSch, 2131 Olympic Blvd., Walnut Creek, 94596. Ages: NA. Ph: (510) 947-2952.
Mt. Diablo Unitarian, 55 Eckley Lane, Walnut Creek, 94598. Ages: 2-5.10 yr. Ph: (510) 932-6902.
Murwood PTA Keyspot—Parkmead, 1920 Magnolia Ave., Walnut Creek, 94595. Ages: 5-11 yr. Ph: (510) 932-8118.
My School, 535 Walnut Ave., Walnut Creek, 94598. Ages: 2.9-5 yr. Ph: (510) 947-1399.
Pied Piper, 2263 Whyte Park Ave., Walnut Creek, 94595. Ages: 2.6-5.9 yr. Ph: (510) 932-3816.
Saybrook, 1355 Walden Rd., Walnut Creek, 94596. Ages: 2-6 yr. Ph: (510) 937-8211.
Saybrook, 1919 Geary Rd., Walnut Creek, 94596. Ages: 2-10 yr. Ph: (510) 937-1478.
Seven Hills, 975 No. San Carlos Dr., Walnut Creek, 94598. Ages: 2-6 yr. Ph: (510) 933-0666.
St. Paul's Co-op, 1924 Trinity Ave., Walnut Creek, 94596. Ages: 2.9-5.9 yr. Ph: (510) 934-2324.
Valle Verde Children's Ctr, 3275 Peachwillow Lane, Walnut Creek, 94598. Ages: 5-12 yr. Ph: (510) 944-5255.
Walnut Acres DCCtr, 450 Wiget Lane, Walnut Creek, 94598. Ages: 4.9-12 yr. Ph: (510) 932-0507.
Walnut Avenue Church, 260 Walnut Ave., Walnut Creek, 94598. Ages: 2-6 yr. Ph: (510) 937-7063.
Walnut Creek Presbyterian Preschool, 1720 Oakland Blvd., Walnut Creek, 94596. Ages: 2.9-6 yr. Ph: (510) 935-1669.
Walnut Heights, 4064 Walnut Blvd., Walnut Creek, 94596. Ages: 4.9-12 yr. Ph: (510) 930-8458.
Woodlands Christian, 2721 Larkey Lane, Walnut Creek, 94596. Ages: 2.9-5.6 yr. Ph: (510) 945-6863.

West Pittsburg
Family Stress Ctr Headstart, 94A Medanos Ave., West Pittsburg, 94565. Ages: 2-5 yr. Ph: (510) 458-6442.
YWCA West Pittsburg CD Ctr, 225 Pacifica Ave., West Pittsburg, 94565. Ages: 2-12 yr. Ph: (510) 458-3787.

Solano County
Benicia
Benicia Child Dev. Unit, 2015 E. Third St., Benicia, 94510. Ages: 2-10 yr. Ph: (707) 745-8435.
Benicia State PreSch, , Benicia, 94510. Ages: 3-5 yr. Ph: (707) 745-8435.
Children's Palace, 525 Military East, Benicia, 94510. Ages: 2.5-5 yr. Ph: (707) 745-1220.
Happy Hearts, 135 Warwick Dr., Benicia, 94510. Ages: 2.6-5 yr. Ph: (707) 746-7053.
Kindercare, 1101 Rose Dr., Benicia, 94510. Ages: 1-12 yr. Ph: (707) 745-0916.
Little School, 602 West K St., Benicia, 94510. Ages: 2.9-6 yr. Ph: (707) 746-1407.
Mary Farmar PreSch, 901 East Military, Benicia, 94510. Ages: 3-5 yr. Ph: (707) 745-1771.
St. Dominic's PreSch, 428 East J St., Benicia, 94510. Ages: 2-6 yr. Ph: (707) 745-4430.

Davis
Bert & Ernie's Preschool, 1401 Cypress Lane, Davis, 95616. Ages: Call center. Ph: (916) 753-4563.
Birch Lane Child Dev. Center, 1700 Birch Lane, Davis, 95616. Ages: Call center. Ph: (916) 758-7251.
Child Development Center, 1207 Sycamore Lane, Davis, 95616. Ages: Call center. Ph: (916) 758-8342.
Davis Montessori School, 2907 Portage Bay Way, Davis, 95616. Ages: Call center. Ph: (916) 753-2030.
Davis Waldorf School, 2277 Road 96, Davis, 95616. Ages: Call center. Ph: (916) 753-1651.
Discovery Preschool & Child Care Center, 1020 F St., Davis, 95616. Ages: Call Center. Ph: (916) 756-2231.
Keane Kids Preschool, 1103 "F" Street, Davis, 95616. Ages: Call center. Ph: (916) 758-4178.
La Rue Park Children's House, 50 Atrium Way, Davis, 95616. Ages: Call center. Ph: (916) 753-8716.
Merryhill Country School, 222 LaVida Way, Davis, 95616. Ages: Call center. Ph: (916) 753-9210.
Montessori Country Day, 1811 Renoir Ave., Davis, 95616. Ages: Call center. Ph: (916) 753-8373.
Pioneer School Age Child Development Center, 5215 Hamel, Davis, 95616. Ages: Call center. Ph: (916) 758-0611.
Redbud Montessori, P.O. Box 1562, Davis, 95617. Ages: Call center. Ph: (916) 753-2623.
Russell Park Child Development Center, 400 Russell Park, Davis, 95616. Ages: Call

172 CONTRA COSTA & SOLANO

center. Ph: (916) 753-2487.
Tender Learning Care, 1009 "L" Street, Davis, 95616. Ages: Call center. Ph: (916) 757-2179.
Tender Learning Care, 1818 Lake Blvd., Davis, 95616. Ages: Call center. Ph: (916) 756-5351.
University Inn Child Care, 340 "A" Street, Davis, 95616. Ages: Call center. Ph: (916) 756-8648.
Valley Oaks School Age Child Development Center, 1450 E. 8th St., Davis, 95616. Ages: Call center. Ph: (916) 753-9223.
West Davis School Age Child Development Center, 1221 Anderson Rd., Davis, 95616. Ages: Call. Ph: (916) 753-3808.

Dixon
Anderson CD Ctr, 415 East C St., Dixon, 95620. Ages: 5-12 yr. Ph: (916) 678-9746.
Dixon Comm. Nursery, 955 East A St., Dixon, 95620. Ages: 2.9-6 yr. Ph: (916) 678-9347.
Dixon Migrant Infant Ctr, 7290 Radio Station Rd., Dixon, 95620. Ages: 0-6 yr. Ph: (916) 678-2113.
Head Start—Dixon, 340 West B St., Dixon, 95620. Ages: 3-5 yr. Ph: (916) 678-2320.
Silveyville CD Ctr, 355 North Almond, Dixon, 95620. Ages: 5-12 yr. Ph: (707) 678-9094.
Warm Fuzzies, 390 East C St., Dixon, 95620. Ages: 2.5-6 yr. Ph: (916) 678-9135.

Fairfield
Fairfield Montessori, 1101 Utah St., Fairfield, 94533. Ages: 2-5 yr. Ph: (707) 427-1442.
Fairfield Parent PreSch, 984 Nightingale Dr., Fairfield, 94533. Ages: 2.9-5 yr. Ph: (707) 425-6777.
Kidderville Nursery, 1657 Kidder Ave., Fairfield, 94533. Ages: 2-5 yr. Ph: (707) 425-8700.
Kindercare, 1611 Wood Creek, Fairfield, 94533. Ages: 6 wk-12 yr. Ph: (707) 426-2275.
Noah's Ark, 1004 Utah St., Fairfield, 94533. Ages: 2-10 yr. Ph: (707) 427-0210.
Solano Christian Academy, 2200 Fairfield, Fairfield, 94533. Ages: 2.9-5 yr. Ph: (707) 422-4788.
St. Mark's Lutheran, 1600 Union Ave., Fairfield, 94533. Ages: 2.9-6 yr. Ph: (707) 422-4742.
Trinity Lutheran, 2075 Dover Ave., Fairfield, 94533. Ages: 2.9-6 yr. Ph: (707) 425-2905.

Mare Island
Mare Island Civilian CCCtr, Bldg. 533 Corner of Walnut & C, Mare Island, 94592. Ages: 2-10 yr. Ph: (707) 557-1708.

Rio Vista
We Care PreSch, 230 Sacramento St., Rio Vista, 94571. Ages: 2-6 yr. Ph: (707) 374-2033.

Suisun
Children's World, 3045 Rockville Rd., Suisun, 94585. Ages: 2-12 yr. Ph: (707) 425-0518.
Children's World, 40 Buena Vista, Suisun, 94585. Ages: 0-12 yr. Ph: (707) 425-1817.
Crescent State PreSch, 400 Mulberry St., Suisun, 94585. Ages: 3-6 yr. Ph: (707) 421-4134.

Vacaville
Bethany Lutheran, 621 So. Orchard, Vacaville, 95688. Ages: 2-6 yr. Ph: (707) 451-6675.
Children's World Learning Ctr, 3561 Alamo Dr., Vacaville, 95687. Ages: 2-12 yr. Ph: (707) 446-6600.
Head Start—Vacaville #1, 120 West St., Vacaville, 95688. Ages: 3-5 yr. Ph: (707) 451-6124.
Head Start—Vacaville #2, 66 Vine St., Vacaville, 95688. Ages: 3-5 yr. Ph: (707) 451-6125.
Kids Klub—Kids R Us, 1600 California Dr., Vacaville, 95688. Ages: 2.5-5 yr. Ph: (707) 449-6539.
Kindercare, 581 Peabody Rd., Vacaville, 95688. Ages: 0-12 yr. Ph: (707) 447-7685.
La Petite Academy, 2501 Nut Tree Rd., Vacaville, 95687. Ages: 2-12 yr. Ph: (707) 447-5252.
Mothers' Day Out, 425 Hemlock, Vacaville, 95688. Ages: 2-4 yr., infants also. Ph: (707) 448-5055.
Noah's Ark, 100 Paden Rd., Vacaville, 95688. Ages: 2-6 yr. Ph: (707) 427-0210.
Orchard Ave. Baptist, 301 N. Orchard Ave., Vacaville, 95688. Ages: 2-6 yr. Ph: (707) 448-5848.
Presbyterian Enrichment PreSch, 425 Hemlock, Vacaville, 95688. Ages: 2.6-6 yr. Ph: (707) 448-1626.
Shepherd of the Hills Lutheran, 580 Trinity Dr., Vacaville, 95687. Ages: 2.9-6 yr. Ph: (707) 448-8599.
Vaca Valley PreSch, 1018 Callen St., Vacaville, 95688. Ages: 2-12 yr. Ph: (707) 448-2674.
Vacaville Christian Academy, 1117 Davis St., Vacaville, 95687. Ages: 6 wk-6 yr. Ph: (707) 446-1776.

Vallejo
Ark Vista—Everest, 425 Corcoran, Vallejo,

DAY CARE

94589. Ages: 2.9-6.7 yr. Ph: (707) 643-2156.
Beverly Hills CDCtr, 1450 Coronel Ave., Vallejo, 94590. Ages: 2.9-12 yr. Ph: (707) 554-8140.
Caring Ctr, 2025 Sonoma Blvd., Vallejo, 94590. Ages: 2-12 yr. Ph: (707) 644-4087.
Castlewood Christian, 3615 Georgia St., Vallejo, 94591. Ages: 2.9-10 yr. Ph: (707) 642-6328.
Federal Terrace, 415 Daniel Ave., Vallejo, 94590. Ages: 2.9-6 yr. Ph: (707) 643-7161.
Grant CD Ctr, 740 Fifth St., Vallejo, 94590. Ages: 2-14 yr. Ph: (707) 648-0043.
Head Start—Vallejo, 1328 Virginia St., Vallejo, 94590. Ages: 3-5 yr. Ph: (707) 645-7845 or 645-7844.
Highland CD Ctr, 1309 Ensign, Vallejo, 94590. Ages: 2.9-6 yr. Ph: (707) 643-4429.
Kiddie Academy, 50 Mariposa St., Vallejo, 94590. Ages: 6 wk-12 yr. Ph: (707) 557-2443.
Kindercare, 35 Rotary Way, Vallejo, 94591. Ages: 0-12 yr. Ph: (707) 557-3007.
La Petite Academy, 470 Avian Dr., Vallejo, 94591. Ages: 2-12 yr. Ph: (707) 642-7500.
New Horizons II, 900 Fairgrounds Dr., Vallejo, 94590. Ages: 0-12 yr. Ph: (707) 644-5066.
New Horizons II, 900 Fairgrounds Drive, Vallejo, 94589. Ages: 0-12. Ph: (707) 644-5066.
Noah's Ark Christian Sch, 2 Andrew Rd., Vallejo, 94589. Ages: 2.5-12 yr. Ph: (707) 644-6465.
North Hills Christian, 200 Admiral Callaghan Lane, Vallejo, 94591. Ages: 2.9-5.9 yr. Ph: (707) 644-5284.
Nurtury—First Presbyterian Church, 1350 Amador St., Vallejo, 94590. Ages: 2-6 yr. Ph: (707) 644-0477.
Reignierd Schools, 2417 Springs Rd., Vallejo, 94591. Ages: 2-5 yr. Ph: (707) 644-1011.
Shining Star Children's House, 707 Heartwood, Vallejo, 94591. Ages: 2.9-6 yr. Ph: (707) 642-5555.
Sonshine Morning PreSch, 210 Locust Dr., Vallejo, 94590. Ages: 2-6 yr. Ph: (707) 643-1077.
St. Basil's PreSch, 1225 Tuolumne St., Vallejo, 94590. Ages: 2.9-5 yr. Ph: (707) 642-5966.
St. Vincent Ferrer PreSch & DC, 400 Florida St., Vallejo, 94590. Ages: 2-6 yr. Ph: (707) 552-6066.
Vallejo Parent Nursery, 500 Amador St., Vallejo, 94590. Ages: 2.6-6 yr. Ph: (707) 644-7576.
Williams PreSch, 15 Poco Way, Vallejo, 94590. Ages: 2.5-5 yr. Ph: (707) 644-7588.
YMCA Gym for Children, 709 Heartwood, Vallejo, 94590. Ages: 2.5-5 yr. Ph: (707) 643-0136.
YMCA—Padan, 1895 Broadway, Vallejo, 94589. Ages: 4.9-12 yr. Ph: (707) 643-0136.

10/Hospitals & Health Services

Insurance Q & A, Directory of Hospitals

GOOD HEALTH CARE. You want it. Where, how do you get it? This chapter will give you an overview of Northern California health care and, although it won't answer all your questions — too complex a business for that — we hope that it will point you in the right directions.

For most people, health care is twined with insurance, in systems that are called "managed care." But many individuals, for a variety of reasons, do not have insurance.

This is a good place to start: with nothing, all options open. Let's use as our seeker for the best of all health care worlds — on a tight budget — a young woman, married, one child. Her choices:

No Insurance—Cash Care

The woman is self-employed or works at a small business that doesn't offer health benefits.

She comes down with the flu. When she goes into the doctor's office, she will be asked by the receptionist, how do you intend to pay? With no insurance, she pays cash (or credit card), usually right there.

She takes her prescription, goes to the pharmacy and pays full cost.

If her child or husband get sick and needs to see a doctor, the same procedure holds. Also the same for treatment of a serious illness, to secure X-rays or hospitalization. It's a cash system.

Medi-Cal

If an illness strikes that impoverishes the family or if the woman, through job loss or simply low wages, cannot afford cash care, the county-state health

Doctors Hospital

Our Commitment To Quality Health Care

Full Service Medical / Surgical Adult Care Center

- 24 Hour Emergency
- Same Day Surgery
- Cardiac Care
- Physical Therapy
- Education/Support Groups
- Nutrition Counseling

Physician Referral Service	223-1011
Senior Status	724-5040
Laser Center	724-7201
Nose & Sinus Center	724-4418
Prostate Treatment Center	1-800-734-7314
Sleep Disorder Center	1-800-640-9440
Lifeline: Emergency Response System	741-2479
TelMed Health Info Tapes	724-5520
Alcohol & Drug Rehabilitation	724-1520

Doctors Hospital
2151 Appian Way
Pinole, CA 94564-2578
(510) 724-5000

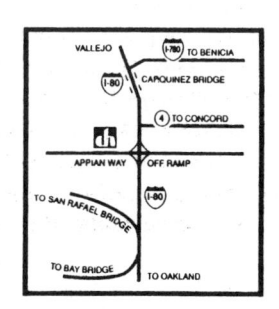

A National Medical Enterprise Health Care Center

Top 25 Baby Names

Contra Costa

Boys	Girls
Michael (217)	Jessica (125)
Matthew (153)	Ashley (105)
Christopher (136)	Amanda (90)
Daniel (119)	Samantha (86)
Nicholas (114)	Jennifer (84)
Andrew (111)	Sarah (81)
Joseph (102)	Nicole (77)
Anthony (95)	Brittany (76)
Ryan (94)	Stephanie (76)
Kyle (93)	Rachel (67)
James (92)	Emily (63)
Robert (89)	Elizabeth (57)
Kevin (88)	Lauren (52)
Brandon (84)	Megan (52)
Joshua (80)	Katherine (50)
Tyler (80)	Danielle (48)
Justin (77)	Kayla (46)
William (77)	Alexandra (44)
Alexander (76)	Michelle (44)
David (75)	Shelby (44)
Eric (72)	Rebecca (43)
John (66)	Melissa (42)
Jonathan (65)	Christina (41)
Jordan (65)	Chelsea (39)
Jacob (64)	Taylor (38)

Solano

Boys	Girls
Michael (107)	Jessica (85)
Christopher (73)	Ashley (49)
Joshua (58)	Samantha (49)
Joseph (57)	Brittany (44)
Matthew (57)	Sarah (39)
Andrew (56)	Jennifer (37)
Anthony (54)	Nicole (33)
Nicholas (54)	Chelsea (30)
Brandon (52)	Danielle (30)
Daniel (51)	Kayla (30)
Jacob (48)	Amber (28)
James (45)	Alyssa (27)
Robert (45)	Elizabeth (27)
Ryan (44)	Megan (27)
Justin (43)	Amanda (26)
David (41)	Lauren (25)
Alexander (36)	Stephanie (24)
Tyler (36)	Emily (23)
Kevin (35)	Courtney (22)
Kyle (32)	Jasmine (21)
William (31)	Mariah (21)
Cody (30)	Melissa (20)
Aaron (29)	Michelle (20)
John (29)	Rachel (20)
Jonathan (29)	Katherine (19)

Source: California Department of Health Services, 1991 birth records. Shown in parentheses is the number of children with the given name.

system will step in. The woman fills out papers to qualify for Medi-Cal, the name of the system (it's known elsewhere as Medicaid), and tries to find a doctor that will treat Medi-Cal patients. Many don't; they say that the paperwork is burdensome and the reimbursement low.

If unable to find an acceptable doctor, the woman could turn to a county hospital or clinic. There she will be treated free or at very low cost.

Drawbacks-Pluses of Medi-Cal

County hospitals and clinics, in the personal experience of one of the editors — who has relatives who work at or use county facilities — have competent doctors and medical personnel. If you keep appointments sharply, often you will be seen with little wait.

If you want immediate treatment for, say, a cold, you register and you wait

HOSPITALS & HEALTH SERVICES 177

How to see a doctor without seeing a bill.

A lot of health plans (perhaps yours) cover only 80% of a doctor's bill. Some even less. And only after you've paid the first $100 or a lot more.

With Kaiser Permanente, one low monthly payment covers virtually all your health care. Including well-baby care, lab tests, x-rays, and much more.

For more information, visit your personnel office or give us a call. In Contra Costa, (510) 946-3485. In Solano, (707) 648-6625.

For over 45 years, we've seen to the health care needs of a lot of people. But without them having to see a lot of doctor bills.

KAISER PERMANENTE
Good People. Good Medicine.

Medical centers in Martinez, Richmond, Vallejo, and Walnut Creek. Medical offices in Antioch and Fairfield. Additional facilities located in 24 other Northern California communities.
© 1991 Kaiser Permanente

Population by Age Groups in Contra Costa County

City or Area	≤5	5-18	19-29	30-54	55+
Alamo	691	2,404	1,074	5,426	2,496
Antioch	6,077	13,110	10,791	22,950	8,455
Bayview-Montalvin	299	965	629	1,502	529
Bethel Island	68	183	238	774	839
Blackhawk	400	1,348	460	3,204	704
Brentwood	751	1,681	1,281	2,578	1,160
Clayton	435	1,723	675	3,313	1,047
Concord	8,569	18,839	21,059	42,202	19,283
Crockett	225	400	482	1,307	795
Danville	1,979	6,168	3,246	14,015	5,496
Discovery Bay	336	789	641	2,546	994
E. Richmond Hts.	201	489	382	1,447	723
El Cerrito	1,191	2,485	3,384	8,340	5,942
El Sobrante	722	1,566	1,533	3,807	2,131
Hercules	1,433	3,631	2,398	7,545	6,630
Kensington	246	556	435	1,981	1,734
Lafayette	1,339	3,967	2,622	9,669	5,612
Martinez	2,238	5,034	5,315	13,605	5,248
Moraga	773	2,589	2,504	5,769	3,918
Oakley	2,019	4,065	3,119	6,948	2,043
Orinda	988	2,704	1,257	6,688	4,841
Pacheco	179	350	537	1,208	1,022
Pinole	1,203	3,171	2,525	6,946	3,420
Pittsburg	4,848	9,952	9,254	16,368	6,475
Pleasant Hill	2,156	4,366	5,437	12,966	6,352
Richmond	7,606	15,499	15,475	31,056	16,600
Rodeo	608	1,615	1,166	2,770	1,347
San Pablo	2,514	5,115	4,946	7,998	4,276
San Ramon	2,526	6,927	5,758	16,291	3,347
Tara Hills	358	821	916	1,911	926
Vine Hill	246	654	562	1,231	477
Walnut Creek	2,629	7,314	8,666	21,385	20,002
West Pittsburg	1,882	3,566	3,447	5,949	2,398
Remainder	3,008	7,299	7,388	17,863	9,131
County Total	60,743	141,345	129,602	309,558	152,727

Source: 1990 Census.

until an urgent-care doctor is free.

If you need a specialist, often the county facility will have one on staff, or will be able to find one at a teaching hospital or other facility. You don't choose the specialist; the county physician does.

The height of health care in Contra Costa

- **Northern California Heart and Lung Institute**—The Number One provider of heart care services in the East Bay with a complete program for the diagnosis and treatment of heart disease. Call **674-2590**.

- **Health and Fitness Institute**—A major new facility whose Centers integrate Occupational Health, Sports Medicine, Corporate Health, and Nutrition and Weight Management. Call **685-7744**.

- **Regional Cancer Center**—A new facility merges medical and radiation oncology in one place. Specialists in many fields apply the latest equipment, technology and treatment in the prevention and care of all types of cancer. Call **674-2190**.

- **Behavioral Medicine Services**—Offers a comprehensive array of services for the effective, caring treatment of psychiatric problems, alcohol and drug dependency and eating disorders in a compassionate environment for healing. Free, confidential evaluation. 24 hour availability. Call **680-6500**.

- **Family Birthplace**—The "Family Birthplace" offers a variety of educational programs and delivery choices with pre-natal and delivery care by an expert staff of physicians and nurses. Call **674-2075**.

MT. DIABLO MEDICAL CENTER

2540 East St., Concord

OPERATED BY THE MT. DIABLO HOSPITAL DISTRICT

County facilities are underfunded and, often, inconveniently located — a major drawback. Some counties, lacking clinics and hospitals, contract with adjoining counties that are equipped. You have to drive some distance for treatment. The paperwork can be demanding.

County hospitals and clinics are not 100 percent free. If you have money or an adequate income, you will be billed for service. Some county hospitals run medical plans designed for people who can pay. These people can ask for a "family" doctor and receive a higher (usually more convenient) level of care.

Let's say the woman lacks money but doesn't want to hassle with a long drive and, possibly, a long wait for treatment of a minor ailment. She can sign up for Medi-Cal to cover treatment of serious illnesses, and for the colds, etc., go to a private doctor for treatment, and pay in cash, ignoring Medi-Cal.

There are many ways to skin the cat, and much depends on circumstances. For the poor and low-income, Medi-Cal is meant to be a system of last resort.

Medicare— Veterans Hospital

If our woman were elderly, she would be eligible for Medicare, the federal insurance system, which covers 80 percent, with limitations, of medical costs or allowable charges. Many people purchase supplemental insurance to bring coverage up to 100 percent (long-term illnesses requiring hospitalization may exhaust some benefits.)

If the woman were a military veteran with a service-related illness, she could seek care at a Veteran's Administration clinic or hospital.

Managed Care

This divides into two systems, Preferred Provider Organizations (PPO) and Health Maintenance Organizations (HMO). Both are popular in California and, if your employer provides health insurance, chances are almost 100 percent you will be pointed toward, or given a choice of, one or the other.

PPOs and HMOs differ among themselves. It is beyond the scope of this book to detail the differences but you should ask if coverage can be revoked or rates increased in the event of serious illness. Also, what is covered, what is not. Cosmetic surgery might not be covered. Psychiatric visits or care might be limited. Ask also how emergency or immediate care is provided.

Preferred Provider

The insurance company approaches certain doctors, clinics, medical facilities and hospitals and tells them: we will send patients to you but you must agree to our prices — a method of controlling costs — and our rules. The young woman chooses her doctor from the list, often extensive, provided by the PPO.

The physician will have practicing privileges at certain local hospitals. The young woman's child contracts pneumonia and must be hospitalized. Dr. X is affiliated with XYZ hospital, which is also signed up with the PPO plan. The

BROOKSIDE HOSPITAL

2000 VALE ROAD
SAN PABLO, CA 94806

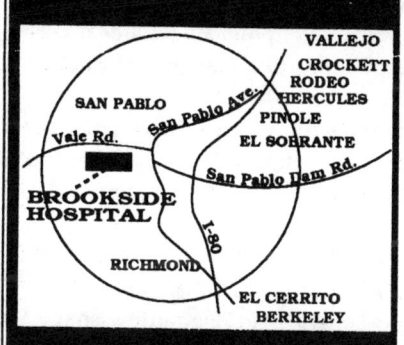

WEST COUNTY'S FIRST, LARGEST & MOST COMPREHENSIVE FULL-SERVICE HOSPITAL.

- Full Range of Hospital Care
- Regional Cancer Center
- Comprehensive Cardiac Care
- Burn & Wound Center
- Breast Care Center
- Skilled nursing facility
- Home health care
- Maternity & Women's Care
- **Free** Physician Referral
- Speakers Bureau & Health Information
- V.I.P. ADVANTAGE –Senior Membership Service
- 24-hour Emergency Services

235-7000

IN CASE OF EMERGENCY CALL 911

EMERGENCY DEPARTMENT
235-3637

THE WEST CONTRA COSTA
COMMUNITY
HEALTH RESOURCE

TTY HEARING IMPAIRED
236-8357

child is treated at XYZ hospital. If the woman used an "outside" doctor or hospital, she would pay extra—the amount depending on the nature of the plan. It is important to know the doctor's affiliations because you may want your hospital care at a certain institution.

Hospitals differ. A children's hospital, for instance, will specialize in children's illnesses and load up on children's medical equipment. A general hospital will have a more rounded program. For convenience, you may want the hospital closest to your home.

If you need specialized treatment, you must, to avoid extra costs, use the PPO-affiliated specialists. The doctor will often guide your choice.

Besides the basic cost for the policy, PPO insurance might charge fees, co-payments or deductibles. A fee might be $5 or $10 a visit. With co-payments, the bill, say, comes to $100. Insurance pays $80, the woman pays $20.

Deductible example: the woman pays the first $250 or the first $2,000 of any medical costs within a year, and the insurer pays bills above $250 or $2,000. The higher the deductible, usually the lower the cost of the policy. The $2,000 deductible is really a form of catastrophic insurance.

Conversely, the higher the premium the more the policy covers. Some policies cover everything (Dental care is usually provided through a separate insurer.) The same for prescription medicines. You may pay for all, part, or nothing, depending on the type plan.

The PPO doctor functions as your personal physician. Often the doctor will have his or her own practice and office, conveniently located. If you need to squeeze in an appointment, the doctor usually will try to be accommodating.

Drawback: PPOs restrict choice.

Health Maintenance Organization (HMO)

The insurance company and medical provider are one and the same. All or almost all medical care is given by the HMO. The woman catches the flu. She sees the HMO doctor at the HMO clinic or hospital. If she becomes pregnant, she sees an HMO obstetrician at the HMO hospital or clinic and delivers her baby there. With HMOs you pay the complete bill if you go outside the system (with obvious exceptions; e.g., emergency care).

HMO's, encourage you to pick a personal physician. The young woman wants a woman doctor; she picks one from the staff. She wants a pediatrician as her child's personal doctor; the HMO, usually, can provide one.

HMO clinics and hospitals bring many specialists and services together under one roof. You can get your eyes examined, your hearing tested, your prescriptions filled, your X-rays taken within an HMO facility (this varies), and much more.

If you need an operation or treatment beyond the capacity of your immediate HMO hospital, the surgery will be done at another HMO hospital within the system.

HOSPITALS & HEALTH SERVICES 183

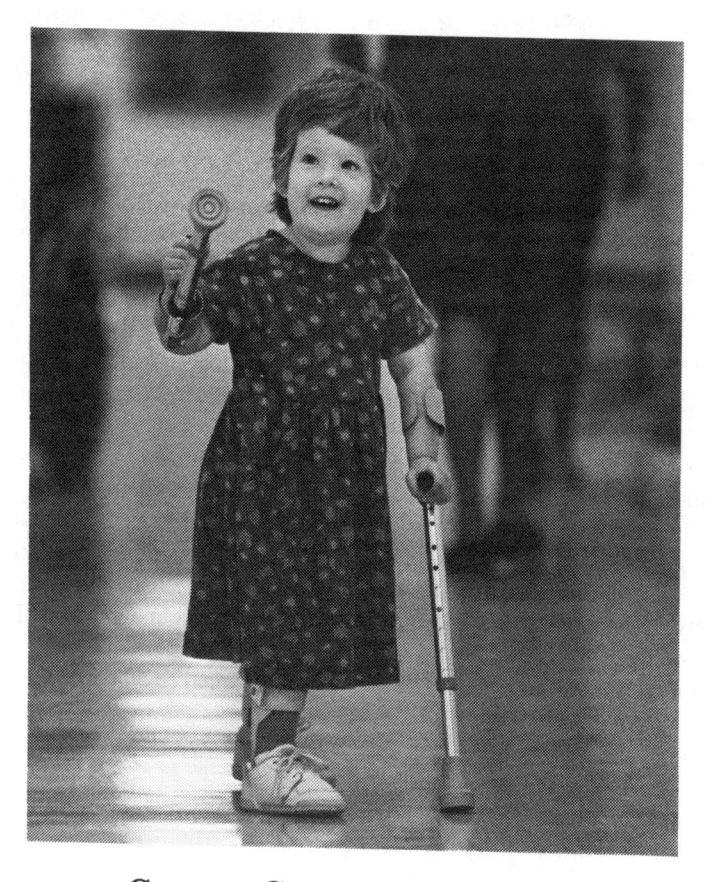

Contra Costa and Solano, we're your children's hospital.

Because we're the only children's hospital for miles around, children come to us from as far away as Hawaii and as close as Contra Costa. And we offer satellite subspecialty services in your area: Walnut Creek and Fairfield. Ask your pediatrician for a referral or call us at 1-800-833-4401.

Children's Hospital Oakland

The pediatric medical center for Northern California

HMO payment plans vary but many HMO clients pay a monthly fee and a small ($5-$15) per visit fee. Often the plan includes low-cost or reduced-cost or free prescriptions.

Drawback: Freedom of choice limited. If HMO facility is not close, the woman will have to drive to another town.

Which is Better: a PPO or an HMO?

This is a competitive field with many claims and counter claims. In recent years, PPOs have signed up many doctors and facilities — increasing the choices of members.

Kaiser Permanente, an HMO, however, remains very popular and enrolls about one out of every three Northern Californians.

If you are receiving medical insurance through your employer, you will be limited to the choices offered. In large groups, unions often have a say in what providers are chosen.

Some individuals will make their choice on price, some on convenience of facilities, others on what's covered, and so on.

Many private hospitals offer Physician Referral Services. You call the hospital, ask for the service and get a list of doctors to choose from. The doctors will be affiliated with the hospital providing the referral. Hospitals and doctors will also tell you what insurance plans they accept for payment, and will send you brochures describing the services the hospital offers.

For Kaiser and other HMOs, call the local hospital or clinic.

A PPO will give you a list of its member doctors and facilities.

Ask plenty of questions. Shop carefully.

Common Questions

The young woman is injured in a car accident and is unconscious. Where will she be taken?

Generally, she will be taken to the closest emergency room or trauma center, where her condition will be stabilized. Her doctor will then have her admitted into a hospital. Or she will be transferred to her HMO hospital or, if indigent, to a county facility.

If her injuries are severe, she most likely will be rushed to a regional trauma center. Trauma centers have specialists and special equipment to treat serious injuries.

Both PPOs and HMOs offer urgent care and emergency care.

The young woman breaks her leg. Her personal doctor is an internist and does not set fractures. What happens?

The personal doctor refers the case to a specialist. Insurance pays the specialist's fee.

In PPO, the woman would generally see a specialist affiliated with the PPO. In an HMO, the specialist would be employed by the HMO.

The Critical Difference In Our Community.

- 24-Hour Physician Staffed
  Emergency Department & Trauma Center

- Complete and Comprehensive
  Medical and Health Care Services

- An Entire Floor Devoted to Maternity
  and Women's Services • **889-5045**

- Eden Heart Institute • **889-5087**
  - Cardiac Catheterization
  - Cardiac Rehabilitation
  - Chest Pain Emergency Service

- Cancer Information • **727-2792**

- Geriatric Services • **727-2719**
  (including transportation and senior housing)

- Adult & Older Adult
  Psychiatric Services • **889-5072**

- Laurel Grove
  Acute Rehabilitation • **727-2755**

EDEN HOSPITAL MEDICAL CENTER
20103 Lake Chabot Road • Castro Valley, CA 94546
(510) 537-1234

Convenient to all of Southern Alameda and Contra Costa counties

Population by Age Groups in Solano County

City or Area	≤5	5-18	19-29	30-54	55+
Benicia	1,926	4,727	3,171	10,603	3,736
Davis*	564	1,354	1,191	1,420	448
Dixon	929	2,334	1,693	3,822	1,496
Fairfield	7,426	15,887	16,142	26,492	10,235
Rio Vista	252	576	442	1,063	942
Suisun City	2,454	5,960	3,788	8,433	1,739
Vacaville	5,791	13,298	14,576	27,925	9,041
Vallejo	9,393	21,171	19,731	38,115	19,304
Remainder	1,572	4,144	3,079	8,651	3,948
County Total	29,743	68,097	62,622	125,104	50,441

Source: 1990 Census. *Yolo County city.

The young woman signs up for an HMO then contracts a rare disease or suffers an injury that requires treatment beyond the capability of the HMO. Will she be treated?

Often yes, but it pays to read the fine print. The HMO will contract treatment out to a facility that specializes in the needed treatment.

The young woman becomes despondent and takes to drink. Will insurance pay for her rehabilitation?

Depends on her insurance. And often her employer. Some may have drug and alcohol rehab plans. Some plans cover psychiatry.

The woman becomes pregnant. Her doctor, who has delivered many babies, wants her to deliver at X Hospital. All the woman's friends say, Y Hospital is much better, nicer, etc. The doctor is not cleared to practice at Y Hospital. Is the woman out of luck?

With a PPO, the woman must deliver at a hospital affiliated with the PPO — or pay the extra cost. If her doctor is not affiliated with that hospital, sometimes a doctor may be given courtesy practicing privileges at a hospital where he or she does not have staff membership. Check with the doctor.

With HMOs, the woman must deliver within the HMO system.

The young woman goes in for minor surgery, which turns into major surgery when the doctor forgets to remove a sponge before sewing up. Upon reviving, she does what?

The obvious answer is that she reaches for the phone and calls the nastiest lawyer in the county. But these days nothing is obvious. Some medical plans require clients to submit complaints to a panel of arbitrators, which decides damages, if any. Read the policy.

The woman's child reaches age 18. Is she covered by the family insurance?

All depends on the insurance. Some policies will cover the children while

Our valley, our home.

QUEEN OF THE VALLEY HOSPITAL
NAPA VALLEY MEDICAL CENTER
(707) 252-4411

A Sisters of St. Joseph of Orange Corporation

they attend college (But attendance may be defined in a certain way, full-time as opposed to part-time.) To protect your coverage, you should read the plan thoroughly.

At work, the woman gets her hand caught in a revolving door and is told she will need six months of therapy during which she can't work. Who pays?

Insurance will usually pay for the medical costs. Workers' Compensation, a state plan that includes many but not all people, may compensate the woman for time lost off the job and may pay for medical costs. If you injure yourself on the job, your employer must file a report with Workers' Comp.

The woman wins a vacation to Switzerland where she falls off an alp, breaks a leg, and spends three days in a Swiss hospital. Her HMO or PPO is 7,000 miles away. Who pays?

Usually the insurance company, but it is wise to check out how to obtain medical services before going on vacation. The woman may have to pay out-of-pocket and then file for reimbursement on her return home.

While working in her kitchen, the woman slips, bangs her head against the stove, gets a nasty cut and becomes woozy. She should:

Call 9-1-1, which will send an ambulance. 9-1-1 is managed by police dispatch. It's the fastest way to get an ambulance. Many insurance policies cover ambulance services. Ask.

What's the difference between a hospital, a clinic, an urgent-care center and a doctor's office?

The hospital has the most services and equipment. The center or clinic has several services and a fair amount of equipment. The office, usually, has the fewest services and the smallest amount of equipment.

Hospitals have beds. If a person must have a serious operation, she goes to a hospital. Hospitals have coronary-care and intensive-care units, emergency care and other specialized, costly treatment units. But many hospitals also run clinics for minor ailments and provide the same services as the medical centers.

Urgent-care or medical centers are sometimes located in neighborhoods, which makes them more convenient for some people. The doctors treat the minor, and often not-so-minor, ailments of patients and send them to hospitals for major surgery and serious sicknesses.

Some doctors form themselves into groups to offer the public a variety of services. Some hospitals have opened neighborhood clinics or centers to attract patients. Kaiser has hospitals in some towns, and clinic-offices in other towns.

The doctor in his or her office treats patients for minor ailments and uses the hospital for surgeries, major illnesses. Many illnesses that required hospitalization years ago are now treated in the office or clinic.

Some hospitals offer programs outside the typical doctor-patient relationships. For example, wellness plans — advice on how to stay healthy or control stress or quit smoking.

HOSPITALS & HEALTH SERVICES 189

Major Hospitals & Medical Offices in or near Contra Costa County

Alta Bates Medical Center: Ashby Campus, 2450 Ashby Ave., Berkeley, 94705. Herrick Campus, 2001 Dwight Way, Berkeley, 94704. Ph. (510) 204-4444. ICU, CCU, OB-GYN, Birth Center, Neonatal Intensive Care, Women's Center, Mental Hewalth Center, Rehabilitation Center, Heart & Vascular Center, Comprehensive Cancer Center, Burn Center, Skilled Nursing, Home Health Care, Orthopedics, Neurosciences, Emergency Services, Chest Pain Emergency Center, Respiratory Services, Surgery & surgical subspecialties, Health Education & Support Groups. 24-hour Healthcare Hotline and Physician Referral: (800) 322-1322. 543 beds.

Brookside Hospital, 2000 Vale Road, San Pablo, 94806. Ph. (510) 235-7000. Emergency Care, Acute Medical/Surgical Care, ICU, CCU, OB-GYN, Outpatient Surgery, Regional Cancer Center, Comprehensive Coronary Care, Burn & Wound Centers with hyperbaric medicine, Pulmonary Medicine, Skilled Nursing, Home Health Care, Breast Care Center, Physical Therapy & Rehab, Nutrition Services, Pharmacy, Health Education, Physician Referral. 326 beds.

Delta Memorial Hospital, 3901 Lone Tree Way, Antioch, 94509. Ph. (510) 779-7200. ICU, CCU, Medical/Surgical, Medical telemetry, Women's Health Center, Family Birth Center, Outpatient Surgery, 24-hour Emergency Services, Urgent Care, Physician Referral, Physical Therapy, Sports Medicine, Pediatrics, Home Health Care, Medical Imaging, Occupational Health, Pulmonary- Cardiac Rehab., Industrial Medicine. 111 bed non-profit health care center.

Doctors Hospital, 2151 Appian Way, Pinole, 94564. Ph. (510) 724-5000. Center for Advanced Surgeries, Cholesterol Treatment Center, Family Foot Center, ICU, CCU, GYN, Emergency Care, Physicians Referral, Physical Therapy, Chemical Dependency, Alcohol Treatment, Radiology, Geriatric Services. Pulmonary-Cardiac Rehab., Sleep Disorder Center, Prostate Treatment Center, Nuclear Medicine, Outpatient Surgery. 137 beds.

Eden Hospital Medical Center, 20103 Lake Chabot Road, Castro Valley, 94546. Ph. (510) 537-1234. ICU, CCU, OB-GYN, Regional Trauma Center, Emergency Services, Urgent Care Center, Physical Medicine & Rehab., Home Health Care, Geriatric Services, Community Cancer Center, Women's Center, Psychiatric, Physical Therapy, Radiology, Pediatric Services, Eating Disorders, Occupational Therapy/Worker Rehabilitation, Acute Rehabilitation, Eye-Care Center, Senior Housing & Transportation. 324 beds.

Health and Fitness Institute, 2231 Galaxy Ct., Concord, 94520. Ph. (510) 685-7744. Center for Occupational Health, Center for Sports Medicine, Center for Corporate Health and Wellness, Center for Nutrition and Weight Management, and Center for Rehabilitation Therapies, Weekly Sports Injury Clinics, 24-hour Sports Injury Hotline.

John Muir Medical Center, 1601 Ygnacio Valley Rd., Walnut Creek, 94598. Ph. (510) 939-3000. Physician Referral, Neuroscience ICU, Medical/Surgical ICU, CCU, Birth Center, OB-GYN, Trauma Center, 24-hour Emergency Services, Physical Medicine and Rehabilitation, Orthopedics, Diabetes Center, Breast Center, Cancer Treatment Center, Cardiac Services, Senior Services and Information, Home Health Services, Full range-Outpatient Services. 347 beds.

Kaiser Permanente Medical Center, 1425 South Main St., Walnut Creek, 94596. Ph. (510) 295-4000. OB, GYN, Emergency Services, Alcohol and Drug Abuse Program, Optometry, Internal Medicine, Neurology, Pediatrics, Podiatry, Surgery, other typical hospital services. 201 Beds.

Kaiser Permanente Medical Center, 200 Muir Road, Martinez, 94553. Ph. (510) 372-1000. Emergency Care, Hospice, Internal Medicine, Pediatrics, Psychiatric Center, Surgery, other hospital services. 150 Beds.

Kaiser Permanente Medical Center, 1330 Cutting Blvd., Richmond, 94604. Ph. (510) 231-4600. Emergency Services, Internal Medicine, OB, GYN, Psychiatry, Pediatrics, other hospital services. 60 Beds.

190 CONTRA COSTA & SOLANO

Kaiser Permanente Medical Offices. Antioch: 3400 Delta Fair Blvd., (510) 779-5000. Walnut Creek: Park Shadelands, 320 Lennon Lane, (510) 906-2000). Pleasanton: 7601 Stoneridge Drive, (510) 847-5000.

Los Medanos Community Hospital, 2311 Loveridge Road, Pittsburg, 94565. Ph. (510) 432-2200. ICU, CCU, OB, GYN, Physician Referral, Physical Therapy, Home Health Care, Diagnostic Services, Cardio-Pulmonary, 24-hour Emergency Services, Industrial Medicine, Optifast, MRI Services, Skilled Nursing. Outpatient Lab. 221 beds.

Merrithew Memorial Hospital & Clinics, 2500 Alhambra Ave., Martinez, 94553. Ph. (510) 370-5000. ICU, CCU, OB, GYN, Emergency Services, Urgent Care, Pediatrics, Psychiatry, Geriatrics, Medical-Psychology for Older Adults, Outpatient Surgery, Outpatient Clinics in Pittsburg, Richmond, Martinez, Concord, Brentwood. 179 beds.

Mt. Diablo Medical Center, 2540 East St., Concord, 94520. Ph. (510) 682-8200. ICU, CCU, 24-Hour Emergency Care, Cardiac Catheterization Lab, Cardiac Emergency Network, Cardiac Rehab, Pulmonary Rehab, Family Birthplace, Home Health Care Services, Lifeline, Regional Cancer Center, Senior Care Program, Male Potency, Health and Fitness Institute, Wellness Programs, Fitness Club Gym, Diabetes Center, Northern California Arthritis Center, Pain Management Center, In/Outpatient Physical, Occupational and Speech Therapy, Industrial Medicine, Outpatient Surgery Center, Physician Referral, Laser Services, Hemodialysis, Pharmacy. 303 beds.

Mt. Diablo Medical Pavilion, 2740 East St., Concord, 94520. Ph. (510) 680-6500. Inpatient Psychiatric Unit, Free Psychiatric Evaluation-, Referral- and 24-hour helpline; Alcohol/Drug 24-hour helpline, Inpatient Medical Detoxification/Rehabilitation, Day Treatment Program, Evening Outpatient Care, 12-Step Recovery Programs- Serenity; Eating disorders, 24-hour helpline, Inpatient Program, Adult and Adolescent Day Treatment, Outpatient Programs; Transitional Care Center, Short Term Skilled Nursing, 24-hour Nursing Care, Post-Operative/Post Illness Rehab Therapy. 72 beds.

San Ramon Regional Medical Center, 6001 Norris Canyon Road, San Ramon, 94583. Ph. (510) 275-9200. Full-service acute care facility, ICU/CCU, 24-hour Emergency Room, Single Room Maternity Obstetrics, Center for Advanced Surgical Procedures, Outpatient Surgery and Diagnostic Treatment Center, Pediatrics, Center for Reproductive Medicine (Infertility Treatment), Ostomy Center, 24-Hour Cardiopulmonary Services, Occupational Medicine, Physician Referral Service, Full-service Laboratory, Complete Diagnostic Imaging, and New Beginnings Chemical Dependency Unit. 125 beds.

Veterans Administration Outpatient Clinic, 150 Muir Road, Martinez, 94553. Ph. (510) 372-2000. Full service clinic offers the following services to eligible veterans: General medicine, ambulatory surgery, mental health care, substance treatment, dermatology, neurology, rehabilitative medicine, radiology, nuclear medicine, ultrasound, MRI, pharmacy, dental. Patients requiring inpatient care are referred to VA Medical Centers in San Francisco, Livermore or Reno.

Walnut Creek Hospital, 175 La Casa Via, Walnut Creek, 94598. Ph. (510) 933-7990. Free-standing psychiatric hospital. Services for children, adolescents, adults. Substance Abuse Program. Free Parent Education classes. Accredited School Program. Free Psychiatric Assessment Service. Family Counseling. Many Groups. 108 beds.

Hospitals & Medical Offices in or near Solano County

First Hospital Vallejo, 525 Oregon Street, Vallejo, 94590. Ph. (707) 648-2200. Mental Health Crisis Line, (800) 222-8220; Psychiatric and Substance Abuse treatment for children, adolescents and adults; specialized women's program; inpatient and partial hospitalization program; outpatient chemical dependency program; free consultation & referral service; speaker's bureau. 61 beds.

Kaiser Permanente Medical Center, 975 Sereno Drive, Vallejo, 94589. Ph. (707) 648-

Over 80 years of history...

In 1907, a registered nurse named Kathleen McConnell opened the Woodland Sanitarium. Miss McConnell sold the Sanitarium in 1911 to four Woodland Physicians who relocated the Sanitarium and founded the Woodland Clinic Hospital and Medical Group.

The Woodland Clinic physicians, in 1960, decided that the community would be better served by a non-profit hospital. In March 1967, the Woodland Clinic relocated to its current location, and Woodland Memorial Hospital opened its doors.

In 1992, Woodland Clinic and Woodland Memorial Hospital formally affiliated and created Woodland Healthcare. This affiliation will allow clinic and hospital physicians to better meet the needs of patients on a regional basis and will position Woodland Healthcare as a strong healthcare resource for the future.

Now, more than eighty years later, Woodland Clinic and Woodland Memorial Hospital continue their commitment to meet the area's healthcare needs by providing the highest quality, comprehensive, multi-specialty care.

As we look towards the future, Woodland Healthcare will honor the same commitment to providing the superior healthcare services that have become the hallmark of Woodland Clinic and Woodland Memorial Hospital.

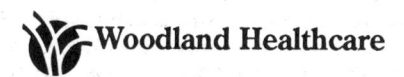

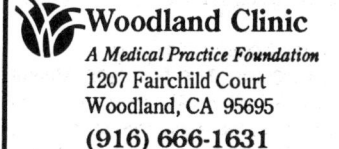

Woodland Healthcare

Woodland Clinic
A Medical Practice Foundation
1207 Fairchild Court
Woodland, CA 95695
(916) 666-1631

Woodland Memorial Hospital
1325 Cottonwood Street
Woodland, CA 95695
(916) 662-3961

6000. Alcohol and Drug Abuse Program, Cardiology, Emergency Services, Labor and Delivery, Rehabilitation Center, Sleep Lab, Surgery, other typical hospital services. 231 beds.

Kaiser Permanente Medical Offices. Fairfield: 1550 Gateway Blvd., (707) 427-4000. Napa: 3285 Claremont Way, (707) 226-5531.

NorthBay Medical Center, 1200 B. Gale Wilson Blvd., Fairfield, 94533. Ph. (707) 429-3600. ICU, CCU, OB, GYN, Emergency Care, Physical Therapy, Physician Referral, Pediatrics, Skilled Nursing, Radiology, Home Health Care, Geriatrics, Cancer Treatment, Radiation Oncology, Trauma Services, Hospice Program, Newborn Intensive Care. 120 beds.

Queen of the Valley Hospital-Napa Valley Medical Center, 1000 Trancas, Napa, 94558. Phone: (707) 252-4411. ICU, CCU, Obstetrics, GYN, Trauma Center, Emergency Care, Pediatric Services, Physical Therapy, Skilled Nursing, Radiology, Home Health Care, Community Cancer Center, Mammography, Regional Heart Center. 180 Beds.

St. Helena Hospital, 650 Sanitarium Road, Deer Park, 94576. Phone: (707) 963-3611. ICU, CCU, Obstetrics/GYN, Emergency Care, Adult Psychiatric Care, Transitional Care, Physicians Referral, Physical Therapy, Alcohol & Chemical Dependency. Outpatient Women's Center in St. Helena. Low-ropes Challenge Course for youths and adults. Residential wellness programs such as Smoking Cessation, McDougall Lifestyle Change Program, and Personalized Health. Regional Heart Center for more than 20 years. 224 beds.

Solano Park Hospital, 2101 Courage Drive, Fairfield, 94533. Ph. (707) 427-8000. Crisis Line: 1-800-955-HOPE. Psychiatric and substance abuse treatment for youths (ages 10-17) and adults. Adult Open, Adult ICU, youth services, partial hospitalization (day treatment). Escape to Reality team-building program. Speaker's Bureau. 80 beds.

Sutter Davis Hospital, Road 99 at Covell Blvd., Davis, 95616. Ph. (916) 756-6440. ICU, CCU, Emergency Care, Physician Referral, Physical Therapy, Radiology, Geriatrics, Lab Services, Weekend Respite, Cardiac Rehabilitation, Health Education, Complete Pharmacy, Respiratory Therapy, Diabetes Education, Outpatient Surgery. 48 beds.

Sutter Solano Medical Center, 300 Hospital Drive, Vallejo, 94589. Ph. (707) 554-4444. ICU, CCU, OB, GYN, Emergency Care, Physician Referral, Pediatrics, Physical Therapy, Radiology, Lab Services, Cardiac Catheterization Heart Institute, Community Health Education. 108 beds.

VacaValley Hospital, 1000 Nut Tree Road, Vacaville, 95687. Ph. (707) 446-4000. Affiliated with NorthBay Medical Center, Fairfield. ICU, CCU, GYN, Emergency Care, Physician Referral, Physical Therapy, Radiology, Home Health Care, Geriatrics, Cancer Treatment, Hospice Program. 50 beds.

Woodland Memorial Hospital, 1325 Cottonwood Street, Woodland, 95695. Ph: (916) 662-3961. ICU, OB/GYN, Emergency Care, Psychiatric, Pediatric Services, Physical Therapy, Skilled Nursing, Radiology, Home Health Care, Outpatient Surgery Center, Speech Therapy Services, Health and Wellness Classes, Family-Centered Maternity Care, Sleep Disorders Center, Cardiac Rehab., Sports Medicine. 122 beds.

Key: ICU, Intensive Care Unit; CCU, Coronary Care Unit; ENT, Ear Nose, Throat; MRI, Magnetic Resonance Imaging; OB, Obstetrics; GYN, Gynecology.

11/Restaurants

Dining Out in Contra Costa & Solano Counties — Pick a City, Then Choose a Restaurant

A LIFETIME OF EATING would not be enough to try all the restaurants in Contra Costa and Solano counties. So, as we all must from time to time, just pick and choose.

Following is a directory of restaurants, listed alphabetically by city and by restaurant, in Contra Costa, then Solano County.

Happy hunting and happy eating!

Contra Costa County
Alamo
Alamo Coffee Shop, 1 Alamo Square, Alamo. Ph: (510) 837-9909. American.
Alamo Palace, 120 Alamo Plaza, Alamo. Ph: (510) 820-1715. Chinese.
Cioni's Seafood Grill, 3160 Danville Blvd., Alamo. Ph: (510) 820-1711. Italian.
Courtyard Cafe, 3195 Danville Blvd., Alamo. Ph: (510) 838-1661.
Don Jose's, 3168 Danville Blvd., Alamo. Ph: (510) 743-8997. Mexican.
Hayama Restaurant, 3160 Danville Blvd., Alamo. Ph: (510) 838-7244. Japanese.
Jitr Thai Restaurant, 115 Alamo Plaza, Alamo. Ph: (510) 838-5583. Thai.
Loard's Ice Cream & Friends, 3160 Danville Blvd., Alamo. Ph: (510) 820-1639.
Luciano's Restaurant, 120 Alamo Plaza, Alamo. Ph: (510) 831-1060. Italian.
Pasta Stop, 215 Alamo Plaza, Alamo. Ph: (510) 831-1115. Italian.

Antioch
99 Express, 2896 Delta Fair Blvd., Antioch. Ph: (510) 754-1888.
A & W Hot Dogs, 2550 Somersville Road, Antioch. Ph: (510) 757-2335. Fast food.
A Tendinha, 603 W. 2nd, Antioch. Ph: (510) 754-6880.
Al's Giant Burgers, 2309 Buchanan Road, Antioch. Ph: (510) 754-4080. American.
Aladino's Pizza, 1324 Sunset Drive, Antioch. Ph: (510) 757-6363. Italian.
Allstar Sports Bar & Grill, 2521 San Jose Drive, Antioch. Ph: (510) 778-9282.
Barney's Hickory Pit, 2734 W. Tregallas Road, Antioch. Ph: (510) 757-9858. Barbecue.
Bridgehead Cafe, 2415 E. 18th, Antioch. Ph: (510) 757-4774.
Bun Bun Chinese Restaurant, 212 G St., Antioch. Ph: (510) 754-1222. Chinese.
Burger King, 2440 Mahogany Way, Antioch. Ph: (510) 757-7830. Fast food.
Cantina Del Rio, 416 W. 2nd St., Antioch. Ph: (510) 778-9338. Mexican.
Carrows Restaurants, 2430 Mahogany Way, Antioch. Ph: (510) 757-7565. American.
Casper's Hot Dogs, 1931 Somersville Road, Antioch. Ph: (510) 757-9540. American.

CONTRA COSTA & SOLANO

Chin's Restaurant, 3800 Delta Fair Blvd., Antioch. Ph: (510) 778-2655. Chinese.
China Express, 3365 Deer Valley Road, Antioch. Ph: (510) 706-4155. Chinese.
Chinese Kitchen, County East Mall, Antioch. Ph: (510) 778-0886. Chinese.
Copper Skillet, 301 E. 18th, Antioch. Ph: (510) 754-0988. American.
Dairy Queen, 607 E. 18th, Antioch. Ph: (510) 757-4845. Fast food.
Denny's Restaurant, 2006 Somersville Road, Antioch. Ph: (510) 754-1360. American.
Down Home Texas Barbeque, 3010 Delta Fair Blvd., Antioch. Ph: (510) 778-7145. Barbecued.
Dragon Inn Restaurant, 2401 Sycamore Drive, Antioch. Ph: (510) 754-8500. Chinese.
Empress Garden, 1721 Alhambra Drive, Antioch. Ph: (510) 778-0546. Chinese.
Ernie's Hot Dogs, 2100 A St., Antioch. Ph: (510) 778-7957. Fast food.
Ernie's Hot Dogs, 3200 E.18th, Antioch. Ph: (510) 754-4710. Fast food.
Farmer Dan International, 3200 E. 18th, Antioch. Ph: (510) 754-4209.
Foster's Freeze, 400 E. 18th, Antioch. Ph: (510) 757-6441. Fast food.
George's Restaurant, 1388 Sunset Drive, Antioch. Ph: (510) 754-9342. American.
George's Rib Palace, 2734 W. Tregallas Road, Antioch. Ph: (510) 706-8860. Barbecue.
Hazel's Drive In, Pittsburg-Antioch Hwy., Antioch. Ph: (510) 757-4772. Fast food.
Hong Kong Restaurant, 1611 A St., Antioch. Ph: (510) 757-7898. Chinese.
Hot Dogs Etc. of Antioch, 2767 Lone Tree Way, Antioch. Ph: (510) 778-3647. American.
Humphrey's Restaurant, 1Marina Plaza, Antioch. Ph: (510) 778-5800.
Il Giardino, 523 Werst 10th St., Antioch. Ph: (510) 754-1355. Italian.
Jack In The Box, 2505 A St., Antioch. Ph: (510) 757-4384. Fast food.
Jerry's Hot Dogs No. 1, 3005 Delta Fair Blvd., Antioch. Ph: (510) 754-4313. Fast food.
Kelly's Restaurant, 408 O St., Antioch. Ph: (510) 757-7315.
Kentucky Fried Chicken, 2410 Mahogany Way, Antioch. Ph: (510) 754-3474. Fast food.
Kentucky Fried Chicken, 317 E. 18th, Antioch. Ph: (510) 757-6664. Fast food.
La Plaza Mexican Restaurant & Cantina, 2370 Buchanan Road, Antioch. Ph: (510) 754-6556. Mexican.
Lin's Buffet, 2730 Delta Fair Blvd., Antioch. Ph: (510) 754-5356. Chinese.
Little Manuel's, 1509 A St., Antioch. Ph: (510) 757-9633. Mexican.
Little Mexico Restaurant, 2100 A St., Antioch. Ph: (510) 778-0905. Mexican.
Little Tai Pei Restaurant, 2715 Contra Loma Blvd., Antioch. Ph: (510) 778-2811. Taiwanese.
Los 3 Amigos, 1123 E. 18th, Antioch. Ph: (510) 778-8775. Mexican.
Lum's Linda Chinese Kitchen, 1884 A St., Antioch. Ph: (510) 706-0882. Chinese.
Lyon's Restaurant, 2009 Somersville Road, Antioch. Ph: (510) 754-0960. American.
Mac's Old House, 3100 E. 18th, Antioch. Ph: (510) 757-9908.
Matchmaker Restaurant, 913 W. 10th St., Antioch. Ph: (510) 757-8500. American.
Milano's Pizza, 2376 Buchanan Road, Antioch. Ph: (510) 754-4050. Pizza.
Miller's Cafe, 0, Antioch. Ph: (510) 757-6999. American.
New Dynasty Chinese Restaurant, 2303 Buchanan Road, Antioch. Ph: (510) 754-3088. Chinese.
No Name Pizza-Antioch, 2500 Sycamore Drive, Antioch. Ph: (510) 778-4900. Pizza.
Okawa Japanese Restaurant, 2327 Buchanan Road, Antioch. Ph: (510) 778-1585. Japanese.
Orange Julius, 2550 Somersville Road, Antioch. Ph: (510) 779-0345. Fast food.
Panther Drive-Inn, 900 A, Antioch. Ph: (510) 757-9839. Fast food.
Paulino's Restaurant, 509 W. 2nd St., Antioch. Ph: (510) 757-6311. Italian.
Pizza Hut, 2713 Contra Loma Blvd., Antioch. Ph: (510) 757-1010. Pizza.
Potato Barge, 105 F, Antioch. Ph: (510) 757-9585.
Quarter LB Big Burger, 3620 Lone Tree Way, Antioch. Ph: (510) 754-7307. Fast food.
Rick's On Second, 619 W. 2nd, Antioch. Ph: (510) 757-5500.
Rickshaw Chinese Food, 2896 Delta Fair Blvd., Antioch. Ph: (510) 754-4501. Chinese.
Rico's Pizza, 3612 Lone Tree Way, Antioch. Ph: (510) 757-3080. Pizza.
Riverview Lodge, Foot of I St., Antioch. Ph: (510) 757-2272. Continental.
Round Table Pizza, 2509 Somersville Road, Antioch. Ph: (510) 754-5747. Pizza.

RESTAURANTS

Round Table Pizza, 2741 Lone Tree Way, Antioch. Ph: (510) 754-8877. Pizza.
Sbarro, 2556 Somersville Road, Antioch. Ph: (510) 779-1505. Italian.
Shanghai Cafe, 740 W. 2nd St., Antioch. Ph: (510) 757-1043. Chinese.
Sizzler Restaurants, 1953 Somersville Road, Antioch. Ph: (510) 754-1993. American.
Sno-White Drive-In, 901 H, Antioch. Ph: (510) 754-6888.
Straw Hat Pizza, 3001 Delrta Fair Blvd, Antioch. Ph: (510) 754-1520. Pizza.
Subway Sandwiches & Salad, 3020 Delta Fair Blvd., Antioch. Ph: (510) 778-9328. Fast food.
Subway Sandwiches & Salads, 3303 Deer Valley Road, Antioch. Ph: (510) 778-6815. Fast food.
Swiss Pretzel Shop, 2550 Somersville Road, Antioch. Ph: (510) 779-9331.
Sylvia's Country Kitchen, 2799 Lone Tree Way, Antioch. Ph: (510) 778-8877.
Taco Bell, 212 E. 18th, Antioch. Ph: (510) 778-2119. Fast food.
Taco Bell, 2404 Mahogany Way, Antioch. Ph: (510) 778-4016. Fast food.
Tai Sun Mandarin Restaurant, 2621 Somersville Road, Antioch. Ph: (510) 778-3844. Chinese.
Tamami's Japanese Restaurant, 2547 San Jose Drive, Antioch. Ph: (510) 778-7584. Japanese.
Tao San Jin, 2378 Buchanan Road, Antioch. Ph: (510) 778-3888. Chinese.
Taqueria Nica, 1068 Sycamore Drive, Antioch. Ph: (510) 757-2360. Mexican.
Taqueria Salsa, 3612 Delta Fair Blvd., Antioch. Ph: (510) 778-9281. Mexican.
The Philly Station, 1806 A, Antioch. Ph: (510) 779-1544.
The Red Caboose, 210 Fulton Shipyard Road, Antioch. Ph: (510) 757-2655.
The Sculapasta, 3676 Delta Fair Blvd., Antioch. Ph: (510) 754-3466. Italian.
Ugly Duck Bar & Grill, 992 Fitzuren Road, Antioch. Ph: (510) 778-5266. American.
Velvet Creamery of Antioch, 3040 Delta Fair Blvd., Antioch. Ph: (510) 754-3971.
Wendy's of Antioch, 1809 A St., Antioch. Ph: (510) 757-1884. Fast food.
Wienerschnitzel, 200 E. 18th, Antioch. Ph: (510) 754-6757. Fast food.
Wiliker's Bar & GBrill, 2890 Delta Fair Blvd., Antioch. Ph: (510) 779-1099.
Windmill Family Restaurant & Bakery, 324 G St., Antioch. Ph: (510) 754-8114.
Wing Wah Restaurant, 1803 W. 10th, Antioch. Ph: (510) 778-3087. Chinese.
Wong's Restaurant, 3704 Lone Tree Way, Antioch. Ph: (510) 754-4411. Chinese.

Bethel Island

Bel-Isle Club, §200 Bethel Island Road, Bethel Island. Ph: (510) 684-3353.
Billeci's Ristorante, 6200 Bethel Island Road, Bethel Island. Ph: (510) 684-3223. Italian.
Boat House Lounge & Cafe, §210 Bethel Island Road, Bethel Island. Ph: (510) 684-2702.
Frank's Cove, 4651 Gateway Road, Bethel Island. Ph: (510) 684-2886.
Hatoba Japanese Restaurant, 6277F Bethel Island Road, Bethel Island. Ph: (510) 684-9890. Japanese.
Island Club Restaurant, 3303 Gateway Road, Bethel Island. Ph: (510) 684-2775.
Kelly's Place, 6277 Bethel Island Road, Bethel Island. Ph: (510) 684-2912.
PaPa Bob's Seafood Restaurant, 6777 Riverview Road, Bethel Island. Ph: (510) 684-0503. Seafood.
Rick's Islander Cafe, 6111 Bethel Island Road, Bethel Island. Ph: (510) 684-0741.
Rusty Porthole, 3895 Willow Road, Bethel Island. Ph: (510) 684-3607.
Sand Trap Restaurant, 3303 Gateway Road, Bethel Island. Ph: (510) 684-2775. Seafood.
The Artist Table, §277 Bethel Island Road, Bethel Island. Ph: (510) 684-3414.
The Boat House, 6210 Bethel Island Road, Bethel Island. Ph: (510) 684-2702. Seafood.
Wally's Restaurant & Deli, 6464 Bethel Island Road, Bethel Island. Ph: (510) 684-3777.
Windmill Family Restaurant & Bakery II, 6256 Bethel Island Road, Bethel Island. Ph: (510) 684-2099.

Blackhawk

Cafe De Paris, 3407 Blackhawk Plaza Cir., Blackhawk. Ph: (510) 736-5006. French.
Florentine Restaurant, 3483 Blackhawk Plaza Circle, Blackhawk. Ph: (510) 736-6060. Italian.
La Fontaine, 3421 Blackhawk Plaza Cir., Blackhawk. Ph: (510) 736-6851.
Ramzi's, 3690 Blackhawk Plaza Cir., Blackhawk. Ph: (510) 736-5051.

Brentwood

Bob's Farmhouse Cafe, 7876 Brentwood Road, Brentwood. Ph: (510) 634-0762.
Brentwood Cafe, 8500 Brentwood Ave., Brentwood. Ph: (510) 634-6503.
Burger King, 1105 2nd, Brentwood. Ph: (510)

196 CONTRA COSTA & SOLANO

634-5739. Fast food.
Chef Chen Restaurant, 8065 Brentwood Blvd., Brentwood. Ph: (510) 634-8062. Chinese.
China Express, 1125 2nd, Brentwood. Ph: (510) 634-6787. Chinese.
Down Home Texas Barbeque, 8335 Brentwood Blvd., Brentwood. Ph: (510) 516-0922. Barbecue.
El Camino Restaurant, Highway 4, Brentwood. Ph: (510) 634-,4011. Mexican.
El Gallito Drive Inn, 8540 Brentwood Blvd., Brentwood. Ph: (510) 634-4992. Mexican.
Little Manuel's, 1272 Highway 4, Brentwood. Ph: (510) 634-2014. Mexican.
Lone Tree Drive-In, Lone Tree Way, Brentwood. Ph: (510) 634-4629. American.
Lord Byron Pizza, 8065 Brentwood Blvd., Brentwood. Ph: (510) 516-7041. Italian.
Margo's Little Bavarian, 71 bSand Creek Road, Brentwood. Ph: (510) 634-9131. Bavarian.
McDonald's, 7455 Brentwood Blvd., Brentwood. Ph: (510) 634-4414. Fast food.
Pee Wee Muldoons, 8065 Brentwood Blvd., Brentwood. Ph: (510) 634-7850.
Quarter LB Big Burger, 8010 Brentwood Blvd., Brentwood. Ph: (510) 634-1440. Fast food.
Rich's Drive-In, 335 Oak St., Brentwood. Ph: (510) §34-3492. American.
Rod's Hickory Pit, 1273 Highway 4, Brentwood. Ph: (510) 634-1522. Barbecue.
Round Table Pizza, 41 San Creek Road, Brentwood. Ph: (510) 634-1700. Pizza.
Sandcreek Grill, 71A West Sand Creek Road, Brentwood. Ph: (510) 634-9081. American.
Silver Skillet Restaurant, 8300 Brentwood Blvd., Brentwood. Ph: (510) 516-1358.
Subway Sandwich & Salad, 7351 Brentwood Blvd., Brentwood. Ph: (510) 634-0207. Fast food.
Sweeney's Station Four, 301 Oak St., Brentwood. Ph: (510) 634-7136. American.
Taco Bell, 7814 Brentwood Blvd., Brentwood. Ph: (510) 634-9102. Fast food.
Taqueria Cha-Cha-Cha, 815 Railroad Ave., Brentwood. Ph: (510) 516-1135. Mexican.
The Canton Garden, 7870 Brentwood Blvd., Brentwood. Ph: (510) 634-5400. Chinese.
Vickie's Sandwich Shop, 735 2nd St., Brentwood. Ph: (510) 634-7220.

Byron

Byron Inn Restaurant, 16141 Byron Hwy., Byron. Ph: (510) 634-9441.
Lazy M Marina, Clifton Court Road, Byron. Ph: (510) 634-4555.

Mural Inn, 3978 Main, Byron. Ph: (510) 634-1657.

Clayton

Carl's Jr., 1530 Kirker Pass Road, Clayton. Ph: (510) 672-9324. Fast food.
China Express, 5431 Clayton Road, Clayton. Ph: (510) 672-2146. Chinese.
Dave's Hot Dogs, 5439 Clayton Road, Clayton. Ph: (510) 672-6716. American.
Gianni's Pizza Pasta Cafe, 5435 Clayton Road, Clayton. Ph: (510) 672-6722. Italian.
La Cocotte, 6115 Main, Clayton. Ph: (510) 672-1333. French.
Peppino's, 1508 Kirker Pass Road, Clayton. Ph: (510) 672-6868. Italian.
Skipolini's Pizza, Main & Diablo, Clayton. Ph: (510) 672-1111. Pizza.
Stagecoach Inn, 6055 Main, Clayton. Ph: (510) 672-1677.
The Royal Oak Pub, 6200 Center, Clayton. Ph: (510) 672-8007.
Villa Clayton Restaurant, 6201 Center, Clayton. Ph: (510) 672-5911.

Concord

Aladino's Pizzeria, 5400 Ygnacio Valley Road, Concord. Ph: (510) 672-6363. Pizza.
Andy's Restaurant, 1089 Oak Grove Road, Concord. Ph: (510) 827-0533.
Arby's Restaurant, 1833 Willow Pass Road, Concord. Ph: (510) 825-2971.
Bakers Square Restaurant & Pie Shop, 1680 Willow Pass Road, Concord. Ph: (510) 689-9365. American.
Barney's Hickory Pit, 3446 Clayton Road, Concord. Ph: (510) 680-9761. Barbecue.
Benihana Of Tokyo, 1989 Diamond Blvd., Concord. Ph: (510) 827-4220. Japanese.
Biagi's Seafood Grotto, 1500 Monument Blvd., Concord. Ph: (510) 676-1595. Seafood.
Burger King, 1 Sun Valley Mall, Concord. Ph: (510) 825-5450. Fast food.
Burger King, 1651 Willow Pass Road, Concord. Ph: (510) 798-7238. Fast food.
Burger King, 2689 Clayton Road, Concord. Ph: (510) 676-7518. Fast food.
Burger King, 5400 Ygnacio Valley Road, Concord. Ph: (510) 672-6090. Fast food.
C C Ole's, 4633 Clayton Road, Concord. Ph: (510) 798-1800. Mexican.
Cactus Cafe, 1390 Willow Pass Road, Concord. Ph: (510) 682-9668.
Cafe Gateway, 1850 Gateway Blvd., Concord. Ph: (510) 680-1991.
Casper's Hot Dogs, 1680 Willow Pass Road, Concord. Ph: (510) 687-4555. Fast food.
Chan's Chinese Buffet, 1671 Willow Pass

RESTAURANTS

Road, Concord. Ph: (510) 687-7874. Chinese.
Charley Brown's, 1981 Diamond Blvd., Concord. Ph: (510) 671-9010. Continental.
Cheese Steak Shop, 3478 Clayton Road, Concord. Ph: (510) 687-6116.
Chen's Mandarin Cuisine, 4340 Clayton Road, Concord. Ph: (510) 676-2353. Chinese.
Chicago Taste, 1847 Willow Pass Road, Concord. Ph: (510) 686-2828.
Chick's Donuts & Coffee Shop, 1801 Willow Pass Road, Concord. Ph: (510) 682-4917. American.
Chili's Grill & Bar, 1501 Concord Ave., Concord. Ph: (510) 676-4062.
China Express, 2250-F Monument Blvd., Concord. Ph: (510) 680-4276. Chinese.
China Express, 2600 Willow Pass Road, Concord. Ph: (510) 825-4105. Chinese.
China Express, 4309 Clayton Road, Concord. Ph: (510) 356-2715. Chinese.
China Pavilion, 2050 Diamond Blvd., Concord. Ph: (510) 827-2212. Chinese.
Concord Inn, 1401 Willow Pass Rd., Concord. Ph: (510) 682-7330. Continental.
Denny's Restaurant, 1313 Willow Pass Road, Concord. Ph: (510) 798-4040. American.
Eduardo's Italian Restaurant, 1901 Salvio, Concord. Ph: (510) 825-1441. Italian.
El Faro Inc., 2280 Monument Blvd., Concord. Ph: (510) 827-0976.
El Morocco, 1311 Meadow Lane, Concord. Ph: (510) 671-0132. Moroccan.
El Rancho Restaurant, 1450 Monument Blvd., Concord. Ph: (510) 685-5582.
El Tapatio, 1802 Willow Pass Road, Concord. Ph: (510) 682-7787. Mexican.
El Tapatio Restaurant, 4475-D Treat Blvd., Concord. Ph: (510) 827-2413, CDA, Mexican.
El Torito Mexican Restaurant & Cantina, 1961 Diamond Blvd., Concord. Ph: (510) 798-7660. Mexican.
Eleni's Coffee Shop, 5400 Ygnacio Valley Blvd., Concord. Ph: (510) 672-4000.
Emil Villa's The Original Hick'ry Pit, 1631 Willow Pass Road, Concord. Ph: (510) 827-9902. Barbecue.
Far East Gardens, 1975 Diamond Blvd., Concord. Ph: (510) 674-0400. Chinese.
Fentons Village Creamery, 1847 Willow Pass Road, Concord. Ph: (510) 689-5190.
Fong Lin Cheng's Chinese Restaurant, 3622 Willow Pass Road, Concord. Ph: (510) 682-3035. Chinese.
Four Corners Pizza, 1880 Monument Blvd.,

Concord. Ph: (510) 680-9751. Italian.
Francisco's, 1800 Monument Blvd., Concord. Ph: (510) 682-1800.
Fred's Place, 2699 Monument Blvd., Concord. Ph: (510) 685-5953.
Fresh Choice Restaurant, 486 Sun Valley Mall, Concord. Ph: (510) 671-7222.
Fuddruckers, 1975 Diamond Blvd., Concord. Ph: (510) 825-1443. American.
Genghis Khan Restaurant, 3505 Clayton Road, Concord. Ph: (510) 685-8886. Chinese.
Giovanni's Bar & Grill, 2325 Clayton Road, Concord. Ph: (510) 686-0503. Italian.
Golden Willow, 2118 Willow Pass Road, Concord. Ph: (510) 827-3228. Chinese.
Goldie's Giant Hamburgers, 2151 Salvio, Concord. Ph: (510) 825-9745.
Green Parrot Restaurant, 108 Sun Valley Mall, Concord. Ph: (510) 671-2372.
Grissini, 1970 Diamond Blvd., Concord. Ph: (510) 680-1700. Italian.
Guadalajara Grill Mexican Restaurant, 5400 Ygnacio Valley Road, Concord. Ph: (510) 672-4430. Mexican.
Hannah's Hot Dogs Etc., 1895 Farm Bureau Road, Concord. Ph: (510) 825-8958.
Hilton Brunch, 1970 Diamond Blvd., Concord. Ph: (510) 827-2000. Continental.
Hobie's Roadhouse, 2045 Mount Diablo, Concord. Ph: (510) 676-4417.
Holiday Inn, Diamond Blvd. & Burnett Ave., Concord. Ph: (510) 687-5500.
Hot Dog Palace, 1990 Grant, Concord. Ph: (510) 676-8723. American.
House of Lui Restaurant, 3491 Clayton Road, Concord. Ph: (510) 676-5670. Chinese.
Hunan Restaurant, 4804 Clayton Road, Concord. Ph: (510) 827-4800. Chinese.
Hungry Hunter, 1400 Willow Pass Road, Concord. Ph: (510) 676-1677. American.
International House of Pancakes, 4619 Clayton Road, Concord. Ph: (510) 687-1124. American.
Jack In The Box, 1710 Monument Blvd., Concord. Ph: (510) 671-7911. Fast food.
Jay's Cafe, 1515 Broadway, Concord. Ph: (510) 825-2800.
Johnny Rockets, 301 Sun Valley Mall, Concord. Ph: (510) 798-8335.
Kasper's Hot Dogs, 3474 Clayton Road, Concord. Ph: (510) 687-1651. Fast food.
Kentucky Fried Chicken, 2160 Monument Blvd., Concord. Ph: (510) 825-1111. Fast food.
Kentucky Fried Chicken, 2650 Willow Pass Road, Concord. Ph: (510) 687-6625. Fast

food.
Kentucky Fried Chicken, 4660 Clayton Road, Concord. Ph: (510) 680-7796. Fast food.
Kiibo, 1975 Diamond Blvd., Ste. D160, Concord. Ph: (510) 671-7112. Japanese.
Knight's Inn, 1250 Contra Costa Blvd., Concord. Ph: (510) 682-4868.
Korea Palace Restaurant, 4436 Clayton Road, Concord. Ph: (510) 674-0180. Korean.
La Rotisserie, 5267 Clayton Road, Concord. Ph: (510) 685-6765.
La Tour Restaurant, 3610 Clayton Road, Concord. Ph: (510) 825-9955.
Lawan Thai Cuisine, 1965 Mt. Diablo St., Concord. Ph: (510) 676-6061. Thai.
Lee's Cafe, 548 Contra Costa Blvd., Concord. Ph: (510) 676-2036. Chinese.
Legends Sports Bar & Grill, 4050 Port Chicago Highway, Concord. Ph: (510) 687-4111.
Lim's Garden, 1140 Meadow Lane, Concord. Ph: (510) 676-0711. Chinese.
Lisa's House of Hot Dogs, 5100-31 Clayton Road, Concord. Ph: (510) 687-7527. American.
Little China Restaurant, 1500 Monument Blvd., Concord. Ph: (510) 685-5231. Chinese.
Los Compadres Mexican Restaurant & Cantina, 2151 Salvio, Concord. Ph: (510) 687-3888. Mexican.
Lunch Break, 5017 Forni Drive, Concord. Ph: (510) 827-0749.
Luping Chinese Restaurant, 4375 Clayton Road, Concord. Ph: (510) 671-7177. Chinese.
Lyon's Restaurant, 4301 Clayton Road, Concord. Ph: (510) 674-0347. American.
Maggie's II, 3606 Willow Pass Road, Concord. Ph: (510) 671-9350.
Manchu Wok Take Out, Sun Valley Mall, Concord. Ph: (510) 685-8880. Manchurian.
Mandarin, 1915 Market, Concord. Ph: (510) 687-5323. Chinese.
Mandarin Garden, 1740 Monument Blvd., Concord. Ph: (510) 686-4442. Chinese.
Mann's Chinese Cuisine, 4115 Concord Blvd., Concord. Ph: (510) 685-2988. Chinese.
Maria Elena's, 2211 Clayton Road, Concord. Ph: (510) 680-6231.
Marie Callender's Restaurants & Bakeries, 2090 Diamond Blvd., Concord. Ph: (510) 827-4930. American.
Maxi Burgers, 2699C Monument Blvd., Concord. Ph: (510) 676-1803. American.

McDonald's, 1691 Monument Blvd., Concord. Ph: (510) 680-7267.
McDonald's, 1847 Willow Pass Road, Concord. Ph: (510) 798-0581.
McDonald's, 4550 Clayton Road, Concord. Ph: (510) 825-5585.
Mediterrean Cafe, 4710 Clayton Road, Concord. Ph: (510) 825-6663.
Mexican Burritos, 1500 Monument Blvd., Concord. Ph: (510) 671-7745. Mexican.
Mexicatessen Chapala, 1819 Colfax, Concord. Ph: (510) 680-2636. Mexican.
Ming Dynasty, 4484 Treat Blvd., Concord. Ph: (510) 689-5830. Chinese.
Moon Yuen Restaurant, 5400 Ygnacio Valley Road, Concord. Ph: (510) §72-3289. Chinese.
Mr. Steak of Concord, 4401 Clayton Road, Concord. Ph: (510) 687-3370. American.
Nation's Giant Hamburgers & Great Pies, 785 Oak Grove Road, Concord. Ph: (510) 798-1750. American.
Numero Uno Taqueria, 1895 Farm Bureau Road, Concord. Ph: (510) 685-4500. Mexican.
Osaka Restaurant, 2650 Monument Blvd., Concord. Ph: (510) 676-1017. Japanese.
Paisano Italian Restaurant & Pizza, 1140 Meadow Lane, Concord. Ph: (510) 676-6450. Italian.
Papa Charlie's, 2765 Clayton Road, Concord. Ph: (510) 676–7272. Italian.
Parkside Cafe, 1924 Grant, Concord. Ph: (510) 827-3765.
Pasta Primavera Cafe, 4425 Treat Blvd., Concord. Ph: (510) 687-5300. Italian.
Peppermill, 1100 Concord Ave., Concord. Ph: (510) 671-2233.
Pizza Hut, 1825 Sutter, Concord. Ph: (510) 680-8200. Pizza.
Pizza Hut, 4375 Clayton Road, Concord. Ph: (510) 689-0254. Pizza.
Plaza Cafe, 1200 Concord Ave., Concord. Ph: (510) 825-6298.
Popeyes Chicken & Biscuits, 1835 Willow Pass Road, Concord. Ph: (510) 685-6618. Fast food.
Quarter LB Big Burger, 3399 Clayton Road, Concord. Ph: (510) 798-3326. Fast food.
Rafael's Fine Mexican Cuisine, 1980 Galindo, Concord. Ph: (510) 686-1178. Mexican.
Rancho Grande Mexican Foods, 1960 Concord Ave., Concord. Ph: (510) 680-9897. Mexican.
Red Lobster Restaurant, 1225 Willow Pass Road, Concord. Ph: (510) 356-2267. Sea-

RESTAURANTS

food.
Red Robin Burger & Spirits Emporiums, 404 Sun Valley Mall, Concord. Ph: (510) 671-9315. American.
Rod's Pizza Parlor, 2191 Solano Way, Concord. Ph: (510) 682-3750. Pizza.
Round Table Pizza, 1743 Willow Pass Road, Concord. Ph: (510) 687-7234. Pizza.
Round Table Pizza, 2960 Treat Blvd., Concord. Ph: (510) 676-1818. Pizza.
Round Table Pizza, 3393 Port Chicago Hwy., Concord. Ph: (510) 825-1993. Pizza.
Round Table Pizza, 3624 Willow Pass Road, Concord. Ph: (510) 671-0400. Pizza.
Round Table Pizza, 4743 Clayton Road, Concord. Ph: (510) 676-6731. Pizza.
Scrumpy's Sandwich Shoppe No. 20, 1035 Detroit Ave., Concord. Ph: (510) 689-0420.
Senor Burrito, 1844 Grant, Concord. Ph: (510) 689-3855. Mexican.
Shalimar Restaurant, 1500 Monument Blvd., Concord. Ph: (510) 675-0229.
Shan Shan Low Restaurant, 1731 Willow Pass Road, Concord. Ph: (510) 685-6311. Chinese.
Sheraton Hotel & Conference Center, 45 John Glenn Drive, Concord. Ph: (510) 825-7700.
Shimmy's Cafe, 2123 Pacheco Blvd., Concord. Ph: (510) 682-8436.
Shinobu, 1800 Monument Blvd., Concord. Ph: (510) 686-1888. Japanese.
Sizzler Restaurants, 1353 Willow Pass Road, Concord. Ph: (510) 687-5830. American.
Sizzler Restaurants, 5400 Ygnacio Valley Road, Concord. Ph: (510) 672-4101. American.
Souperb Salads, 1975 Diamond Blvd., Concord. Ph: (510) 827-2161.
Spring Garden, 785 Oak Grove, Concord. Ph: (510) 827-1900. Chinese.
Straw Hat Pizza, 3501 Clayton Road, Concord. Ph: (510) 689-0556. Pizza.
Straw Hat Pizza, 5358 Clayton Road, Concord. Ph: (510) 689-4610. Pizza.
Strictly To Go Pizzeria, 4702 Clayton Road, Concord. Ph: (510) 671-2777. Pizza.
Subway Sandwiches, 4701 Clayton Road, Concord. Ph: (510) 825-3382. Fast food.
Subway Sandwiches & Salads, 2995 Monument Blvd., Concord. Ph: (510) 825-7363. Fast food.
Sugar Plum Coffee Shop, 1815 Colfax, Concord. Ph: (510) 689-1738. American.
Sun And Moon Restaurant, 2081 Salvio, Concord. Ph: (510) 682-4452. Chinese.
Sun Lim Chinese Cuisine, 288 Sun Valley Mall, Concord. Ph: (510) 686-0789. Chinese.
Suwa's Japanese Restaurant, 2151-E Salvio St., Concord. Ph: (510) 825-3201. Japanese.
T.R.'s Bar & Grill, 2001 Salvio St., Concord. Ph: (510) 827-4660. American.
Tachi Sushi Bar, 5400 Ygnacio Valley Road, Concord. Ph: (510) 672-1431. Japanese.
Taco Bell, 1698 Monument Blvd., Concord. Ph: (510) 687-0166. Fast food.
Taco Bell, 2475 Olivera Road, Concord. Ph: (510) 680-9888. Fast food.
Taco Bell, 286 Sun Valley Mall, Concord. Ph: (510) 680-6345. Fast food.
Taco Bell, 4530 Clayton Road, Concord. Ph: (510) 825-4460. Fast food.
Taiwan Village, 4485 Clayton Road, Concord. Ph: (510) 689-8970. Chinese.
Taqueria Mexican Grill, 4787 Clayton Road, Concord. Ph: (510) 680-0914. Mexican.
Taqueria Mexican Grill Concord, 1847 Willow Pass Road, Concord. Ph: (510) 676-3367. Mexican.
Teddy House, 2186 Solano Way, Concord. Ph: (510) 825-6222. American.
Teriyaki Express, 2118 Willow Pass Road, Concord. Ph: (510) 686-3171. Japanese.
The Chinese Kitchen, 3426 Clayton Road, Concord. Ph: (510) 682-1825. Chinese.
The Front Room Restaurant & Bar, 1990 Concord Ave., Concord. Ph: (510) 676-5070.
The Lunch Express, 1950 Market, Concord. Ph: (510) 682-7977.
The Old Spaghetti Factory, 1955 Mt. Diablo St., Concord. Ph: (510) 687-5030. Italian.
The Original Mel's, 4600 Clayton Road, Concord. Ph: (510) 798-7745.
Time Out Sports Bar, 1822 Grant, Concord. Ph: (510) 798-1811.
Togo's Eatery, 1768 Willow Pass Road, Concord. Ph: (510) 685-8600. Fast food.
Togo's Eatery, 4475 Treat Blvd., Concord. Ph: (510) 687-1711. Fast food.
Tokyo Express, 5356 Clayton Road, Concord. Ph: (510) 682-1326. Japanese.
TR's Bar & Grill, 2001 Salvio, Concord. Ph: (510) 827-4660. American.
Treats Sidewalk Cafe & Bakery, 2300 Clayton Road, Concord. Ph: (510) 685-6212.
Tropical Squeeze, 282 Sun Valley Mall, Concord. Ph: (510) 685-6055.
Underdog, 22 Dana Plaza, Concord. Ph: (510) 687-9664.
Upper Level Bar & Grill, 2118 Willow Pass Road, Concord. Ph: (510) 682-9693.
Vie De France, 480 Sun Valley Mall, Con-

200 CONTRA COSTA & SOLANO

cord. Ph: (510) 685-3400. French.
Wah Yuen, 5267 Clayton Road, Suite 7, Concord. Ph: (510) 680-7817. Chinese.
Wat Phou Restaurant, 1823 Broadway, Concord. Ph: (510) 827-1538. Thai.
Wendy's, 1551 Monument Blvd., Concord. Ph: (510) 671-2790. Fast food.
Whistle Stop Cafe, 4669 Clayton Road, Concord. Ph: (510) 825-0803.
Wienerschnitzel, 4320 Clayton Road, Concord. Ph: (510) 671-0696.
Woung Luang Thai Cuisine, 1965 Mount Diablo, Concord. Ph: (510) 825-3787. Thai.
Yet Wah, 4635 Clayton Road, Concord. Ph: (510) 671-7044. Chinese.
Yvonne T's, 2118 Mount Diablo, Concord. Ph: (510) 680-1656.
Zips Hot Dogs, 2380 Salvio, Concord. Ph: (510) 686-6518. American.

Crockett
Four Corners Pizza-N-Pasta, 628 2nd Ave., Crockett. Ph: (510) 787-1083. Italian.
Nantucket Fish Co., 1306 Pomona Street, Crockett. Ph: (510) 787-2233. Seafood.
Rosy's Kitchen, 1207 Pomona, Crockett. Ph: (510) 787-1628.
Valona Delicatessen & Cafe, 1323 Pomona, Crockett. Ph: (510) 787-2022.
Yet Wah Mandarin Cuisine, 20050 San Pablo Ave., Crockett. Ph: (510) 787-3011. Chinese.
Yozen Frogurts, 1322 Pomona, Crockett. Ph: (510) 787-1430.

Danville
Azetca Restarante, 558 San Ramon Valley Blvd., Danville. Ph: (510) 820-3809. Mexican.
Blackhawk Grill, 3530 Plaza Circle, Danville. Ph: (510) 736-4295. American.
Bob's Big Boy Family Restaurant, 387 Diablo Road, Danville. Ph: (510) 838-9222. American.
Bridges Restaurant, 44 Church, Danville. Ph: (510) 820-7200. Continental.
Burger King, 444 Front, Danville. Ph: (510) 820-5077. Fast food.
China Paradise Restaurant, 3446 Camino Tassajara, Danville. Ph: (510) 736-1221. Chinese.
Country Gourmet & Co., 100 Sycamore Valley Road West, Danville. Ph: (510) 837-1098.
Country Waffles, 130 Hartz Ave., Danville. Ph: (510) 838-0651.
Danville Hotel, 411 Hartz Ave., Danville. Ph: (510) 837-6627. American.
Denny's Restaurant, 807 Camino Ramon, Danville. Ph: (510) 820-8240. American.
Don Pepe's Restaurant, 171 Hartz Ave., Danville. Ph: (510) 837-4552. Mexican.
Father Nature's Shed, 172 E. Prospect Ave., Danville. Ph: (510) 820-3160.
Faz Restaurant & Bar, 600 Hartz Ave., Danville. Ph: (510) 838-1320. Mediterranean.
Frankie G's, 267 Hartz Ave., Danville. Ph: (510) 837-7117.
Grand China Restaurant, 105 Town & Country Drive, Danville. Ph: (510) 820-8887. Chinese.
Great Impasta Inc., 318 Sycamore Valley Road West, Danville. Ph: (510) 831-9363. Italian.
Imperial Chinese Seafood Restaurant, 150 Hartz Ave., Danville. Ph: (510) 820-6088. Chinese.
Kentucky Fried Chicken, 700 Hartz Way, Danville. Ph: (510) 837-5549. Fast food.
La Ultima, 263 S. Hartz, Danville. Ph: (510) 838-9705. Mexican.
La Ultima New Mexico Food, 445 Hartz Ave., Danville. Ph: (510) 838-9705. Mexican.
Luna Loca Mexican Restaurant, 500 Sycamore Valley Road West, Danville. Ph: (510) 831-3644.
Lyon's Restaurant, 185 Railroad Blvd., Danville. Ph: (510) 838-1027. American.
Marcello's Restaurant, 515 San Ramon Valley Blvd., Danville. Ph: (510) 838-8144.
Nattika Thai Cuisine, 301 Hartz Ave., Danville. Ph: (510) 838-0644. Thai.
Pastavino Ristorante, 111 Town & Country Drive, Danville. Ph: (510) 820-9111. Italian.
Pete's Brass Rail & Car Wash, 331 Hartz Ave., Danville. Ph: (510) 820-8281.
Saro's Ristorante, 254 Rose St., Danville. Ph: (510) 838-2008. Italian.
Sen Dai Teriyaki, 101C Town & Country Drive, Danville. Ph: (510) 937-1027. Japanese.
Sesame Restaruant, 59 Danville Square, Danville. Ph: (510) 820-2111. Chinese.
Sun's Chinese Restaurant, 426 Diablo Road, Danville. Ph: (510) 820-2736. Chinese.
Sushi Bar Hana, 165 W. Prospect Ave., Danville. Ph: (510) 820-0670. Japanese.
Taqueria Express, 3452 Camino Tassajara, Danville. Ph: (510) 736-0535. Mexican.
Taqueria Mexican Grill Danville, 348 Hartz Ave., Danville. Ph: (510) 838-7292. Mexican.
The Copper Skillet, 501 Hartz Ave., Danville. Ph: (510) 743-0801.

RESTAURANTS 201

The Village Cafe, 105 Town & Country Drive, Danville. Ph: (510) 837-7760. American.
Tony Roma's-A Place For Ribs, 200 Sycamore Valley Road West, Danville. Ph: (510) 831-1818. Barbecue.
Vally Medlyn's Coffee Shop, 330 Hartz Ave., Danville. Ph: (510) 837-4040. American.
Windy City West, 356 Hartz Ave., Danville. Ph: (510) 820-4840.
Windy City West Pasta, 120 E. Prospect Ave., Danville. Ph: (510) 820-2427. Italian.
Yuki of Tokyo, 200 Hartz Ave., Danville. Ph: (510) 838-2505. Japanese.
Yvonne T's, 103 Town & Country Drive, Danville. Ph: (510) 837-2397.

El Cerrito

Armadillo Pizza, 10180 San Pablo Ave., El Cerrito. Ph: (510) 528-7777. Mexican.
Burger King, 6021 Central Ave., El Cerrito. Ph: (510) 525-6377. Fast food.
Cafe Viale, 100 El Cerrito Plaza, El Cerrito. Ph: (510) 526-9429.
Carrows Restaurant, 6120 Potrero Ave., El Cerrito. Ph: (510) 235-3209. American.
Chef Choy Chinese Restaurant, 10166 San Pablo Ave., El Cerrito. Ph: (510) 525-9240. Chinese.
Chevys Mexican Restaurant, 6 El Cerrito Plaza, El Cerrito. Ph: (510) 526-2551. Mexican.
Church's Fried Chicken, 11575 San Pablo Ave., El Cerrito. Ph: (510) 215-0141. Fast food.
El Amigo, 10561 San Pablo Ave., El Cerrito. Ph: (510) 526-3066. Mexican.
El Patio Chuckburger, 10682 San Pablo Ave., El Cerrito. Ph: (510) 527-1210.
Fatapple's Restaurant & Bakery, 7525 Fairmont Ave., El Cerrito. Ph: (510) 528-3433.
Golden Dynasty Restaurant, 10140 San Pablo Ave., El Cerrito. Ph: (510) 524-7851. Chinese.
Gou Bu Li Chinese Restaurant, 10684 San Pablo Ave., El Cerrito. Ph: (510) 525-5362. Chinese.
Green Garden Coffee Shop, 11265 San Pablo Ave., El Cerrito. Ph: (510) 231-0182.
International House of Pancakes, 11701 San Pablo Ave., El Cerrito. Ph: (510) 232-0177.
Jack In The Box, 10409 San Pablo Ave., El Cerrito. Ph: (510) 525-6271. Fast food.
Kentucky Fried Chicken, 10175 San Pablo Ave., El Cerrito. Ph: (510) 528-0125. Fast food.

King Chwan Chinese Restaurant, 225 El Cerrito Plaza, El Cerrito. Ph: (510) 525-8737. Chinese.
Kirby's Restaurant, 10 El Cerrito Plaza, El Cerrito. Ph: (510) 524-1086. American.
Krung Tep Thai Cuisine, 11224 San Pablo Ave., El Cerrito. Ph: (510) 232-9316. Thai.
Little Ange's, 6115 Potrero Ave., El Cerrito. Ph: (510) 232-8979.
Little Hong Kong Restaurant, 10350 San Pablo Ave., El Cerrito. Ph: (510) 524-7599. Chinese.
Lotus Pizza, 10550 San Pablo Ave., El Cerrito. Ph: (510) 524-8000. Italian.
Mandarin House, 10443 San Pablo Ave., El Cerrito. Ph: (510) 524-6035. Chinese.
Marlo's Italian Cuisine, 11299 San Pablo Ave., El Cerrito. Ph: (510) 237-0033. Italian.
McDonald's, 11821 San Pablo Ave., El Cerrito. Ph: (510) 232-2121. Fast food.
Mogami Japanese Restaurant, 10887 San Pablo Ave., El Cerrito. Ph: (510) 233-8780. Japanese.
Nation's Giant Hamburgers & Great Pies, 6060 Central Ave., El Cerrito. Ph: (510) 528-8888. American.
Nib's Burgers, 10841 San Pablo Ave., El Cerrito. Ph: (510) 233-6620. American.
Oriental Restaurant, 10264 San Pablo Ave., El Cerrito. Ph: (510) 526-5188. Chinese.
Original Peking Restaurant, 10675 San Pablo Ave., El Cerrito. Ph: (510) 524-8772. Chinese.
Pizza Hut, 11775 San Pablo Ave., El Cerrito. Ph: (510) 232-2400. Italian.
Shem's Place, 9935 San Pablo Ave., El Cerrito. Ph: (510) 525-8313.
Sizzler Restaurants, 11344 San Pablo Ave., El Cerrito. Ph: (510) 235-7355. American.
Subway Sandwiches & Salads Inc., 10398 San Pablo Ave., El Cerrito. Ph: (510) 527-4300. Fast food.
Thai Gourmet Kitchen & Pizza, 7516 Fairmount Ave., El Cerrito. Ph: (510) 525-9080. Thai & Mexican.
The Juice House, 340 El Cerrito Plaza, El Cerrito. Ph: (510) 526-2037.
The Junket, 235 El Cerrito Plaza, El Cerrito. Ph: (510) 524-4622.
The Red Onion, 11900 San Pablo Ave., El Cerrito. Ph: (510) 236-9462. American.
The Shutter, 10066 San Pablo Ave., El Cerrito. Ph: (510) 525-4227.
Tokyo House, 10546 San Pablo Ave., El Cerrito. Ph: (510) 527-9733. Japanese.
Top Burritos, 10390 San Pablo Ave., El Cerrito. Ph: (510) 525-8355. Mexican.

Top Thai Cuisine, 10621 San Pablo Ave., El Cerrito. Ph: (510) 528-0709. Thai.
Wienerschnitzel, 11101 San Pablo Ave., El Cerrito. Ph: (510) 232-0800. Fast food.
Yokohama Japanease Restaurant, 11880 San Pablo Ave., El Cerrito. Ph: (510) 234-0821. Japanese.
Yusan's, 11866 San Pablo Ave., El Cerrito. Ph: (510) 233-0606. Japanese.

El Sobrante

Coffe Shop, 5094 Appian Way, El Sobrante. Ph: (510) 222-2248. American.
El Sobrante Number One, 3873 San Pablo Dam Road, El Sobrante. Ph: (510) 222-6960.
El Tumi Restaurant, 3748 San Pablo Dam Road, El Sobrante. Ph: (510) 222-0607. Mexican.
Hong Kong Express, 3340 San Pablo Dam Road, El Sobrante. Ph: (510) 223-0688. Chinese.
Jack-In-The-Box Drive Thru Restaurants, 4080 San Pablo Dam Road, El Sobrante. Ph: (510) 223-3354. Fast food.
Jo-Ba-Ja's, 3721 San Pablo Dam Road, El Sobrante. Ph: (510) 223-0702.
Joe's Pizza Factory, 4203 Valley View Road, El Sobrante. Ph: (510) 222-9925. Italian.
Kentucky Fried Chicken, 3300 San Pablo Dam Road, El Sobrante. Ph: (510) 222-6973. Fast food.
Let's Do Lunch, 4592 Appian Way, El Sobrante. Ph: (510) 223-5315.
Mandarin House-El Sobrante, ,5047 Appian Way, El Sobrante. Ph: (510) 223-2060. Chinese.
McDonald's, 3320 San Pablo Dam Road, El Sobrante. Ph: (510) 223-9838. Fast food.
Ocean Yacht, 3741 San Pablo Dam Road, El Sobrante. Ph: (510) 222-8191.
P-J's Restaurant & Cocktail Lounge, 3721 San Pablo Dam Road, El Sobrante. Ph: (510) 222-0221.
Poker Pizza, 5090 Appian Way, El Sobrante. Ph: (510) 223-5151. Italian.
Sam's Dog House, 3857 San Pablo Dam Road, El Sobrante. Ph: (510) 223-8870. American.
Subway Sandwich & Salads, 3800 San Pablo Dam Road, El Sobrante. Ph: (510) 223-7566. Fast food.
Taco Bell, 4068 San Pablo Dam Road, El Sobrante. Ph: (510) 222-8220. Fast food.
The Lion's Den Restaurant, 4241 Valley View Road, El Sobrante. Ph: (510) 222-7523.
The Original Red Onion, 4783 Appian Way, El Sobrante. Ph: (510) 223-6856. American.
Trevino's Restaurant, 11795 San Pablo Ave., El Camino. Ph: (510) 234-7462.

Hercules

Burgerama, 1581 Sycamore Ave., Hercules. Ph: (510) 799-3637. American.
Cafe Nobel, 825 Alfred Nobel Drive, Her-

Drumming up an appetite

RESTAURANTS

cules. Ph: (510) 724-7636.
Chess Cafe, 1511 Sycamore Ave., Hercules. Ph: (510) 799-9719.
Dragon Terrace, 1581 Sycamore Ave., Hercules. Ph: (510) 799-3838. Chinese.
Jamalos Pizza & Pasta, 844 Willow Ave., Hercules. Ph: (510) 799-3391. Italian.
McDonald's, 1570 Sycamore Ave., Hercules. Ph: (510) 245-0912. Fast food.
Oriental Food To Go, 1572 Sycamore Ave., Hercules. Ph: (510) 799-5800. Chinese.
Subway Sandwiches & Salads, 1572 Sycamore Ave., Hercules. Ph: (510) 799-6230. Fast food.
Willow Garden Restaurant, 844 Willow Ave., Hercules. Ph: (510) 799-0778.

Kensington

Ali's, 385 Colusa Ave., Kensington. Ph: (510) 526-1500. Moroccan.

Lafayette

Cafe Barbara, 1005 Brown Ave., Lafayette. Ph: (510) 284-9390.
Cape Cod House, 3666 Mt. Diablo Blvd., Lafayette. Ph: (510) 283-8288. Seafood.
Chaiyos Thai Cuisine, 3555 Mount Diablo Blvd., Lafayette. Ph: (510) 283-8883. Thai.
Duck Club Restaurant, 3287 Mount Diablo Blvd., Lafayette. Ph: (510) 283-7108. Continental.
El Charro, 3339 Mount Diablo Blvd., Lafayette. Ph: (510) 283-2345. Mexican.
Express Cafe, 3732 Mount Diablo Blvd., Lafayette. Ph: (510) 283-7170.
Fish-N-Chips Piccadilly Circus, 3596 Mount Diablo Blvd., Lafayette. Ph: (510) 284-5770.
Flavio's, 3604 Mount Diablo Blvd., Lafayette. Ph: (510) 284-2515. Italian.
Freddie's Pizzeria, 3614 Mount Diablo Blvd., Lafayette. Ph: (510) 284-9110. Italian.
Hungry Hunter, 3201 Mount Diablo Blvd., Lafayette. Ph: (510) 938-3938. American.
Jack-In-The-Box, 3407 Mount Diablo Blvd., Lafayette. Ph: (510) 284-1371. Fast food.
Kaffee Barbara Restaurant, 1005 Brown Ave., Lafayette. Ph: (510) 284-9390.
Kentucky Fried Chicken, 3455 Mount Diablo Blvd., Lafayette. Ph: (510) 284-7310. Fast food.
Killarney Restaurant, 3535 Mount Diablo Blvd., Lafayette. Ph: (510) 284-7822. Fast food.
Le Marquis, 3524 B Mount Diablo Blvd., Lafayette. Ph: (510) 284-4322.
Loard's Ice Cream, 3590 Mount Diablo Blvd., Lafayette. Ph: (510) 283-2353.
Los Gallos, 3707 Mt. Diablo Blvd., Lafayette. Ph: (510) 283-4033. Mexican.
Marquis, 3524 Mount Diablo Blvd., Lafayette. Ph: (510) 284-4422. French.
Millie's Kitchen, 1018 Oak Hill Road, Lafayette. Ph: (510) 283-2397.
Miraku, 3740 Mount Diablo Blvd., Lafayette. Ph: (510) 284-5700. Japanese.
Pasta Stop, 3569 Mount Diablo Blvd., Lafayette. Ph: (510) 283-1620. Italian.
Petar's, 32 Lafayette Cir., Lafayette. Ph: (510) 284-7117. Continental.
Plaza Bistro, 3685 Mount Diablo Blvd., Lafayette. Ph: (510) 284-2446.
Round Table Pizza, 3637 Mount Diablo Blvd., Lafayette. Ph: (510) 283-0404. Pizza.
Royal Cafe, 3518 Mount Diablo Blvd., Lafayette. Ph: (510) 283-3370.
Ruby Restaurant, 3444 Mount Diablo Blvd., Lafayette. Ph: (510) 283-7272.
Senor Nero Mexican Restaurant, 3606 Mount Diablo Blvd., Lafayette. Ph: (510) 283-1313. Mexican.
Station One, 3343 Mount Diablo Blvd., Lafayette. Ph: (510) 283-3233. American.
Taco Bell, 3510A Mount Diablo Blvd., Lafayette. Ph: (510) 284-1754. Fast food.
Tang's Restaurant, 3555 Mt. Diablo Blvd., Lafayette. Ph: (510) 284-7569. Chinese.
The Great Wall, 3500 Golden Gate Way, Lafayette. Ph: (510) 284-3500. Chinese.
The Squirrels, 998 Moraga Blvd., Lafayette. Ph: (510) 284-7830. American.
Togo's, 3647 Mount Diablo Blvd., Lafayette. Ph: (510) 283-5950. Fast food.
Tokyo Chicken, 3406 Mt. Diablo Blvd., Lafayette. Ph: (510) 283-3890. Japanese.
Tourelle, 3565 Mount Diablo Blvd., Lafayette. Ph: (510) 284-3565. Continental.

Martinez

Amato's, 414 Ferry Street, Martinez. Ph: (510) 313-0523. Italian.
Bella Roma Pizza, 4040 Alhambra Ave., Martinez. Ph: (510) 228-4935. Pizza.
Burger King, 6638 Alhambra Ave., Martinez. Ph: (510) 933-8778. Fast food.
Burger King, 7 Muir Road, Martinez. Ph: (510) 228-1292. Fast food.
Cafe Bohemia, 514 Main Street, Martinez. Ph: (510) 228-0301. Czechoslovakian.
Cafe Romano, 533 Main St., Martinez. Ph: (510) 370-0700. Italian.
Canton Restaurant, 719 Main St., Martinez. Ph: (510) 228-0100. Chinese.
Carrows Cafe & Bakery, 500 Center Ave., Martinez. Ph: (510) 228-0600. American.
Chicken Asado, 1311 Pine, Martinez. Ph: (510) 229-2199.
China Villa, 2376 Pacheco Blvd., Martinez.

204 CONTRA COSTA & SOLANO

Ph: (510) 229-4078. Chinese.
Chris' Snack Bar, 725 Court, Martinez. Ph: (510) 228-7351.
Connie's California Continental Cuisine, 1333 Pine, Martinez. Ph: (510) 228-5486. California.
Creative Croissants, 1029 Arnold Drive, Martinez. Ph: (510) 228-8938.
Dimaggio's Restaurant, 701 Main, Martinez. Ph: (510) 229-1525.
Domino's Pizza, 1622 Pacheco Blvd., Martinez. Ph: (510) 372-5555. Pizza.
Donna's Restaurant, 929 Alhambra Ave., Martinez. Ph: (510) 228-9009.
Down Home Texas BBQ-No. 4, 2250 Pacheco Blvd., Martinez. Ph: (510) 370-0147. Barbecue.
Family Kitchen No. 2, 825 Escobar, Martinez. Ph: (510) 228-0660.
Ferry Street Station, 600 Ferry, Martinez. Ph: (510) 228-9220.
Fortune City Restaurant, 6635 Alhambra Ave., Martinez. Ph: (510) 933-4572. Chinese.
Foster's Old Fashioned Freeze, 1500 Pacheco Blvd., Martinez. Ph: (510) 372-8693. American.
Fubar's, 1150 Arnold Drive, Martinez. Ph: (510) 370-1282. American.
George's Deli & Restaurant, 889 Howe Road, Martinez. Ph: (510) 370-0740. American.
Giovanni's Deli & Catering, 601 Main, Martinez. Ph: (510) 228-2452. Italian.
Grand China, 1135-G Arnold Drive, Martinez. Ph: (510) 372-3322. Chinese.
Gung Ho Kitchen, 1170 Arnold Drive, Martinez. Ph: (510) 228-8888.
Gyro Place, 729 Ferry, Martinez. Ph: (510) 228-7445.
Hangar One, 4966 Pacheco Blvd., Martinez. Ph: (510) 229-5666.
Haute Stuff, 521 Main Street, Martinez. Ph: (510) 229-0521. California Cuisine.
International House of Pancakes, 1190 Arnold Drive, Martinez. Phone: (510) 228-3322.
Jack-In-The-Box Restaurant, 3955 Alhambra Ave., Martinez. Ph: (510) 229-2288. Fast food.
Jalisco Grill, 6635 Alhambra Ave., Martinez. Ph: (510) 944-5516. Mexican.
Joe's Martinez Bar & Grill, 3925 Alhambra Ave., Martinez. Ph: (510) 228-8700.
Kentucky Fried Chicken, 4025 Alhambra Ave., Martinez. Ph: (510) 229-2244. Fast food.
Kingsway Fish & Chips, 732 Main, Martinez. Ph: (510) 228-6333.
La Casita, 924 Court, Martinez. Ph: (510) 372-0536. Mexican.
Le Beau's Bar & Grill, 436 Ferry, Martinez. Ph: (510) 372-8941. Creole-Cajun.
Louie Bertola's, 611 Escobar, Martinez. Ph: (510) 372-0688. Italian.
McDonald's, 1155 Arnold Drive, Martinez. Ph: (510) 229-0757.
Mr. Philly, 1170 Arnold Drive, Martinez. Ph: (510) 228-6668.
Mr. T's Coffee Shop, 3206 Pacheco Blvd., Martinez. Ph: (510) 3206 Pacheco Blvd. Martinez.
Numero Uno Taqueria, 1125-D. Arnold Drive, Martinez. Ph: (510) 370-9800. Mexican.
Peggs Cafe Grill, 3210 Pacheco Blvd., Martinez. Ph: (510) 370-6379.
Peking-Tokyo, 522 Center Ave., Martinez. Ph: (510) 372-3366. Chinese-Japanese.
Pizza Hut, 6648 Alhambra Ave., Martinez. Ph: (510) 256-0788. Pizza.
Quarter LB Big Burger, 3792 Pacheco Blvd., Martinez. Ph: (510) 228-9941. Fast food.
Ristorante Ze', 823 Main Street, Martinez. Ph: (510) 228-7795. Italian.
Ron's Cafe, 1350 Arnold Drive, Martinez. Ph: (510) 229-3474.
Round Table Pizza, 504 Center, Martinez. Ph: (510) 370-0626. Pizza.
Taco Bell, 11 Muir Road, Martinez. Ph: (510) 372-9585. Fast food.
The Albatross, 15 N. Court, Martinez. Ph: (510) 228-3800.
The Family Kitchen Martinez Creamery, 825 Escobar, Martinez. Ph: (510) 372-7033.
The Savoy Restaurant, 633 Escobar, Martinez. Ph: (510) 938-2911.
Vicki's Hot Dogs, 925 Main, Martinez. Ph: (510) 229-3595. American.
Weird Harold's, 621 Las Juntas, Martinez. Ph: (510) 372-5788.
Wendy's, 1330 Arnold Drive, Martinez. Ph: (510) 229-5947. Fast food.
Wendy's, 3455 Alhambra Ave., Martinez. Ph: (510) 370-1275. Fast food.
Wing Wah Restaurant, 822 Escobar, Martinez. Ph: (510) 372-0842. Chinese.
Wink's Restaurant, 3835 Alhambra Ave., Martinez. Ph: (510) 372-7609.

Moraga

Chef Chao, 343 Rheem Blvd., Moraga. Ph: (510) 376-1740. Chinese.
Chez Maurice, 360 Park, Moraga. Ph: (510) 376-1655. French.
Fireside Grill, 489 Moraga Road, Moraga. Ph: (510) 376-5127.

RESTAURANTS

Jack-In-The-Box, 1440 Moraga Way, Moraga. Ph: (510) 376-0642. Fast food.
Mondello's Cucina Italiana, 337 Rheem Blvd., Moraga. Ph: (510) 376-2533. Italian.
Moraga Coffee Shop, 1419 Moraga Way, Moraga. Ph: (510) 376-3832. American.
Moraga Country Club, 1600 Saint Andrews Dr., Moraga. Ph: (510) 376-1943. Continental.
Nation's Giant Hamburgers & Great Pies, 400 Park, Moraga. Ph: (510) 376-8888. American.
New Taipei Restaurant, 380 Park, Moraga. Ph: (510) 376-8558. Chinese.
Pepe's, 556 Center St., Moraga. Ph: (510) 376-4030. Mexican.
Round Table Pizza, 361 Rheem Blvd., Moraga. Ph: (510) 376-1411. Pizza.
Shangri-La Restaurant, 1460 Moraga Road, Moraga. Ph: (510) 376-0809. Chinese.
Taco Bell, 410 Moraga Road, Moraga. Ph: (510) 376-8071. Fast food.

Oakley

Becky's Restaurant, 144 Main, Oakley. Ph: (510) 625-1333.
Burger King, 2505 Main, Oakley. Ph: (510) 625-0338. Fast food.
Buzz Inn, Main Street, Oakley. Ph: (510) 625-0234.
Ernie's Hot Dogs, Highway 4, Oakley. Ph: (510) 625-1515. Fast food.
Little Manuel's, 142 Main St., Oakley. Ph: (510) 625-2449. Mexican.
Mr. Wong's Chinese Restaurant, 2005 Main, Oakley. Ph: (510) 625-0607. Chinese.
Pasta Cafe, 2085 Main, Oakley. Ph: (510) 625-4594. Italian.
Raley's Hot Wok, 2075 Main, Oakley. Ph: (510) 625-0744. Chinese.
Round Table Pizza, 3070 Main, Oakley. Ph: (510) 625-1700. Pizza.
Silver River Restaurant, 276 Main, Oakley. Ph: (510) 625-9783.
Taco Bell, 2015 Main, Oakley. Ph: (510) 625-9929. Fast food.
The Snack Shop, 3921 Main, Oakley. Ph: (510) 625-9351.

Orinda

Alexander Lanzone, 65 Moraga Way, Orinda. Ph: (510) 253-1322.
Alexander Ristorante, 65 Moraga Way, Orinda. Ph: (510) 253-1322. Italian.
Burritos & Dreams, 15 Moraga Way, Orinda. Ph: (510) 254-1693. Mexican.
Caffe Plaza, 87 Orinda Way, Orinda. Ph: (510) 254-2084.
Casa Orinda, 20 Bryant Way, Orinda. Ph: (510) 254-2981. American.
Chef Han, 1 Camino Sobrante, Orinda. Ph: (510) 254-1606.
Don Jose's Mexican Restaurant, 1 Orinda Way, Orinda. Ph: (510) 254-1957. Mexican.
Hama-Yu, 99 Oringa Way, Orinda. Ph: (510) 254-7260. Japanese.
Nation's Giant Hamburgers & Great Pies, 76 Moraga Way, Orinda. Ph: (510) 254-8888. American.
OB's At Pine Grove, 4 Orinda Way, Orinda. Ph: (510) 254-7§13.
Orinda Szechwan-Chinese Restaurant, 79 Orinda Way, Orinda. Ph: (510) 254-2020. Chinese.
Pasta Cuisine, 2 Theatre Square, Orinda. Ph: (510) 254-5423. Italian.
Pasta Stop, 1 Camino Sobrante, Orinda. Ph: (510) 254-8133. Italian.
Serika Restaurant, 2 Theatre Square, Orinda. Ph: (510) 254-7088. Japanese.
Szechwan Restaurant, 79 Orinda Way, Orinda. Ph: (510) 254-2020. Chinese.
Village Inn Cafe, 290 Village Square, Orinda. Ph: (510) 254-6080.
Village Pizza, 19A-B Orinda Way, Orinda. Ph: (510) 254-1200. Pizza.
Vintage House, 25 Orinda Way, Orinda. Ph: (510) 254-7733.

Pacheco

California Grand, 5867 Pacheco Blvd., Pacheco. Ph: (510) 685-8397.
Hop Sing's Kitchen, 5868 Pacheco Blvd., Pacheco. Ph: (510) 786-3360. Chinese.
Hot Dog Heaven, 5860 Pacheco Blvd., Pacheco. Ph: (510) 680-1705. American.
Los Panchos Mexican Restaurant, 5850 Pacheco Blvd., Pacheco. Ph: (510) 689-4430. Mexican.
Maggie's I, 5224 Pacheco Blvd., Pacheco. Ph: (510) 680-8934.
Run Burger Run, 5830 Pacheco Blvd., Pacheco. Ph: (510) 676-7900. American.
Wendy's, 5943 Pacheco Blvd., Pacheco. Ph: (510) 686-2790. Fast food.
Won Kee Kitchen, 5867 Pacheco Blvd., Pacheco. Ph: (510) 685-0847. Chinese.

Pinole

Alfonso's Mexican Restaurant, 624E San Pablo Ave., Pinole. Ph: (510) 724-7998. Mexican.
Blackie's Maryland Fried Chicken, 600 Tennant Ave., Pinole. Ph: (510) 724-4851.
Burger King, 1571 Fitzgerald Drive, Pinole. Ph: (510) 223-0377. Fast food.
Carl's Jr. Restaurant, 1550 Fitzgerald Drive, Pinole. Ph: (510) 223-2562. Fast food.

206 CONTRA COSTA & SOLANO

Foster's Freeze, 993 San Pablo Ave., Pinole. Ph: (510) 724-8782. Fast food.
House of Hunan, 2700 Pinole Valley Road, Pinole. Ph: (510) 758-2028. Chinese.
Hunan Villa Chinese Restaurant, 632-A San Pablo Ave., Pinole. Ph: (510) 724-1368. Chinese.
Jack In The Box, 2689 Pinole Valley Road, Pinole. Ph: (510) 758-2346. Fast food.
Kentucky Fried Chicken, 1544 Fitzgerald Drive, Pinole. Ph: (510) 222-6742. Fast food.
La Spaghettata, 2772 Pinole Valley Road, Pinole. Ph: (510) 262-9202. Sicilian.
Long John Silver's Seafood Shoppe, 1541 Fitzgerald Drive, Pinole. Ph: (510) 222-1413. Fast food.
Lord Shiva Indian Cuisine, 1501 Tara Hills Dricve, Pinole. Ph: (510) 724-3605. Indian.
Mandarin House, 5047 Appian Way, Pinole. Ph: (510) 223-2060. Chinese.
Poko, 1569 Tara Hills Drive, Pinole. Ph: (510) 724-8106.
Rickshaw Restaurant, 1560 Fitzgerald Drive, Pinole. Ph: (510) 222-6677. Chinese.
Round Table Pizza, 1596 Fitzgerald Drive, Pinole. Ph: (510) 222-9988. Pizza.
Schober's Restaurant, 1300 Pinole Valley Road, Pinole. Ph: (510) 724-1554. Continental.
Sizzler Restaurants, 1515 Fitzgerald Drive, Pinole. Ph: (510) 222-3468. American.
Tachikawa Japanese Restaurant, 632 San Pablo Ave., Pinole. Ph: (510) 724-2090. Japanese.
The Alley, 2265 Pear, Pinole. Ph: (510) 724-5312.
The Embers, 600 San Pablo Ave., Pinole. Ph: (510) 724-4949.
The Persimmon Tree, 2454 San Pablo Ave., Pinole. Ph: (510) 724-1040.
The Red Onion, 2870 Pinole Valley Road, Pinole. Ph: (510) 758-9462. American.
Uncle Chung's Szechuan, 2550 Appian Way, Pinole. Ph: (510) 222-8881. Chinese.
Wendy's, 1581 Fitsgerald Drive, Pinole. Ph: (510) 262-0242. Fast food.
Zip's Restaurant, 2727 Pinole Valley Road, Pinole. Ph: (510) 758-6171. American.

Pittsburg

Al's Snack Shop, E. 17th & Railroad Ave., Pittsburg. Ph: (510) 439-9691.
Arby's Restaurants, 2243 Loveridge Road, Pittsburg. Ph: (510) 473-0232. American.
Ben's Burgers, 2775 Willow Pass Road, Pittsburg. Ph: (510) 458-4040. American.
Birrieria Y Taqueria Yahualica, 13 S. Bella Monte Ave., Pittsburg. Ph: (510) 458-5549. Mexican.
Blew Whale Cafe, 306 Railroad Ave., Pittsburg. Ph: (510) 427-1076.
Burger King, 2162 Railroad Ave., Pittsburg. Ph: (510) 432-2297. Fast food.
Burger King, 604 Bailey Road, Pittsburg. Ph: (510) 458-9311. Fast food.
C & C's Bar-B-Que, 785 Railroad Ave., Pittsburg. Ph: (510) 439-1955.
Canton's Kitchen, 184 Atlantic Ave., Pittsburg. Ph: (510) 439-3033. Chinese.
Carl's Jr. Restaurants, 4595 Century Blvd., Pittsburg. Ph: (510) 754-5423. Fast food.
Carlo's Pizzeria, 2099 Railroad Ave., Pittsburg. Ph: (510) 432-2848. Italian.
Casa Veronica Mexican Restaurant, 700 Railroad Ave., Pittsburg. Ph: (510) 432-7440. Mexican.
Chico's Mexican Restaurant, 162 Atlantic Ave., Pittsburg. Ph: (510) 427-5596. Mexican.
China Express, 660 Bailey Road, Pittsburg. Ph: (510) 458-6087. Chinese.
China Restaurant, 368 Leslie Drive, Pittsburg. Ph: (510) 432-8822. Chinese.
Copper Skillet, 3745 Railroad Ave., Pittsburg. Ph: (510) 439-3060. American.
Domino's Pizza, 3724 Railroad Ave., Pittsburg, 427-3030, Italian. Pizza.
Down Home Texas Barbeque III, 2175 Railroad Ave., Pittsburg. Ph: (510) 439-3305. Barbecue.
Frito Bandido, 2447 Willow Pass Road, Pittsburg. Ph: (510) 458-8340. Mexican.
George's Coffee Shop, 3712 Railroad Ave., Pittsburg. Ph: (510) 427-0407. American.
Guadalajara Restaurant, 2474 Willow Pass Road, Pittsburg. Ph: (510) 458-5287. Mexican.
Hamburger Stand, 2285 Railroad Ave., Pittsburg. Ph: (510) 432-7648. American.
Jack In The Box, 2135 Railroad Ave., Pittsburg. Ph: (510) 432-3378. Fast food.
Joseph's Hot Dogs, 602 Port Chicago Hwy., Pittsburg. Ph: (510) 458-2307. Fast food.
Juarez Mexican Food, 3811 Railroad Ave., Pittsburg. Ph: (510) 432-2135. Mexican.
Kentucky Fried Chicken, 2155 Railroad Ave., Pittsburg. Ph: (510) 439-2101. Fast food.
La Marina, 395 Railroad Ave., Pittsburg. Ph: (510) 439-1222.
Liberty Hotel Restaurant, 200 E. 3rd, Pittsburg. Ph: (510) 427-1770.
Los Gordos, 205 Port Chicago Hwy., Pittsburg. Ph: (510) 458-5377. Mexican.
Los Medanos Lanes, 1411 East Leland Road, Pittsburg. Ph: (510) 432-2695.

Mariza's Food To Go, 2273 Railroad Ave., Pittsburg. Ph: (510) 432-6985. Fast food.
McAvoy Harbor Restaurant, 780 Port Chicago Hwy., Pittsburg. Ph: (510) 709-1357.
McDonald's, 460 Atlantic Ave., Pittsburg. Ph: (510) 432-4081. Fast food.
Nation's Giant Hamburgers & Great Pies, 3789 Railroad Ave., Pittsburg. Ph: (510) 432-3103. American.
New Mecca, 324 Railroad Ave., Pittsburg. Ph: (510) 432-7433.
Nicki's Cafe, 2921 Harbor, Pittsburg. Ph: (510) 432-9766.
Norma's Bar-B-Q, 1996 Harbor, Pittsburg. Ph: (510) 432-27880. Barbecue.
Olive Garden Italian Restaurant, 4195 Century Blvd., Pittsburg. Ph: (510) 778-6208. Italian.
Padrinos, 745 Railroad Ave., Pittsburg. Ph: (510) 427-9000.
Prima Donna Cake Box, 135 East Leland Road, Pittsburg. Ph: (510) 432-4385.
Round Table Pizza, 1331 Buchanan Road, Pittsburg. Ph: (510) 432-1000. Pizza.
Round Table Pizza, 408 Bailey Road, Pittsburg. Ph: (510) 348-2244. Pizza.
Royal Palace Restaurant, 2909 Railroad Ave., Pittsburg. Ph: (510) 427-1090. Chinese.
Rudy's Restaurant, 2222 Railroad Ave., Pittsburg. Ph: (510) 439-1992.
Sandra Country Kitchen, 690 Railroad Ave., Pittsburg. Ph: (510) 427-9360.
Snooker Pete's, 3788 Railroad Ave., Pittsburg. Ph: (510) 439-9090.
Straw Hat Pizza, 2905 Railroad Ave., Pittsburg. Ph: (510) 432-2100. Pizza.
Subway Sandwiches & Salads, 532 Bailey Road, Pittsburg. Ph: (510) 458-8018. Fast food.
Sun On Restaurant, 1317 Buchanan Road, Pittsburg. Ph: (510) 439-3959. Chinese.
Super Taco Mexican Food To Go, 295 E. 10th, Pittsburg. Ph: (510) 439-3320. Mexican.
Taco Bell, 2111 Loveridge Road, Pittsburg. Ph: (510) 432-2873. Fast food.
Taco Bell, 2713 Willow Pass Road, Pittsburg. Ph: (510) 458-9956. Fast food.
That's Amore, 453 Railroad Ave., Pittsburg. Ph: (510) 432-3581.
The Cheese Steak Shop, 4581 Century Blvd., Pittsburg. Ph: (510) 706-0625.
Togo's Eatery, 2901 Railroad Ave., Pittsburg. Ph: (510) 432-8441. Fast food.
Tom's Elegant Steak House, 2921 Harbor, Pittsburg. Ph: (510) 427-1970.

Tung's Chinese Restaurant, 149 Atlantic Ave., Pittsburg. Ph: (510) 427-0932. Chinese.
Western Sizzlin Restaurant, 140 East Leland Road, Pittsburg. Ph: (510) 427-1060.
Zio Nicolo's, 2222 Golf Club Road, Pittsburg. Ph: (510) 432-1700.

Pleasant Hill

Almond Bud Villa Chinese Cuisine, 2344 Monument Blvd., Pleasant Hill. Ph: (510) 686-2961. Chinese.
Andy's Monument Coffee Shop, 2265 Contra Costa Blvd., Pleasant Hill. Ph: (510) 798-4119.
Arooj Restaurant, 2371 Contra Costa Blvd., Pleasant Hill. Ph: (510) 934-7740.
Back Forty Texas Bar-B-Q, 1941 Oak Park Blvd., Pleasant Hill. Ph: (510) 935-1440.
Bangkok Restaurant, 1910 Oak Park Blvd., Pleasant Hill. Ph: (510) 937-4368. Thai.
Bud's Burgers, 1432 Contra Costa Blvd., Pleasant Hill. Ph: (510) 798-4233. American.
Burger King, 677 Contra Costa Blvd., Pleasant Hill. Ph: (510) 689-2644. Fast food.
Burger Road, 1625 Contra Costa Blvd., Pleasant Hill. Ph: (510) 798-5339. American.
Cafe Milano, 716 Contra Costa Blvd., Pleasant Hill. Ph: (510) 682-3333. Iranian-Persian.
Carlos Murphy's, 999 Contra Costa Blvd., Pleasant Hill. Ph: (510) 827-0655.

After soccer a pizza would be nice

CONTRA COSTA & SOLANO

Carrows Restaurant, 624 Contra Costa Blvd., Pleasant Hill. Ph: (510) 689-5757. American.

Casper's Hot Dogs, 6 Vivian Drive, Pleasant Hill. Ph: (510) 687-6030. Fast food.

Chevys Mexican Restaurant, 650 Ellinwood Way, Pleasant Hill. Ph: (510) 685-6651. Mexican.

China Garden, 2223 Morello Ave., Pleasant Hill. Ph: (510) 676-8585. Chinese.

Coco's Family Restaurant, 3202 Buskirk Ave., Pleasant Hill. Ph: (510) 937-2710. American.

Confettis Restaurant & Pasta Market, 1900 Contra Costa Blvd., Pleasant Hill. Ph: (510) 687-1680. Italian.

Dallimonti's Family Style Restaurant, 1932 Oak Park Blvd., Pleasant Hill. Ph: (510) 944-5224. Italian.

El Tapatio Restaurant, 40 Golf Club Road, Pleasant Hill. Ph: (510) 676-2420. Mexican.

Emperor Restaurant, 2001 Contra Costa Blvd., Pleasant Hill. Ph: (510) 671-9100.

Flambeau's, 205 Coggins Drive, Pleasant Hill. Ph: (510) 933-4894. French.

Gene's Restaurant, 2237 Morello Ave., Pleasant Hill. Ph: (510) 676-8778. Filipino.

Giant Chef Burger Inc., 10 Golf Club Road, Pleasant Hill. Ph: (510) 689-6094. Hamburgers & Hot Dogs.

Golden Ching Chinese Restaurant, 2653 Pleasant Hill Road, Pleasant Hill. Ph: (510) 934-9393. Chinese.

Golden Oak Restaurant, 2618 Pleasant Hill Road, Pleasant Hill. Ph: (510) 256-8899. American.

India Restaurant, 2371 Contra Costa Blvd., Pleasant Hill. Ph: (510) 934-7740.

Jack-In-The-Box Drive-Thru, 1817 Contgra Costa Blvd., Pleasant Hill. Ph: (510) 685-3542. Fast food.

Kentucky Fried Chicken, 635 Contra Costa Blvd., Pleasant Hill. Ph: (510) 689-6381. Fast food.

Lee Wah Restaurant, 1428 Contra Costa Blvd., Pleasant Hill. Ph: (510) 798-4885. Chinese.

Lisa's House of Hot Dogs, 240 Golf Club Road, Pleasant Hill. Ph: (510) 687-6454. American.

Lyon's Restaurant, 2059 Contra Costa Blvd., Pleasant Hill. Ph: (510) 682-1668. American.

Mary's Pizza Shack, 1420 Contra Costa Blvd., Pleasant Hill. Ph: (510) 356-2797. Italian.

McDonald's, 65 Chilpancingo Pkwy, Pleasant Hill. Ph: (510) 680-9571. Fast food.

Melo's, 1660 Contra Costa Blvd., Pleasant Hill. Ph: (510) 687-1880. Italian.

Mexican Burritos, 2101 Contra Costa Blvd., Pleasant Hill. Ph: (510) 687-3870. Mexican.

Ming Wah Restaurant, 2290 Monument Blvd., Pleasant Hill. Ph: (510) 827-3450. Chinese.

Nation's Giant Hamburgers & Great Pies, 2195 Contra Costa Blvd., Pleasant Hill. Ph: (510) 798-4280. American.

Pacific Fresh, 550 Ellinwood Way, Pleasant Hill. Ph: (510) 827-3474. Seafood.

Pazzo Ristorante, 1420 Contra Costa Blvd., Pleasant Hill. Ph: (510) 676-4332. Italian.

Pizza Hut, 1749 Contra Costa Blvd., Pleasant Hill. Ph: (510) 686-1616. Pizza.

Plaza Cafe, 1912 Contra Costa Blvd., Pleasant Hill. Ph: (510) 827-2811. American.

Round Table Pizza, 1938 Oak Park Blvd., Pleasant Hill. Ph: (510) 930-9004. Pizza.

Round Table Pizza, 2609 Pleasant Hill Road, Pleasant Hill. Ph: (510) 934-6996. Pizza.

Round Table Pizza, 85 Chilpancingo Pkwy., Pleasant Hill. Ph: (510) 798-3355. Pizza.

Shams Pizza Cafe, 716 Contra Costa Blvd., Pleasant Hill. Ph: (510) 685-5764. Italian.

Smuggler's Cove Restaurant, 205 Coggins Drive, Pleasant Hill. Ph: (510) 930-9900. Seafood.

Straw Hat Pizza, 2221 Morello Ave., Pleasant Hill. Ph: (510) 689-6666. Pizza.

Stuart Anderson's Black Angus Restaurant, 3195 N. Main, Pleasant Hill. Ph: (510) 938-9900. American.

Subway Sandwiches & Salads, 1300 Contra Costa Blvd., Pleasant Hill. Ph: (510) 676-7821. Fast food.

Sun Sun Garden, 1675 Contra Costa Blvd., Pleasant Hill. Ph: (510) 686-9190. Chinese.

Sunshine Cafe, 1908 Oak Park Blvd., Pleasant Hill. Ph: (510) 938-5180. American.

Taco Bell, 1700 Contra Costa Blvd., Pleasant Hill. Ph: (510) 680-9544. Fast food.

Taco Grande, 508 Contra Costa Blvd., Pleasant Hill. Ph: (510) 680-9664. Mexican.

Thai Village Restaurant, 670 Gregory Lane, Pleasant Hill. Ph: (510) 256-0289. Thai.

The Bistro, 3478 Buskirk Ave., Pleasant Hill. Ph: (510) 933-1208.

The Velvet Turtle, 100 Chilpancingo Pkwy., Pleasant Hill. Ph: (510) 825-4511. Continental.

Tien Tu Kitchen, 41 Woodsworth Lane, Pleasant Hill. Ph: (510) 682-5150. Chinese.

Togo's Eatery, 2239 Morello Ave., Pleasant Hill. Ph: (510) 798-5886. Fast food.

Tsingtao, 1958 Contra Costa Blvd., Pleasant Hill. Ph: (510) 687-7669. Chinese.

Tsingtao Restaurant, 1958 Contra Costa Blvd., Pleasant Hill. Ph: (510) 671-7669. Chinese.
Velvet Turtle, 100 Chilpacingo Pkwy, Pleasant Hill. Ph: (510) 825-4511. Continental.
Zakuro, 150 Longbrook Ray, Pleasant Hill. Ph: (510) 827-9393. Japanese.
Zio Fraedo's, 701 Gregory Lane, Pleasant Hill. Ph: (510) 933-9091.

Point Richmond
Baltic Restaurant, 135 Park Pl., Point Richmond. Ph: (510) 235-2532. Continental.
Point Orient, 199 Park Place, Point Richmond. Ph: (510) 237-4999. Chinese.

Port Costa
Bull Valley Inn, 14 Canyon Lakes Drive, Port Costa. Ph: (510) 787-2244.
Bull Valley Inn, 14 Canyon Lakes Drive, Port Costa. Ph: (510) 787-2244.
Warehouse Cafe, 5 Canyon Lakes Drive, Port Costa. Ph: (510) 787-1827.

Rheem
La Fonda No 3, 556 Center, Rheem. Ph: (510) 376-4030.
Tamami's Japanese Restaurant, 356 Park, Rheem. Ph: (510) 376-2872. Japanese.
Tommy G's Valley Cafe, 552 Center, Rheem. Ph: (510) 376-6500.
Villa China, 581 Moraga Road, Rheem. Ph: (510) 376-7839. Chinese.

Richmond
All's Fare, 1210 Brickyard Cove Road, Richmond. Ph: (510) 232-1500.
Bakers Square Restaurant & Pie Shop, 12323 San Pablo Ave., Richmond. Ph: (510) 232-6350.
Big Red's, 801 Marina Way South, Richmond. Ph: (510) 234-0904.
Bill's Snack Bar, 100 37th, Richmond. Ph: (510) 232-4539.
Boon Restaurant, 1249 23rd, Richmond. Ph: (510) 233-4818.
Burger King, 12999 San Pablo Ave., Richmond. Ph: (510) 237-4665. Fast food.
Candy's Dream Pie Factory, 570 Harbour Way, Richmond. Ph: (510) 236-2692.
Casper's Hot Dogs, 2530 MacDonald Ave., Richmond. Ph: (510) 235-6492. Fast food.
Chapala's Mexican Cafe, 201 Tewksbury, Richmond. Ph: (510) 236-6725. Mexican.
Chevys Mexican Restaurant, 3101 Garrity Way, Richmond. Ph: (510) 222-9802. Mexican.
Chinese Restaurant, 2409 MacDonald Ave., Richmond. Ph: (510) 236-2222. Chinese.
Chino's Taqueria, 3231 MacDonald Ave., Richmond. Ph: (510) 620-0830. Mexican.

Dalian Restaurant, 12288 San Pablo Ave., Richmond. Ph: (510) 236-4247.
Ducre House of Chicken, 512 5th, Richmond. Ph: (510) 236-6767.
Easter's Coffee Shop, 1802 Cutting Blvd., Richmond. Ph: (510) 233-4457.
Edie's Cafe, 145 Tewksbury Ave., Richmond. Ph: (510) 237-6136.
Ernie Goods Bar B.Q., 2401 MacDonald Ave., Richmond. Ph: (510) 237-2346. Barbecued.
Francisco's Restaurant, 332 MacDonald Ave., Richmond. Ph: (510) 231-º132.
Fujiyama Japanese Steak House, 3044 Hilltop Mall Road, Richmond. Ph: (510) 222-8282. Japanese.
Galley Cafe, Point San Pablo Yacht Harbor, Richmond. Ph: (510) 233-0570.
General Franks Hot Dogs, 221 Tewksbury, Richmond. Ph: (510) 233-2523.
Ginny's Pizza, 353 24th, Richmond. Ph: (510) 236-1977. Pizza.
Golden China Mandarin Restaurant, 2800 Hilltop Mall Road., Suite 250, Richmond. Ph: (510) 222-7620. Chinese.
Golden Oyster Cafe, 12811 San Pablo Ave., Richmond. Ph: (510) 236-4755.
Golden Palace Restaurant, 3829 MacDonald Ave., Richmond. Ph: (510) 233-5332. Chinese.
Golden Star Cafe, 1400 MacDonald Ave., Richmond. Ph: (510) 234-0573. American.
Great American Hamburger & Pie Co., 35 E. Richmond Ave., Richmond. Ph: (510) 233-2223. American.
H. Salt Esquire Fish & Chips, 12929 San Pablo Ave., Richmond. Ph: (510) 232-3884. Fast food.
Hawthorne's At Marina Bay, 1900 Esplanade Dr., Richmond. Ph: (510) 620-0400. Seafood.
Hidden City Cafe, 109 Park Place, Richmond. Ph: (510) 232-9738.
Hilltop Subway Sandwiches & Salads, 2800 Hilltop Mall Road, Richmond. Ph: (510) 758-6528.
Himalaya Restaurant & Sweets, 12469 San Pablo Ave., Richmond. Ph: (510) 236-4148.
Honolulu Cafe, 12056 San Pablo Ave., Richmond. Ph: (510) 234-7148. Hawaiian.
Hotel Mac, 50 Washington Ave., Richmond. Ph: (510) 233-0576. Continental.
Hunan Chef Restaurant, 130 Railroad Ave., Richmond. Ph: (510) 233-5151. Chinese.
Il Buco D'Italia, 1105 MacDonald Ave., Richmond. Ph: (510) 233-4700. Italian.
Johnny's Diner, 171 Harbour Way South,

Richmond. Ph: (510) 232-5986.
Junmaie Guey Restaurant, 12221 San Pablo Ave., Richmond. Ph: (510) 234-9898. Chinese.
Kentucky Fried Chicken, 1203 MacDonald Ave., Richmond. Ph: (510) 235-3244. Fast food.
Kentucky Fried Chicken, 12951 San Pablo Ave., Richmond. Ph: (510) 232-2311. Fast food.
Kikuya, 12860 San Pablo Ave., Richmond. Ph: (510) 233-0551. Japanese.
La Flor de Jalisco Restaurant, 12889 San Pablo Ave., Richmond. Ph: (510) 232-7754. Mexican.
Le Cordon Bleu, 205 Cutting Blvd., Richmond. Ph: (510) 232-4014. French.
Little China, 152 Washington Ave., Richmond. Ph: (510) 236-9382. Chinese.
Little Louie's, 49 Washington Ave., Richmond. Ph: (510) 235-3108.
Lorraine's Fish Poultry & Bar-B-Q, 3051 Cutting Blvd., Richmond. Ph: (510) 232-3732.
Los Cerros Mexican Restaurant, 4705 Valley View Road, Richmond. Ph: (510) 222-2955. Mexican.
Manchbu Wok, 2132 Hilltop Mall Road, Richmond. Ph: (510) 222-5620. Manchurian.
Marge's Cafe, 12620 San Pablo Ave., Richmond. Ph: (510) 236-0385.
Master Bilal Fish & Chips, 2900 Cutting Blvd., Richmond. Ph: (510) 237-9494.
McDonald's, 2301 MacDonald Ave., Richmond. Ph: (510) 233-7824. Fast food.
McDonald's, 2443 Hilltop Mall Road, Richmond. Ph: (510) 222-8746. Fast food.
Mr. Pizza Man, 353 24th, Richmond. Ph: (510) 234-9900. Pizza.
Nation's Giant Hamburgers & Great Pies, 1100 23rd, Richmond. Ph: (510) 234-1445. American.
New Garden Restaurant, 12372 San Pablo Ave., Richmond. Ph: (510) 232-0141. Chinese.
Olive Garden Italian Restaurant, 2960 Hilltop Mall Road, Richmond. Ph: (510) 223-6192. Italian.
Pablo's Restaurant, 9120 23rd St., Richmond. Ph: (510) 215-0646. Mexican.
People's Choice Barbecue, 3419 Cutting Blvd., Richmond. Ph: (510) 233-4083.
Pepito's Deli, 1087 23rd, Richmond. Ph: (510) 232-9750. Mexican.
Point Panchos Mexican Restaurant, 915 Cutting Blvd., Richmond. Ph: (510) 237-3000. Mexican.

Popeye's Famous Fried Chicken, 1000 Nevin Ave., Richmond. Ph: (510) 232-8877. Fast food.
Portumex Restaurant, 721 23rd, Richmond. Ph: (510) 237-7513. Mexican.
Pup Hut, 12505 San Pablo Ave., Richmond. Ph: (510) 235-5456.
R & B Coffee Shop & Catering, 1801 Cutting Blvd., Richmond. Ph: (510) 234-5932.
Red Lobster Restaurant, 3190 Klose Way, Richmond. Ph: (510) 223-9750. Seafood.
Red's Seafood Restaurant, 2207 MacDonald Ave., Richmond. Ph: (510) 235-6855. Seafood.
Rin's Thai Cuisine, 12200 San Pablo Ave., Richmond. Ph: (510) 232-5542. Thai.
Ron's King Burger, 3330 Cutting Blvd., Richmond. Ph: (510) 233-1112.
Roscoe Hofbrau, 353 24th, Richmond. Ph: (510) 236-1977.
Royal Pizza, 12221 San Pablo Ave., Richmond. Ph: (510) 237-3641. Pizza.
Sbarro The Italian Eatery, 2449 Hilltop Mall Road, Richmond. Ph: (510) 223-9986. Italian.
Shogun Oriental Cuisine, 3044 Hilltop Mall Road, Richmond. Ph: (510) 222-8282. Chinese.
Snapper's Seafood Restaurant, 1501 Ohio Ave., Richmond. Ph: (510) 235-6328. Seafood.
Steve's Restaurant Catering & Cook Shop, 3529 Waller Ave., Richmond. Ph: (510) 237-3686.
Sudduth Reba, 1501 3rd, Richmond. Ph: (510) 234-0957.
Sun Lim Chinese Cuisine, 2453 Hilltop Mall Road, Richmond. Ph: (510) 223-9497. Chinese.
Super Carnitas Restaurant, 1212 Cutting Blvd., Richmond. Ph: (510) 232-6453. Mexican.
T S Piane's, 4705 Valley Viuew Road, Richmond. Ph: (510) 758-9340.
Taco Bell, 2129 Hilltop Mall Road, Richmond. Ph: (510) 223-7035. Fast food.
Taco Bell, 4532 MacDonald Ave., Richmond. Ph: (510) 236-3138. Fast food.
Tajkesri Cuisine of India, 12221 San Pablo Ave., Richmond. Ph: (510) 233-3817. Indian.
Taqueria La Bamba, 12345 San Pablo Ave., Richmond. Ph: (510) 235-2288. Mexican.
Tarabini's Deli, 322 Harbour Way, Richmond. Ph: (510) 232-4712.
The Point, 2 W. Richmond Ave., Richmond. Ph: (510) 233-4295.

RESTAURANTS

Touch of Class Cajun, 421 Grove St., Richmond. Ph: (510) 236-6747. Cajun.
Uncle Sam Restaurant, 4705 Valley View Road, Richmond. Ph: (510) 223-2776.
Wendy's, 12201 San Pablo Ave., Richmond. Ph: (510) 236-7649. Fast food.
White Knight, 3150 Pierce, Richmond. Ph: (510) 527-1725. Hofbrau.

Rodeo

D's Giant Burger, 358 Parker Ave., Rodeo. Ph: (510) 799-0800. American.
El Sol, 224 Pacific Ave., Rodeo. Ph: (510) 799-7070. Mexican.
Flippy's Family Restaurant, 240 Parker Ave., Rodeo. Ph: (510) 799-4400.
Happy Wok, 677 Parker Ave., Rodeo. Ph: (510) 799-1448. Chinese.
Mountain Mike's Pizza Restaurant, 687 Parker Ave., Rodeo. Ph: (510) 799-6500. Pizza.
Rickie's Corner, 18 Parker Ave., Rodeo. Ph: (510) 799-5222. Italian.
Silver Dollar Too, 13 Pacific Ave., Rodeo. Ph: (510) 245-8909.
Tony's Cafe, 685 Parker Ave., Rodeo. Ph: (510) 799-3207.

San Pablo

Anna's Cafe, 847 Madeline Road, San Pablo. Ph: (510) 223-6035.
Cabo Taqueria, 13501 San Pablo Ave., San Pablo. Ph: (510) 236-2226. Mexican.
Casper's Hot Dogs, 14417 San Pablo Ave., San Pablo. Ph: (510) 232-5600. Fast food.
Catfish Wally's, 14555 San Pablo Ave., San Pablo. Ph: (510) 234-0439.
Chepes Restaurant, 1742 Rumrill Blvd., San Pablo. Ph: (510) 237-7605.
China Express, 100 El Portal Shopping Center, San Pablo. Ph: (510) 232-1604. Chinese.
China Express Restaurant, 1841 23rd, San Pablo. Ph: (510) 235-4669. Chinese.
Chris' Kitchen, 1260 Rumrill Blvd, San Pablo. Ph: (510) 235-9117.
Denny's Restaurant, 2526 San Pablo Dam Road, San Pablo. Ph: (510) 232-6813. American.
Dragon Palace, 291 El Poertal Shopping Center, San Pablo. Ph: (510) 232-2370. Chinese.
Duang Chanh Thai Restaurant, 2037 23rd, San Pablo. Ph: (510) 237-0696. Thai.
El Tapatio, 2031 23rd, San Pablo. Ph: (510) 236-0202. Mexican.
Foster Freeze, 1890 23rd St., San Pablo. Ph: (510) 232-5710. Fast food.
Gonzalez Mexican Restaurant, 12955 San Pablo Ave., San Pablo. Ph: (510) 234-2285. Mexican.
Hacienda, 12020 San Pablo Ave., San Pablo. Ph: (510) 235-2000. Mexican.
Hambrick's Giant Hamburgers, 13th & Market, San Pablo. Ph: (510) 233-7255. American.
Hickory Post, 13255 San Pablo Ave., San Pablo. Ph: (510) 232-4433. Barbecued.
Jack-In-The-Box Drive Thru Restaurants, 14395 San Pablo Ave., San Pablo. Ph: (510) 232-0905. Fast food.
Jasmine Restaurant, 14272 San Palbo Ave., San Pablo. Ph: (510) 235-6845. Chinese.
Kan Thai Food, 1811 23rd, San Pablo. Ph: (510) 215-6352. Thai.
Kentucky Fried Chicken, 14621 San Pablo Ave., San Pablo. Ph: (510) 237-8500. Fast food.
King Pizza, 1762 Rumrill Blvd., San Pablo. Ph: (510) 232-2662. Pizza.
Liao's Foods, 1829 Rumrill Blvd, San Pablo. Ph: (510) 234-2929.
Mandarin Restaurant, 14465 San Pablo Ave., San Pablo. Ph: (510) 234-4645. Chnese.
McDonald's, 14480 San Pablo Ave., San Pablo. Ph: (510) 237-2605. Fast food.
Nation's Giant Hamburgers & Great Pies, 13296 San Pablo Ave., San Pablo. Ph: (510) 234-1330. American.
Nation's Giant Hamburgers & Great Pies, 16396 San Pablo Ave., San Pablo. Ph: (510) 724-5530. American.
Ocean Dragon Restaurant, 13993 San Pablo Ave., San Pablo. Ph: (510) 234-2565. Chinese.
Old San Francisco Pizza Co., 2325 Road 20, San Pablo. Ph: (510) 232-9644. Italian.
Rainbow Garden, 20237 23rd St., San Pablo. Ph: (510) 237-0696. Chinese.
Rhodes English Fish & Chip Shop, 14402 San Pablo Ave., San Pablo. Ph: (510) 234-8767. English.
Rickshaw Restaurant, 299 El Portal Shopping Center, San Pablo. Ph: (510) 231-0881. Chinese.
Sam Uen Chinese Restaurant, 3556 San Pablo Dam Road, San Pablo. Ph: (510) 222-3910. Chinese.
San Pablo Family Cafe, 2554 El Portal Drive, San Pablo. Ph: (510) 236-1161. American.
Seven Mares Seafood Mexican Restaurant, 14401 San Pablo Ave., San Pablo. Ph: (510) 236-3818. Mexican.
Sukie's Country Kitchen, 900 El Portal Shopping Center, San Pablo. Ph: (510) 233-5856.

Taco Bell, 40 San Pablo Town Center, San Pablo. Ph: (510) 215-1971. Fast food.
Taqueria Michoacan, 1811 23rd, San Pablo. Ph: (510) 236-7593. Mexican.
Taqueria Morelia, 16376 San Pablo Ave., San Pablo. Ph: (510) 724-2700. Mexican.
V P's Restaurant, 2215 Church Lane, San Pablo. Ph: (510) 232-6717. American.
Wally's Hickory Pit, 14559 San Pablo Ave., San Pablo. Ph: (510) 234-6664. American.
Wienerschnitzel, 14260 San Pablo Ave., San Pablo. Ph: (510) 620-9460. Fast food.

San Ramon

Bobby McGee's Conglomeration, 3110 Crow Canyon Place, San Ramon. Ph: (510) 866-8883. American.
Buon Appetito Deli & Cafe, 12949 Alcosta Blvd., San Ramon. Ph: (510) 830-1021.
Burger King, 3250 Crow Canyon Road, San Ramon. Ph: (510) 866-1102. Fast food.
Cafe Dolce, 2527 Camino Ramon, San Ramon. Ph: (510) 275-9968.
Cafe Vivoli, 3104 Crow Canyon Place, San Ramon. Ph: (510) 830-2960.
Caramba Burritos Etc., 12165 Alcosta Blvd., San Ramon. Ph: (510) 833-8896. Mexican.
Carl's Jr. Restaurants, 3131 Crow Canyon Place, San Ramon. Ph: (510) 866-1156. Fast food.
Charley Brown's, 680 Bollinger Canyon Way, San Ramon. Ph: (510) 735-6800.
Chatillon, 21314A San Ramon Valley Blvd., San Ramon. Ph: (510) 828-7910.
Checkers Grill, 4000 Executive Pkwy., San Ramon. Ph: (510) 830-0890.
China Cafe, 12153 Alcosta Blvd., San Ramon. Ph: (510) 829-3550. Chinese.
China Panda Restaurant, 2211 San Ramon Valley Blvd., San Ramon. Ph: (510) 838-8044. Chinese.
Chung Hei Low Chinese Restaurant, 2550 San Ramon Valley Blvd., San Ramon. Ph: (510) 838-2347. Chinese.
Croutons, 2540 San Ramon Valley Road, San Ramon. Ph: (510) 838-5878.
Crystal Gardens Restaurant, 100 Market Place, San Ramon. Ph: (510) 830-0330.
El Nuevo Chaparral, 2450 San Ramon Valley Blvd., San Ramon. Ph: (510) 820-6225.
Friday's, 2410 San Ramon Valley Blvd., San Ramon. Ph: (510) 820-0401.
Garcia's Mexican Restaurants, 2431 San Ramon Valley Blvd., San Ramon. Ph: (510) 838-0500. Mexican.
Half Crown Fish & Chips, 2550L San Ramon Valley Blvd., San Ramon. Ph: (510) 837-9137.
Hop Sings, 3191 Crow Canyon Place, San Ramon. Ph: (510) 866-9478. Chinese.
Kentucky Fried Chicken, 2020 San Ramon Valley Blvd., San Ramon. Ph: (510) 820-2124. Fast food.
Le Chateaubriand, 2065 San Ramon Valley Blvd., San Ramon. Ph: (510) 820-7274. French.
Marie Callender's Restaurants & Bakeries, 250 Market Place, San Ramon. Ph: (510) 838-9000. American.
Max's Diner, 2015 Crow Canyon Place, San Ramon. Ph: (510) 277-9300. American.
Miraku Japanese Cuisine, 2416 San Ramon Valley Blvd., San Ramon. Ph: (510) 820-8107. Japanese.
Mr. Philly Steak, 1061 Market Place, San Ramon. Ph: (510) 830-1144.
Mudd's Restaurant, 10 Boardwalk, San Ramon. Ph: (510) 837-9287.
Nation's Giant Hamburgers & Great Pies, 2426 San Ramon Valley Blvd., San Ramon. Ph: (510) 831-8882. American.
Nikki's Bar-B-Que, 3141 Crow Canyon Place, San Ramon. Ph: (510) 866-1314.
Orient Express, 2475 San Ramon Valley Blvd., San Ramon. Ph: (510) 743-9516.
Pacific Pasta, 192 Market Place, San Ramon. Ph: (510) 275-1266. Italian.
Pappy's Restaurant, 2217 San Ramon Valley Blvd., San Ramon. Ph: (510) 820-2453.
Pasta Primavera Cafe, 3124 Crow Canyon Place, San Ramon. Ph: (510) 830-9500. Italian.
Peking Tokyo Restaurant, 5000 Bollinger Canyon Way, San Ramon. Ph: (510) 735-8880. Chinese-Japanese.
Pelican Grill, 2323 San Ramon Valley Blvd., San Ramon. Ph: (510) 820-7282.
Ruggie's, 3191L Crow Canyon Place, San Ramon. Ph: (510) 866-9460.
Rusty's American Cafe, 2323 San Ramon Valley Blvd., San Ramon. Ph: (510) 820-7282.
Sakura Japanese Cuisine, 3151 Crow Canyon Place, San Ramon. Ph: (510) 277-1628. Japanese.
Sidelines Sports Bar & Grill, 500 Bollinger Canyon Way, San Ramon. Ph: (510) 735-1806.
Sizzler Restaurants, 3150 Crown Canyon Road, San Ramon. Ph: (510) 866-7181. American.
Sun Sun Garden, 21314-G San Ramon Valley Blvd., San Ramon. Ph: (510) 829-5517. Chinese.
Taco Grande, 400 Market Place, San Ramon.

RESTAURANTS 213

Ph: (510) 277-9444. Mexican.
Tengu Restaurant, 2550 San Ramon Valley Blvd., San Ramon. Ph: (510) 831-3777. Japanese.
The Brass Door, 2154 San Ramon Valley Blvd., San Ramon. Ph: (510) 94583.
The Dog House, 3211 Crown Canyon Place, San Ramon. Ph: (510) 866-8757. American.
The Fisherman, 200 Montgomery St., San Ramon. Ph: (510) 866-7066. Seafood.
The Hot Dog Spot, 1061 Market Place, San Ramon. Ph: (510) 830-4694. American.
Togo's, 2550 San Ramon Valley Blvd., San Ramon. Ph: (510) 831-3596. Fast food.
Uncle Yu's Szechuan No. 2, 2005 Crow Canyon Place, San Ramon. Ph: (510) 275-1818. Chinese.
Y Not Falafel, 2410 San Ramon Valley Blvd., San Ramon. Ph: (510) 837-5222.

Walnut Creek

Abernathy's, 1411 Locust, Walnut Creek. Ph: (510) 934-9490.
All In Good Taste, 2228 Oak Grove Road, Walnut Creek. Ph: (510) 945-0580.
Arturo's Mexican Cuisine, 2383 North Main, Walnut Creek. Ph: (510) 937-7891. Mexican.
Blazing Burgers, 1510 N. Main, Walnut Creek. Ph: (510) 932-7577. American.
Boudin Sourdough Bakery & Cafe, 67 Broadway Lane, Walnut Creek. Ph: (510) 935-4375.
Boundary Oak Restaurant, 3800 Valley Vista Road, Walnut Creek. Ph: (510) 935-8121.
Broadway Cafe, 1250 Newell Ave., Walnut Creek, 5110, 935-2126.
Broadway East Restaurant, 1448 South Main, Walnut Creek. Ph: (510) 932-6666. Chinese.
Burger King, 1799 N. Broadway, Walnut Creek. Ph: (510) 937-5129. Fast food.
Burger King, 2855 N. Main, Walnut Creek. Ph: (510) 930-6826. Fast food.
Buttercup Kitchen, 2387 North Main, Walnut Creek. Ph: (510) 938-2270.
Cafe 21, 2121 N. California Blvd., Walnut Creek. Ph: (510) 935-1122.
Cafe Dolce, 100 Pringle Ave., Walnut Creek. Ph: (510) 935-2233.
Cafe India, 1521 North Main, Walnut Creek. Ph: (510) 944-5403. Indian.
Cafe Salzburg, 1555 Bonanza, Walnut Creek. Ph: (510) 939-7345.
Calda Calda, 1646 California, Walnut Creek. Ph: (510) 939-5555.
California Cafe, 1540 North California Blvd., Walnut Creek. Ph: (510) 938-9977. American.
Casper's Hot Dogs, 1280A Newell Hill Place, Walnut Creek. Ph: (510) 930-9154. American.
Central Shack, 1450 Treat Blvd., Walnut Creek. Ph: (510) 939-1261.
Cheese Steak Shop, 1626 Cypress, Walnut Creek. Ph: (510) 934-7017.
Chez Dyon, 1450 Centeral Road, Walnut Creek. Ph: (510) 945-1343. Continental.
Chi Ho's, 1627 N. Broadway, Walnut Creek. Ph: (510) 932-2828.
China Restaurant, 2580 North Main Street, Walnut Creek. Ph: (510) 937-2031. Mandarin.
China Village, 1849 Ygnacio Valley Road, Walnut Creek. Ph: (510) 944-1006. Chinese.
Chinatown Express Inc., 2064 Treat Blvd., Walnut Creek. Ph: (510) 933-3278. Chinese.
Chuck's Steak Room, 2580 N. Main St., Walnut Creek. Ph: (510) 937-2032. American.
Coffee Coffee, 1646 North California Blvd., Walnut Creek. Ph: (510) 947-6763. Espresso-Coffee.
Copper Skillet Restaurant, 700 Bancroft Road, Walnut Creek, 5110, 937-2240.
Courtyard Bistro, 2210 Oak Grove Road, Walnut Creek. Ph: (510) 933-6264.
Creative Croussants, 24 Broadway Lane, Walnut Creek. Ph: (510) 930-9609.
Crogan's Bar and Grill, 1387 Locust St., Walnut Creek. Ph: (510) 933-7800. American.
Cruchon's, 2599 N. Main, Walnut Creek. Ph: (510) 937-0682.
Daruma Japanese Restaurant, 1520 N. Main St., Walnut Creek. Ph: (510) 934-3523. Japanese.
Denny's Restaurant, 660 Ygnacio Valley Road, Walnut Creek. Ph: (510) 938-2424. American.
Elvie's Hamburgers, 2861 Ygnacio Valley Road, Walnut Creek. Ph: (510) 934-4737. American.
Emil Villa's The Original Hick'ry Pit, 1495 S. Main, Walnut Creek. Ph: (510) 935-7450. Barbecue.
Foster's Old Fashion Freeze, 2300 N. Main, Walnut Creek. Ph: (510) 934-1535. Fast food.
George's Giant Hamburger, 1491 E. Newell Ave., Walnut Creek. Ph: (510) 939-4888.
House of Saki, 1716 N. Main, Walnut Creek.

Ph: (510) 930-8811. Japanese.
Hubcaps, 1548 Bonanza, Walnut Creek. Ph: (510) 945-6960.
Ilpavone, 2291 Olympic Blvd., Walnut Creek. Ph: (510) 939-9060. Italian.
Jack-In-The-Box, 2295 N. Main, Walnut Creek. Ph: (510) 944-5690. Fast food.
Jade Garden, 2907 Ygnacio Valley Rd., Walnut Creek. Ph: (510) 934-7688. Chinese.
Joe's Restaurant, 1908 Tice Valley Blvd., Walnut Creek. Ph: (510) 938-5637.
Johnny Angels, 2033 N. Main, Walnut Creek. Ph: (510) 939-6949.
Johnny Angels, 2033 North Main Street, Walnut Creek. Ph: (510) 939-6949. Mediterranean.
Jun-Jun Japanese Restaurant, 1989 North Main, Walnut Creek. Ph: (510) 947-1174. Japanese.
Kentucky Fried Chicken, 1520 Olympic Blvd., Walnut Creek. Ph: (510) 935-3011. Fast food.
King Sea, 140 N. Civic Drive, Walnut Creek. Ph: (510) 937-2700. Seafood.
King Tsin Restaurant, 2280 Oak Grove Road, Walnut Creek. Ph: (510) 935-1238. Chinese.
La Cigale, 2195 North Broadway, Walnut Creek. Ph: (510) 937-8800. French.
La Fogata Mexican & American Food, 1315 North Main, Walnut Creek. Ph: (510) 934-8121. Mexican.
La Ultima, 1516 Bonanza St., Walnut Creek. Ph: (510) 937-0383. Mexican.
Le Virage, 2211 N. Main, Walnut Creek. Ph: (510) 933-8484. French-Continental.
Little Europe, 1516 N. Main, Walnut Creek. Ph: (510) 945-1165.
Locust Street Deli-Cafe, 1552 Locust, Walnut Creek. Ph: (510) 945-6669.
Lori's, 2730 N. Main St., Walnut Creek. Ph: (510) 935-5674. American.
Lyon's Restaurant, 1750 N. Main, Walnut Creek. Ph: (510) 935-4666. American.
Magic Garlic Restaurant, 2910 N. Main, Walnut Creek. Ph: (510) 938-6868.
Mai Thai, 1414 N. Main, Walnut Creek. Ph: (510) 937-7887. Thai.
Main Street Cafe, 1329 N. Main, Walnut Creek. Ph: (510) 935-2356.
Main Street Grill, 2355 N. Main, Walnut Creek. Ph: (510) 934-2000.
Margaritaville, 1829 Mt. Diablo Blvd., Walnut Creek. Ph: (510) 944-6595. Mexican.
Marie Callender's Restaurants & Bakeries, 1101 S. California Blvd., Walnut Creek. Ph: (510) 943-7100. American.

Mariposa Chinese Cuisine, 1670 Locust, Walnut Creek. Ph: (510) 933-8883. Chinese.
Max's Opera Cafe, 1676 North California Blvd., Walnut Creek. Ph: (510) 932-3434. American.
Maximillian's, 1604 Locust St., Walnut Creek. Ph: (510) 932-1474. Continental.
McDonald's, 1380 N. California Blvd., Walnut Creek. Ph: (510) 932-7740. Fast food.
Miraku, 2131 North Broadway, Walnut Creek. Ph: (510) 932-1112. Japanese.
Montecatini Restaurant, 1528 Civic Drive, Walnut Creek. Ph: (510) 943-6608.
Mr. Lucky's, 1527 Locust, Walnut Creek. Ph: (510) 935-7778.
New York Pizza, 1534 Locust, Walnut Creek. Ph: (510) 939-2222. Italian.
Noga Corner, 1394 N. Main, Walnut Creek. Ph: (510) 934-4591.
Original Hot Dog Place, 1420 Lincoln Ave., Walnut Creek. Ph: (510) 256-7302. American.
Our Place Cafe, 2400 Olympic Blvd., Walnut Creek. Ph: (510) 938-4474.
Papagottso's Pizza & Pasta, 1995 Main, Walnut Creek. Ph: (510) 938-4040. Italian.
Pasta Primavera Cafe, 2929 N. Main, Walnut Creek. Ph: (510) 930-7775. Italian.
Pasta Primavera Too, 2997 N. Main, Walnut Creek. Ph: (510) 930-7774. Italian.
Peking Restaurant, 2580 N. Main St., Walnut Creek. Ph: (510) 937-2030. Chinese.
Pepito's Mexican Restaurant, 704 Bancroft Road, Walnut Creek. Ph: (510) 256-8266. Mexican.
Pinky's Pizza Parlor of Walnut Creek, 1379 S. California Blvd., Walnut Creek. Ph: (510) 932-2728. Italian.
Pita King, 1607 Palos Verdes Mall, Walnut Creek. Ph: (510) 945-0386.
Prima Cafe & Wine Merchants, 1522 N. Main, Walnut Creek. Ph: (510) 935-7780.
Ristorante Toscano, 1520 Palos Verdes Mall, Walnut Creek. Ph: (510) 934-3737. Italian.
Round Table Pizza, 1512 N. Main, Walnut Creek. Ph: (510) 939-6066. Pizza.
Round Table Pizza, 1865 Ygnacio Valley Road, Walnut Creek. Ph: (510) 930-9400. Pizza.
Round Table Pizza, 55 Broadway, Walnut Creek. Ph: (510) 932-1833. Pizza.
Savoy, P.O. Box 514, Walnut Creek. Ph: (510) 935-8121. Continental.
Scott's Seafood Grill & Bar, 1333 North California Blvd., Walnut Creek. Ph: (510) 934-1300. Seafood.

RESTAURANTS 215

Sepp's Chicago-Style Pizza, 1606 N. Main, Walnut Creek. Ph: (510) 930-7377. Italian.
Sizzler Restaurants, 1940 N. Main, Walnut Creek. Ph: (510) 937-4060. American.
Sontaree's Melting Pot, 1532 N. Main, Walnut Creek. Ph: (510) 937-1006. Thai.
Sorrento - Broadway No. 2, 2065 N. Broadway, Walnut Creek. Ph: (510) 938-3367. Italian.
Sorrento - Treat No. 1, 2064 Treat Blvd., Walnut Creek. Ph: (510) 938-3366. Italian.
Sorrento Restaurant & Pizza, 2065 North Broadway, Walnut Creek. Ph: (510) 938-3367. Italian.
Spiedini Ristorante, 101 Ygnacio Valley Road, Walnut Creek. Ph: (510) 939-2100. Italian.
Spring Flower, 1815 Ygnacio Valley Road, Walnut Creek. Ph: (510) 933-1900. Chinese.
Station One, 1603 Palos Verdes Mall, Walnut Creek. Ph: (510) 933-4450.
Sue's House of Hot Dogs, 2270 Oak Grove Road, Walnut Creek. Ph: (510) 930-7654.
Sunrise Bistro, 1559 Botelho Drive, Walnut Creek. Ph: (510) 930-0122.
Sunrise Cafe & Bakery, 1355 S. California Blvd., Walnut Creek. Ph: (510) 930-0240.
Szechwan Garden, 1651 Botelho Drive, Walnut Creek. Ph: (510) 938-8384.
Taco Bell, 2400 N. Main, Walnut Creek. Ph: (510) 932-9414. Fast food.
Tang's Restaurant, 1523 East St., Walnut Creek. Ph: (510) 945-1400. Chinese.
Tao's Grill, 1345 Treat Blvd., Walnut Creek. Ph: (510) 934-3850. Chinese.
Taqueria Mexican Grill Walnut Creek, 1359 Locust, Walnut Creek. Ph: (510) 932-8987. Mexican.
The Cantina, 1470 North Broadway, Walnut Creek. Ph: (510) 946-1010. Mexican.
The Encore, 1101 Civic Drive, Walnut Creek. Ph: (510) 932-4833.
The Golden City Restaurant, 2932 North Main, Walnut Creek. Ph: (510) 935-3233. Chinese.
The Greenery Restaurant, 1551 Marchbanks Drive, Walnut Creek. Ph: (510) 937-1270.
The Sandwich Tree, 1990 N. California Blvd., Walnut Creek. Ph: (510) 943-1088.
The Savoy Restaurant at Boundary Oak, 3800 ValleyVista Road, Walnut Creek. Ph: (510) 935-8121.
Theatre Cafe, 1655 N. Main, Walnut Creek. Ph: (510) 935-7779.
Togo's, 1321 Locust, Walnut Creek. Ph: (510) 930-9147. Fast food.
Togo's, 2975 Ygnacio Valley Road, Walnut Creek. Ph: (510) 935-4966. Fast food.
Tsuru Hachi Sushi Bar, 2997 N. Main St., Walnut Creek. Ph: (510) 256-9350. Sushi.
Viggy's Take & Bake Pizza, 1485 Newell Ave., Walnut Creek. Ph: (510) 932-1186. Italian.
Viva Mexican Restaurant, 1101 Civic Drive, Walnut Creek. Ph: (510) 945-8888. Mexican.
Walnut Creek Hofbrau House, 1401 Mount Diablo Blvd., Walnut Creek. Ph: (510) 947-2928.
Wan Fu Chinese Restaurant, 1375 N. Broadway, Walnut Creek. Ph: (510) 938-2288. Chinese.
Wendy's Old Fashioned Hamburgers, 2955 N. Main, Walnut Creek. Ph: (510) 937-7269. Fast food.
Wonderland Cafe, 313 N. Civic Drive, Walnut Creek. Ph: (510) 256-6690.

West Pittsburg
T'Bones, 3355 Willow Pass Road, West Pittsburg. Ph: (510) 458-1323. American.

Solano County
Benicia
Burger Burger Cafe, 191 Military East, Benicia. Ph: (707) 745-2333. American.
Burger King, 118 Warwick Drive, Benicia. Ph: (707) 747-6100. Fast food.
Burger King, 1980 Columbus Pkwy., Benicia. Ph: (707) 746-1980. Fast food.
Burger King, 828 Southampton Road, Benicia. Ph: (707) 746-7005. Fast food.
Captain Blyther's, 123 First St., Benicia. Ph: (707) 745-4082.
China Garden Restaurant, 498 Military East, Benicia. Ph: (707) 745-8130. Chinese.
Cliff's Pleasant View Recreation, 810 W. 9th St., Benicia. Ph: (707) 745-9985.
Enseneda Restaurant, 864 Southampton Road, Benicia. Ph: (707) 745-5536.
First Street Cafe, 440 First St., Benicia. Ph: (707) 745-4404.
Fong's Chinese Cuisine, 718 First, Benicia. Ph: (707) 745-5359. Chinese.
Gina's Benicia Bay Restaurant, 920 First St., Benicia. Ph: (707) 745-8811.
Happy Hot Dog, 866 Southampton Road, Benicia. Ph: (707) 745-2232. American.
Happy House Chinese Restaurant, 408 Military East, Benicia. Ph: (707) 746-1708. Chinese.
Kentucky Fried Chicken, 155 Military East, Benicia. Ph: (707) 745-4186. Fast food.
Lai Wah Chinese Restaurant, 2040 Colum-

216 CONTRA COSTA & SOLANO

bus Pkwy., Benicia. Ph: (707) 747-1688. Chinese.
Mabel's Cafe, 635 First St., Benicia. Ph: (707) 746-7068.
Mi-Casita Restaurant, 818 First, Benicia. Ph: (707) 747-1269. Mexican.
Morgan's Grill, 1034 First St., Benicia. Ph: (707) 745-4466.
Pacifica Pizza, 915 First, Benicia. Ph: (707) 746-1790. Italian.
Papa's Family Restaurant, 800 Southampton Road, Benicia. Ph: (707) 745-0314. Greek.
Pizza Pirate, 72 Solano Square, Benicia. Ph: (707) 745-1667. Pizza.
Rickshaw Restaurant, 836 Southampton Road, Benicia. Ph: (707) 746-7535. Chinese.
Robert's China Garden Restaurant, 498 Military East, Benicia. Ph: (707) 745-5355. Chinese.
Rosie's Hot Dogs, 131A First, Benicia. Ph: (707) 745-4476.
Rosie's Hot Dogs, 3001 Bayshore Road, Benicia. Ph: (707) 745-1154.
Round Table Pizza, 878 Southampton Road, Benicia. Ph: (707) 746-7000. Pizza.
San'wich Station, 685 Stone Road, Benicia. Ph: (707) 745-8833.
Sandoval's Mexican Foods & Catering, 2032 Columbus Pkwy., Benicia. Ph: (707) 747-0515. Mexican.
Sandoval's Mexican Foods & Catering, 640 First, Benicia. Ph: (707) 746-7830. Mexican.
Sundowner Restaurant, 1401 E. Fifth, Benicia. Ph: (707) 745-2600.
Szechwan House, 500 First St., Benicia. Ph: (707) 745-4743.
The Wet Noodle, 129 First, Benicia. Ph: (707) 746-8505.
Tia Theresa, 120 West H St., Benicia. Ph: (707) 745-2535.
Union Hotel Restaurant, 401 First St., Benicia. Ph: (707) 746-0105.
Washington House Deli Cafe, 333AS First St., Benicia. Ph: (707) 745-3364.
Waterfront Cafe & Bistro, 127 First, Benicia. Ph: (707) 745-4635.
Cordelia
Bravos Pizza Shop, 364 Pittman Road, Cordelia. Ph: (707) 864-6400. Italian.
Burger King, 190 Pittman Road, Cordelia. Ph: (707) 864-8466. Fast food.
Morgan's Old San Francisco Express, I-80 & Suisun Valley Road, Cordelia. Ph: (707) 864-1900.
Red Top Coffee Shop, I-80, Cordelia. Ph: (707) 864-1221. American.
The Old San Francisco Express, 4560 Central Way, Cordelia. Ph: (707) 864-1900.
Dixon
Arby's, 1425 Ary Lane, Dixon. Ph: (916) 678-0318. American.
Burger King, 1350 Stratford Ave., Dixon. Ph: (916) 678-6800. Fast food.
Cattlemens Restaurants, I-80 & Currey Road, Dixon. Ph: (916) 678-5518. American.
Chevy's Mexican Restaurant, 1470 Ary Lane, Dixon. Ph: (916) 678-5101.
Chez Helene French Bakery & Cafe, 180 S. First, Dixon. Ph: (916) 678-9382. French.
Country Oak Restaurant, 127 N. First St., Dixon. Ph: (916) 678-5866. American.
Cueva's Restaurant, 143 North 1st St., Dixon. Ph: (916) 678-9685. Mexican.
Dawson Cigar Store, 105 N. First, Dixon. Ph: (916) 678-2067. American.
Denny's Dixon, 1250 Stratford Ave., Dixon. Ph: (916) 678-1002. American.
El Charro Cafe, 116 N. First, Dixon. Ph: (916) 678-5969. Mexican.
Frank's Bar & Restaurant, 100 S. First, Dixon. Ph: (916) 678-6190. American.
Frosty Drive-In, 171 West A, Dixon. Ph: (916) 678-2624. Fast food.
George's Orange, 6134 Dixon Ave. West, Dixon. Ph: (916) 678-1222.
Golden Dragon, 470 N. Adams St., Dixon. Ph: (916) 678-9681. Chinese.
International House of Pancakes, 1435 Ary Lane, Dixon. Ph: (916) 678-5153. American.
Kim & Ned's, 119 N. First St., Dixon. Ph: (916) 678-4134. Chinese.
Los Altos, 7800 Batavia Road, Dixon. Ph: (916) 678-5122. Mexican.
McDonald's Restaurant, 1410 Ary Lane, Dixon. Ph: (916) 678-1256. Fast food.
Mi Nidito Mexican Restaurant, 1005 N. Adams, Dixon. Ph: (916) 678-5888. Mexican.
Nana & Papa's Caffe & Ristorante, 180 West A St., Dixon. Ph: (916) 678-7267.
Taco Bell, 1421 Ary Lane, Dixon. Ph: (916) 678-9790. Fast food.
Tacos La Adelita, 162 West A, Dixon. Ph: (916) 678-0477. Mexican.
Fairfield
Arby's Restaurant, Solano Mall, Fairfield. Ph: (707) 427-3276. American.
Bakers Square Restaurant & Pie Shop, 2190 Texas, Fairfield. Ph: (707) 428-3519.
Beamer's, 1430 North Texas, Fairfield. Ph: (707) 426-4186.

RESTAURANTS 217

Big John's Submarine Sandwiches, 1807 North Texas, Fairfield. Ph: (707) 422-7111.
Big Valley Hof Brau, 201 Travis Blvd., Fairfield. Ph: (707) 426-3485.
Birdcage Wok Restaurant, 2731 North Texas, Fairfield. Ph: (707) 429-4790. Chinese.
Burger King, 1475 Holiday Lane, Fairfield. Ph: (707) 429-4648. Fast food.
Burger King, 2415 North Texas, Fairfield. Ph: (707) 425-3873. Fast food.
Cann's Q Barbeque, 1513 W. Texas, Fairfield. Ph: (707) 425-7000.
Carl's Jr., 1401A Solano Mall, Fairfield. Ph: (707) 422-9263. Fast food.
Carl's Jr., 2380 North Texas, Fairfield. Ph: (707) 425-6993. Fast food.
Carl's Jr., 4400 Central Way, Fairfield. Ph: (707) 864-2122. Fast food.
Chevy's Mexican Restaurant, 1730 Travis Blvd., Fairfield. Ph: (707) 425-8374. Mexican.
Chicken-Mania, 1657 North Texas, Fairfield. Ph: (707) 428-4097.
Chick-fil-A of Solano Mall, 1443B Solano Mall, Fairfield. Ph: (707) 427-3317.
China Palace, 715 Jackson St., Fairfield. Ph: (707) 422-5019. Chinese.
Chuck E. Cheese Pizza Time Theatre, 1027 Oliver Road, Fairfield. Ph: (707) 426-4500. Pizza.
Church's Fried Chicken, 2370 North Texas, Fairfield. Ph: (707) 426-4008. Fast food.
Dairy Queen, 1730 West Texas, Fairfield. Ph: (707) 425-1535. Fast food.
Dave's Giant Hamburger, 1055 North Texas, Fairfield. Ph: (707) 425-1818. Fast food.
Denny's Restaurant, 1360 Holiday Lane, Fairfield. Ph: (707) 422-6511. American.
Denny's Restaurant, 2980 Travis Blvd., Fairfield. Ph: (707) 425-0303. American.
Domino's Pizza, 1239 Western, Fairfield. Ph: (707) 427-1170. Pizza.
Downtown Deli, 714 Texas, Fairfield. Ph: (707) 429-3354.
Dragon Palace Chinese Restaurant, 594 Parker Road, Fairfield. Ph: (707) 437-6671. Chinese.
El Azteca Mexican Food, 1731 North Texas, Fairfield. Ph: (707) 422-2108. Mexican.
Fairfield Landing, 2440 Martin Road, Fairfield. Ph: (707) 429-2370.
Favela's Taqueria, 1215 Texas, Fairfield. Ph: (707) 421-2045. Mexican.
Frank & Yuen's Chinese Restaurant, 1955 W. Texas St., Fairfield. Ph: (707) 428-3230. Chinese.

Geri-Towne Pizza, 3027 Travis Blvd., Fairfield. Ph: (707) 429-4660. Italian.
Gordito's Mexican Restaurant, 1025 Oliver Road, Fairfield. Ph: (707) 425-9833. Mexican.
Great China, 1972-A N. Texas St., Fairfield. Ph: (707) 426-2593. Chinese.
Green Valley Foods, 2320 Courage Drive, Fairfield. Ph: (707) 428-1541.
Han Kung, 739 Texas St., Fairfield. Ph: (707) 426-0202. Mongolian.
Happy Steak Restaurant, 1767 North Texas, Fairfield. Ph: (707) 428-5170. American.
Holiday Inn, 1350 Holiday Lane, Fairfield. Ph: (707) 422-4111.
Imperial Tandori Chicken, 2617 North Texas, Fairfield. Ph: (707) 429-0875.
Izuma Restaurant, 2773 N. Texas St., Fairfield. Ph: (707) 422-3114. Japanese.
Jack In The Box Restaurants, 1965 Texas, Fairfield. Ph: (707) 429-2772. Fast food.
Jack-In-The-Box, 1980 North Texas, Fairfield. Ph: (707) 426-5039. Fast food.
Jade Garden, 1431 Travis Blvd., Fairfield. Ph: (707) 422-2717. Chinese.
Johanne's Hot Dogs, 1708 Texas, Fairfield. Ph: (707) 422-6666. American.
Kentucky Fried Chicken, 2277 North Texas, Fairfield. Ph: (707) 422-5220. Fast food.
La Hacienda Restaurant, 720 Madison St., Fairfield. Ph: (707) 429-8360.
La Ramada Mexican Food, 146 Acacia, Fairfield. Ph: (707) 425-2947. Mexican.
La Taqueria Mexican Food, 1809 North Texas, Fairfield. Ph: (707) 427-1592. Mexican.
Las Flautas, 1360 Solano Mall, Fairfield. Ph: (707) 427-2270. Mexican.
Le Chalet, 3035 Travis Blvd., Fairfield. Ph: (707) 426-3753.
Little Mayon Restaurant, 1924 North Texas, Fairfield. Ph: (707) 426-0249.
Lyon's Restaurant, 2390 North Texas, Fairfield. Ph: (707) 429-5330. American.
Main Smorgas Board, 1720 Texas, Fairfield. Ph: (707) 422-8797.
Mandarin Restaurant, 219 Texas St., Fairfield. Ph: (707) 428-9736. Chinese.
Margaritas Village, 146 Acacia, Fairfield. Ph: (707) 425-0406.
Marie Callender's Restaurants & Bakeries, 1750 Travis Blvd., Fairfield. Ph: (707) 428-4745. American.
Mary's Pizza Shack, 1500 Oliver Road, Fairfield. Ph: (707) 422-2700. Pizza.
McDonald's Hamburgers, 2212 North Texas, Fairfield. Ph: (707) 421-2867. Fast food.

McDonald's Hamburgers, 3080 Travis Blvd., Fairfield. Ph: (707) 422-1044. Fast food.
McDonald's Restaurant, 4440 Central Place, Fairfield. Ph: (707) 864-9701. Fast food.
Moon Room Cocktail Lounge, 3333 North Texas, Fairfield. Ph: (707) 429-1515.
Muffin Treat Restaurant, 3333 N. Texas St., Fairfield. Ph: (707) 422-2908.
Nation's Giant Hambergers & Great Pies, 1955 Texas, Fairfield. Ph: (707) 425-1800. American.
New China Restaurant, 1343 O.iver Road, Fairfield. Ph: (707) 429-8562.
New Manila Express Restaurant, 2704 North Texas, Fairfield. Ph: (707) 422-9397. Filipino.
North Shore Seafood Grill, 1470 Holiday Lane, Fairfield. Ph: (707) 428-3474.
Omelette House Cafe, 1690 Texas, Fairfield. Ph: (707) 425-5074.
Omodaka Japanese Restaurant, 1972 North Texas, Fairfield. Ph: (707) 427-2434. Japanese.
Orange Julius, 1467 Travis, Fairfield. Ph: (707) 428-9699. Fast food.
Pagoda, 2155 N. Texas St., Fairfield. Ph: (707) 425-6817.
Parker's Snack Bar, 630 Union Ave., Fairfield. Ph: (707) 426-2973.
Pearl Fish Factory, 1831 North Texas, Fairfield. Ph: (707) 427-3474.
Peking Restaurant, 3073 Travis Blvd., Fairfield. Ph: (707) 425-0207. Chinese.
Pelayo's Mexican Restaurant, 1972 N. Texas St., Fairfield. Ph: (707) 427-3385. Mexican.
Pepe's Mexican Restaurant, 620 Jackson, Fairfield. Ph: (707) 428-3413. Mexican.
Pietro's, 407 Cernon, Fairfield. Ph: (707) 446-1771.
Pietro's, 711 Madison St., Fairfield. Ph: (707) 422-4497. Italian.
Pizza Hut, 1803 North Texas, Fairfield. Ph: (707) 422-0221. Pizza.
Professor's Pizza, 1230 Western, Fairfield. Ph: (707) 428-4545. Italian.
Puerto Vallarta Restaurant, 720 Madison, Fairfield. Ph: (707) 422-1240. Mexican.
S & L Thai Restaurant, 419 Texas, Fairfield. Ph: (707) 426-6499. Thai.
Sbarro The Italian Eatery, 1377 Travis Blvd., Fairfield. Ph: (707) 427-1637. Italian.
Shakey's Restaurant, 2281 N. Texas St., Fairfield. Ph: (707) 422-5951. Pizza.
Six Fortunes Restaurant, 844 Texas St., Fairfield. Ph: (707) 425-8908.
Sizzler, 1795 Pennsylvania Ave., Fairfield. Ph: (707) 427-8436. American.

Skipper's Seafood N' Chowder House, 2285 North Texas, Fairfield. Ph: (707) 425-9449.
SL Thai Restaurant, 419 Texas St., Fairfield. Ph: (707) 426-6499.
Subway Sandwiches & Salads, 1914 Texas, Fairfield. Ph: (707) 428-3938.
Sunrise International Restaurant, 1720 N. Texas St., Fairfield. Ph: (707) 422-3474.
Taco Bell, 1661 North Texas, Fairfield. Ph: (707) 426-3231. Fast food.
Taqueria Tampico, 2785 North Texas, Fairfield. Ph: (707) 426-9766. Mexican.
Teriyaki Kitchen, 3079 Travis Blvd., Fairfield. Ph: (707) 427-2448. Japanese.
The New China Restaurant, 1343 Oliver Road, Fairfield. Ph: (707) 429-8562. Chinese.
The Restaurant at Rancho Solano, 3250 Rancho Solano Parkway, Fairfield. Ph: (707) 427-8917.
Togo's Eatery, 1350 Gateway Blvd., Fairfield. Ph: (707) 425-8646.
Tomiyoshi Japanese Restaurant, 740 Texa St., Fairfield. Ph: (707) 425-3311. Japanese.
Tony Roma's of Fairfield, 1620 Pennsylvania Ave., Fairfield. Ph: (707) 428-4414.
Wendy's Old Fashioned Hamburgers, 2045 North Texas, Fairfield. Ph: (707) 429-2199. Fast food.
West Texas Southern Cafe, 900 Texas, Fairfield. Ph: (707) 422-4151.
Wild Willey's, 1955 W. Texas St., Fairfield. Ph: (707) 425-1938.
Wokman, 1500 Oliver Road, Fairfield. Ph: (707) 427-3558. Chinese.
You's Burger, 715 2nd, Fairfield. Ph: (707) 425-8781.

Suisun

Arby's, 4445 Central Place, Suisun. Ph: (707) 864-2729. American.
Babs Delta Diner, 501 Main, Suisun. Ph: (707) 421-1926.
BJ's Soul Food Restaurant, 607 Marina Center, Suisun. Ph: (707) 421-1904.
Carl's Jr., 2828 Sunset Ave., Suisun. Ph: (707) 422-9511. Fast food.
D's Bar B Q, 108 Sunset Center, Suisun. Ph: (707) 429-5335.
Dynasty Restaurant, 254 Sunset Ave., Suisun. Ph: (707) 426-6222. Chinese.
El Tapatio Cafe, 2982 Rockville Road, Suisun. Ph: (707) 425-9622. Mexican.
Gerry Lane Inc., 1879 Rockville Road, Suisun. Ph: (707) 864-0460.
HJ's Pub, 605 Main St., Suisun. Ph: (707) 425-7319.

RESTAURANTS 219

Jason's, 100 Suisun Valley Road, Suisun. Ph: (707) 864-0223. American.
Kentucky Fried Chicken, 173 Sunset Ave., Suisun. Ph: (707) 427-2521. Fast food.
Kimo's Favorite Island Foods & Cake Shoppe, 258 Sunset Ave., Suisun. Ph: (707) 427-1008. Hawaiian.
La Copa De Oro Taqueria, 415 Main, Suisun. Ph: (707) 429-5871. Mexican.
London Fish & Chips, 108 Sunset Center, Suisun. Ph: (707) 421-0635.
Main 627, A Restaurant, 627 Main St., Suisun. Ph: (707) 428-6270.
Mankas Corner Restaurant, Mankas Corner Road, Suisun. Ph: (707) 425-3207.
McDonald's Hamburgers, 109 Sunset Center, Suisun. Ph: (707) 426-6235. Fast food.
Mullins Pub & Grill, 605 Main, Suisun. Ph: (707) 421-9567.
Myrna's, 4171 Suisun Valley Road, Suisun. Ph: (707) 864-2507.
Pedro's Latino Food, 104 Sunset Center, Suisun. Ph: (707) 421-8003. Mexican.
Port of Subs, 274 Sunset Ave., Suisun. Ph: (707) 422-7762.
Puerto Vallarta, 301B Main, Suisun. Ph: (707) 429-9384. Mexican.
Raley's Chinese Food To Go, 270 Sunset Ave., Suisun. Ph: (707) 426-1391. Chinese.
Rockville Inn, 4163 Suisun Valley Road, Suisun. Ph: (707) 864-4325.
Rod's Pizza, 104-A Sunset Center, Suisun. Ph: (707) 427-1163. Pizza.
Sports Unlimited, 250 Sunset Ave., Suisun. Ph: (707) 429-7172.
Suisun Thai Cafe, 301 Marina Centrer, Suisun. Ph: (707) 422-8204. Thai.
Taqueria Azteca, 288 Sunset Ave., Suisun. Ph: (707) 421-8809. Mexican.
Tasuke Japanese Restaurant, Main & Spring, Suisun. Ph: (707) 427-1221. Japanese.
The Burrito Palace, 307 Alder, Suisun. Ph: (707) 429-1969. Mexican.
Wings N Thngs, 507 Marina Center, Suisun. Ph: (707) 427-0618.
Golden Grill, 108-G Sunset Shopping Center, Suisun City. Ph: (707) 425-6555. Chinese.
Zowie's Cafe, 701 Main St., Suisun City. Ph: (707) 422-1613.

Travis

Hanger 21, 666 Parker Road, Travis. Ph: (707) 437-9376.
Koreana Restaurant, 574 Parker Road, Travis. Ph: (707) 437-4822. Korean.
La Salsa Mexican Taqueria, 520 Partker Road, Travis. Ph: (707) 437-5186. Mexican.
Pizza Pit, 670 Parker Road, Travis. Ph: (707) 437-1100. Pizza.
Star Deli, 666 Parker Road, Travis. Ph: (707) 437-3610.

Vacaville

A & W Family Restaurant, 936 Merchant, Vacaville. Ph: (707) 448-5990. Fast food.
Arby's, 1347 E. Monte Vista Ave., Vacaville. Ph: (707) 446-6029. American.
Bakers Square Restaurant & Pie Shop, 951 Merchant, Vacaville. Ph: (707) 449-0566.
Black Oak Restaurant, I-80 & US 505, Vacaville. Ph: (707) 448-1311. American.
Brookhill Restaurant, 888 Alamo Drive, Vacaville. Ph: (707) 449-3686.
Burger King, 1330 E. Monte Vista, Vacaville. Ph: (707) 446-7400. Fast food.
Buttercup Pantry Restaurant & Bakery, 400 Orange Drive, Vacaville. Ph: (707) 451-0234.
Cafe Carmel, 126 S. Orchard Ave., Vacaville. Ph: (707) 448-9544.
Carl's Jr., 98 Peabody Court, Vacaville. Ph: (707) 446-8119. Fast food.
Chin Hua, 2018 Nut Tree Road, Vacaville. Ph: (707) 447-3223. Chinese.
China House Restaurant, 513 Main St., Vacaville. Ph: (707) 446-8068. Chinese.
China Village, 120 Peabody Road, Vacaville. Ph: (707) 449-0915. Chinese.
Coffee Tree, Nut Tree Road, Vacaville. Ph: (707) 448-8435. American.
Downtown Coffee Shop, 374 Merchant, Vacaville. Ph: (707) 448-0490. American.
E&W Take Out, 1110 E. Marshall Road, Vacaville. Ph: (707) 448-7669. Fast food.
E. Charro, 1401 E. Monte Vista, Vacaville. Ph: (707) 446-8345.
El Azteca Mexican Food II, 102 Peabody Road, Vacaville. Ph: (707) 448-7231. Mexican.
El Caracol, 201 Dobbins, Vacaville. Ph: (707) 449-3798. Mexican.
El Charro Mexican Foods, 1401 E. Monte Vista Ave., Vacaville. Ph: (707) 446-8345. Mexican.
El Pajaro Mexican Restaurant, 871 Merchant St., Vacaville. Ph: (707) 448-4788.
El Patio Restaurant, 3039 Alamo Drive, Vacaville. Ph: (707) 447-8226. Mexican.
Emil Villa's The Original Hick'ry Pit, 960 Orange Drive, Vacaville. Ph: (707) 446-7427.
Fabulous Franks, 3015 Alamo Drive, Vacaville. Ph: (707) 446-3030.
Food Pavilion, 324 Nut Tree Road, Vacaville.

220   CONTRA COSTA & SOLANO

Ph: (707) 449-8494.
Fosters Old Fashion Freeze, 653 Merchant, Vacaville. Ph: (707) 448-1400. Fast food.
Georges Steak Den, 107 Peabody Road, Vacaville. Ph: (707) 448-3377. American.
Golden Dragon, 519 Main, Vacaville. Ph: (707) 446-1285. Chinese.
Great Wall Chinese Restaurant, 3019 Alamo Drive, Vacaville. Ph: (707) 447-5667. Chinese.
Hamburger Stand, 149 Peabody Road, Vacaville. Ph: (707) 447-9483. American.
Helen & Ned's Restaurant, 751 E. Monte Vista Ave., Vacaville. Ph: (707) 448-8822.
Heritage House Cafe, 303 Merchant, Vacaville. Ph: (707) 448-3900.
Hong Kong Restaurant, 760 Merchant St., Vacaville. Ph: (707) 448-8133. Chinese.
Jack-In-The-Box, 1035 Alamo Drive, Vacaville. Ph: (707) 446-2645. Fast food.
Jack-In-The-Box Drive-Thru, 290 E. Monte Vista Ave., Vacaville. Ph: (707) 448-9828. Fast food.
Jessy's Burgers & Burritos, 819 Davis, Vacaville. Ph: (707) 448-9505. American.
Kentucky Fried Chicken, 780 Merchant, Vacaville. Ph: (707) 448-7141. Fast food.
Kim & Ned's Express Chinese Food Takeout, 324 Nut Tree Road, Vacaville. Ph: (707) 446-9599. Chinese.
La Maison, 537 Main St., Vacaville. Ph: (707) 447-0737. French.
La Posada, 871 Merchant, Vacaville. Ph: (707) 451-9252. Mexican.
Le Deli Cafe, 312 Cernon, Vacaville. Ph: (707) 447-7782.
Le Fever Mattson, 130 Allison Court, Vacaville. Ph: (707) 449-8500.
Little Caesar's Pizza, 1041 Alamo Drive, Vacaville. Ph: (707) 447-6000. Italian.
Long John Silver's Seafood Shoppe, 1327 E. Monte Vista Ave., Vacaville. Ph: (707) 425-2670.
Louie's Place, 240 Nut Tree Road, Vacaville. Ph: (707) 451-1133.
Lyon's Restaurant, 909 Merchant St., Vacaville. Ph: (707) 447-4600. American.
McDonald's Hamburgers, 1310 E. Monte Vista Ave., Vacaville. Ph: (707) 449-8275. Fast food.
Merchant & Main Grill & Bar, 349 Merchant St., Vacaville. Ph: (707) 446-0368.
Murillo's Restaurants, 1581 E. Monte Vista Ave., Vacaville. Ph: (707) 447-3704. Mexican.
Murillo's Restaurants, 633 Merchant, Vacaville. Ph: (707) 448-3395. Mexican.

Nation's Giant Hamburgers & Great Pies, 100 Browns Valley Pkwy., Vacaville. Ph: (707) 446-8881. American.
Nut Tree Restaurant, Monte Vista Exit from I-80, Vacaville. Ph: (707) 448-1818.
Papa Joe's Gourmet Restaurant, 324 Nut Tree Road, Vacaville. Ph: (707) 446-9669.
Pelayo's Mexican Restaurant, 1160 E. Monte Vista Ave., Vacaville. Ph: (707) 449-9365. Mexican.
Penelope's, 547 Main, Vacaville. Ph: (707) 449-8933.
Piccolo's Pizza, 883 Markham Ave., Vacaville. Ph: (707) 451-ª207. Italian.
Pietro's No. 1, 407 Cernon, Vacaville. Ph: (707) 446-1771. Italian.
Pietro's No. 2, 679 Merchant St., Vacaville. Ph: (707) 448-4588.
Premier Foods, 290 E. Monte Vista Ave., Vacaville. Ph: (707) 448-4446.
Rod's Pizza, 631 Elmira Road, Vacaville. Ph: (707) 448-4349. Pizza.
Sacca Properties, 810 Alamo Drive, Vacaville. Ph: (707) 449-3469.
Shanghai Express, 500 Elmira Road, Vacaville. Ph: (707) 451-3388. Chinese.
Sizzler, 1350 E. Monte Vista Ave., Vacaville. Ph: (707) 446-1505. American.
Sonora Desert Taqueria, 1040-B E. Monte Vista Ave., Vacaville. Ph: (707) 448-7792.
Stir Fry Chinese Food, 959 Alamo Drive, Vacaville. Ph: (707) 447-7053. Chinese.
Subway Sandwiches, 741 E. Monte Vista Ave., Vacaville. Ph: (707) 446-1944.
Sun Garden Restaurant, I-80 at I-505, Vacaville. Ph: (707) 446-3838.
Sushi Sen, 121 Peabody Road, Vacaville. Ph: (707) 447-2161. Japanese.
Taco Bell, 120 Parker, Vacaville. Ph: (707) 447-4305. Fast food.
Taco Bell, 1481 E. Monte Vista Ave., Vacaville. Ph: (707) 449-8852. Fast food.
The Buckhorn, Railroad & Main, Vacaville. Ph: (916) 795-4503.
The Happy Mug, 348 Merchant, Vacaville. Ph: (707) 447-9514.
The Original Mels Inc., 591 Orange Drive, Vacaville. Ph: (707) 451-3693.
The Sandwich Shop, 217 Parker, Vacaville. Ph: (707) 449-1988.
Togo's Eatery, 132 Peabody Road, Vacaville. Ph: (707) 448-1447.
Vaca Joe's, 980 Leisure Town Road, Vacaville. Ph: (707) 447-4633.
Wah Shine, 145 Peabody Road, Vacaville. Ph: (707) 448-0785. Chinese.
Wendy's of Vacaville, 1377 E. Monte Vista

Ave., Vacaville. Ph: (707) 446-8669. Fast food.
Wren's Cafe, 1005 Merchant, Vacaville. Ph: (707) 446-4259.
Yen King Chinese Restaurant, 136 Browns Valley Park Way, Vacaville. Ph: (707) 449-4217. Chinese.

Vallejo

Anthony's Restaurant, 1711 Solano Ave., Vallejo. Ph: (707) 557-0494.
Arby's Roast Beef Sandwich Restaurant, 3201 Sonoma Blvd., Vallejo. Ph: (707) 649-2729.
B & W Cafe, 2632 Sonoma Blvd., Vallejo. Ph: (707) 644-2592.
Black Angus Restaurant, 124 Plaza Drive, Vallejo. Ph: (707) 647-0595. Amercian.
Brook's Ranch Restaurant, 720 Admiral Callaghan Lane, Vallejo. Ph: (707) 647-0198.
Bud's Burgers, 117b Maritime Academy Drive, Vallejo. Ph: (707) 647-7407. American.
Bud's Burgers, 1339 Springs Road, Vallejo. Ph: (707) 641-1012. American.
Bud's Burgers, 3849b Sonoma Blvd, Vallejo. Ph: (707) 642-3252. American.
Burger King, 1 Mariposa, Vallejo. Ph: (707) 554-8344. Fast food.
Burger King, 1598 Fairgrounds Drive, Vallejo. Ph: (707) 644-1598. Fast food.
Burger King, 3606 Sonoma Blvd., Vallejo. Ph: (707) 552-1511. Fast food.
Caesar's Dinner House, 315 Tennessee St., Vallejo. Ph: (707) 552-4648.
Cajun Joe, 601 Tennessee St., Vallejo. Ph: (707) 553-7866.
Canton Ocean, 860 Tuolumne St., Vallejo. Ph: (707) 552-3663.
Carnitas Estrella, 2907 Sonoma Blvd., Vallejo. Ph: (707) 552-8024.
Chateau De Crepe Inc., 2001 Marine World Pkwy., Vallejo. Ph: (707) 552-7373.
Chef George's Bar-B-Q, 18 Laurel, Vallejo. Ph: (707) 647-2825.
Chevy's Mexican Restaurant, 157 Plaza Drive, Vallejo. Ph: (707) 644-1373. Mexican.
Chicken Express, 1075 Redwood, Vallejo. Ph: (707) 642-6454.
China Barn of Vallejo, 320 Tuolumne, Vallejo. Ph: (707) 642-1523. Chinese.
China Cafe, 512 Sacramento St., Vallejo. Ph: (707) 648-0797.
China Express, 774 Admiral Callaghan Lane, Vallejo. Ph: (707) 554-1307. Chinese.
Church's Fried Chicken, 1920 Solano Ave., Vallejo. Ph: (707) 642-8118.
Circus Coffee Shop, 306 Georgia, Vallejo. Ph: (707) 552-7613.
City Lights Cafe & Catering, 415 Virginia, Vallejo. Ph: (707) 557-9200.

Kids galore in the suburbs

222 CONTRA COSTA & SOLANO

D's Eat & Run, 1300 Georgia, Vallejo. Ph: (707) 644-6499.
Dad's Barbecue, 2909 Sonoma Blvd., Vallejo. Ph: (707) 552-4399.
Dairy Queen, 2120 Springs Road, Vallejo. Ph: (707) 643-0221. Fast food.
Dairyland, 818 Tennessee, Vallejo. Ph: (707) 644-2663.
Denny's Restaurant, 415 Santa Clara, Vallejo. Ph: (707) 552-0439. American.
Denny's Restaurant, 4355 Sonoma Blvd., Vallejo. Ph: (707) 644-6100. American.
Dodwell Company, 3570 Sonoma Blvd., Vallejo. Ph: (707) 644-4202.
Dot's Baking Pantry & Catering, 535 Georgia St., Vallejo. Ph: (707) 552-8212.
El Nopal, 406 Virginia, Vallejo. Ph: (707) 557-0456. Mexican.
Foster's Old Fashion Freeze, 1143 Tennessee, Vallejo. Ph: (707) 644-8518. Fast food.
Freddie's China Barn, 320 Tuolumne St., Vallejo. Ph: (707) 642-1523.
G & L Cafe, 1030 Tennessee, Vallejo. Ph: (707) 554-4221. American.
Gold Rush Pizza & Potato Co., 35 Admiral Callaghan Lane, Vallejo. Ph: (707) 642-8485.
Golden Bubble Restaurant & Cocktail Lounge, 2272 Sacramento, Vallejo. Ph: (707) 642-4343.
Golden Ox, 4300 Sonoma Blvd., Vallejo. Ph: (707) 649-1007.
Gonzalez' Mexican Restaurant, 2164 Springs Road, Vallejo. Ph: (707) 644-3846.
Grotto, 3 Curtola Parkway, Vallejo. Ph: (707) 644-4743.
Gumbah's Italian Beef, 138 Tennessee, Vallejo. Ph: (707) 648-1100. Italian.
Harbor House Restaurant, 23 Harbor Way, Vallejo. Ph: (707) 642-8984.
Harvey's Lounge & Restaurant, 2234 Sacramento, Vallejo. Ph: (707) 642-9515.
Hi-Tops Sports Grill, 480 Redwood, Vallejo. Ph: (707) 557-4133.
Holiday Inn, 1000 Fairgrounds Drive, Vallejo. Ph: (707) 644-1200.
Honey Bears, 314 Georgia, Vallejo. Ph: (707) 557-8988.
Hong Kong Kitchen, 320 Fairgrounds Drive, Vallejo. Ph: (707) 644-6826. Chinese.
Hop Hing's Chinese Restaurant, 3624 Sonoma Blvd., Vallejo. Ph: (707) 554-3614. Chinese.
House of Soul, 1526 Solano Ave., Vallejo. Ph: (707) 644-3792.
Hwy 37 Cafe, 1510 Marine World Pkwy., Vallejo. Ph: (707) 553-1210.

International House of Pancakes, 1400 Tennessee, Vallejo. Ph: (707) 643-0972. American.
Italia Pizzeria, 23 Tennessee, Vallejo. Ph: (707) 644-5907. Italian.
J's Garden Restaurant, 134 Robles Drive, Vallejo. Ph: (707) 552-9700.
Jack-In-The-Box Restaurant, 400 Broadway, Vallejo. Ph: (707) 554-3312. Fast food.
Jack-In-The-Box Restaurants, 1610 Marine World Pkwy., Vallejo. Ph: (707) 552-8307. Fast food.
Jarearn Thai & Chinese Cuisine, 907 Tennessee, Vallejo. Ph: (707) 557-4834. Thai & Chinese.
Jay's Place, 405 Wilson Ave., Vallejo. Ph: (707) 644-2806.
Jaya Chinese Restaurant, 2215 Sonoma Blvd., Vallejo. Ph: (707) 648-1388. Chinese.
JJ Winfield's Restaurant, 901 Redwood, Vallejo. Ph: (707) 644-3603.
JP's Seafood Burger Deli, 3420 Sonoma Blvd., Vallejo. Ph: (707) 557-6903.
Kenito's Burritos, 333 Tennessee St., Vallejo. Ph: (707) 647-1447. Mexican.
Kentucky Fried Chicken, 1201 Georgia, Vallejo. Ph: (707) 643-2524. Fast food.
Kentucky Fried Chicken, 991 Redwood, Vallejo. Ph: (707) 643-8207. Fast food.
Kwongnan Restaurant, 405 York St., Vallejo. Ph: (707) 554-1696. Chinese.
La Bufa Mexican Restaurant, 1622 Sonoma Blvd., Vallejo. Ph: (707) 552-8878. Mexican.
La Prima Pizza, 170 Robles Way, Vallejo. Ph: (707) 648-0600. Mexican.
Ling Nam Noodle House, 972 Admiral Callaghan Lane, Vallejo. Ph: (707) 553-8837. Chinese.
Long John Silver Seafood Shoppe, 1015 Redwood, Vallejo. Ph: (707) 553-1449. Fast food.
Lourd's Tastes & Sounds, 1524 Sonoma Blvd., Vallejo. Ph: (707) 554-3488.
Lyon's Restaurant, 980 Admiral Callaghan Lane, Vallejo, u707, 557-4551. American.
Maggie's Hamburgers, 700 Benicia Road, Vallejo. Ph: (707) 643-9149. American.
Mandarin, 734 Lincoln Road East, Vallejo. Ph: (707) 552-8911. Chinese.
Manila Sunset Restaurant, 1601 Marine World Pkwy., Vallejo. Ph: (707) 554-8211. Filipino.
Mario's Cafe Italiano, 308 Pennsylvania, Vallejo. Ph: (707) 644-6625. Italian.
Matthew's Fine Foods, 414 Georgia St., Vallejo. Ph: (707) 642-0744.

RESTAURANTS 223

McDonald's, 2565 Springs Road, Vallejo. Ph: (707) 552-9798. Fast food.
McDonald's, 3289 Sonoma Blvd., Vallejo. Ph: (707) 643-6220. Fast food.
McDonald's, 902 Admiral Callaghan Lane., Vallejo. Ph: (707) 552-7497. Fast food.
McDonald's, Railroad Ave., Mare Island, Vallejo. Ph: (707) 552-3400. Fast food.
Micado Restaurant, 524 Tuolumne St., Vallejo. Ph: (707) 642-1122.
Mike's Fish Grotto, 1922 Broadway, Vallejo. Ph: (707) 643-6420.
Misaki Japanese Restaurant, 2138 Springs Road, Vallejo. Ph: (707) 642-0313.
Moe's Delights, 480 Redwood, Vallejo. Ph: (707) 648-1714.
Molinar's Mexico Lindo, 541 Benicia Road, Vallejo. Ph: (707) 742-1101.
Myrna's Bakery Cafe, 630 Tennessee, Vallejo. Ph: (707) 553-9786.
Napoli Pizzeria, 124 Tennessee St., Vallejo. Ph: (707) 644-9270.
Nation's Giant Hamburgers & Great Pies, 2525 Sonoma Blvd., Vallejo. Ph: (707) 554-8888. American.
Nitti Gritti Family Restaurant, 2065 Solano Ave., Vallejo. Ph: (707) 642-4411.
Nujo's Pizza, 1833 Springs Road, Vallejo. Ph: (707) 648-9971.
One Mile House, 1120 Broadway, Vallejo. Ph: (707) 648-9323.
Oriental Express, 3335 Sonoma Blvd., Vallejo. Ph: (707) 645-1926. Chinese.
Palby's Restaurant, 3860 Napa-Vallejo Highway, Vallejo. Ph: (707) 648-9399.
Parker's Snack Bar, 355 Tuolumne, Vallejo. Ph: (707) 557-9653.
Peking Palace, 2621 Springs Road, Vallejo. Ph: (707) 557-4601. Chinese.
Pepe's Mexican Restaurant, 105 Couch St., Vallejo. Ph: (707) 557-0542. Mexican.
Philippine Village Cafe, 738 Sonoma Blvd., Vallejo. Ph: (707) 644-9987. Filipino.
Pink Dawn Chinese Restaurant, 1601 Marine World Pkwy., Vallejo. Ph: (707) 557-7785. Chinese.
Pizza Hut, 5 Flemingtowne Center, Vallejo. Ph: (707) 644-4051. Pizza.
Pizza Hut, 905 Broadway, Vallejo. Ph: (707) 645-0505. Pizza.
Pizza King, 1624 Fairgrounds Drive, Vallejo. Ph: (707) 553-9112. Pizza.
Pizza Pirate, 972 Admiral Callaghan Lane, Vallejo. Ph: (707) 648-3300. Pizza.
Pluto's Hot Dogs, 529 Broadway, Vallejo. Ph: (707) 554-2040. American.
Popeye's Chicken, 1601 Marine World Pkwy., Vallejo. Ph: (707) 643-9223. Fast food.
Princess Garden, 3611 Sonoma Blvd., Vallejo. Ph: (707) 648-0808.
Princess Garden, 960 Admiral Callaghan Lane, Vallejo. Ph: (707) 643-0202.
Rafael's Bar & Restaurant, 301 Nebraska, Vallejo. Ph: (707) 645-1333.
Raley's Superstores Chinese Food To Go, 4300 Sonoma Blvd., Vallejo. Ph: (707) 642-0820. Chinese.
Redwood Inn, 125 Flemingtowne Center, Vallejo. Ph: (707) 553-8598.
Remark's Harbor House, 23 Harbor Way, Vallejo. Ph: (707) 642-8984.
Richard's Inn, 2200 Redwood St., Vallejo. Ph: (707) 644-4457.
Rickshaw Chinese Food, 4300 Sonoma Blvd., Vallejo. Ph: (707) 643-4837. Chinese.
Right Touch BBQ, 423 Lincoln Road West, Vallejo. Ph: (707) 552-3385.
Rod's Hickory Pit, 199 Lincoln Road West, Vallejo. Ph: (707) 642-8989.
Round Table Pizza, 2633 Springs Road, Vallejo. Ph: (707) 642-4494. Pizza.
Round Table Pizza, 27 Rancho Square, Vallejo. Ph: (707) 642-6545. Pizza.
Round Table Pizza, 4300 Sonoma Blvd., Vallejo. Ph: (707) 552-9747. Pizza.
Round Table Pizza, 742 Admiral Callaghan Lane, Vallejo. Ph: (707) 554-4033. Pizza.
Rudy's Louisiana Seafood, 324 Mini Drive, Vallejo. Ph: (707) 642-9716. Seafood.
Sac's Tasty Hot Dogs, 2445 Springs Road, Vallejo. Ph: (707) 642-2442.
Shima Japanese Restaurant, 3335 Sonoma Blvd., Vallejo. Ph: (707) 553-1738. Japanese.
Silahis Restaurant, 3315 Sonoma Blvd., Vallejo. Ph: (707) 644-2131.
Sizzler Restaurants, 3740 Sonoma Blvd., Vallejo. Ph: (707) 552-0100.
Smorgabob's Buffet, 910 Lincoln Road East, Vallejo. Ph: (707) 552-7425.
South Villa Chinese Restaurant, 758 Admiral Callaghan Lane, Vallejo. Ph: (707) 557-2125.
Straw Hat Pizza, 3780 Sonoma Blvd., Vallejo. Ph: (707) 644-5541. Pizza.
Subway Sandwiches & Salad, 1601 Marine World Pkwy. #114, Vallejo. Ph: (707) 557-0751. Fast food.
Subway Sandwiches & Salad, 2045 Springs Road, Vallejo. Ph: (707) 552-2279. Fast food.
Subway Sandwiches & Salad, 617 Tennessee, Vallejo. Ph: (707) 647-3667. Fast food.
Subway Sandwiches & Salad, 976 Admiral

Callaghan Lane, Vallejo. Ph: (707) 642-8246. Fast food.
Swensen's Ice Cream Restaurant, 972 Admiral Callaghan Lane., Vallejo. Ph: (707) 642-4469. American.
Szechuan Chinese Cuisine, 2079 Solano Ave., Vallejo. Ph: (707) 554-4657.
Taco Bell, 3600 Sonoma Blvd., Vallejo. Ph: (707) 553-1111. Fast food.
Taco Bell, 974 Admiral Callaghan Lane, Vallejo. Ph: (707) 648-2402. Fast food.
Taco's La Playita, 920 Marin, Vallejo. Ph: (707) 647-0695. Mexican.
Tacos Jalisco, 3440 Sonoma Blvd., Vallejo. Ph: (707) 647-0554. Mexican.
The Joy of Eating, 1828 Springs Road, Vallejo. Ph: (707) 644-5315.
The Original Scotty's, 1645 Tennessee, Vallejo. Ph: (707) 644-2051.
The Sardine Can, 0 Harbor Way, Vallejo. Ph: (707) 553-9492.
Tia Lupe's Taqueria, 301 Georgia, Vallejo. Ph: (707) 552-3811. Mexican.
Togo's Eatery, 3656 Sonoma Blvd., Vallejo. Ph: (707) 552-8646.
Tonelli's Restaurant, 6240 Napa Vallejo Highway, Vallejo. Ph: (707) 642-8807. Continental.
Uncle Chang's, 145 Plaza Drive, Vallejo. Ph: (707) 645-1611. Chinese.
Uncle Sam, 785 Sereno Drive, Vallejo. Ph: (707) 647-0378.
Vallejo Fish & Chips & Hamburgers, 613 Tennessee, Vallejo. Ph: (707) 644-3474.
Wendy's, 118 Plaza Drive, Vallejo. Ph: (707) 645-0884. Fast food.
Western Restaurants, 44 Admiral Callaghan Lane, Vallejo. Ph: (707) 647-1362.
Wharf, Georgia Street Wharf, Vallejo. Ph: (707) 648-1966.
Wok Inn, 42 Springtowne Shopping Center, Vallejo. Ph: (707) 648-1000. Chinese.
Zamorano Restaurant, 635 Broadway, Vallejo. Ph: (707) 644-9441.
Zarducci's Pizza, 3365 Sonoma Blvd., Vallejo. Ph: (707) 644-5656. Italian.

12/Fun & Games

Regional Parks and Preserves, Trails, Museums — Sports & Entertainment for Adults and Children

FUN IN CONTRA COSTA and Solano counties draws from four traditions, the first symbolized by conservationist John Muir, the second by the martini, the third by Abner Doubleday, the fourth by a whale at Marine World. Muir, who lived in Martinez, stands for the pleasures of hill and trail, and the martini, supposedly concocted in Martinez, for delights of bar, table and band.

Doubleday invented baseball. Thousands of people in the two counties find great happiness in organized sports. People go to Marine World not to participate but to observe: fish, whales and other animals. Other observation events include theater, movies, art shows and college and professional sports.

In all traditions, the East and North Bay have done well. First the outdoors.

The Regional Parks

The East Bay Regional Park District, encompassing Contra Costa County and Alameda County, includes 46 regional parks comprising 60,000 acres with more than 500 miles of internal trails and 100-plus miles of nine connecting trails. For general information on any of the park district activities or locations, call (510) 635-0135. Reservations for group picnic areas, youth-group day and overnight camping are available by calling (510) 636-1684. Reservations for backpacking and family overnight camping are available by calling (510) 562-2267.

• **Briones Regional Park.** 5,303 acres. Wildflowers in spring and views of Suisun Bay and Mount Tamalpais. Red-tailed hawks, golden eagles fly overhead. In summer, hike open grasslands, woodlands, around the four ponds.

Hiking, equestrian, nature trails, picnicking, barbecue pits, camping, children's play area. Parking fee. Try Briones-to-Mount Diablo Trail on

Pleasant Hill Road, north of Acalanes High. Trail open to Heather Farms Park in Walnut Creek with portions used by hikers, bicyclers, joggers and horseback riders. Enter via Reliez Valley Road or Alhambra Valley Road or take San Pablo Dam Road off Highway 24, then to Bear Creek Road and park entrance.

• **Contra Loma Regional Park.** 776 acres. Cool blue waters, olive trees, greenery make this one of the most popular in county. Located on Frederickson Lane, south of Antioch. Swimming, fishing, hiking, boating, picnicking. Bathhouse, food concession, boat rentals. Parking, boating fees.

Take Highway 24 or Highway 680 north to Highway 4, then east on 4 to L Street and Contra Loma Boulevard. Go south and watch for signs.

• **Tassajara Creek Regional Park.** 451 acres south of San Ramon. Quiet, undeveloped place for picnicking, kite flying, hiking, equestrian use. Take I-580 to Tassajara Road exit then north to parking lot and bridge to trails.

• **Tilden Regional Park.** 2,078 acres adjacent to El Cerrito, Kensington in Berkeley hills, spreading to Orinda.

In season at Lake Anza: swimming, sandy beach, bathhouse complex, large turfed area, food concession. Year-round fishing. At Environmental Education Center and Nature Area: interpretive programs, exhibits, puppet shows, Little Farm, Jewel Lake, all-weather nature trails. Tilden Public Golf Course: 18 holes, driving range, pro shop, Tee Clubhouse restaurant.

In other park areas, a merry-go-round, food concession and children's playhouse, Redwood Valley Railroad and Golden Gate Steamers (scale model steam locomotives), playfields, horseshoe pits, picnicking, Native Plant Botanic Garden and Visitor Center, Inspiration Point, hilltop vistas, reservable areas for group picnicking and youth group camping. Brazilian Building available for social events, meetings, business functions by reservation.

Hiking, jogging, bicycling, equestrian trails throughout. Backpacking access via East Bay Skyline Trail. One of the best parks in the Bay Area.

• **Wildcat Canyon Regional Park.** 2,419 acres in the hills east of Richmond, north of Tilden. Access from Tilden Nature Area and via Clark-Boas Trail.

Bicycling, birdwatching. Hiking, equestrian, jogging trails. Kite flying, blanket picnicking, interpretive programs.

• **Black Diamond Mine Regional Park.** 3,809 acres, near Pittsburg and Antioch. Welsh immigrants once mined coal fields located at long-gone towns of Nortonville, Somersville, Stewartville. Tours of some mines. Poignant miners' graveyard. (They had it tough in those days.) Barbecue pits, swimming, nature area, hiking trails, picnicking. Fee. Reservations: (510) 757-2620. Take Highway 4 to Somersville Road exit, then south to park entrance.

• **Morgan Territory Regional Preserve.** 2,164 acres north of Livermore and southeast of Clayton. Take Morgan Territory Road. Birdwatching, hiking, equestrian and jogging trails, kite flying, picturesque ponds, views of the eastern slope of Mount Diablo. Blanket picnicking.

- **Little Hills Ranch Regional Recreation Area.** 25 acres. Adjacent to Las Trampas Regional Wilderness, south of Alamo and west of Danville. Take Crow Canyon Road off Highway 580 or 680, then to Bollinger Canyon Road. From there four and a half miles to entrance.

Reservations for group picnicking or for entire park. Hiking, hayrides, horseback riding, swimming pool, stable area and covered arena, two pavilions, turfed area for sports, trout pond, barbecue pits. Phone (510) 462-1400.

- **Martinez Regional Shoreline.** Two miles long, flat, 343 acres. Gravel paths, pond, marshes. A great place to take Suzy or Johnny for a walk. Playgrounds, pier for fishing and feeding ducks. Restaurant. Soccer, baseball fields, off-road bicycle course, bocce ball courts. Marina.

Take Highway 4 to Alhambra Avenue exit, north to Marina Vista and signs to marina. Free.

- **Miller Knox Regional Shoreline.** 259 acres. On bay side of Point Richmond. Landscaped picnic area, secluded cove, beach, hilltop view of Bay and surrounding shore. Reservations for group picnics. Jogging and bicycling trails, swimming, fishing, kite flying.

Take Garrard Boulevard south through automobile tunnel to Dornan Drive and park entrance.

- **Point Isabel Regional Shoreline.** 21 acres at west end of Central Avenue in El Cerrito. Walking, bicycling trail. Fishing, birdwatching, kite flying, picnicking and dog walking.

Take Interstate 80 to Central Avenue exit, then west to park.

- **Point Pinole Regional Shoreline.** 2,147 acres. Beautiful park. Fine fishing pier. Three-mile shoreline. Good views, a beach, trails, a marsh and stands of eucalyptus. A shuttle runs from the parking lot to pier. No license required for pier fishing. Jogging, bicycling, restrooms, picnic tables.

From Interstate 80, take Hilltop west to San Pablo Avenue, then north to Atlas Road, left on Atlas until you see the park signs. Fee for parking, shuttle. Phone (510) 635-0135.

Wilderness

Predominantly natural areas for enjoyment far from urban scene.

- **Las Trampas Regional Wilderness.** 3,298 acres. No development other than parking lot, trail system. Bisected by Bollinger Creek. Rocky Ridge, west of creek, accessible from parking lot via paved road to 2,024-foot summit. At 1,760-foot level hike west along East Bay Municipal Utility District trail to the Valle Vista staging area on Canyon Road. On clear day, see Mount Tamalpais, cities around Bay.

Abundant wildlife, birdwatching. Picnic areas with barbecue pits near parking lot. Overnight equestrian camping area and other special-use areas available by reservation. Call (510) 562-7275. Horseback riding available at stables near park entrance. Phone (510) 838-7546.

Take Crow Canyon Road exit off Highway 580 or 680, then to Bollinger Canyon Road, 4.5 miles to entrance.

Trails

Linear parkland for walking, jogging, bicycling, and horseback riding. Five hundred miles of trails are within parks, plus the following 106 miles which connect the parks:

- **East Bay Skyline National Trail.** 31-mile trail for hiking, backpacking, horseback riding full length, and for bicycling in part. Connects six regional parks: Wildcat Canyon, Tilden, Sibley Volcanic, Huckleberry Botanic, Redwood, Chabot regional parks.

Trail meets entrance road to Chabot Family Camp near the southern end of the trail, Proctor Gate in Chabot, Castro Valley.

- **Contra Costa Canal.** Popular 12-mile hiking trail. Winds mostly through Central County. Pathway for hiking, bicycling, horseback riding.

Trail begins at Hidden Lakes Drive and Center Ave. in Martinez, follows canal south before turning east through Walnut Creek and Concord. Canal once supplied irrigation water to the farms. Watch the kiddies. Canal has drowned more than a few.

Indoors and Out

If regional parks aren't enough to put a claim on your time, try museums or shopping malls or a cruise on the Sacramento. Or even a beer brewery in Fairfield.

- **Alexander Lindsay Junior Museum.** Walnut Creek. A natural history museum specializing in the feathery, furry and scaly residents of Contra Costa, from song birds to rattlers. Also, a hospital for injured wildlife. Pet library: take a rabbit or other animal home. Great for children.

Located in Larkey Park, which has a pool, picnic tables, tennis, basketball courts, playground. Buena Vista Avenue and First Avenue. (510) 935-1978.

- **Alvarado Square.** San Pablo. Early California, handsomely and accurately restored, the residence of a governor of California. Indian artifacts. Also, a 1920 farmhouse with iron stove and oak furniture. Maple Hall is popular for meetings and weddings. Saturday and Sunday afternoons. Church Lane and San Pablo Avenue.

- **AMTRAK.** Three stations in Contra Costa County, Antioch, Martinez, Richmond, and one in Davis. The trains are a pleasant surprise. Plenty of leg room. Bar car. View windows. Instead of driving to Sacramento to see the state buildings, take a train and double the thrill, or ride the rails to the Reno casinos.

- **Anheuser-Busch Brewery**, Fairfield. See how beer is brewed. Tours Monday through Friday. By appointment only. No charge. Short film precedes tour. Just south of Interstate 80 on Busch Boulevard. (707) 429-7595.

- **The Behring Auto Museum.** Located at Blackhawk in the Danville

Hills. Dramatic art deco building houses over 200 vintage vehicles, of which 120 are on display at one time. Value estimated at $100 million-plus, just for those on display.

Displays of cars rotate every month. Ken Behring made big bucks building Blackhawk and retirement towns in Florida and now owns — along with another local developer, Ken Hofmann — the Seattle Seahawks. UC Berkeley Museum opened in the Auto Museum complex in June, 1991.

The complex is open 10 a.m.-5 p.m. Tuesday through Sunday. Open until 9 p.m. on Wednesday and Friday nights. Tickets—$7 for adults, $4 for children if visiting both museums.

Take Sycamore Valley Road east of Interstate 680, about five miles to Blackhawk Plaza Circle. Phone (510) 736-2280.

• **Concord Pavilion.** John Denver, Bette Midler, Waylon and Willie, Dave Brubeck — they have all played the Pavilion, a great cultural showplace.

The outdoor pavilion is also used for musicals, jazz festivals, graduations, boxing and religious events. A relaxed, family place. Picnics on the lawn, great view of Mt. Diablo. 2000 Kirker Pass Road. Box office, 1870 Adobe St., Concord. Tickets are available at BASS and Ticketron. Phone (510) 67-MUSIC.

• **The Delta.** A recreation paradise. Fishing (sturgeon, striped bass, catfish), hunting, boating, water skiing, swimming, houseboating. Some people rent houseboats and spend weeks cruising Delta waterways.

To get a feel for what the Delta has to offer, take Highway 4 to Stockton or the Antioch Bridge up to Isleton or Highway 12 to Rio Vista. Meander. Take the side roads. In the summer, farmers set up vegetable stands and, for a fee, allow city slickers to pick berries and other goodies. If dining out, try crayfish, a Delta delicacy.

Many river cities have marinas, and some rent boats. Be careful. The currents are strong.

• **East Brother Light Station.** Want to get away from it all yet remain in the thick of things? Try bed-and-breakfast in a restored Victorian situated on a small island, just north of the Richmond-San Rafael Bridge. Great Bay views. Antiques. Museum. Old lighthouse equipment. Also, day trips. Boat leaves from Point San Pablo. Phone for reservations. (510) 233-2385.

• **Golden Gate Fields Racetrack.** Thoroughbred racing. The season runs February to June. Golden Gate Fields, located in Albany, is less than a half hour from most Contra Costa cities. Take the Gilman Street exit off Interstate 80.

• **John Muir Home** and Martinez Adobe, a relic from the ranchero days, located one behind the other in Martinez. Interesting, pretty, historic. Muir was a great conservationist and a devoted family man, and the place captures his spirit. Take Alhambra Avenue off Hwy. 4 and you're there. Adults $1. Wednesday through Sunday, 10 a.m. to 4:30 p.m. (510) 228-8860.

• **Lafayette Reservoir.** An outdoor pearl in the heart of suburbia and one of the favorite jogging spots of Contra Costa, beloved by Yups and Dinks (Double Income No Kids). No traffic, scenic views. Also fishing, boating and picnicking. Park road leads directly off Mt. Diablo Boulevard, Lafayette's main business street. Phone (510) 284-9669.

• **Marine World-Africa USA.** Located in Vallejo. Major theme park. Draws people from throughout Northern California. Your chance to see lions, tigers, elephants, seals, whales and dolphins. Feed and pet some aforementioned. Restaurants. Kind of place where you spend a day or two. General admission $21.95, kids $16.95, seniors $18.95. Parking $3. Price covers all except animal rides. In winter, open Wednesday through Sunday. In summer, seven days a week. I-80 to Highway 37, go west. Phone (707) 643-6722.

• **Martinez Waterfront.** Baseball fields, a fishing pier, a marsh, a marina, trails, bocce ball courts. Martinez is one of the leading bocce towns in the nation. If you live near Martinez or work there, form your own team and join.

• **Mt. Diablo State Park.** Another recreation cornucopia, 18,000 acres, trails galore, magnificent views, caves, rock climbing, fossils embedded in rocks, camping and picnicking, bobcats, mountain lions, foxes, coyotes. Open 8 a.m. to sundown, $5 per car. Camping $12 overnight.

Drive to summit, 3,849 feet. From Walnut Creek, take Northgate Road; from Danville, Diablo Road. Fee. Phone (510) 837-2525.

• **Point Richmond.** Easily missed, bordered by a freeway, warehouses, and industry, Point Richmond is one of the most captivating neighborhoods in Contra Costa County, a touch of riffraff not the least of its charms.

A grand natatorium (indoor swimming pool), churches, tennis courts, excellent bars and restaurants, diners and sandwich shops, mom-and-pop stores, mansions and apartments, a shoreline park, a theater, an elementary school, a library — the Point has them all, and all within walking distance. In the watering holes and eating places, the Chevron people talk oil, the racing crowd ponders the daily entries at Golden Gate Fields, the political mob debates the maneuverings of government. On the windward side of the Point, residents sip martinis and watch the sun sink beyond the Golden Gate. Jack London found Point Richmond bars congenial, and madams appreciated the community's sympathy toward struggling entrepreneurs.

From I-80, take Cutting or Hoffman Boulevard to Garrard Boulevard, turn left, turn right on Richmond Avenue and you're in the heart of town.

• **Port Costa.** Former grain-shipping center and railroad town. Small and, by California standards, quaint. About 250 residents. Two restaurants, shops. Partially collapsed, the scenic road to Martinez is passable to joggers and cyclists. To reach Port Costa by car, take McEwen Road off Highway 4, west of Martinez or Pomona Street and Carquinez Drive east from Crockett.

• **Regional Center for the Arts.** Bob Hope was on hand to celebrate the grand opening in summer, 1990. Expect the best the East Bay has to offer in musicals, drama, comedy and symphony. Located at 1601 Civic Drive., Walnut

Creek. Phone (510) 943-7469.

• **St. Mary's College.** Moraga. Beautiful church, the bell tower a copy of the 15th century cathedral in Cuernavaca, Mexico. Hearst Art Gallery, Spanish architecture, rare art works. Perfect for a Sunday afternoon stroll. Picnic grounds (make reservations with security department). For football and basketball fans, exciting college games. Masses. Moraga Road to St. Mary's Road. (510) 376-4411.

• **San Pablo Dam.** Located between El Sobrante and Orinda, the reservoir is stocked with bass and trout and equipped for picnics. A nice place to sail, hike or relax. Take a spin on Bear Creek Road, behind the reservoir. Picturesque. Entrance off San Pablo Dam Road. Phone (510) 223-8489.

• **Shadelands Ranch Museum.** Walnut Creek. A turn-of-the century ranch that gives visitors a look at how old-time Contra Costans lived and worked. 2660 Ygnacio Valley Road. (510) 935-7871. Run by the Walnut Creek Historical Society. In recent years, Contra Costa history has become popular. Several cities — Martinez, Richmond, Pittsburg — have museums.

• **Shopping Malls.** Hilltop in Richmond, SunValley in Concord, Solano Mall in Fairfield, Stoneridge in Pleasanton, plus about four dozen smaller centers. Parks are nice, softball is fun but for sheer ecstasy few pursuits beat spending money.

Contra Costa is attracting the better specialty shops and gourmet stores.

• **Tao House.** Danville home of playwright Eugene O'Neill, designed by wife, Carlotta, built in 1937. Here in a room overlooking San Ramon Valley, O'Neill brooded and wrote some of his most famous plays: "The Iceman Cometh," "Moon for the Misbegotten," "Long Day's Journey into Night."

Tao House is open for tours, but neighbors are discouraging frequent visits. For more information, call the John Muir House, also run by the National Park Service. (510) 228-8860.

Playing Around

As inviting as these places sound, many Contra Costans and Solano residents ignore them for other places and activities. Softball leagues in some towns draw more than a thousand players. Bowling also counts its players by the thousands. Most cities in Contra Costa and Solano have golf courses, many of them open to the public. Besides the parks mentioned, dozens more are spotted around the East and North Bay. Bicycle and jogging trails wind their way throughout the countryside.

Soccer, football and baseball leagues every year sign up thousands of children. Aerobics exercise is another activity that is attracting participants, mostly women, in large numbers. Exercise clubs and spas have long been popular in the larger cities. Those interested will have no trouble finding roller and ice-skating rinks, miniature golf courses, rifle-pistol-shotgun ranges, poker parlors and racquetball courts.

Art and Culture

Art guilds and galleries, dance schools (good enough to draw the attention of the Joffrey), bands, symphonies, choral groups, little theater — they're out there.

Every town is hooked to cable television, a cultural revolution that has doubled and, in some cases, tripled the number of channels available to local residents. Sales of video recorders are booming and movie-rental stores do a roaring business. Despite the video recorders, movie theaters still attract long lines for first-run shows. In recent years several movie complexes of multiple screens have opened in both counties. Berkeley, a short drive, usually has the latest foreign films.

On the Road

Contra Costa and Solano counties are within an hour's drive of many of the major attractions of Northern California. The wine country is to the north, San Francisco a short drive west, Great America an hour's drive south, the state capital to the northeast. You can finish dessert at 6:15 p.m. in Walnut Creek and make the Oakland Coliseum with time to spare for an A's game. The shows and slot machines of Reno and Tahoe are within a few hours' drive.

Food, Wine and Song

Do you like to dine out? Contra Costa and Solano restaurants with rare exceptions do not boast the quality of the best of San Francisco's but the local places are improving quickly. There's an old story being acted out: Where money ventures, culture and cuisine inevitably follow.

Many cities have traditional celebrations: Art in the Park in Martinez, the Walnut Festival in Walnut Creek, the Seafood Festival in Pittsburg, several "Concours d'Elegance," "Juneteenth" festivities in Richmond and Pittsburg, rousing Fourth-of-July fairs and fireworks.

In Solano County, Benicia, Fairfield, Suisun City, Vacaville, Dixon and Vallejo celebrate town events. Travis Air Force Base has an annual air show that draws thousands of people.

The Contra Costa and Solano county fairs, which feature top-name stars, draw tens of thousands of people. The John Muir Medical Center Film Festival (medical) attracts national attention.

How to Sort Out Choices

A suggestion: subscribe to a newspaper. Most papers run excellent community-events calendars.

15/Regional Recreation

What the San Francisco Bay Region Has to Offer

WHERE TO PLAY, where to spend the weekend? Northern California offers many amusements. Here is a list of the major ones by county.

Always call ahead. Some places are open seasonally, some only a few days weekly. Some require reservations. A few are free, most charge.

Alameda County

- **Children's Fairyland.** Off Grand Avenue at the north end of Lake Merritt in downtown Oakland. Mother Goose, Alice in Wonderland, Chesire Cat, etc. Merry-go-round, ferris wheel. Puppets, clowns, slides, mazes. (510) 832-3609.
- **Crown Memorial State Beach.** One of the few beaches on the Bay, 383 acres in city of Alameda. Day camps, turfed play areas, 2.5 miles of beach. Estuary and reserve, wading, sunbathing, swimming, fishing. I-880 to downtown Oakland. Webster Street west to end. (510) 521-6887.
- **Dunsmuir House and Gardens.** Gothic house and garden, 2960 Peralta Court, Oakland. Exit 106th Ave. from Interstate 580. (510) 562-0328.
- **East Bay Regional Park District.** Covers Alameda and Contra Costa counties. Parks, lakes, hiking trails, botanical gardens, Victorian farms, estuaries, wilderness areas. Fishing, swimming, boating, golfing, much more. For brochures, maps, (510) 531-9300.
- **Golden Gate Fields Racetrack.** Thoroughbred racing, January to June. In Albany, I-80 to Gilman St. (510) 526-3020.
- **Lawrence Hall of Science.** Science museum for adults and children. Hands-on fun, computers rabbits, snakes, brain games, astronomy, Nobel medals, classes, all fortified by strong connection to UC-Berkeley. Often features robotic, life-sized dinosaurs and whales. Store sells science toys. Located in Berkeley Hills. Highway 24 to Fish Ranch Road, to Grizzly Peak Road, left on Centennial Drive. Also can be reached from rear of university. (510) 642-5132.
- **Magnes Memorial Museum.** Art and artifacts of Jewish culture. Library, history, tours. 2911 Russell St., Berkeley. Ph. (510) 849-2710.
- **McConaghy House,** 18701 Hesperian Blvd., Hayward, next to Kennedy Park. Furnished Victorian farmhouse. Tours. (510) 276-3010.
- **Meek Estate.** Renovated and furnished five-story Victorian. Ballroom, library, solarium, bedrooms. Picnic grounds. Hampton and Boston Roads, Hayward. (510) 581-0223.
- **Mission San Jose.** 43300 Mission Blvd., Fremont. Built in 1797, destroyed in 1868 earthquake, restored. Picturesque building. Slide show, artifacts, history of Ohlone Indian. (510) 657-1797.
- **Navy-Marine Corps Museum.** Treasure Island in San Francisco Bay. Navy and Marine Corps paintings, memorabilia. Call (415) 395-5067.

234 CONTRA COSTA & SOLANO

- **Oakland Museum.** Located at 1000 Oak St. in downtown. California art, history and natural history. First class. (510) 834-2413.
- **Paramount Theatre,** 2025 Broadway, Oakland. "Art Deco" at its finest. Parquet floors, gold ceiling, sculptures. (510) 465-6400.
- **Steam locomotive rides.** Sunol. Abandoned line overhauled and put in service with rides for public. Leaves from hamlet of Sunol, off I-680 south of Pleasanton. (510) 862-9063.
- **University of California, Berkeley.** Bookstores, libraries, museums, lectures, concerts, ballet. University Avenue off I-80 and go east. For performances, call (510) 642-9988. For tours, (510) 642-5215. Sports tickets, (510) 642-5150.

San Francisco

- **Academy of Sciences.** Located in Golden Gate Park, it contains: Morrison Planetarium, information and show schedules, (415) 750-7141; Laserium, laser light shows with rock, classical, contemporary music, (415) 750-7138; Natural History Museum, displays of wildlife, rocks, universe; Steinhart Aquarium, great white sharks, penguins, sea life from around the world. (415) 750-7145.
- **Alcatraz.** Former federal prison, now a national park. Ferries from Pier 41, Fisherman's Wharf. Carry jackets, comfortable shoes. (415) 546-2805.
- **Ansel Adams Center.** Museum of photography. 250 Fourth St., (415) 495-7000.
- **Asian Art Museum.** Art works over the centuries. Eighth Avenue and Kennedy Drive, Golden Gate Park, (415) 668-8921.
- **Cable Car Museum.** In addition to photographs and memorabilia of the city's 128-year love affair with its cable car, there is an underground viewing room to watch the cables at work. Washington and Mason streets. (415) 474-1887.
- **DeYoung Memorial Museum.** American art, colonial through 20th century, as well as art of Africa, Oceania, Americas. Touring collections also featured. Golden Gate Park. (415) 863-3330.
- **Exploratorium.** Hands-on center focusing on physical sciences and human perception. Palace of Fine Arts, Lyon Street and Marina Boulevard. (415) 561-0360.
- **Fisherman's Wharf.** Former center of San Francisco's commercial fishing industry, now collection of restaurants and shops; historic sailing ships. At end of Embarcadero.
- **Fleishhacker Zoo.** Tuxedo Junction penguin exhibit, gorilla world, antique carousel and primate exhibits among the features. Sloat Boulevard at 45th Avenue, San Francisco. (415) 753-7083.
- **Fort Mason.** Once the command post for all U.S. forces in the west. Theaters, restaurants, workshops, art galleries, liberty ships. Marina Boulevard at Laguna, San Francisco. (415) 441-5705.
- **Haas-Lilienthal House.** Elaborate gables and Queen Anne-style circular tower adorn this 106-year-old mansion. 2007 Franklin St., San Francisco. (415) 441-3000.
- **Mission Dolores.** Founded in 1776, built in 1791, the city's oldest building includes museum and cemetery garden. (415) 621-8203.
- **Museum of Modern Art.** Touring and permanent collections of art and photography. Van Ness Avenue and McAllister Street. (415) 252-4177.
- **National Maritime Park.** Liberty ships, schooners, models and nautical history displays, bookstore, museum. Pier 45, Fisherman's Wharf at foot of Hyde Street. (415) 556-8177.
- **Old Mint.** A survivor of the 1906 quake and fire. Three million dollars of gold bars, coin collection. Fifth and Mission. (415) 744-6830.
- **Pier 39.** Located next to Fisherman's Wharf. Shops, restaurants, and amusements. Entertainment by jugglers and musicians. Seals frolic in waters immediately to west. (415) 981-7437.
- **Presidio Museum.** Exhibits of early San Francisco military history, Presidio and Spanish-American War, 1906 quake and fire. Lincoln Boulevard at Funston Street. (415) 921-8193.
- **Strybing Arboretum.** Giant greenhouse; home to more than 6,000 plant and tree species. Ninth Avenue at Lincoln Way. (415) 661-1316.

Marin County

- **Angel Island.** Off Tiburon. West Coast Ellis Island. Chinese immigrants were detained here. Picnicking. Trails. Beaches. Views. Ferry from Tiburon. Park (415) 435-1915. Ferry (415) 546-2896.
- **Bay Area Discovery Museum,** Sausalito, 557 East Fort Baker Road. Live fish, murals of Bay habitats, pretend salmon fishing, science corner, boat making, story telling, and more. (415) 332-7674.
- **Bay Model Visitors' Center.** 2100 Bridgeway in Sausalito. How the rivers and estuary and currents of the Bay interact. A model. Natural history exhibits. (415) 332-3870.
- **Golden Gate Bridge.** You can't walk across the Bay Bridge or the San Rafael. You can the Golden Gate. It's worth it.
- **Golden Gate National Recreation Area.** The general name given the big park purchase made by the feds in the 1970s. Includes Muir Woods, Point Reyes and Headlands, (415) 556-0560.
- **Marin Civic Center, San Rafael.** What Marin County inspired in Frank Lloyd Wright. Public building. Stop any time. Civic Center Drive or San Pedro Road off of Hwy. 101. Tours. (415) 499-6104
- **Marin Headlands,** the land just west of Golden Gate Bridge. Spectacular vistas of San

REGIONAL RECREATION 235

Looking for that special San Francisco shop, restaurant, fun spot? We've got a number of them!

PIER 39

All the things you've always loved about San Francisco you'll love about PIER 39:

Great varieties of restaurants, 10 at last count.

More than 100 unique specialty shops on two scenic levels.

Great views. Golden Gate Bridge. Alcatraz. Sunsets over the Bay and city skyline.

Cruise the Bay on our own Blue & Gold Fleet. Enjoy a spin on the Breyers Venetian Carousel, tour the city on our motorized Cable Cars or hurtle into another dimension on Turbo Ride.

Always something exciting going on here! Jugglers. Mimes. Acrobats. And PIER 39's famous, unrehearsed sea lion performances!

PIER 39 is located two blocks east of Fisherman's Wharf at Beach and The Embarcadero.

Call 415-705-5495 for more information.

That total San Francisco sensation? It all adds up to 39.

(PIER 39)

236 CONTRA COSTA & SOLANO

Oakland A's 1993 Schedule*

[Schedule calendar grids for April through September 1993 showing home and away games]

☐ Home Games

*Tentative schedule, subject to change.

Francisco, the Golden Gate, the Pacific. Artillery fortifications. Take Sausalito exit closest to bridge, pick up Bunker Road. Information (415) 331-1540.

- **Mt. Tamalpais.** See Farallones, Sierra, Richmond, Oakland, San Fran. Many trails to top. Hwy. 101 to Shoreline Highway (north of Sausalito), to Panoramic Highway off Route 1. (415) 388-2070.
- **Muir Woods.** Giant coast redwoods. Highway 101 to Shoreline Highway to Panoramic Highway. (415) 388-2595.
- **Point Reyes.** The Pacific Coast. One big park. Lighthouse. Trails. Earthquake country, where the San Andreas Fault goes to sea. (415) 663-1092. Off Highway 1.
- **Marin Museum of American Indian.** 2200 Novato Blvd., Novato. Artifacts. (415) 897-4064.

Napa

- **Lake Berryessa.** Lake-reservoir located in eastern part of the county, off of Highway 128. Boating, water sports. Scenic drive.
- **Wine Country.** Napa is synonymous with wine and, over the last few decades, the wineries have gone to great lengths to welcome visitors with tours and tastings and, lately, with entertainment, such as jazz festivals. Many restaurants. Spas that tap into mineral springs. For day's tour, take Highway 29 out of Vallejo, go to Calistoga, return on Silverado Trail.

REGIONAL RECREATION 237

San Francisco Giants 1993 Schedule*

*Tentative schedule, subject to change.

- **Wine Train.** From Napa to St. Helena and back. Old train activated to tour the valley in style. Dine and sip (wine) on board. Features many local vintages. (800) 427-4124.

Sonoma

- **Armstrong Redwoods.** Grove of giants. Located outside Guerneville. Armstrong Woods Road from Highway 116. (707) 869-2015.
- **Farm Trails.** If you want to pick what you eat straight from vine or tree, Sonoma County farmers will lay out the welcome mat. About 165 farms and wineries have formed into a "farm trails" group. For free map, call (707) 586-3276.
- **Fort Ross.** What Russians built when they lived in California. A detailed restoration. Interesting. Just off Highway 1, above Jenner. State park. Info. (707) 847-3286.
- **Glen Ellen.** Where Jack London, California's favorite son, wrote and lived. Ruins of London mansion, the Wolf House. Above city of Sonoma, off Highway 12, in Sonoma Valley wine country. Jack London State Historic Park. (707) 938-5216.
- **Luther Burbank Home and Gardens.** Perhaps the most famous green thumb in California, Burbank made everything grow. Santa Rosa and Sonoma avenues in Santa Rosa. (707) 524-5445.
- **Mt. St. Helena.** Views, trails, hiking, geologically interesting. Highest mountain in Bay Area,

4,343 feet. Looks like volcano but isn't. Hwy. 29 to Robert Louis Stevenson State Park. (707) 942-4575.
- **Russian River.** A nice drive in winter, nicer in summer, when the river is dammed to raise the level for canoeing and swimming. Canoe rentals, public beaches along river, including some in Guerneville. On Highway 101, about 5 miles above Santa Rosa you'll see the signs.
- **Sonoma Coast.** Highway 1. Start at Bodega Bay or Jenner. Rugged. Great views. To see seals, stroll beach at Goat Rock near Jenner. Restaurants, resorts along route.
- **Sonoma Mission.** The last mission built on El Camino Real, the King's Highway. Nicely restored. Downtown City of Sonoma. (707) 938-1519.
- **Sonoma Plaza.** Where Mariano Vallejo quartered and trained his soldiers and ran his vast estate. Bear Flag Rebellion began here. Restored barracks. Mission close by and, within a half mile, the home of Vallejo. Highway 12 to middle of City of Sonoma. (707) 938-1519.
- **Whale Watching.** Migrating south between November and February, the California Grey Whale often passes within a half mile of shore. Same on return trip in a few months. Watch from Bodega Head State Park, Salt Point State Park, and bluffs of state beach along Sonoma coast. (707) 847-3221.
- **Wine Country.** For the quick tour, drive Highway 12 south to north, or travel the Redwood Highway north of Santa Rosa. Wineries are all along both routes. Also in Alexander and Dry Creek Valleys, the Russian River area.

San Mateo County
- **Acres of Orchids.** 1450 El Camino Real, South San Francisco. Flowers by the thousands in garden patio setting of retail sales house, a laboratory. Orchids grown and cloned. (415) 871-5655
- **Año Nuevo State Reserve.** 1,192 acres. 27 miles south of Half Moon Bay on Highway 1. Where elephants seals mate. Fishing, nature and hiking trails, exhibits. (415) 879-0595.
- **Bay Meadows Racetrack.** On San Mateo County Fairgrounds. Off Highway 101 at Hillsdale Boulevard. Thoroughbred racing., Labor Day through January. (415) 574-RACE.
- **Coyote Point Beach Park & Museum.** Peninsula Avenue exit off Highway 101 in Burlingame and head east. Exhibits on humans' ties with nature, aquarium, computer games, films, giant mural. Large bee tube. (415) 342-7755.
- **Filoli House & Garden.** On Cañada Road in Woodside, south of the Highway 92-Interstate 280 intersection. Tours of modified Georgian-style mansion, 17 acres of formal gardens. (415) 364-2880.
- **Sunset Magazine & Gardens.** Middlefield and Willow roads, Menlo Park. Tours of gardens and test kitchens of Sunset magazine. (415) 324-5479.
- **Whale watching.** Migration off California coast from December through March. Whales visible from many places along coast, but best place to view is from boat. Tours from Pillar Point Harbor in Half Moon Bay. Capt. John's Fishing Trips, (415) 728-3377; Huck Finn Fishing Trips, (415) 726-7133; Oceanic Society, (415) 474-3385.

Santa Clara County
- **Barbie Hall of Fame.** 460 Waverly St., Palo Alto. Barbie dolls from all over. (415) 326-5841.
- **Children's Discovery Museum,** 180 Woz Way, San Jose. Hands-on exhibits; technology, science, humanities and arts. (408) 298-5437.
- **Great America.** Located in the city of Santa Clara, off Great America Parkway. First-class amusement park, 100-plus attractions, many spine-tingling. Games. Musical reviews. (408) 988-1800.
- **Lick Observatory.** Atop Mt. Hamilton, southeast of San Jose, one of the most powerful observatories in the world. Scenic. Tours. (408) 554-4023.
- **Rosicrucian Museum.** Park and Naglee Avenues, San Jose. Egyptian, Babylonian and Assyrian artifacts, including tools, jars and jewelry. Also mummies. Next to museum are a planetarium and science museum. (408) 287-2807.
- **San Jose Flea Market.** 12000 Berryessa Road, between Highway 101 and Interstate 680, San Jose. One of the great bazaars of the West Coast. Open Wednesdays through Sundays. Draws 50,000 to 75,000 on weekends. Also includes farmers' markets and kiddie amusements. (408) 453-1110.
- **San Jose Historical Museum.** 635 Phelan St., San Jose. Old Santa Clara County recreated at Kelley Park — an Indian acorn granary, the Pacific Hotel, a candy store, an electric tower, a 1920s gas station, a dental building, stables and more. Nearby: a petting zoo, and Japanese Friendship Park, six acres of waterfalls, stone bridges, bonsai plants. (408) 287-2290.
- **Stanford University.** Palo Alto. Beautiful campus, a delight to tour. Spanish architecture. Hoover Tower (views). Several museums. Palo Alto is also a good shopping town.
- **Villa Montalvo.** Located just outside Saratoga on Saratoga-Los Gatos Road. Italian Renaissance villa. Shows and programs on cultural subjects. The grounds, 175 acres, are maintained as a public arboretum. (408) 741-3421.
- **Winchester Mystery House.** 525 South Winchester Blvd., San Jose. Heiress of the shooting Winchesters pumped about $5 million into this four-story, eccentric, 160-room house. Rifle collection. Garden. Cafe. Tours. (408) 247-2101.

14/Newcomer's Guide

Where to Get a Driver's License, Register to Vote, Register Your Child for School, and More...

FOR NEWCOMERS to Contra Costa and Solano counties here are tips on getting started in your new town and answers to frequently asked questions.

Voter Registration

You must be 18 years and a citizen. Go to the nearest post office and ask for a voter registration postcard. Fill it out and pop it into the mail box. Or register in person at most county offices, or political party headquarters, which are listed in the phone book.

For more information on voting, call the elections office at (510) 646-4166 in Contra Costa County and (707) 421-6675 in Solano County.

Before every election, the county will mail you a sample ballot with the location of your poll.

Ballots are marked in ink and placed in a box. No voting machines.

School Registration

Because of crowding in some schools, it is a good idea to register your children early to get your school of choice. It's also prudent, in some situations, to make sure you are in a school attendance zone that you think you're in. When a school district opens a new school or revamps programs, it often changes attendance boundaries. Look in a phone directory, business section, under the name of the school district, and make a phone call.

To get into kindergarten, your child must turn five before December 3 of the year he or she enters the grade. For first grade, your child must be six before Dec. 3. If he is six on Dec. 4, if she is a mature Jan. 6 birthday girl, speak to the school. There may be some wiggle room.

For registration, you are required to show proof of immunization for polio, diphtheria, tetanus, pertussis (whooping cough), measles, rubella, and mumps. If the kid is seven or older, you can skip mumps and pertussis.

Dog Licensing

Contra Costa County Animal Services, 4849 Imhoff Place, Martinez, near the junction of Highway 4 and Interstate 680. (510) 646-2995. Registration requires proof of rabies shot. For West County residents, 651 Pinole Shores Road, Pinole. Phone (510) 374-3966.

Cost: $21 per year if Rover is intact, $7 if not. Low cost spay-neutering-immunization clinic at Imhoff site. Also adopt a dog or cat.

Solano County Animal Control, 2510 Claybank Road, Fairfield, Phone (707) 421-7486. Licenses can also be purchased at following city halls: Vallejo, Vacaville, Benicia, Dixon, Rio Vista.

License $10.60 for unaltered, $5.30 for fixed, $2.65 for seniors (the humans, not the dogs). Some cities have extra fees. Bring rabies proof.

Driving

California has the most stringent smog requirements in the country. If your out-of-state car or truck is not equipped to meet the requirements, you pay a $300 penalty. You have 20 days from the time you enter the state to register your vehicles. After that you pay an added penalty and face a ticket-fine.

For registration, go to any office of the Department of Motor Vehicles. Bring your smog certificate, your registration card and your license plates.

Registration is simple, but the fees can be hefty. The basic fee is 2 percent of market value. A $10,000 car would cost $200, a $15,000 car, $300, a $20,000 car $400 — plus about $40 in miscellaneous cost. These incidentally, are annual fees.

If you are a California resident, all you need to do is complete a change of address form, which can be obtained by calling one of the following Dept. of Motor Vehicles Offices :
- Concord: 2075 Meridian Park Blvd. Phone (510) 671-2876.
- El Cerrito: 6400 Manila Ave. Phone (510) 235-9171.
- Fairfield: 445 Pacific Ave. Phone (707) 428-2052.
- Pittsburg: 1399 Buchanan Rd. Phone (510) 432-4748.
- Vallejo: 200 Couch. Phone (707) 648-4170.
- Walnut Creek: 1910 North Broadway, Phone 935-4464.

Age Requirements for Driving

To obtain a driver's license, you must be 16 years old, pass a state-certified Driver's Education (classroom) and Driver's Training (behind-the-wheel) course, and written and driving tests at DMV. Once you pass, your license is usually renewed by mail. Retesting is rare, unless your driving record is poor.

High schools used to offer driving courses but these are rapidly disappearing due to state budget cuts. Private driving schools have moved in to fill the gap. Courses average about $250.

Teenagers older than 15 who are in driver's training can be issued a permit, which allows them to drive accompanied by an 18-year-old licensed driver.

If no driver's education program has been completed, you must be at least 17 years old to apply for a driver's license. You must pass a written test, simple eye exam and a behind-the-wheel test.

Rules of the Road
  • Turning Rules. If signs don't say no, you can turn right on a red light (after making a full stop), and make a U-turn at an intersection.
  • Stop for pedestrians. Law.
  • Insurance. Must have it to drive.

Earthquakes
They're fun and great topics of conversation, until you get caught in a big one. Then they are not so funny. At the beginning of your phone book is some advice about what to do before, during and after a temblor. It's worth reading.

Garbage service
The garbage fellows come once a week. Rates vary by city but figure $18 to $25 a month for two cans.

Besides the cans, almost every home will receive recycling bins for plastics, glass and cans. Pickup weekly, usually the same day as garbage.

To get rid of car batteries and used motor oils and water-soluble paints, call your local garbage firm and ask about disposal sites. Or call city hall.

Don't burn your garbage in the fireplace or outside. Don't burn leaves. Against the law.

Property Taxes
The average property tax rate in California is 1.25 percent. If you buy a $250,000 home this year, your property tax is $3,125. Once the basic tax is established, it goes up very little from year to year.

"Average" needs to be emphasized. Some jurisdictions have tacked costs on to the property tax; some have not.

Property taxes are paid in two installments - March and November. They are generally collected automatically through impound accounts set up when you purchase a home, but check your sale documents carefully. Sometimes homeowners are billed directly.

Some cities, to fund parks and lights and other amenities in new subdivisions, have installed what is called the Mello-Roos tax. Realtors are required to give you complete information on all taxes.

If you buy a resale home in an established neighborhood, Mello-Roos almost never enters the picture.

Disclosure laws

California requires Realtors to give detailed reports on every home sold — a good law and it recently was expanded to include earthquake fault info.

Sales Tax

In Contra Costa County, it is 8.25 percent. In Solano County, it's 7.25 percent. May drop slightly in June.

Gas and Electricity

Most homes are heated with natural gas. Average heating bill is $56.75 a month; average electric bill $62.

Almost never between May and September, and rarely between April and October, will you need to heat your home. Air conditioners are used throughout the summer but on many days they're not needed. PG&E, the utility, will give you advice on insulating your home.

Cable TV Service

Almost all East Bay homes are served by cable. Rates vary according to channels accessed but a basic rate is about $20 a month. Installation is extra. For clear radio reception, often a cable connection is required.

Phones

Pacific Bell charges $34.75 to run a line to your house. It charges extra for jack installation. If you're handy, you can do the jack wiring and installation yourself. Many homes will have the jacks in place.

The basic monthly charge is $8.35 but with taxes, access to interstate calling, and other miscellaneous items the true basic for many people is $12 to $15.

Bottled Water

If the direct source for your town's water is the Sierra, then you may not need bottled water. If the source is the Delta, many people take the bottled, especially in summers (salinity).

Fences

If you want to build one, check with city hall. Often there are restrictions on height.

Tipping

It's not done in the Bay Area as much as it is done in other parts of the country. Tip the newspaper delivery person, cab drivers, waiters and waitresses, and, at the holidays, people who perform regular personal services: yard maintenance, child care, housekeeping.

Don't tip the supermarket employee who carries bags to your car. Don't tip telephone or cable TV installers. Your garbage collector will usually be a Teamster. No beer. No money. Maybe a little cake or box of candy at Christmas.

California has a liquor law that can put a person in violation for as little as one drink. If a garbage collector gets nailed for drunk driving, it will probably cost him his job.

Some people give the mailman or mail lady a little holiday gift; most don't.

Casual Labor

If you need help moving in, the community colleges and St. Mary's College run job boards for students. You call, the job is posted, applicants call you. If you offer too little, you won't get anyone. Try $7 to $7.50 an hour.

See Chapter 8 for college phone numbers. Ask for Job Placement.

Smoking

In public, increasingly frowned on and, in restaurants in certain cities, forbidden. The trend is to discourage the weed.

Dress

Lawyer, executive or professional? Wear a tie and jacket if you're a man, a two- or three-piece suit if a woman.

For almost all social occasions, even, in some circles, weddings and funerals, the dress is casual. The person who wears a tie to a restaurant on Friday or Saturday often stands out (depends a little on the town. Lamorinda tends to formality.)

Dress formal for dinner in San Francisco and the theater (but even here, many men go in sportscoats, no tie; women in slacks).

Advice from one woman who follows the fashions: steer clear of earth tones; Californians favor bright colors. Avoid trendy casual, go for classic.

15/New Housing

Homes for Sale, Homes Being Built for 1993 in Contra Costa, Solano and Other Counties

SHOPPING FOR A new home? This chapter gives an overview of new housing underway in Contra Costa, Solano and nearby counties. Smaller projects are generally ignored. If you know where you want to live, drive that town or ask the local planning department what's new in housing.

Prices change. Incidentals such as landscaping fees may not be included. In the 1980s, to pay for services, cities increased fees on home construction. Usually, these fees are included in the home prices but in what is known as Mello-Roos districts, the fees are often assessed like tax payments (in addition to house payments). Nothing secret. By law developers are required to disclose all fees. But the prices listed below may not include some fees.

After rocketing in the 1980s, home prices, new and resale, stabilized and in many instances dropped. Some developers, particularly in towns with many new units, have gotten very competitive in pricing. Listed alphabetically by county, city and development, the following directory covers what's available at time of publication. For latest information, call the developers for brochures.

Alameda County
Fremont
Mission Heights, Ponderosa Homes, 67 Pilgrim Loop, Fremont. Ph: (510) 651-7143. Single-family, 4-5 bedrooms, 3-3.5 baths, from low $600,000's.
Hayward
Prominence, Presley Homes, atop Hayward hills off Hayward Boulevard. Ph: (510) 537-7350. Single-family, 3,4 and 5 bedrooms. Call for prices.
Livermore
Amber Ridge, Pulte Home Corp., First Street and No. Mines, Livermore. Ph: (510) 449-1637. Single-family detached, 4-5 bedrooms, $320,000-$400,000.

NEW HOUSING 245

Vets: VA Financing...

DON'T DREAM THE AMERICAN DREAM. OWN IT AT FOXWOOD.

With our great prices and VA financing, your dream of owning a home can become a reality sooner than you think at Foxwood. These 2, 3 and 4 bedroom single-family homes are loaded with amenities, including air conditioning, vaulted ceilings, large yards and 2 and 3 car garages (per plan).

The quiet location is near Travis Air Force Base, schools, shopping and recreation. Seven floor plans are available, priced from the low $100,000s. From Hwy. 80 in Vacaville, take the Alamo exit, turn right on Nut Tree Road and follow the signs.
(707) 447-6559.

FOXWOOD

O'BRIEN & HICKS INC.
THE ANDEN GROUP

Map not to scale; prices effective as of publication deadline.

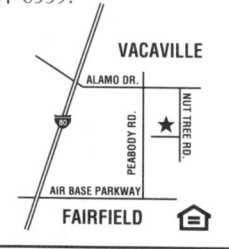

VACAVILLE
ALAMO DR.
PEABODY RD.
NUT TREE RD.
AIR BASE PARKWAY
FAIRFIELD

Monticello, Standard Pacific, 624 Zermatt St., Livermore. Ph: (510) 447-7777. Single-family, 3-5 bedrooms, from upper $200,000's.

Vintage Lane, Diablo Pacific Properties, Arroyo Rd. & Bess Dr., Livermore. Ph: (510) 373-6300. Single-family, 5 bedrooms, 3.5 baths, $500,000-$550,000

Windmill Springs, McBail Homes, Mines Road and East Avenue, Livermore. Ph: (510) 449-5458. Single-family detached, 3-4 bedrooms, 2-3 baths, $214,950-$349,950.

Union City

The Village at Ponderosa Landing, Ponderosa Homes, 31417 Marlin Court, Union City. Ph: (510) 471-2140. Single-family detached, 3-5 bedrooms, 2-3 baths, from the mid $200,000's.

Contra Costa County
Alamo

Alamo Estates, Paul C. Petersen-Whitecliff Homes, Alamo. Ph: (510) 439-7833. Single-family detached, call Bruce Kittess.

Antioch

Almondridge, McBail Homes, Off East 18th, Antioch. Ph: (510) 778-3246. Single-family detached, 3 & 4 bedrooms, 2-2.5 baths, $149,000-$179,950.

California Heritage, Kaufman & Broad of No. Ca., 5266 Prewett Ranch, Antioch. Ph: (510) 829-4500. Single-family detached, 3-4 bedrooms, 2-3 baths, VA Financing Available, $153,990-$178,990.

Casablanca, O'Brien & Hicks-The Anden Group, 639 Eaker Way, Antioch. Ph: (510) 757-1213. Single-family detached, 3 & 4 bedrooms, 2-3 bath, 6,000 sq. ft. lots, $139,990-$205,990.

Deerfield Heights, Ponderosa Homes, 4524 Wildcat Circle, Antioch. Ph: (510) 778-5533. Single-family detached, 4-5 bedrooms, 2-3 baths, from the low $200,000's.

Diablo Hills, Pacwest Development Corp., 5059 Sundance Way, Antioch. Ph: (510) 754-1788. Unique architectural styles, 3-5 bedrooms, from the $160,000's.

Lone Tree Estates, Davidon Homes, 2713 Joshua Court, Antioch. Ph: (510) 778-3092. Single-family detached, 4-5 bedrooms, 2.5-3 baths, $204,990-$249,990.

Montclair, Standard Pacific, 4513 Angel Court, Antioch. Ph: (510) 778-4422. 3-4 bedroom executive homes, low $200,000's.

New Horizons at Meadow Creek Estates, A.D. Seeno Const. Co., 4908 Chism Way, Antioch. Ph: (510) 778-0357. Single-family, 3-4 bedrooms, from $170,000's.

Shelbourne Classic Collection, Citation Homes Northern, 2405 Shelbourne Way, Antioch. Ph: (510) 757-6755. Single-family detached, up to 5 bedrooms, 3-car garage, $178,900-$223,900.

Sterling Place, Pulte Home Corporation, Davison and Vandenberg, Antioch. Ph: (510) 779-1116. Single-family, 3-4 bedrooms, mid $160,000-$200,000.

Sunrise Pointe at Meadow Creek Estates, A.D. Seeno Const. Co., 5109 Woodmont Way, Antioch. Ph: (510) 754-3701. Single-family, 3-4 bedrooms, from $140,000's.

Wildhorse Ridge, Centex Homes, 4017 Pillsburg Court, Antioch. Ph: (510) 779-9606. Single-family detached, 3-5 bedrooms, 2-3 baths, 1857-2672 sq. ft. lots, You pick the lot and house you like, we build it just like a custom home, $189,000-$251,000.

"Quality First."

When a family notices our attention to all details, large and small, and expresses their appreciation with a simple "thanks", it truly makes our day.

Because of all the things we do to make our homes beautiful, comfortable and affordable, nothing is more important to us than your family's complete satisfaction. To us the quality of our homes is best measured by the quality of your life.

Our commitment to your family is to give you the best new home and the best all around customer service in the business. We take pride in our work, having happy customers is proof that the job is well done.

Visit a Citation Northern community today... and see how we're building better home values for your family.

Visit Our Contra Costa and Solano County Communities

VINTAGE
Green Valley
Fairfield
(707) 864-5041

SHELBOURNE
Classic Collection
Antioch
(510) 757-6755

COMING SOON
Call (510) 372-0300

SEASCAPE
at Glen Cove
Vallejo/Benicia

SEA BREEZE
Martinez

Brentwood

Edgewood, A.D. Seeno Const. Co., 1170 Glenwillow Way, Brentwood. Ph: (510) 516-2093. Single-family, 3-5 bedrooms, from $150,000's.

Four Seasons, Pulte Home Corporation, Balfour and Claremont, Brentwood. Ph: (510) 516-7001. Single-family detached, 4 bedroom, low $190,000's to $220,000.

Twin Gables, Pulte Home Corporation, Balfour and Claremont, Brentwood, Single-family detached, 3-4 bedrooms, detached garages and bonus space, low $140,000's-$170,000.

Walnut Woods, A.D. Seeno Const. Co., 369 Madrone Place, Brentwood. Ph: (510) 516-0109. Single-family, 3-5 bedrooms, from low $200,000's.

Byron

Balboa Cove, The Hofmann Company, Discovery Bay 4507 Cove Lane, Byron. Ph: (510) 634-0500. Single-family homes in the recreation-oriented Discovery Bay, master-planned community, 1,775-2,150 sq. ft., from low $160,000's.

Discovery Bay

Country Club Villas, The Hofmann Company, Discovery Bay 2325 Firwood Court, Byron. Ph: (510) 634-6121. Golf course villas in recreation-oriented Discovery Bay, master-planned community, 1,840-2,157 sq. ft., from low $200,000's.

Discovery Bay Lots, The Hofmann Company, Discovery Bay 2076 Windward Point, Byron. Ph: (510) 634-2105. Waterfront lots, from low-$130,000's.

Clayton

Black Diamond, Presley Homes, off Oakhurst Drive, Clayton. Ph: (510) 762-7886. Duets, 2-3 bedrooms, golf course. Call for prices.

Chaparrel Springs, Presley Homes, off Oakhurst Drive, Clayton. Ph: (510) 672-1115. Townhomes, 2-3 bedrooms, golf course. Call for prices.

Diablo Ridge, Presley Homes, off Oakhurst Drive, Clayton. Condominium-resort, 2-3 bedrooms, golf course.

Oak Hollow, Presley Homes, off Oakhurst Drive, Clayton. Patio homes, 2-3 bedrooms, golf course.

Eagle Peak, Presley Homes, off Oakhurst Drive, Clayton. Ph: (510) 672-3085. Single-family, 3-5 bedrooms, semi-custom, golf course. Call for prices.

Windmill Canyon, off Oakhurst Drive, Clayton. Ph: (510) 672-0504. Single-family, 3-4 bedrooms, golf course. Call for prices.

Concord

Canyon Creek, A.D. Seeno Const. Co., 2199 Bluerock Circle, Concord. Ph: (510) 686-5777. Single-family, 3-5 bedrooms, from $260,000's.

Pavilion Place, Standard Pacific, 1523 Allegro Ave., Concord. Ph: (510) 825-4422. Single-family, 3-4 bedrooms, from $229,000.

Spring Ridge, A.D. Seeno Const. Co., 2199 Bluerock Circle, Concord. Ph: (510) 686-5777. Single-family, 3-5 bedrooms, from $290,000's.

Danville

Cimarron Hills, Davidon Homes, 105 Cimarron Court, Danville. Ph: (510) 736-5666. Single-family detached, 4-5 bedrooms, 2.5-3 baths, $462,990-$553,990.

Heritage Park Townhomes, Davidon Homes, 109 Heritage Park Drive, Danville. Ph: (510) 736-0568. Townhomes, 3 bedrooms, 2.5 baths, $248,990-$274,990.

Vista Tassajara Crown Collection, Standard Pacific, 110 Parkhaven Drive,

NEW HOUSING 249

Country Club Living From Under $200,000.

Just 4 miles from Walnut Creek in the heart of Contra Costa County, the Oakhurst Country Club offers homes to fit a variety of lifestyles. The centerpiece of Oakhurst is a championship 18-hole golf course rated in 1991 as one of the top 5 public courses in Northern California. Models open daily.

CHAPARREL SPRINGS
2 & 3 bedroom townhomes
(510) 672-1115

WINDMILL CANYON
3 & 4 bedroom family homes
(510) 672-0504

DIABLO RIDGE
2 & 3 bedroom resort condominiums
COMING SOON

BLACK DIAMOND
2 & 3 bedroom duet homes
(510) 672-7886

EAGLE PEAK
3, 4 & 5 bedroom semi-custom homes (510) 672-3085

OAK HOLLOW
2 & 3 bedroom patio homes
COMING SOON

OAKHURST COUNTRY CLUB

250 CONTRA COSTA & SOLANO

Ph: (510) 736-0568. Townhomes, 3 bedrooms, 2.5 baths, $248,990-$274,990.
Vista Tassajara Crown Collection, Standard Pacific, 110 Parkhaven Drive, Danville. Ph: (510) 736-1866.
Vista Tassajara Empire Collection, Standard Pacific, 17 Lakefield Court, Danville. Ph: (510) 736-1676.

Martinez

Elderwood Glen, Davidon Homes, 109 Woodglen Lane, Martinez. Ph: (510) 372-0506. Single-family detached, 4 bedrooms, 2.5-3 baths, $361,490-$409,990.
New Hidden Pond, Davidon Homes, 811 Hidden Pond Lane, Martinez. Ph: (510) 228-6987. single-family detached, 3-4 bedrooms, 2.5-3 baths, $465,990-$537,990.
Stonehurst, Security Owners Corp., Vaca Creek Road at Alhambra Valley Road, Martinez. Ph: (510) 228-5872. Custom homes on 1 to 2.5 acre lots, lots start at $250,000.

Oakley

California Dawn, Kaufman & Broad of No. Ca., 4504 Waterford Way, Oakley. Ph: (510) 829-4500. Single-family detached, 3-4 bedrooms, 2.5 baths, VA financing available, $132,990-$152,990.
Fairhaven Parc, A.D. Seeno Const. Co., 1792 Fairhaven Court, Oakley. Ph: (510) 625-1311. Single-family, 3-4 bedrooms, from $130,000's.
The Willows, The Hofmann Co., 1320 Walnut Meadows Dr., Oakley. Ph: (510) 625-5611. Single-family homes, 3-4 bedrooms, 1321-1702 sq. ft., from low $140,000's.

Pittsburg

California Seasons, Kaufman & Broad of No. Ca., 4 Harmony Court, Pittsburg. Ph: (510) 829-4500. Single-family detached, 3-4 bedrooms, 2-3 baths, VA financing available, $156,990-$186,990.
Marina Park, Paul C. Petersen-Whitecliff Homes, 140 Heron Drive, Pittsburg. Ph: (510) 427-4663.

San Ramon

Bent Creek Estates, Ponderosa Homes, 608 Helena Creek Court, San Ramon. Ph: (510) 833-9056. Single-family detached, 4-5 bedrooms, 2-3 baths, from the mid $300,000's.
Bent Creek Parc, Ponderosa Homes, 201 Hat Creek Court, San Ramon. Ph: (510) 828-1311. Single-family detached, 3 to 5 bedrooms, 2-3 baths, in the low $300,000's.
Old Ranch Estates, Davidon Homes, 1150 Timbercreek Road, San Ramon. Ph: (510) 803-9545. Single-family detached, 4-5 bedrooms, 2.5-3 baths, $361,990-$505,990.
Vista Pointe, Vermillion Group, Inc., 902 Vista Pointe Drive, San Ramon. Ph: (510) 735-2850. Single-family detached, from $280,000.

Walnut Creek

Blackwood Estates, Davidon Homes, 2186 Ridgepointe Court, Walnut Creek. Ph: (510) 256-0669. Single-family detached, 4-5 bedrooms, 2.5-3 baths, $480,990-$673,990.
Northgate Meadows, Diablo Pacific Properties, Arbolado Dr. & Northgate Rd., Walnut Creek. Ph: (510) 256-1300. Single-family, 5 bedrooms, 3,5 baths, $600,000-$725,000.
Vista Paraiso, Diablo Pacific Properties, Arbolado Dr. & Woodfern Ct., Walnut

NEW HOUSING 251

THE MOST COMPLETE GUIDE TO NEW HOME COMMUNITIES...
AS CLOSE AS YOUR PHONE

Homes For Sale
HOMEBUYER'S MONTHLY
SINCE 1971 - NORTHERN CALIFORNIA'S MOST COMPREHENSIVE GUIDE TO BETTER NEW HOME COMMUNITIES

How To Use Homebuyer's Monthly
Page 6

Special Feature
Weston Ranch
Page 20

Carriage Oaks in Vallejo...
Where It's All Happening
See page 10.

AND WE'LL SEND IT TO YOU
FREE!

Homes For Sale features virtually every new home development for sale in the Bay Area, Sacramento and Central Valley. Full color photos, prices, specifications and our detailed maps help you find the home that's right for you.

If you'd like to make house hunting easier just call...

1-800-257-6031

1-800-442-3579 outside California
between 8 a.m. & 2 p.m. weekdays for your issue of
Homes For Sale for Northern California.

Homes For Sale magazine is not affiliated with any realtor, builder, or sales agency of any kind. The call and the magazine are free. There is no obligation involved whatsoever.

Marin County
Novato

Wildwood Glen, McBail Homes, Corner of Olive & Samrose, East Novato. Ph: (707) 763-4333. Single-family detached, lots 6,000 sq. ft. to 1.25 acres, 3-5 bedrooms, 2,023-3,150 sq. ft., $360,000-$500,000.

Napa County
Napa

The Grove at Silverado, O'Brien & Hicks— Westholme Partners, 900 Augusta Circle, Napa. Ph: (707) 224-1261. Condominium attached & detached, 2-3 bedrooms, 2-3.5 baths, golf course views, country club memberships, $500,000-$790,000.

Greater Sacramento Area and the Sacramento Valley
Cameron Park

Oakcrest Estates, Winncrest Homes, 4009 El Norte Road, Cameron Park. Ph: (916) 933-4609. Single-family detached, 3-4 bedrooms, 2-3 baths, 1,415-2,230 sq. ft., from mid $150,000's.

Davis

Scarborough Faire at Mace Ranch, Centex Homes, 3060 Hortaleza Place, Davis. Ph: (916) 757-1075. Single-family detached, 3-4 bedrooms, 2-3 baths, front porches, $178,000-$211,500.

Elk Grove

Fallbrook Estates, Winncrest Homes, 9211 Whittemore Drive, Elk Grove. Ph: (916) 686-8501. Single-family detached, 3-4 bedrooms, 2-3 baths, 1,415-2,230 sq. ft., from mid $140,000's.

Las Brisas at Laguna Creek, Pacwest Development Corp., 9136 Acorn Ridge Circle, Elk Grove, (916) 684-2644. 3-5 bedrooms, unique architectural style, from mid $170,000's.

Legacy Park, Richmond American Homes, 9408 Erlton Court, Elk Grove. Ph: (916) 683-1991. Single-family detached, 3-5 bedrooms, 2-3 baths, 1,863-2,650 sq. ft., $191,990-$236,990.

Meridian Pointe, Winncrest Homes, 9211 Edisto Way, Elk Grove. Ph: (916) 684-5660. Single-family detached, plus half-plexes, 3-4 bedrooms, 2-3 baths, 1,310-2,045 sq. ft., half-plexes from low $120,000's, single from high $140,000's.

Somerset at Laguna Park, Winncrest Homes, 6709 Risata Way, Elk Grove. Ph: (916) 684-7083. Single-family detached, 2-3 bedrooms, 2-2.5 baths, 1,140-1,635 sq. ft., from low $120,000's.

Stonegate, Pacwest Development Corp., 8906 Marlayna Ct., Elk Grove. Ph: (916) 684-7030. 3-4 bedrooms, unique architectural style, from mid $130,000's.

The Pavilions at Camden Passage, Citation Homes Northern, 8723 W. Camden Drive, Elk Grove. Ph: (916) 685-8880. Single-family detached, up to 5 bedrooms, 4 baths, 3-car garage, large lots, $229,000-$262,000.

The Vintage Collection at Laguna Park, Winncrest Homes, 6312 Di Lusso Drive, Elk Grove. Ph: (916) 684-7868. Single-family detached, 3-4 bedrooms, 2-2.5 baths, 1,245-1,835 sq. ft., from mid $130,000's.

Twin Gables, Pulte Home Corporation, Laguna West, Elk Grove, Single-family detached, 3-4 bedrooms, detached garage, bonus space, $160,000-$190,000.

Elverta

Northbrook, Winncrest Homes, 8100 Orchid Tree Way, Elverta. Ph: (916) 334-

4474. Single-family detached, 3-4 bedrooms, 2-3 baths, 1,710-2,200 sq. ft., from mid $140,000's.

Folsom

Briggs Ranch Classics Series, Winncrest Homes, 102 Riggins Court, Folsom. Ph: (916) 985-2357. Single-family detached, 3-4 bedrooms, 2-3 baths, 1,730-2,280 sq. ft., from low $200,000's.

Briggs Ranch Estates, Winncrest Homes, 240 Briggs Ranch Drive, Folsom. Ph: (916) 985-4552. Custom Lots, .25 acre, from $84,000.

Bryncliffe at Los Cerros, Morrison Homes, 148 Cruickshank, Folsom. Ph: (916) 983-0566. Single-family detached, 3-6 bedrooms, 2-3 baths, $230,450-$275,450.

Silvertrace, Richmond American Homes, 433 Turnpike Drive, Folsom. Ph: (916) 985-0252. Single-family detached, 4-6 bedrooms, 2.5-4 bedrooms, $220,000-$285,000.

Galt

Garland Ranch, Morrison Homes, 908 Lake Canyon Ave., Galt. Ph: (209) 745-0311. Single-family detached, 3-4 bedrooms, 2-2.5 baths, $158,900-$178,950.

Granite Bay

Treelake Village, The Lusk Co. and K.H. Moss Co., 9500 Swan Lake Drive, Granite Bay. Ph: (916) 791-5111. Custom Lots, $63,000-$140,000.

Loomis

Los Lagos, The Hofmann Company, 5935 Via Madrid, Loomis. Ph: (916) 972-7110. Custom building sites in the rolling hills of Loomis, from high $120,000's.

Modesto

Las Brisas, Security Owners Corporation, Kansas Ave. near Rosemore Ave., Modesto. Ph: (209) 577-2001. Single-family detached, 3-4 bedrooms, 1-2 stories, $139,950-$159,950.

Silver Springs, Pacwest Development Corporation, 3633 Jarena Drive, Modesto. Ph: (209) 523-7976. Executive, customized homes, 3-5 bedrooms, from mid $120,000's.

Rancho Murieta

Rancho Murieta South Classic Series, Winncrest Homes, 15164 Reynosa Drive, Rancho Murieta, (800) 834-5401. Single-family detached, plus half-plexes, 2-4 bedrooms, 2-3 baths, 1,260-2,300 sq. ft., half-plexes from high $130,000's, single from mid $180,000's.

Rancho Murieta South Masters Series, Winncrest Homes, 15256 Abierto Drive, Rancho Murieta, (800) 339-4681. Single-family detached, 3-5 bedrooms, 2-3 baths, 2,110-2,575 sq. ft., from low $220,000's, custom golf course lots also available from $59,900.

Rancho Murieta South Vintage Series, Winncrest Homes, 14825 Reynosa Drive, Rancho Murieta, (800) 675-8456. Single-family detached, plus half-plexes, 3 bedrooms, 2-2.5 baths, 1,115-1,745 sq. ft., half-plexes from high $120,000's, single from high $140,000's.

Rocklin

Las Palmas at Stanford Ranch, Pacwest Development Corp., 5306 Swindon Road, Rocklin. Ph: (916) 624-4176. 3-5 bedrooms, unique architectural style, from mid $190,000's.

Mirada at Stanford Ranch, Pacific Scene, 5004 Charter Road, Rocklin. Ph: (916)

254 CONTRA COSTA & SOLANO

624-9558. Single-family detached, 3-4 bedrooms, one-story, 2-3-car garages, 1,250-1,750 sq. ft., from $149,990.

Parkside at Stanford Ranch, The Lusk Company, 5928 Pebble Creek Drive, Rocklin. Ph: (916) 632-3102. Single-family, 3-4 bedrooms, 2.5-3 baths, 3-car garage, from $179,000.

Stanford Ranch, Stanford Ranch, Inc., Sunset Blvd. & Stanford Ranch Rd., Rocklin. Ph: (916) 965-7100. Single-family detached, 3-5 bedrooms, 10 builders, $130,000's-$300,000's.

Roseville

Kerry Downs, Richmond American Homes, 1000 Killarney Court, Roseville. Ph: (916) 969-0456. Single-family detached, 3-5 bedrooms, 2-3 baths, $180,990-$223,990.

Lansdowne, Ryder Homes of No. Ca., 203 Shelley Court, Roseville. Ph: (916) 771-2312. Single-family detached, 3-4 bedrooms, 3 baths, $160,000-$190,000.

Sterling Place, Pulte Home Corporation, Woodcreek Oaks Blvd. & Camino Capistrano, Roseville. Ph: (916) 638-1054. Single-family detached, 3-4 bedrooms, $120,000-$180,000.

Villa Cabernet, The Hofmann Company, 250 Union St., Roseville. Ph: (916) 773-0779. Single-family, 1,195-1,950 sq. ft., 2-4 bedrooms, from high $120,000's.

Sacramento

Antelope Pointe, Winncrest Homes, 3447 Loneridge Court, Sacramento. Ph: (916) 332-7495. Single-family detached, 3-4 bedrooms, 2-2.5 baths, 1,150-1,900 sq. ft., from mid $120,000's.

Chelsea, Morrison Homes, 8916 Palmerson, Sacramento. Ph: (916) 729-5314. Single-family detached, 3-4 bedrooms, 2-3 baths, $140,100-$159,150.

Laguna Creek III, Pacific Scene, Sacramento. Ph: (916) 339-1600. Single-family detached, 1,200-1,700 sq. ft., 3-4 bedrooms, from low $120,000.

Morningside, Morrison Homes, 8409 Hillsbrook Drive, Sacramento. Ph: (916) 729-2934. Single-family detached, 3-4 bedrooms, 2-2.5 baths, $130,250-$147,250.

Steamboat Bend, The Hofmann Company, 7784 Amherst St., Sacramento. Ph: (916) 665-2020. Single-family homes, 1,121-1,596 sq. ft., 3-4 bedrooms, from high $80,000's.

The Cottages at Antelope Park, Winncrest Homes, 4524 Antelope Park Way, Sacramento. Ph: (916) 721-4929. Single-family detached, 3-4 bedrooms, 2-3 baths, 1,017-1,565 sq. ft., from low $100,000's.

Thornbury, Morrison Homes, 8708 Redwater Drive, Sacramento. Ph: (916) 729-3513. Single-family detached, 3-4 bedrooms, 2.5 baths, $150,950-$172,150.

Windbridge Villas, Winncrest Homes, 7750 Windbridge Drive, Sacramento. Ph: (916) 391-6447. Half-plexes, 2 bedrooms, 2 baths, 896-1,230 sq. ft., from low $110,000's.

Winters

The Villages at Putah Creek, GOMA Development, Putah Creek, Winters. Ph: (415) 459-1445. Single-family, 3 bedrooms, 2-2.5 baths, 1 and 2 stories, mid $100,000's.

Yuba City

Pheasant Pointe, The Hofmann Company, 2440 Dove Court, Yuba City. Ph: (916) 755-0208. Single-family, 1,318-2,203 sq. ft., 3-4 bedrooms, from high $110,000's.

NEW HOUSING

West Sacramento
Windsor Meadows, A.D. Seeno Const. Co., 3074 Susan Ct., West Sacramento. Ph: (916) 371-3700. Single-family, 3-4 bedrooms, from upper $130,000's.

Santa Clara County
Cupertino
Seven Springs, The Gregory Group, 11591 Seven Springs Pkwy., Cupertino. Ph: (408) 996-8222. Single-family home, several plans available, 1,950-2,440 sq. ft., High $400,000's to mid $500,000's.

Milpitas
Stonegate, Alta Pacific Housing Partners, 1222 Cracolice Lane off Dempsey, Milpitas. Ph: (408) 945-9015. Single-family, 3-4 bedrooms, from mid $200,000's.

Morgan Hill
Eldorado II, Standard Pacific, 17052 Heatherwood Way, Morgan Hill. Ph: (408) 778-2233. 4-5 bedroom executive home, from low $400,000's.

Palo Alto
Palo Alto Central, Summerhill Homes, California Ave. & Park Blvd., Palo Alto. Ph: (415) 325-7192. Condominiums, 1-2 bedrooms, $200,000's.

San Jose
Beacon Hill, Trigon Development Co., 160 Knightshaven, San Jose. Ph: (408) 227-2745. Single-family detached, large hillside view lots, from the mid $300,000's.

Bordeaux, Standard Pacific, 3233 Delta Road, San Jose. Ph: (408) 270-3334. Single-family, 3-5 bedrooms, from upper $300,000's.

Carnegie Square, Barry Swensen Builder, 24th and Santa Clara Streets, San Jose. Ph: (408) 971-7653. 68 condominiums, 2 bedrooms, 1-2 baths, mid $100,000's.

Rosecreek, Davidson, Kavanagh & Brezzo, 1911 Rosenelf Circle, San Jose. Ph: (408) 259-9872. Single-family, 4-5 bedrooms, from mid $200,000's.

Ryland Mews, Barry Swensen Builder, 430 North First Street, San Jose. Ph: (408) 971-7653. 131 condominium and townhome-style 1-3 bedroom homes, from the low $100,000's.

San Pedro Square, Barry Swensen Builder, San Pedro at Ayers, San Jose. Ph: (408) 298-1800. 50-unit low-density condominiums and townhomes, 2-3 bedrrooms, $200,000-$300,000.

Waterside, O'Brien & Hicks-Westholme Partners, 1096 Summerplace Drive, San Jose. Ph: (408) 298-4692. Condominium attached, 1-2 bedrrooms, 1-2.5 baths, 2 pools, spa & tennis courts, $98,000-$166,000.

Sunnyvale
Expressions, Summerhill Homes, California & Pajaro Court, Sunnyvale. Ph: (408) 739-2767. Townhomes, 2-3 bedrooms, mid $200,000's.

Traditions, Davidson Kavanagh & Brezzo, 1176 La Rochelle Terrace, Sunnyvale. Ph: (408) 745-0174. Townhomes, 2-3 bedrooms, den, up to 2,150 sq. ft., from mid $200,000.

San Joaquin County
Stockton
Delta Vista at Weston Ranch, Standard Pacific, Stockton. Ph: (209) 982-5555. Single-family, 3-4 bedrooms, from upper $100,000's.

Wedgewood Park, Busby Dev. Co., West 8th St. and Fresno Ave., Stockton. Ph: (209) 466-2044. Single-family detached, 3-4 bedrooms, 1-2 stories, $109,590-

$129,950.

Tracy

California Marquis, Kaufman & Broad of No. Ca., 910 Arches Court, Tracy. Ph: (209) 829-4500. Single-family detached, 3-4 bedrooms, 2-2.5 baths, VA financing available, $140,990-$165,990.

Chantilly, Standard Pacific, 646 Shaw Court, Tracy. Ph: (209) 832-3453. Single-family, 3-4 bedrooms, from $159,000.

Circle B Ranch, Bright Development, Tracy Blvd. at W. Mt. Diablo, Tracy. Ph: (209) 836-9586. Single-family, 3-4 bedrooms, 2-2.5 baths, $152,950-$179,950.

Fox Hollow, Ryder Homes of No. Ca., 1860 Fox Tail Way, Tracy. Ph: (209) 832-8462. Single-family detached, 3-4 bedrooms, 2 baths, $148,0000-$167,000.

Harvest Country West, H.C.W. Co., 1925 Harvest Landing Ct., Tracy. Ph: (510) 830-8700. Single-family, 4-5 bedrooms, 2.5-3 baths, $179,000-$294,000.

Normandy, Standard Pacific, Tracy. Ph: (209) 832-2111. Single-family, 3-4 bedrooms, from low $200,000's.

The Village at Summergate, The Lusk Company, 2351 Westbury Court, Tracy. Ph: (209) 835-3503. Condominiums, 2-3 bedrooms, 2.5 baths, attached 2-car garage, from $99,500.

San Mateo County
Redwood Shores

Hampton at Redwood Shores, A-M Greystone Homes, 581 Shoal Circle, Redwood Shores. Ph: (415) 594-9348. Townhomes, 1-3 bedrooms, 5 plans available, from mid $200,000's.

San Carlos

San Carlos Highlands, Paul C. Petersen-Whitecliff Homes, 197 Glasgow Lane, San Carlos. Ph: (415) 592-9922. Single-family detached, 4 bedrooms, 3 baths, $599,950-$749,350.

Solano County
Benicia

Classic Homes, Southampton Co., Kearny & McCall streets, Benicia. Ph: (707) 745-2112. Single-family detached, 4-5 bedrooms luxury homes, tile roofs, 3-car garage, 5 floor plans from 2,475-3,375 sq. ft., $300,000-$375,000.

Encore Homes, Southampton, Benet Court, Benicia. Ph: (707) 745-2112. Single-family detached, 3-4 bedrooms, tile roofs, $210,000-$265,000.

Fairfield

Castle Rock, Centex Homes, 2423 Trevino Way, Fairfield. Ph: (707) 426-5211. Single-family detached, 3-5 bedrooms, 2-3 baths, closets galore, 3-car garages, large lots, $197,000-$270,000.

Diablo Vista, Miller-Sorg Group, Rancho Solano, Fairfield. Ph: (707) 428-1007. Single-family detached, up to 5 bedrooms, 3 baths, from the mid $200,000's.

Dover Park Estates II, The Hofmann Company, 1119 Spruce Way, Fairfield. Ph: (707) 425-5298. Single-family, 3-4 bedrooms, 1,945-2,581 sq. ft., from the mid $190,000's.

Fairway Estates, Miller-Sorg Group, Rancho Solano, Fairfield. Ph: (707) 428-1009. Single-family detached, up to 5 bedrooms, 3 baths, 3-car garages, 3 fireplaces, from the low $300,000's.

First Green at Rancho Solano, Centex Homes, 3287 Quail Hollow Drive, Fairfield, . Single-family detached, 2-5 bedrooms, 2-3 baths, country club location, fully-landscaped, turn-key homes, $288,000-$405,000.

NEW HOUSING 257

Le Parc at Southbrook, A.D. Seeno Const. Co., 4691 Wildwood Way, Fairfield. Ph: (707) 864-0382. Single-family, 3-4 bedrooms, from $130,000's.

Spyglass Summit, Security Owners Corporation, Oliver Road and Waterman Blvd., Fairfield. Ph: (707) 425-2396. Single-family detached, 3-5 bedrooms, one and two stories, $234,950-$269,950.

Vintage Green Valley, Citation Homes Northern, 608 Pavilion Drive, Fairfield. Ph: (707) 864-5041. Single-family detached, up to 6 bedrooms, 3-car garage, large lots, $242,000-$310,000.

Suisun

Eastridge in Green Valley, The Hofmann Company, 906 Eastridge Drive, Suisun. Ph: (707) 864-0292. Custom building sites in beautiful Green Valley, from the low $120,000's.

Lawler Montero, The Hofmann Company, Lawler Ranch 1312 Potrero Circle, Suisun. Ph: (707) 429-1179. Single-family, 3-4 bedrooms, 1,940-2,580 sq. ft., from the high $170,000's.

Lawler Valencia, The Hofmann Company, Lawler Ranch 243 Seabury, Suisun. Ph: (707) 421-8012. Single-family, 2-3 bedrooms, 1,190-1,945 sq. ft., from the high $130,000's.

Parkside, A.D. Seeno Const. Co., 205 Cloverleaf Circle, Suisun. Ph: (707) 428-5938. Single-family, 3-4 bedrooms, from $120,000's.

Villages at Heritage Park, A.D. Seeno Const. Co., 278 Tamarisk Circle, Suisun. Ph: (707) 428-5911. Single-family, 3-4 bedrooms, from $130,000's.

Vacaville

Farmington, Condiotti Enterprise, 145 Audrey Place, Vacaville. Ph: (707) 447-5363. Single-family, $140,000-$170,000.

The Cottages at Foxwood, O'Brien & Hicks— Westholme Partners, 800 Turquoise St., Vacaville. Ph: (707) 447-6559. Single-family detached, 2-4 bedrooms, 2-2.5 baths, 4,500 sq. ft. lots, $129,950-$155,950.

The Manors at Foxwood, O'Brient & Hicks-Westholme Partners, 906 Calcite Court, Vacaville. Ph: (707) 452-8456. Single-family detached, 3-4 bedrooms, 2-3 baths, 6,000 sq. ft. lots, $161,950-$181,950.

Vista del Cerro, The Hofmann Company, 795 Shannon Drive, Vacaville. Ph: (707) 446-2710. Single-family, 3-5 bedrooms, 1,752-2,480 sq. ft., from high $170,00's.

Vallejo

Carriage Oaks, The Lusk Company, 513 Carousel Drive, Vallejo. Ph: (707) 557-5972. Single-family, 3-4 bedrooms, 2-3 baths, $155,000-$203,000.

Clearpointe II, Centex Homes, 276 Clearpointe Drive, Vallejo. Ph: (707) 643-7731. Single-family paired homes, 3-4 bedrooms, 2-car garage, front & rear yards, $159,900-$184,900.

Seascape at Glen Cove, Citation Homes Northern, 1030 Suncliff, Vallejo. Ph: (707) 372-0300. Four-plex condominiums, garage, from low $100,000's.

Somerset Hills, Davidon Homes, 296 Devonshire Court, Vallejo. Ph: (707) 553-1383. Single-family detached, 4-5 bedrooms, 2.5-3 baths, $240,000-$300,000.

Sonoma County
Geyserville

Geyser Ridge, Benjamin Tuxhorn, 44 Bosworth Lane, Geyserville. Ph: (707) 857-3101. Single-family, 3-4 bedrooms, Victorian, $194,500-$234,900.

Petaluma

Adobe Creek Golf Estates, Christopherson Homes, 1901 Frates Road, Petaluma.

Ph: (707) 769-0469. Single-family, 4-5 bedrooms, mid $300,000's to low $400,000's.

Cader Farms, Ryder Homes of No. California, 507 Greenwich St., Petaluma. Ph: (707) 778-0811. Single-family detached, 3-5 bedrooms, 3 baths, $253,000-$305,000.

Graystone, McBail Co., Petaluma. Ph: (707) 762-6906. Single-family detached, 3-5 bedrooms, 1,500-3,000 sq. ft., low $200,000's to high $200,000's.

Sonoma Glen, Delco Builders & Developers Inc., 1604 Merlot Court, Petaluma. Ph: (510) 762-1074. Single-family detached, 3-5 bedrooms, 2-3 baths, 2-3-car garages, $236,950-$309,950.

Santa Rosa

Deer Meadows, Christopherson Homes, 3707 Deauville Place, Santa Rosa. Ph: (707) 546-3448. Executive homes, extras, mid $300,000's to high $400,000's.

Kensington, Keith Development, Devonshire Place, Santa Rosa. Ph: (707) 525-1358. Single-family, $299,950-$399,950.

Wyndham, Cobblestone Development, Santa Rosa. Ph: (707) 525-1358. Single-family, $150,000-$230,000.

West Petaluma

Victoria, A.D. Seeno Co., 1249 B St., West Petaluma. Ph: (707) 765-2333. Single-family, 3-5 bedrooms, from mid $200,000's.

Windsor

California Arbor, Kaufman Broad, Leafhaven Lane, Windsor. Ph: (707) 838-1050. Single-family, 3-4 bedrooms, from high $100,000's.

California Creekside, Kaufman Broad, Lazy Creek Drive, Windsor. Ph: (707) 836-0146. Single-family, 3-4 bedrooms, from high $100,000's.

16/Jobs, Salaries & Food Prices

Trends — What Job Sectors Show Promise

CONTRA COSTA AND, to a lesser extent Solano County, usually weather recessions better than other California counties because their economies are diverse. Nonetheless, in 1992, the recession took its toll in both counties. Unemployment, notched up about another point in each county, and stores reported sluggish holiday sales (although better than 1991). Interest rates dropped sharply, perking up the housing market, but no one predicted an immediate return to the boom times of a few years ago.

In Walnut Creek, Dow Chemical announced it was closing its research center, and the Navy continued its cutbacks at Mare Island. On the plus side, highway construction is roaring. A plant is being opened in Pittsburg to build BART cars. A veterans hospital is to be built at Travis in Fairfield.

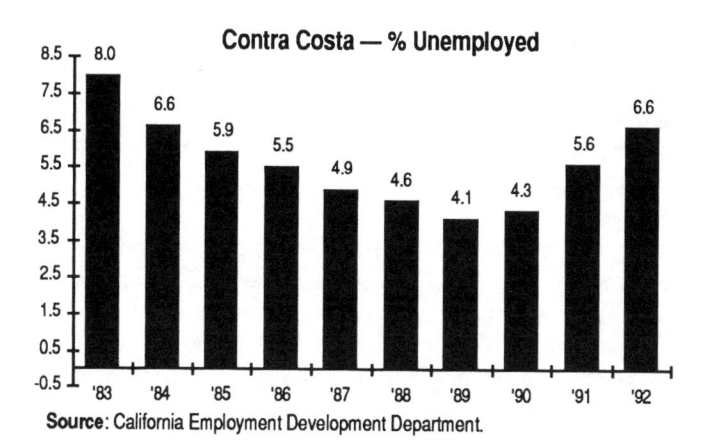

Contra Costa — % Unemployed

Year	% Unemployed
'83	8.0
'84	6.6
'85	5.9
'86	5.5
'87	4.9
'88	4.6
'89	4.1
'90	4.3
'91	5.6
'92	6.6

Source: California Employment Development Department.

Job Outlook by Industry for Contra Costa County

Job Sector	1990	*1997	Change
Nonagricultural employ.	296,900	337,500	40,600
Mining	2,800	2,90000	100
Construction	21,400	24,300	2,900
Manufacturing	31,700	34,100	2,400
Nondurable goods	20,800	22,400	1,600
Printing & publishing	3,300	3,900	600
Chemicals	4,700	5,100	400
Petroleum	9,200	9,800	600
Other nondurable goods	3,600	3,600	0
Durable goods	10,900	11,700	800
Electronics & inst.	4,300	4,800	500
Other durable goods	6,600	6,900	300
Transport & public util.	20,000	22,500	2,500
Transportation	6,700	8,200	1,500
Communications & util.	13,300	14,300	1,000
Wholesale trade	11,100	12,400	1,300
Retail Trade Total	61,600	70,4000	8,800
Department & apparel	11,200	12,400	1,200
Food Stores	9,700	10,500	800
Auto Dealers & Ser. Sta.	5,900	6,600	700
Restaurants & bars	19,400	22,800	3,400
Other retail trade	15,400	18,100	2,700
Finance, insurance, real estate	27,300	29,800	2,500
Finance	15,200	16,000	800
Insurance & real estate	12,100	13,800	1,700
Services Total	77,300	95,300	18,000
Hotels & motels	1,900	2,200	300
Bus. services	19,000	26,200	7,200
Auto & misc. repair	3,500	4,100	600
Health services	19,600	25,000	5,400
Engineering & man. ser.	9,900	11,000	1,100
Other Services	23,400	26,800	3,400
Government Total	43,700	45,800	2,100
Federal government	7,100	7,200	3,400
State and local	36,600	38,600	2,000

Source: California Economic Development Department. *Projected

Emphasing local projects is misleading because many residents work in other counties, particularly San Francisco and Oakland. Unemployment in these areas has risen but not as much as in Southern California.

The information in this chapter will tell you where the new jobs are being created. But remember many positions open in replacement jobs. Newspaper classifieds still carry pages of jobs. Good luck!

Call Us for Your Refuse & Recycling Needs

BFI-Pleasant Hill Bayshore Disposal, Inc., offers up-to-date and convenient recycling and refuse service for business and residential customers.

Call us about curbside recycling of glass, plastics, newspapers and cardboard and aluminum and tin cans.

We also recycle old car batteries, used motor oil, used anti-freeze and latex paint for residential customers at our collection centers in Antioch, Benicia, Pacheco and Rodeo.

Serving:
Antioch, Clayton, Clyde, parts of Concord, Martinez, Mt. View, Pacheco, Pleasant Hill, Rodeo and West Pittsburg in Contra Costa County

The city of Benicia in Solano County

(510) 685-4711

BFI Pleasant Hill Bayshore Disposal, Inc.

441 N. Buchanan Circle, Pacheco, CA 94553

What They Earn

Position	Annual Salary
Accountant	$32,000
Accounting Clerk, experienced	$16,640-$20,800
Administrative Assistant	$20,800
Aircraft Applicator	$21,840
Alarm-Security Tech trainee	$14,560
Appliance Rep	$19,200
Assembler	$18,720-$19,760
Assistant Controller	$42,000
Auto Mechanic, experienced	to $39,520
Baker, union, apprentice	$17,472
Bank Teller, experienced	$19,656-$22,800
Bartender, no experience	$8,840-$14,560
Blinds & Drapery Installer	$7,000-$10,000
Bookkeeper	$18,720
Bus Driver, school district	$14,107-$16,810
Cafeteria Assistant	$13,957-$17,576
Carpenter, journeyman	$52,000
Carpenter Helper	$16,640-$24,960
Carpet Cleaners	$10,400-$18,720
Collection Representative	$20,800-$22,880
Computer Operator	$12,480-$22,880
Construction, all phases	$20,800-$29,120
Copy Machine Operator	$12,480
Courier	$20,280
Credit Analyst	$25,300
Customer Service Rep	$23,520
Data Entry, experienced	to $25,480
Dental Assistant	$27,040-$31,200
Dispatcher	to $25,000
Drycleaning Counter Worker	$12,480
Electronics Assembler	$13,000-$21,840
General Office Help	$8,840
Guard	$8,840-16,640
Health Spa Fitness Worker	$20,000
Housing Management Supervisor, city	$38,280-46,188
Industrial Waste Inspector, city	$34,116-$41,484
Instructional Aide, no experience	$10,400-$12,168
Insurance Agent	$36,000
Landscape Supervisor	$29,000

What They Earn

Position	Annual Salary
Legal Secretary	$28,080
Librarian, govt.	$32,496-$39,480
Loan Processor	$24,960
Locksmith-Security Tech Trainee	$14,560-$18,720
Machinist, experienced	$14,560-$40,560
Medical Assistant, no experience	$12,480-$14,560
Medical Office, Billing	$24,000
Medical Transcriptionist	$31,200
Nurse, LVN,	$26,484-$33,816
Nurse, RN,	$42,576-$51,876
Office Assistant	$12,480
Office Machine Servicer, experienced	$16,640-$21,320
Operating Engineer, experienced	$27,040-$54,080
Optical Technician	$22,880
Order Entry Clerk	$14,560-18,720
Paralegal Specialist, experienced	$19,200-$28,800
Pest Control Technician	$23,400
Photographer, trade magazine	$14,560
Pizza Delivery	$16,640-$24,960
Pressman	$19,760-$22,880
Production Worker	$16,557
Programer II, govt.	$34,300-$51,500
Receptionist	$16,640
Restaurant Cook-Banquets	to $35,000
Retail Clerk	$12,480
Secretary	$12,480-$26,000
Security Guard	$9,880-$13,520
Sheet Metal Worker	$16,640
Short Order Cook, no experience	$9,360-$15,080
Software Engineer	to $70,000
Switchboard Operator-Receptionist	$14,560-$17,680
Teacher, experienced	$35,600
Teachers-Aides	$10,920-$17,160
Teacher, substitute	by day $70
Training & Placement Specialist	$14,500-$18,000
Truck Driver, experienced	to $28,080
X-ray Technologist	to $62,400

Source: Survey of local and Bay Area help-wanted advertising in summer and fall, 1992.

Grocery Prices

Item	High	Low	Avg
Apple Juice, frozen, cheapest, 12 oz.	$1.55	$0.99	$1.30
Apple Pie, Mrs. Smith's, 26 oz.	$3.39	$2.89	$3.17
Apples, Red Delicious, 1 lb.	$0.59	$0.47	$0.54
Aspirin, cheapest, 100 pills	$4.49	$0.99	$3.02
Baby Food, Gerber, bananas, 4 oz. jar	$0.43	$0.37	$0.39
Baby Food, Gerber, spinach, 4 oz. jar	$0.43	$0.37	$0.39
Bacon, Armour, 1 lb.	$2.99	$1.38	$2.39
Bananas, 1 lb.	$0.49	$0.45	$0.48
Beef, chuck roast, 1 lb.	$2.28	$2.18	$2.15
Beef, ground round, 1 lb.	$2.48	$1.78	$2.02
Beer, Budweiser, 6-pack, cans	$3.99	$3.79	$3.92
Beer, Coors, 6-pack, cans	$3.99	$3.79	$3.92
Bleach, Clorox, 1 gal.	$1.91	$0.89	$1.35
Bread, sourdough, Colombo, 1 lb.	$1.73	$1.46	$1.61
Bread, white, cheapest, 1 lb.	$0.63	$0.55	$0.59
Broccoli, bunch	$0.89	$0.68	$0.79
Butter, Challenge, 1 lb.	$1.65	$1.15	$1.46
Cabbage, 1 lb.	$0.39	$0.27	$0.35
Cantaloupe, 1 lb.	$0.49	$0.39	$0.45
Carrots, fresh, 1 lb.	$0.39	$0.33	$0.37
Cat food, 9 Lives, 5.5 oz.	$0.37	$0.29	$0.34
Charcoal, Kingsford, 10 lbs.	$3.99	$2.85	$3.38
Cheese, Swiss, 1 lb.	$3.79	$2.98	$3.39
Chicken, fryer, 1 lb.	$0.99	$0.78	$0.92
Chili, Dennison, 15 oz. can	$1.29	$0.79	$1.06
Cigarettes, Marlboro Lights, carton	$21.39	$19.99	$20.79
Coca Cola, six-pack, 12 oz. cans	$2.29	$1.39	$1.98
Coffee, Folgers, 1 lb. 10 oz.	$3.68	$3.39	$3.49
Cookies, Oreo, 1 lb.	$2.89	$1.99	$2.59
Corn Flakes, Kellogg, 15 oz.	$2.99	$1.69	$2.13
Diapers, Pampers, box of 36	$9.99	$9.29	$9.79
Dishwashing liquid, Joy, 22 oz.	$1.59	$1.49	$1.54
Dog Food, Kal Kan, 14 oz. can	$0.71	$0.62	$0.67
Eggs, large, Grade AA, doz.	$1.50	$1.25	$1.41
Flour, Gold Medal, 5 lbs.	$1.35	$1.19	$1.28
Frozen Yogurt, Dreyers, half gal.	$4.39	$4.19	$4.29
Gin, Beefeater, 750 ml.	$14.88	$13.99	$14.44
Grapefruit, 1 lb.	$0.60	$0.33	$0.44
Grapenuts, Post, 16 oz.	$3.85	$2.45	$3.00
Ham, 1.5-lb. tin	$5.49	$4.98	$5.24
Ice Cream, store brand, vanilla half gal.	$2.19	$1.98	$2.09

Grocery Prices

Item	High	Low	Avg
Ketchup, Del Monte, 32 oz.	$1.75	$1.49	$1.61
Ketchup, Heinz, 28 oz.	$2.79	$1.19	$1.88
Lamb, leg of, 1 lb.	$2.99	$2.58	$2.85
Laundry Detergent, Tide, 39 oz.	$3.33	$2.89	$3.11
Lettuce, Iceberg, head	$0.99	$0.78	$0.92
Margarine, Imperial, whipped, 1-lb. tub	$1.55	$1.09	$1.40
Mayonnaise, Best Foods, 1 qt.	$2.59	$2.25	$2.48
Milk, skim, half gallon	$1.29	$1.19	$1.23
Milk, whole, half gallon	$1.31	$1.25	$1.28
Mixed vegetables, frozen, 10 oz.	$0.77	$0.56	$0.67
Mushrooms, 1 lb.	$2.39	$0.99	$1.75
Olive Oil, cheapest, 17 oz.	$3.99	$3.29	$3.62
Onions, 1 lb.	$0.39	$0.27	$0.33
Orange juice, frozen, cheapest, 12 oz.	$1.19	$0.79	$0.92
Oranges, fresh, 1 lb.	$0.49	$0.33	$0.40
Peanuts, cocktail, Planter's, 12 oz.	$2.79	$2.29	$2.51
Peas, frozen, 10 oz.	$0.69	$0.56	$0.65
Pork, chops, 1 lb.	$3.79	$2.38	$2.92
Potato Chips, Eagle, 6.5 oz.	$1.59	$1.39	$1.52
Potatoes, 1 lb.	$0.39	$0.33	$0.37
Raisins, bulk, 1 lb.	$1.55	$1.19	$1.37
Red Snapper, fresh, 1 lb.	$3.88	$2.78	$3.32
Rice, Hinode, 5 lbs.	$2.25	$1.99	$2.08
Seven-Up, 6-pack, cans	$2.99	$2.25	$2.51
Soap, bar, Ivory, 4-pack	$1.79	$1.19	$1.39
Soup, Campbell, Chicken Noodle, 10 oz. can	$0.61	$0.47	$0.52
Soy Sauce, Kikkoman, 20 oz.	$2.39	$2.15	$2.31
Spaghetti, cheapest, 1 lb.	$0.99	$0.72	$0.89
Sugar, cheapest, 5 lbs.	$1.83	$1.59	$1.67
Toilet Tissue, 4-roll pack, cheapest	$0.99	$0.77	$0.85
Tomatoes, Beefsteak	$0.79	$0.49	$0.67
Toothpaste, Crest, 6.4 oz.	$2.29	$2.19	$2.26
Tortillas, cheapest, 15 oz.	$1.69	$1.19	$1.36
Tuna, Starkist, 6.125 oz.	$1.59	$0.73	$1.27
Turkey, ground, 1 lb.	$2.89	$2.38	$2.62
Turkey, whole, hen, 1 lb.	$1.29	$0.98	$1.15
Vegetable Oil, Wesson, 24 oz.	$1.59	$1.15	$1.34
Whiskey, Cutty Sark, 750 ml.	$13.99	$13.88	$13.94
Whiskey, Johnnie Walker Red, 750 ml.	$19.99	$15.99	$17.99
Wine, Burgundy, Gallo, 1.5 liter	$4.88	$3.59	$4.15

Source: Survey of three supermarkets in fall, 1992. Prices are the highest, lowest and average of those found at the three stores.

Job Outlook by Industry for Solano County

Job Sector	1989	*1996	Change
Nonag. employ.	92,700	113,600	20,900
Mining & construction	7,800	10,100	2,300
Manufacturing	7,100	8,700	1,600
Nondurable goods	4,600	5,100	500
Food & kindred prod.	2,300	2,100	-200
Other nondurables	2,300	3,000	700
Durable goods	2,500	3,600	1,100
Transport & public util.	3,700	4,700	1,000
Transportation	2,400	2,900	500
Comm. & util.	1,300	1,800	500
Wholesale trade	2,300	3,000	700
Retail Trade Total	20,900	26,200	5,300
Dept. & apparel stores	3,100	3,800	700
Food stores	3,700	4,800	1,100
Auto dealers & ser. sta.	2,600	2,900	300
Restaurants & bars	8,100	10,200	2,100
Other retail trade	3,400	4,500	1,100
Finance, insurance, real estate	3,200	6,600	3,400
Finance	1,600	4,300	2,700
Insurance & real estate	1,600	2,300	700
Services Total	17,600	24,400	6,800
Hotels & motels	600	900	300
Personal services	1,000	1,300	300
Bus. services	2,800	4,000	1,200
Health services	6,000	8,500	2,500
Other services	7,200	9,700	2,500
Government Total	30,100	29,900	-200
Federal government	14,800	12,200	-2,600
State and local	15,300	17,700	2,400

Source: California Economic Development Department. *Projected.

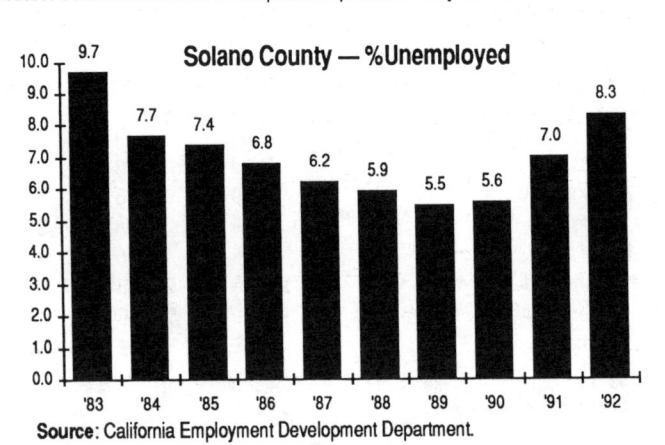

Solano County — %Unemployed

Year	%
'83	9.7
'84	7.7
'85	7.4
'86	6.8
'87	6.2
'88	5.9
'89	5.5
'90	5.6
'91	7.0
'92	8.3

Source: California Employment Development Department.

17/Commuting

Miles to the Bay Bridge, Commute Times on BART, Wide Choice of Buses Locally and to San Francisco

THANKS TO LOCAL BONDS and federal funds, improvements are being made to East Bay freeways and BART that will cut minutes off the commuting. The bad news is that construction is further impeding traffic flows.

Improvements: Recent and Coming.
• BART extensions to West Pittsburg and Dublin-Pleasanton are under construction. When they arrive in few years, residents in East Contra Costa and the San Ramon Valley will enjoy a faster, more comfortable commute.
• Willow Pass, the hilly bottleneck on Highway 4 between Concord and Pittsburg, was widened and is now being graded. For 1993, traffic will still jam in the mornings and before 4 p.m. on most weekdays.
• Construction has started to overhaul one of the worst bottlenecks in the county, the I-680-Highway 24 interchange at Walnut Creek. Work should be completed by 1995.
Traffic almost every morning is backed up to Pleasant Hill and evenings, into Lafayette. After the interchange, traffic usually picks up.
• After years of lawsuits and delays, the green light was given in 1992 for major improvements on Interstate 80, from Pinole to Emeryville. The freeway now suffers major delays but worse are expected at certain times during construction.
• Two lanes were added to the Martinez-Benicia Bridge and to Interstate 680, to about Pleasant Hill. It's amazing how much traffic an extra lane will carry.
• The I-580 connector in Richmond was completed, joining I-80 with the Richmond-San Rafael Bridge.

Driving Miles
Contra Costa — To the Bay Bridge

City	I-680/H-24	I-80/H-4
Alamo*	23	NA
Antioch	41	46
Brentwood	52	59
Concord	22	31
Crockett	NA	21
Danville*	28	NA
El Cerrito	NA	6
El Sobrante	NA	10
Hercules	NA	16
Lafayette	13	NA
Martinez	26	25
Moraga	13	NA
Oakley	47	54
Orinda	10	NA
Pinole	NA	14
Pittsburg	37	40
Pleasant Hill	22	33
Richmond	NA	9
Rodeo	NA	18
San Pablo	NA	10
San Ramon*	34	NA
Walnut Creek	18	40

Note: These are approximations. A traveler from Concord or Walnut Creek, two of the larger cities in Contra Costa, could easily add another five miles depending upon his starting point within the city. Of bridges, the Bay Bridge is a little over 8 miles long, the San Mateo about 7, the Dumbarton about 3. **Key:** NA, not applicable. Either exits were not available or the freeway was judged to be too distant for a reasonable measurement. *Drivers from Alamo, Danville and San Ramon can use Interstate 580 as an alternate route to the Bay Bridge with respective distances of 40, 37 and 32 miles.

• Interstate 680, south of Walnut Creek has been widened in some parts and is being widened in others.

Quake Aftermath

Interstate 80, as it nears the Bay Bridge, remains a mess. The 1989 earthquake destroyed a section of the freeway in Oakland and it has yet to be rebuilt. Traffic coming from Fremont and Hayward or going south from Vallejo and Richmond has to be detoured.

BART IS YOUR TICKET TO THE BAY AREA

The easiest way to tour the Bay Area is to pick up a BART ticket and step aboard.

Our clean, comfortable trains run every day until midnight and kids 4 and under ride FREE!

Here are just a few places of interest you careach on BART:

■ **SHOPPING** - BART is the perfect shopping companion because we stop where you shop. BART serves over 2000 stores and retail centers

■ **RESTAURANTS** - BART is easily accessible to thousands of fine restaurants throughout the greater Bay Area. Then leave the driving to us!

■ **SPORTS EVENTS** - Don't hassle with fighting the traffic to the Oakland Coliseum or other sporting events. Take BART and you'll have even more fun!

■ **PERFORMING ARTS** - From the San Francisco Opera House to the Orpheum Theatre, BART gives you a front row seat.

■ **AIR TRAVEL** - Save money on parking by taking BART right to the Oakland Coleseum/Airport station plus a short shuttle.

BART is your ticket to everything from the major financial districts to museums and historical sites.

For more information, please call - **(510)464-6000**

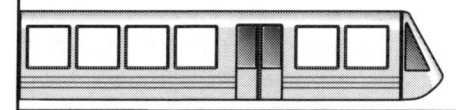

Means of Transportation to Work in Solano

Town or City	HM	WK	BK	MC	MV	BS	TC	BART
Benicia	3	2	*0	1	90	1	0	2
Davis**	3	4	22	1	67	3	0	0
Dixon	2	2	1	*0	94	*0	0	0
Fairfield	2	2	1	1	92	1	0	*0
Rio Vista	2	9	2	1	86	0	0	0
Suisun City	2	1	*0	1	93	2	0	*0
Vacaville	2	2	1	*0	94	1	0	*0
Vallejo	3	3	1	1	88	2	0	1
Solano County	3	3	1	1	90	1	0	1

Source: 1990 Census. **Key**: HM (work at home); WK (walk); BK (bike); MC (motorcycle); MV (motor vehicle including car, truck or van); BS (bus); TC (trolley or street car); BART (Bay Area Rapid Transit). Figures are percent of population, rounded to the nearest whole number. *Less than 0.5 percent. **Yolo County city.

Besides overloading the open freeways, the detours force abrupt lane changes. Be extra careful.

Time-saving Strategies

What can be done to save time?

• Buy a good map book and keep it in the car. The editors favor Thomas Guides. Sooner than later you will find yourself jammed on the freeway and in desperate need of an alternate route. They're out there.

Pleasant Hill Road bypasses the bottleneck at Walnut Creek. Treat Boulevard parallels Ygnacio Valley Road, often clogged. Concord Avenue parallels the more congested Clayton Valley Road. San Pablo Avenue, recently improved, is, at times, a better road than I-80 in the West County.

Fairfield and Vacaville commuters can sometimes duck congestion at the Benicia Bridge by detouring along Second Street in Benicia.

Crow Canyon Road will whisk you toward Oakland when I-580 is jammed. But don't speed.

Rumrill Road in Richmond leads directly to the San Rafael Bridge.

• Listen to traffic reports on the radio. Helicopters and planes give immediate news of jams. Avoid trouble before you get on the road.

• Buy bridge ticket books, and a $20 BART ticket. The bridge books will save you money and a few minutes. The BART ticket will save your sanity. That $20 ticket will speed you through the gate.

• Join a car pool. The Bay Bridge has a lane for pools (at least three persons per vehicle). No toll. You whip to the head of the line. So popular is this lane that drivers, shy a body or two, cruise BART stations in search of passengers.

Means of Transportation to Work in Contra Costa

Town or City	HM	WK	BK	MC	MV	BS	TC	BART
Alamo	4	1	*0	*0	91	*0	0	3
Antioch	2	1	*0	1	93	1	0	1
Bayview-Montalvin	1	2	0	*0	91	3	0	3
Bethel Island	9	3	1	0	85	0	0	1
Blackhawk	4	1	0	0	92	0	0	2
Brentwood	1	6	1	1	89	1	0	*0
Clayton	3	1	*0	*0	88	*0	0	6
Concord	3	2	1	1	84	2	0	7
Crockett	4	3	0	*0	88	1	0	3
Danville	4	1	*0	*0	89	*0	0	3
Discovery Bay	3	1	*0	0	94	0	0	0
East Richmond Hts.	3	1	1	1	87	1	0	7
El Cerrito	4	2	2	*0	73	4	*0	13
El Sobrante	3	*0	*0	1	90	1	*0	4
Hercules	2	*0	*0	*0	91	2	*0	4
Kensington	9	2	1	*0	74	7	0	6
Lafayette	7	2	*0	*0	78	*0	*0	10
Martinez	2	2	1	1	88	1	0	4
Moraga	3	3	1	*0	82	1	*0	8
Oakley	3	1	*0	*0	93	1	0	1
Orinda	7	1	*0	*0	81	*0	0	10
Pacheco	4	4	1	1	86	0	0	3
Pinole	2	1	0	*0	90	1	*0	3
Pittsburg	2	2	*0	*0	91	1	*0	3
Pleasant Hill	3	2	1	1	83	1	*0	8
Richmond	3	3	1	*0	80	5	*0	7
Rodeo	2	1	*0	*0	91	1	0	3
San Pablo	1	3	1	*0	82	5	0	6
San Ramon	3	1	1	*0	93	*0	0	1
Tara Hills	2	1	0	1	92	2	0	2
Walnut Creek	4	2	1	*0	81	1	*0	9
West Pittsburg	2	1	*0	1	88	1	*0	4
Contra Costa County	3	2	1	*0	85	2	*0	6

Source: 1990 Census. **Key**: HM (work at home); WK (walk); BK (bike); MC (motorcycle); MV (motor vehicle including car, truck or van); BS (bus); TC (trolley or street car); BART (Bay Area Rapid Transit). Figures are percent of population, rounded to the nearest whole number. *Less than 0.5 percent.

Commuter's BART Guide
(Time in Minutes)

Station	Oakland	Berkeley	SF
Concord	30	37	47
El Cerrito Del Norte	17	10	34
El Cerrito Plaza	17	10	30
Lafayette	16	23	33
Orinda	10	17	27
Pleasant Hill	24	31	41
Richmond	21	15	38
Walnut Creek	21	28	38

Note: The table provides a guide to typical commuting times from BART stations to three reference stations—MacArthur Station in Oakland, Berkeley, and Embarcadero, the first stop in San Francisco. There are typically 12- to 15-minute intervals between departures on the same line.

RIDES, phone (415) 861-POOL, will help you find a car pool in your town — no charge. In the typical arrangement, passengers meet at one or two spots and are dropped off in one or two destinations. The pools go all over. All that's needed are passengers and a driver. If you want to set up your own pool, RIDES will help you find passengers. Passengers split the cost which is based on the type of van, mileage and operating expenses. The driver gets a free commute and use of the van.

• Avoid the peak hours. If you can leave for work — it gets earlier every year — about 6:30 a.m. and hit the freeway home before 4 p.m., you might make the 6 o'clock news.

On Fridays during winter, it is especially important to leave early or late. The Crockett and the Martinez bridges are the main roads to the Sierra and ski country. They jam early Friday afternoons.

BART

Take BART. The train breakdowns are fewer, the cars nice, the ride smooth, the fare on the high side: $2.65 from Concord to downtown San Francisco. But parking in the City runs much higher, and among alternatives to the freeway BART is the best. Passengers from Concord and Richmond, the last stops in Contra Costa County, are assured seats on the way in.

For BART information in East Contra Costa, call (510) 754-2278, in Central Contra Costa (510) 933-2278, in West Contra Costa, (510) 236-2278.

The Buses

Take the County Connection or one of the other bus systems. Increasingly,

Serving Alamo, Clayton, Concord, Danville, Lafayette, Martinez, Moraga, Orinda, Pacheco, Pleasant Hill, San Ramon, and Walnut Creek.

Buses operate every day except Sundays, New Year's Day, Memorial Day, July 4th, Labor Day, Thanksgiving and Christmas Day. Saturday schedules are used on President's Day. For schedule and route information phone:

676-7500

Central Contra Costa Transit Authority
Transportation Center
1990 N. California Blvd., Suite 100
Walnut Creek, CA 94596

The County Connection

Driving Miles
Solano County — to Bay Bridge & Concord

City	Bay Bridge	Concord
Benicia	27	6
Cordelia	31	16
Davis	75	49
Dixon	55	42
Fairfield	37	22
Suisun City	38	21
Vacaville	41	26
Vallejo	22	NA

Note: These are approximations. A traveler from Fairfield or Vacaville, two of the larger cities in Solano County, could easily add another five miles depending upon his starting point within the city. Bay Bridge distances were measured along Interstate 80, Concord distances along Interstate 680 via the Benicia Bridge.

buses will work better than cars. If you can't find parking at the BART station, take the bus to the station or drive to an outlying lot and take a station bus.

• **The County Connection** runs buses throughout Central Contra Costa. Towns served include Martinez, Pleasant Hill, Concord, Walnut Creek, Clayton, Lafayette, Orinda, Moraga, San Ramon, Danville, Alamo, Pleasanton (Stoneridge Mall). Phone (510) 676-7500.

County Connection also runs buses to special events: UC Berkeley games, shows at the Concord Pavilion. Also a free shuttle from Walnut Creek's Broadway Plaza to BART station.

• **BART** runs express buses from East and West Contra Costa cities to the Concord and Richmond BART stations. Phone (510) 754-2278 in East Contra Costa, and (510) 236-2278 in West Contra Costa.

• **Tri Delta Transit** provides bus service to East Contra Costa. Fixed bus routes serve West Pittsburg, Pittsburg, Antioch. Dial-A-Ride serves Brentwood. Bus service is also available for Bethel Island and Discovery Bay. For information, call (510) 754-4040. For Dial-A-Ride, (510) 754-3060.

• **WESTCAT** (West Contra Costa County Transit Authority) runs buses through the communities of Crockett, Port Costa, Rodeo, Hercules, Pinole, Montara Bay, Bayview and Tara Hills. The last three are unincorporated neighborhoods near Pinole.

WESTCAT also offers Dial-A-Ride, door-to-door service for the elderly and handicapped. In addition, WESTCAT buses connect with AC-Transit buses that run to Hilltop Mall Shopping Center and BART stations. For WESTCAT schedules and location of stops, call (510) 724-7433.

• **AC Transit** serves the West Contra Costa cities of Richmond, El Cerrito,

San Pablo and El Sobrante. Buses run to the BART stations in Richmond and El Cerrito. Phone (510) 232-5665.

DUI

Driving under the influence. If you drive 5 or 10 miles over the limit on the freeway, chances are the cops won't flag you down. If they see you weaving or driving erratically, they'll usually go after you.

State law has been tightened to point where two or three drinks can put you over the limit. No preaching. But if you're tippling, it might save you a lot of grief and money to line up a safe driver.

Ygnacio — I Told You So

For years Walnut Creek residents have muttered bitter mutters about the traffic that comes over Ygnacio Valley Road from Concord and East Contra Costa. If it weren't for THEM, traffic along Ygnacio, one of the most heavily traveled arteries in that city, would be much less.

A study was done: they're right. Three out of ten cars came from East Contra Costa, three more from Concord, and one in ten came from Clayton.

Park and Ride

Many people do. They drive their vehicles to certain destinations, park, and hitch a ride in the cars, vans and pickups of other car pools. Much is arranged informally.

BART has park and ride lots in:
- Antioch. North of Highway 4 on east side of Hillcrest Avenue.
- Concord. East side of Port Chicago Highway near Panoramic Court.
- West Pittsburg. South of Highway 4 on west side of Bailey Road.

Buses carry passengers from these lots to BART stations. For information, (510) 464-6000.

18/Weather

Pacific High, Summer Fog, Rainy Months Affect All — from the Bay on up through the Delta

WHEN IS THE best time to have a picnic or reroof a home or stage an outdoor wedding? Although generally delightful, the local weather is fickle but some predictions can be safely made. For one, rain rarely falls in the summer months. Wettest months are December and January.

Contra Costa Public Works Department figures show that the true rainfall in July and August is about one hundredth of an inch. You're thinking, "I'll have the wedding, but watch — on that day that little bit of rain will fall." Take a chance.

Mild, Diverse Climate

The Bay Area enjoys one of the mildest climates on earth and one of the most diverse. While Antioch and Byron residents swelter in 90-degree sunshine, fishermen at Stinson Beach in Marin County may shiver in parkas. On the Contra Costa side of the Caldecott Tunnel, the sun shines. On the Alameda side, during the summer, the sun often hides behind ocean fog and the air becomes chilly. In the early winter, this pattern reverses: Contra Costa County is often chilled by "valley fog" while Alameda County, shielded by the hills, enjoys winter sunshine.

The Extremes

Temperatures rarely drop below freezing, but almost every winter in recent years Mt. Diablo has donned a mantle of snow. In the 1975-76 season, the county endured one of the worst droughts of the century. ("Endured" is not quite precise. We had a glorious Indian Summer throughout the winter, but water had to be rationed.)

Solano Weather Patterns

LIKE CONTRA COSTA, Solano County straddles two systems, the coastal and the continental. Vallejo, on San Pablo Bay, is cooler in the summer than Vacaville, located inland.

Just east of the Benicia bridge is Suisun Bay. In Indian, Suisun means "west wind." Solano County gets strong winds blowing through the Carquinez Strait and up to Sacramento. Not for nothing have wind-powered generators been installed at Collinsville.

Wind conditions vary by town and topography. Benicia, which looks down the Carquinez Strait, often gets gusts, and driving the Luther Gibson freeway (Benicia to Cordelia I-680) is occasionally a both-hands-on-the-wheel experience.

Measured at Travis, winds in July average 20 m.p.h. This drops to 18 in August and to 7 by November. In January and February, the winds reverse, shooting fog from the San Joaquin Valley into San Francisco Bay. Winter fog causes accidents and demands careful driving.

Here is a sampling of temperatures taken at Vallejo and Vacaville on March 5-11, 1989, and July 5-11, 1989.

Winter Pattern

Date	Vallejo Hi	Vallejo Lo	Vacaville Hi	Vacaville Lo
March 5	53	41	51	40
March 6	61	48	62	47
March 7	61	48	68	51
March 8	59	50	63	53
March 9	59	52	62	50
March 10	63	51	65	54
March 11	65	48	69	50

Summer Pattern

Date	Vallejo Hi	Vallejo Lo	Vacaville Hi	Vacaville Lo
July 5	90	54	100	54
July 6	98	54	105	56
July 7	87	59	*110	56
July 8	86	59	106	62
July 9	79	55	95	56
July 10	77	56	95	56
July 11	69	54	94	58

NOTE: Rare for March, rain fell on all seven days: Vallejo total 1.45 inches, Vacaville 2 inches.
*The hottest day of the year.

Average Annual Rainfall by City

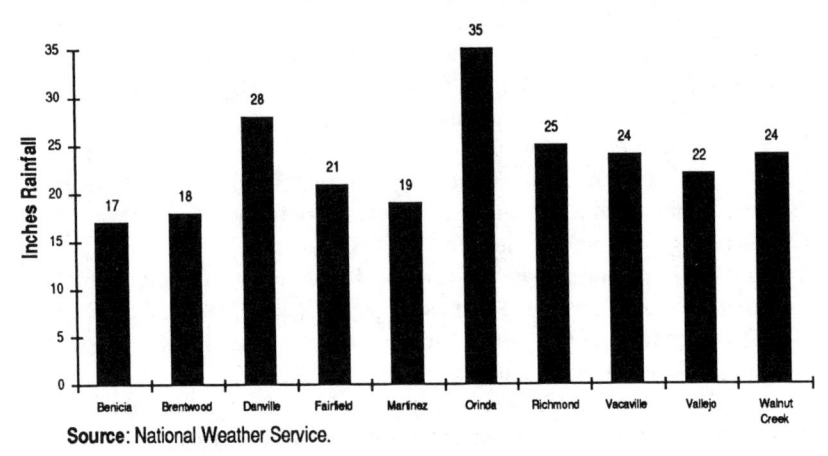

City	Inches Rainfall
Benicia	17
Brentwood	18
Danville	28
Fairfield	21
Martinez	19
Orinda	35
Richmond	25
Vacaville	24
Vallejo	22
Walnut Creek	24

Source: National Weather Service.

In the 1982-83 season, Contra Costa and Solano counties suffered through one of the heaviest rains of the century. The last few years have been drought. As we go to press, it appears this season will be deliciously wet.

Understanding Contra Costa weather is easy, if you know the roles played by five actors: the sun, the Pacific, the Golden Gate, the hills and the Central Valley.

The Sun

In the spring and summer the sun moves north, creating a mass of air called the Pacific High. The Pacific High blocks storms from the California coast and dispatches winds to the coast. In the fall the sun moves south, taking the Pacific High with it. The winds slough off for a few months, then in bluster the storms. Toward spring, the storms will abate as the Pacific High settles into place.

The Pacific

Speeding across the Pacific, the spring and summer winds pick up moisture and, at the coast, strip the warm water from the surface and bring up the frigid. Cold water exposed to warm wet air makes a thick fog. In summer months San Francisco often looks like it is about to be buried by cotton candy.

The Golden Gate

This fog would love to scoot over to the East Bay, but Mt. Tamalpais and the hills running up the San Francisco peninsula stop or greatly impede its progress except where there are openings. Of the half dozen or so major gaps, the biggest is the Golden Gate.

The fog shoots through the Golden Gate in the spring and summer, visually

Rainfall Distribution by Month

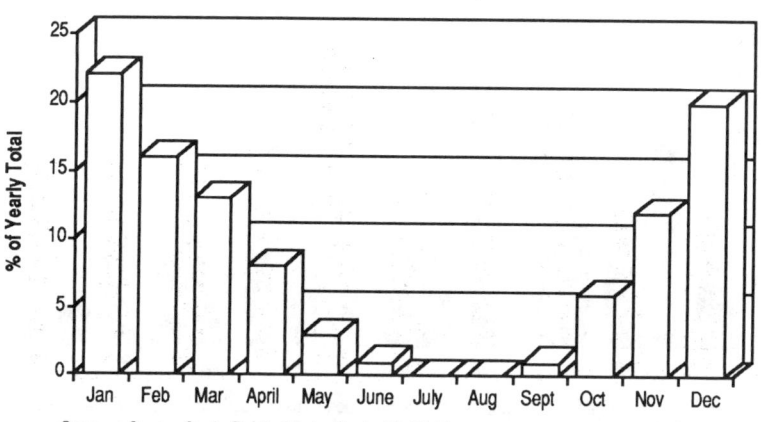

Source: Contra Costa Public Works Dept., Mt. Diablo.

delighting motorists on the Bay Bridge, and bangs into the Berkeley hills. Without the hills, Lafayette, Orinda and Moraga and much of Central Contra Costa would be decidedly cooler. As it is, some fog does spill over, giving the Lafayette-Orinda area cooler summers than the East County. El Cerrito, almost opposite the Golden Gate, catches some fog, but Richmond and other towns in the West County usually escape with just the cooler air.

The Central Valley

Also known as the San Joaquin Valley and located about 75 miles inland, the Central Valley is more influenced by continental weather than coastal. In the summer this means heat. Rising hot air pulls in cold air like a vacuum. The Central Valley sucks in the coastal air through openings in the East Bay hills, mainly the Carquinez Strait, until the Valley cools. Then the Valley says to the coast: no more cool air, thank you. The suction gone, the winds taper off for a few days.

With the winds down, the fog stays offshore and San Francisco enjoys some sunny days. Meanwhile, lacking the cooling fog, the Valley heats up

Average Daily Temperature

City	Ja	Fb	Mr	Ap	My	Ju	Jy	Au	Sp	Oc	No	Dc
San Fran.	51	55	55	55	57	59	60	61	63	62	60	53
Richmond	50	54	55	57	61	63	64	64	66	63	56	51
Mt. Diablo	48	49	49	53	60	66	72	72	71	65	54	50
Antioch	45	51	54	59	65	71	73	73	70	63	52	48

Source: National Climatic Center, Asheville, N.C. Averages of 10 years, 1974-83.

Average Annual Rainfall

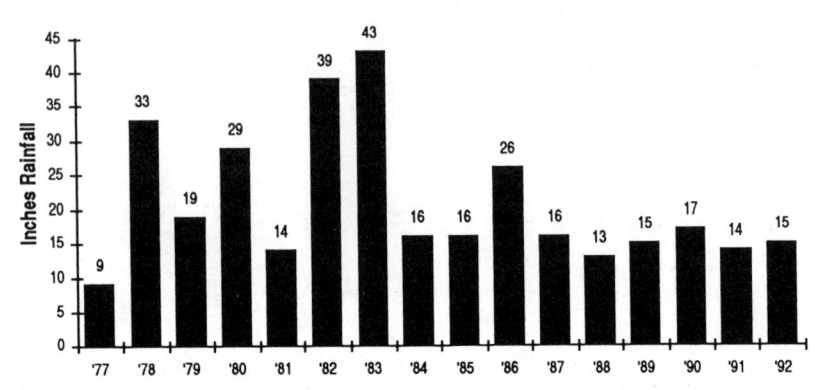

Year	Inches Rainfall
'77	9
'78	33
'79	19
'80	29
'81	14
'82	39
'83	43
'84	16
'85	16
'86	26
'87	16
'88	13
'89	15
'90	17
'91	14
'92	15

Source: Contra Costa Public Works Dept., Walnut Creek Station. Totals for season ending June 30.

again, creating the vacuum that pulls in the fog and renews the cycle.

This cycle has its daily counterpart. As the sun's rays weaken in the late afternoon, the fog will often steal across the Bay to be burned off the following morning by the robust sunlight.

In the fall and winter the temperatures are reversed. The Central Valley grows colder and the Pacific Ocean, which is warmer than the land in winter, sends its balmy breezes over the coast.

Again the hills impede the coastal flow. San Francisco, in the winter, is warmer than Berkeley, which is warmer than Orinda and Walnut Creek and Danville. These towns are warmer than Antioch and Brentwood.

Also in the winter, "Valley" fog, attracted to warm air, moves toward the Bay Area but, except for openings like the Carquinez Strait, is blocked by the hills.

The Hills

Besides blocking the fog, the hills greatly influence the rain pattern. When storm clouds rise to pass over a hillside, they cool and drop much of their rain. Orinda and Moraga, which stand against the Oakland-Berkeley hills, get the most rain in Contra Costa, Brentwood and the East County the least.

Records kept over 100 years put the average annual rainfall atop Mt. Diablo, 3,849 feet, at 25 inches. But about 1,000 feet lower, at the junction of roads from Walnut Creek and Danville, the annual rainfall is 22 inches.

Minor variations like this are common throughout Central Contra Costa County. The rain dances to the tune of the hills. In the San Ramon Valley, rain gauges placed on the Las Trampas ridges catch a few more inches annually than those placed on hills east of the freeway. The clouds that pour 32 inches on the hills above Orinda can manage only 28 inches at the Lafayette Reservoir and 22 inches at the outskirts of Walnut Creek (100-year records).

Lastly, the hills buffer some towns against the wind. Martinez and Benicia are built on the Carquinez Strait, one directly across from the other. Benicia has a great view of the strait but suffers when the wind comes whistling through the inland passage. Martinez, nestled in the Alhambra Valley, sees less in the way of views but suffers less from the winds (although the waterfront gets gusty).

That basically is how the weather works (see, it wasn't hard), but, unfortunately for regularity's sake, the actors often forget their lines or fail to show up. Rainfall figures at the Walnut Creek station show how undependable nature can be. Totals ranged from 7 inches in 1976, the height of the mid-Seventies drought, to 39 and 43 inches in 1982 and 1983, respectively, when El Niño acted up.

Even when erratic, however, the weather is almost always mild. Rainy winters cause slides and road washouts and bring many complaints but, as much as Contra Costans grumble, they shiver with delight when they sit in front of the television and see what mischief Nature raises in the rest of the nation.

Weather Tidbits: First, Sunshine

Like sunshine? You are in the right place. Records show that during daylight hours the sun shines in New York City 60 percent of the time; in Boston, 57 percent; in Detroit, 53 percent; and in Seattle, 43 percent. In San Francisco, the sun shines during 66 percent of daylight hours. Atop Mt. Tamalpais, where conditions are comparable to those in Contra Costa County, the sun shines 73 percent of daylight hours.

Humidity

Although moist, the coastal climate is rarely muggy. The fog keeps the temperature too low. Summer heat is usually dry.

19/Crime

Putting Crime in Perspective — the Numbers, How to Weigh Them, Taking Precautions

IF YOU'RE RENTING AN APARTMENT OR BUYING a house, keep in mind that although vandals, muggers and murderers can strike anywhere, they do most of their damage in sections where the poor reside.

Which is not to say that the middle class and rich are universally good. The Savings and Loans thieves, generally silvered at birth, ruined many and did the country great harm. The rich and middle class have their violent and their murderers.

Nor is it to say that the poor are universally criminal. The great majority of poor and low-income people obey the law and live good lives, and in many countries the connection between poverty and crime is weak. After World War II, almost all Japanese were impoverished but social values kept crime low.

In this country, however, violent crime is most likely to be committed by the down-and-out, the abused, the addicted, the demented and the aimless, especially if they are young. These persons, because of their backgrounds and actions, are likely to be poor and live in low-income neighborhoods.

FBI Reports

In its annual reports, the FBI correlates crimes by age, by sex, and by other categories. Women are more peaceful than men. In homicides, the chances are about 10 to 1 he did it, says FBI.

The old are more law-abiding than the young. The FBI reports that in 1991 persons age 12 through 29 accounted for 61 percent of all arrests.

Opportunity

Many crimes are crimes of easy opportunity (which is why precautions and

Crime Statistics by City
Contra Costa County

City	Population	Rate	Homicides
Antioch	63,490	69	6
Concord	113,667	66	3
Danville	31,958	23	0
El Cerrito	23,345	86	0
Hercules	17,179	25	0
Lafayette	23,990	25	1
Martinez	32,470	41	0
Moraga	16,182	12	1
Orinda	16,988	18	0
Pinole	17,823	71	0
Pittsburg	48,554	64	4
Pleasant Hill	32,242	74	1
Richmond	89,246	123	61
San Pablo	25,682	111	7
San Ramon	36,038	32	0
Walnut Creek	61,830	47	3
Unincorporated	—	—	20

Solano County

City	Population	Rate	Homicides
Benicia	24,946	38	2
Davis*	47,171	72	0
Dixon	10,617	49	0
Fairfield	78,819	75	8
Suisun City	23,158	52	1
Vacaville	72,967	43	1
Vallejo	111,473	81	13

Crime in Other Cities

City	Population	Rate	Homicides
Atlanta	403,085	190	205
Honolulu	856,432	87	29
New York	7,350,023	92	2,154
Oakland	379,995	122	149
San Francisco	739,039	94	95
San Jose	798,m542	54	53
Washington, D.C.	598,000	108	482

Source: Annual 1992 FBI crime report which uses 1991 data, including population estimates based on the 1990 census. Rate is all reported crimes per 1,000 residents. Homicides include murders and non-negligent manslaughter. The FBI does not rank unincorporated towns or cities below 10,000 population. * Yolo County city.

safeguards do help; they discourage the often easily discouraged.)

When the violent and the criminal strike, they generally attack or rob their neighbors, often their friends and relatives, studies have shown.

Between rich and the poor, crime moves across a spectrum. In middle-class towns, crime rates are middling. Within these communities, the poorer sections will often be afflicted with higher crime than the others.

Washington, D.C., is notorious for its crime. Yet, according to the Washington Post, police studies show that the neighborhoods that have suffered high crime for decades are the ones that now suffer the most; and that crime in middle- and upper-income neighborhoods is no more serious than it has been in times past.

(But the violence in the poorer neighborhoods has worsened, mainly because of drugs and easy access to weapons. And the middle class and rich neighborhoods may be taking stronger precautions than before. It's not just location.)

Bay Area Pattern

The same pattern holds in the Bay Area. East Oakland, high crime; Oakland hills, low. Bayview district in San Francisco, high; Twin Peaks, Pacific Heights, low.

In Contra Costa County, San Pablo, North Richmond and Richmond in some of its flatland neighborhoods suffer the most crime. These sections are among the poorest in the county.

When you move away from these neighborhoods, crime drops sharply. The El Sobrante section of Richmond is about as safe, say, as Concord.

From a slightly different perspective, San Jose, about equal to Contra Costa in population, year in and out has fewer homicides than Contra Costa — 53 in 1991 vs. about 106. Which is the safer?

Compared one to one, San Jose. Compared by section, it depends on the section. Contra Costa has 16 cities with a population over 10,000, the cutoff number for tracking by the FBI. In 1991, these cities had 86 homicides. Of the 86, however, Richmond accounted for 61.

The remaining 15 cities, with a population of about 561,000, counted 25 homicides — which is not small. You should always take precautions. But the contrast in numbers shows how misleading overall tallies can be.

How safe is the street you're thinking about moving onto? For a rough measure, take a look at the school rankings. As most children attend school in their immediate neighborhoods, the rankings reflect the social climate. Very low rankings indicate trouble; many kids not learning, drifting.

The Random Element

Is any town or neighborhood 100 percent safe? As long as human beings roam the earth, the answer is no. The "safest" place will still be prey to the random element. Blackhawk, a gated community, stills calls out sheriff's deputies; domestic disputes.

Some places are safer than others. It's tempting to say, pick the safest place possible. But the reality is that your income will limit your choices. We can't all live in Blackhawk.

There's a flip side to crime that's rarely advertised. Felons lower home prices. The higher the crime generally the cheaper the house. Many cities have transition neighborhoods, where crime is a problem but housing is cheap or the location in other ways is attractive. Often the commute to the job center is short.

Choose your address with care. Look for tell-tale signs: bars on windows, men idling at liquor stores, very low school rankings.

Remember, statistics are one thing, the real thing is painfully real. Take precautions: alarms, neighborhood watches, good locks.

Subject Index

—A—
A. Lindsay Jr. Museum, 228
AC Transit, 274
Acalanes schools, 27-28
Alamo, 50-51
Alvarado Square, 228
Amtrak, 228
Anheuser-Busch, 228
Antioch, 51-52, 130
Antioch schools, 28-30
—B—
Baby names, Contra Costa, 176
Baby names, Solano, 176
BART, 9, 23, 267, 270, 272, 274, 275
Bay Bridge, 268
Behring Auto Museum, 228-229
Benicia, 93, 97, 99, 100, 112-115
Benicia schools, 102-104
Bethel Island, 52-53
Black Diamond Park, 226
Blackhawk, 50, 51, 53-55
Brentwood, 55-56
Brentwood schools, 30
Briones Park, 225-226
Byron, 56-58
Byron schools, 30-32
—C—
California State University, Hayward, 153-154
Canyon Elementary, 32
Catholic Schools, 150-151
Carquinez Strait, 100
Car pools, 272
Clayton, 58-59
Caldecott Tunnel, 23-276
Center for Higher Education, 23, 155
Chapman College, 155
College admissions, 133, 134, 135, 147, 148, 154
Commuting mode, Contra Costa, 271
Commuting mode, Solano, 270
Concord, 23, 59-61
Concord Pavilion, 23, 229
Contra Costa Canal, 228
Contra Costa Center, 154
Contra Costa College, 153
Contra Loma Park, 226
Cordelia, 115-116
County Connection, 273-274
Crime ratings, Contra Costa, 283
Crime ratings, Solano, 283
Crockett, 61
—D—
Danville, 61-64
Davis, 116-117
Day-care directory, Contra Costa, 164-171
Day-care directory, Solano, 171-173
Delta, The, 229
Diablo, 64
Diablo Valley College, 153
Discovery Bay, 64-65
Dixon, 117-118
Dixon Unified schools, 104
Dog licenses, 240
Drivers Licenses, 240
Driving distances, Contra Costa, 268
Driving distances, Solano, 274
Dropout rates, 137
—E-F-G—
East Bay Regional Park District, 225
East Bay Skyline Trail, 228
East Brother Light Station, 229
El Cerrito, 65-66, 132
El Sobrante, 66
Ethnic makeup, Contra Costa, 24
Ethnic makeup, Solano, 101
Ethnic school enrollment, Contra Costa, 141
Ethnic school enrollment, Solano, 141
Fairfield, 118-122
Fairfield-Suisun Unified schools, 104-107
Food prices, 264-265
Golden Gate Fields Race-track, 229
Golden Gate University, 155
—H-I-J-K—
Hercules, 66-67
Home prices, Contra Costa, 54, 57, 74-75
Home prices, Solano, 114, 115, 127
Hospital directory, Contra Costa, 189-190
Hospital directory, Solano, 190-192
Income, Contra Costa, 12
Income, Solano, 94
Job outlook, Contra Costa, 260
Job outlook, Solano, 266
John F. Kennedy University, 155
John Swett schools, 32
Kensington, 67-68, 132
Knightsen schools, 32-33
—L—
Lafayette, 68-69
Lafayette Reservoir, 229
Lafayette schools, 33
Las Trampas Wilderness, 227-228
Liberty School District, 33
Little Hills Recreation Area, 227
Los Medanos College, 153
—M—
Mare Island Naval Shipyard, 99, 100
Marine World-Africa USA, 94, 225, 230
Marsh, John, 17, 19
Martinez, 41, 69-73, 130
Martinez schools, 33-34
Martinez shoreline, 227
Martinez waterfront, 230
Martinez-Benicia Bridge, 100-112
Miller-Knox Park, 227
Moraga, 73-76
Moraga schools, 34
Morgan Territory Preserve, 226
Mt. Diablo School District, 34-38
Mt. Diablo State Park, 9, 230
Muir, John, 225, 229
—N-O—
New homes directory, 244-258
Oakland Athletics, 13, 236
Oakley, 76-77
Oakley schools, 38-39
Ohlone Indians, 17
Orinda, 77-78, 130
Orinda schools, 39
—P-Q-R—
Pinole, 78-79
Pittsburg, 23, 79-81
Pittsburg schools, 39-40
Pleasant Hill, 23, 81-82
Point Isabel, 227
Point Pinole shoreline, 227
Point Richmond, 230
Population, Contra Costa, 10, 16, 22, 178
Population, Solano, 94, 95, 96-97, 100
Port Chicago, 23
Port Costa, 230
Presidential voting, Contra Costa, 21
Presidential voting, Solano, 99
Private schools directory, Contra Costa, 155-161
Private schools directory, Solano, 161-162, 186
Rainfall, 278, 279, 280
Regional Center for the Performing Arts, 230-231
Religion, Contra Costa, 18-19
Religion, Solano, 98
Rent, Contra Costa, 63, 70
Rent, Solano, 120, 121
Restaurant directory, Contra Costa, 193-215
Restaurant directory, Solano, 215-224
Richmond, 23, 82-85

INDEX 287

Advertisers' Index

Developers
Citation Homes 247
O'Brien & Hicks 245
Oakhurst Country Club 249

Garbage Disposal & Recycling
Pleasant Hill Bayshore 261

Hospitals
Childrens Hospital-Oakland 183
Doctors Hospital 175
Eden Hospital 185
Kaiser Permanente .... Inside Back Cover, 177
Mt. Diablo Medical Center 179
Queen of the Valley Hospital 187
West Contra Costa Hospital 181
Woodland Memorial Hospital 191

Industry
Shell Oil Co. 71

Lenders
I. C. M. Mortgage 19
Western Financial Savings 17

Private Schools
Academy School 156
Brighton Elementary 159
Christian Center School 159
Contra Costa Christian High School 161
Diablo Valley Montessori 157
Fountainhead Montessori 158
Head Royce School 157
Spectrum Center 160

Private Schools
Woodlands Christian School 161

Publications
Homebuyers Monthly 251

Realtors & Relocation Services
Better Homes and Gardens Heritage
 Real Estate 69
Better Homes Realty 5
Better Homes Realty, Roger Stumbo 49
Century 21 .... 29, 31, 103
Coldwell Banker, Heidi Slocomb 27
Coldwell Banker, Mary Ann
 Patison .... Inside Front Cover, 37
Corporate Homes of America 11
Executive Living 21
Grubb & Ellis, Marianna Bottari 89
John M. Grubb Relocation 23
Kappel & Kappel Inc. 119, 125
Mason-McDuffie, Jeanne Pennell 39
Muir West Realty 73
National Relocation 13
Prudential California Realty, Bob, Sandy and Kelly
 McDougall 47

Regional Recreation
Pier 39 235

Title Insurance Companies
American Title Insurance 55
Old Republic Title Company 7

Transit
BART 269
County Connection 273

Richmond Unified School District, 40-45, 143
Rio Vista, 122
Rodeo, 85-86
—S—
Salaries, 262-263
San Francisco Giants, 237
San Pablo, 86-87, 130
San Pablo Dam, 231
San Ramon, 23, 24, 87-89
San Ramon Valley Unified schools, 45-48
SAT scores, Contra Costa, 130
SAT scores, Solano, 131
School enrollments, Contra Costa, 139
School enrollments, Solano, 139

School rankings, Contra Costa, 27-49
School rankings, Solano, 102-111
School registration, 239-240
School vacations, Contra Costa, 139
School vacations, Solano, 139
Shadelands Ranch Museum, 231
Shakespeare Festival, 13, 78
Solano Community College, 153
St. Mary's College, 15, 155, 231
Suisun Bay, 100
Suisun City, 122-124
—T-U-V—
Tao House, 231
Tassajara Creek Park, 226

Temperatures, 277, 279
Tilden Park, 226
Travis Air Force Base, 118, 119, 120
Travis Unified schools, 107
Tri Delta Transit, 274
Unemployment rate, Contra Costa, 259
Unemployment rate, Solano, 266
University of California, Berkeley, 11, 43, 153
University of Phoenix, 155
University of San Francisco, 155
Vacaville, 124-126
Vacaville Unified schools, 107-109
Vallejo, 94, 97, 126-

128, 130
Vallejo City Unified schools, 109-111
Voter registration, Contra Costa, 20, 239
Voter registration, Solano, 99, 239
—W-X-Y-Z—
Walnut Creek, 13, 89-91
Walnut Creek elementary schools, 48
West Pittsburg, 91
WESTCAT, 274
Wildcat Canyon Park, 226

How to Order McCormack's Guides by Mail or Fax

Please fill out appropriate form and send with check to: McCormack's Guides, P.O. Box 190, Martinez, CA 94553. Or fax your order and we will include bill with shipment. Fax: (510) 228-7223. Ph: (510) 229-3581

For single orders or orders totaling 19 or less

In blank next to title, write in number of copies ordered:

____ Alameda County '93 (includes Tracy & Manteca) $6.95
____ Contra Costa & Solano '93 $6.95
____ Marin, Napa & Sonoma '93 $6.95
____ Sacramento County '93 $6.95
____ San Francisco & San Mateo County '93 $6.95
____ Santa Clara County '93 $6.95

Please add shipping charge of $2 for first book, $1.50 per book thereafter. California residents add 8.25% sales tax to cover price.

Name/Company: _____

Address: _____

City: _____ State: _____ Zip: _____

Amount Enclosed: _____ Phone: (____) _____

Buy 20 or more and SAVE!

If your order adds up to 20 or more, you qualify for the bulk rate. You also save on shipping & handling. **Ask about discounts for orders of 100 or more.**

In blank next to title, write in number of copies ordered:

____ Alameda County '93 (includes Tracy & Manteca) $3.50
____ Contra Costa & Solano '93 $3.50
____ Marin, Napa & Sonoma '93 $3.50
____ Sacramento County '93 $3.50
____ San Francisco & San Mateo County '93 $3.50
____ Santa Clara County '93 $3.50

Please add shipping charge of 30 cents per book. California residents add 8.25% sales tax to cover price.

Name/Company: _____

Address: _____

City: _____ State: _____ Zip: _____

Amount Enclosed: _____ Phone: (____) _____

____ Check here to receive information about placing an ad in McCormack's Guides. Or Phone (510) 229-3904 or 229-3581.

This book contains adult language, descriptions of surgical procedures and suicidal thoughts. All of the events depicted in this book are real. Where permission could not be sought, names have been changed to respect privacy.

Copyright © Amy Kate Carter 2021

The author asserts the moral right to be identified as the author of this work.

Published by Amy Kate Carter via Kindle Direct Publishing (KDP).

All rights reserved. No part of this publication may be reproduced, stored in a retrieval system, or transmitted in any form or by any means, electronic, mechanical, photocopying, recording or otherwise without the prior permission of the author.

This book is sold subject to condition that it shall not by way of trade or otherwise, be lent, resold, hired out or otherwise circulated without the author's prior consent in any form of binding or cover other than that in which it is published and without a similar condition being imposed on the subsequent purchaser.

Acknowledgements

This book would not have been written without the help, encouragement and advice of some truly amazing people. Sam, thank you for proofreading the first draft. Becky, thank you for creating the beautiful cover artwork. Kate, thank you for painstakingly editing the manuscript. Kelly, thank you for all your advice on sexual health matters covered in the book. Serena, thank you for your unshakable belief in me and encouragement when the going got tough.

Thank you to the Northamptonshire gender clinic for your support, help and guidance throughout my transition. You are all amazing, I will never forget you. Special thanks to Lynne for sorting out my appointments and keeping me calm when things went wrong, and to Rhiannon, for helping me to find my female voice.

Thank you to the Nuffield hospital in Brighton for looking after me and making my gender affirmation surgery one of the most incredible experiences of my life. Thank you so very much for your care and compassion. Thank you to Mr Charles Coker, brilliant surgeon and thoroughly nice man. You have given me the most amazing gift and for that, I will always be grateful.

Thank you to my wonderful friends and family, my mum, my daughter and my sister for believing in me and being there for me when I couldn't get the words out and I felt like giving up. You are my tribe and I love you all.